W9-CKD-303

*Number one, you just have to have teachers more directly involved in education. Teachers feel they're the last ones to be asked. . . . You just don't get the teachers' input into these things. It always comes down from the administrators, from the politicians, from the union, from the public, whatever, but it always comes from the top down. It rarely gets from the bottom up. It's like teachers aren't respected, so why should they have their word? And you just get to the point that you really just don't care about it. . . . Most teachers feel that they are continually being pushed in every direction, and there's no support from anywhere for them these days. Students, parents, press, high administration, government, nothing seems to be on the side of the teachers.*

— A Dade County Public School Teacher

*SUNY Series, Teacher Preparation and Development*
*Alan R. Tom, editor*

# Teachers

## *The Missing Voice in Education*

Marilyn M. Cohn
and
Robert B. Kottkamp

STATE UNIVERSITY OF NEW YORK PRESS

129875

Published by
State University of New York Press, Albany

© 1993  State University of New York

All rights reserved

Printed in the United States of America

No part of this book may be used or reproduced
in any manner whatsoever without written permission
except in the case of brief quotations embodied in
critical articles and reviews.

For information, address State University of New York Press,
State University Plaza, Albany, N.Y., 12246

Production by Marilyn P. Semerad
Marketing by Bernadette LaManna

**Library of Congress Cataloging-in-Publication Data**

Cohn, Marilyn M.
    Teachers : the missing voice in education / Marilyn M. Cohn and
Robert B. Kottkamp.
        p.    cm. — (SUNY series, teacher preparation and development)
    Includes bibliographical references (p.    ) and index.
    ISBN 0-7914-1341-1. — ISBN 0-7914-1342-X (pbk.)
    1. Teachers—Florida—Dade County—Case studies. 2. Educational
change—Florida—Dade County—Case studies. 3. Education—Social
aspects—Florida—Dade County—Case studies. I. Kottkamp, Robert
B. II. Title. III. Series: SUNY series in teacher preparation and
development.
LB1775.3.F6C64  1993
371.1′009759′38—dc20                                                92-14008
                                                                            CIP

10 9 8 7 6 5 4 3 2 1

*To "Karen" and her teacher colleagues everywhere who continue to give their best measure in the face of great challenges.*

# Contents

129875

# List of Tables

# Foreword

Reform movements are not new to American education; they have occurred almost every decade since the beginning of the century. What is new about the current reform movement is the increased attention to teachers and students as both the *primary* objects and subjects of change. This has caused us to examine the prevailing values that have driven change strategies over the past twenty years, and the impact they have had on the teacher and the teacher/student relationship. While much has been written on school reform, no single book has combined the gathering of "objective" empirical data from outside with the voices of teachers on the inside attempting to deal with these questions.

In 1975 when Dan Lortie's book, *Schoolteacher*, was published, the educational world was surprised to learn about the "endemic uncertainties" that teachers felt about what they taught and what they hoped students learned. The field was equally surprised when Lortie explicated the meaning and significance of the "psychic rewards" that teachers received when students learned, and their disappointments when they didn't. Exploring the "real world" of the teacher, her isolation from other adults and her total dependence on a "good" and enabling principal, revealed a much more complicated world of schools and teachers than had been known before.

Lortie's book was subsequently followed by other studies that explained the complexities of schools as cultures (with their patterned ways of organizing work) and the difficulties of making piecemeal changes instead of dealing with the school's culture as a whole. Changing schools and their practices, we were beginning to realize, was not just a matter of mandate or program but, rather, a joining together of such complex and varied things as teachers' commitment and motivation, opportunities for teachers to learn new ideas, to meet, to discuss and plan with other teach-

ers, and to receive continuous support from enlightened leadership as new practices were implemented in the classroom. The
teacher's sense of her own efficacy in relation to her students,
the importance of a supportive culture for her continuous learning, and her increased understanding of the change process all
were necessary conditions for change. It was important, then,
that policies created at sometimes a great distance from the
schools also enabled teachers to engage in these kinds of practices at the school level.

Within this context this book allows us now to hear the voices
of contemporary teachers struggling to create rich learning environments for students. That this is occurring within an increasingly fragmented society with obvious deleterious effects on students, and during a period when prescriptive policies that continue
to erode the kinds of conditions needed to support change for
schools and teachers are still being enacted, heightens the perti-
nence and poignancy of this book.

No one will be able to read *Teachers: The Missing Voice in Education* without empathizing with and feeling the agony of Karen,
one of the teachers whose personal and professional lives we
come to know well. As Karen struggles to teach all of her students, we begin to see the powerful influence of the school with
its uniform mandates, constricting the possibilities for dealing
with the variability of today's students. Understanding Karen's
particular problems helps us to understand more fully those of
every teacher.

This book does not romanticize teaching, however. Rather, this
is a book that provides an important social, political and cultural
analysis of school reform, bringing to the surface underlying tensions that exist in our schools and in our society. These tensions
include pressure for reform that favors bureaucratic control over
professional control, external control over teacher control and
autonomy, standardization—often confused with a need for standards—which would discourage the need for teacher flexibility to
deal with increased student variability, and concern for competence that is prescriptive (what everyone should know) as opposed
to encouraging excitement about learning (what motivates and
interests students).

While the data in this book anticipated the current quest for
restructuring schools and teacher professionalism, the book supports this quest, joining these ideas with the necessity for teachers
to be engaged, active, and key players in transforming schools.
This book educates us not only as to why we must change our

schools, but it also shows us how, and under what conditions. In this informed analysis, dispassionate—in its meticulous collection and interpretation of data—and passionate—in its strong conviction that the teacher's voice has been missing—we have the book that we need to help us move forward.

ANN LIEBERMAN

Teachers College, Columbia University

# Preface

## The Missing Voice of Teachers

The importance of education is an unassailable axiom of our national ideology. As a people we believe that education is a bulwark for preserving our political and economic system. We believe that education is the basis for solving current and future problems. We say that in the long run, the effectiveness of our schools is more important than that of the military. Our President symbolizes the centrality of education by saying he wishes to be remembered as the "education president."

Our accomplishments have not matched our beliefs and aspirations. For the past decade, this nation has had a growing sense that our educational system has failed us. We have appointed expert commissions to figure out why; others have appointed themselves to do the same. We have debated the question with a rhetoric of crisis. We have looked for causes, and because we tend to think in concrete terms—especially in terms of persons—we have sought villains to blame for our problems: We have found them in our two million teachers. First we publicly denounced them. Then we designed policies to make teachers "toe the line" and prod our students to perform better on standardized tests. But still we have the nagging sense that education is in trouble—that perhaps it is even getting worse.

This book is about the teachers who live at the center of the maelstrom of rhetoric, vilification, and conflict over making our educational system better. They have been expected to "shape up" and implement the reforms that others have developed. They have been treated more like uninformed hired hands than professionals to whom we entrust our most precious asset. They have been the last to be consulted when we consider what is broken and how to fix it. Their voices have not and still do not inform the actions taken to rectify what reformers believe to be the matter with education in the United States.

The absence of teachers from the dialogue and decision-making on reform has been a serious omission. It has yielded faulty definitions of the problem, solutions that compound rather than confront the problem, and a demeaned and demoralized teaching force. Efforts to improve education are doomed to failure until teachers become respected partners in the process. If reform is to be successful, their voices and views must be included in any attempts to improve and alter their work. Although their involvement cannot insure success, their absence will guarantee continued failure.

In this book, we hear the views of contemporary teachers, in their unity and division, in their complexity and simplicity. We listen to what they say and take note of what they do not or cannot say. We feel their joy, but also their pain. We make public their side of the story.

Their accounts are compelling and illuminating. Their vivid images portray teachers as victims rather than villains. We learn of the staggering challenges they face. We are reminded that teaching and learning are interpersonal processes. We come to understand how well-intentioned attempts to make teachers accountable have essentially ignored the human side of the equation. We begin to see with increasing clarity how reform policies and practices are leading us away from, not toward, our educational aspirations. We recognize an urgent need for a break in the existing paradigm of reform—a rethinking of school improvement and how to achieve it. For us, this complicated process begins with reexamining our educational purposes and problems from a new perspective, that of the classroom teacher.

## *The Dade County Study: The Perspective of the Classroom Teacher*

The teacher voices and perspectives in this book were collected in a study, "Teacher Work Rewards and Incentives: 1964-1984," funded by the National Institute of Education (NIE) and conducted by Eugene F. Provenzo, Jr., Marilyn M. Cohn, and Robert B. Kottkamp during 1984 and 1985 in Dade County (Miami), Florida. Gary N. McCloskey, O.S.A., joined the project during the summer of 1985. The major purpose of the study was to explore how powerful social changes over two decades had affected teachers and wrought a decline in their rewards and incentives. Its overall design, however, permitted a much broader examination of the meanings teachers construct from their work.

The benchmark for assessing change in the experience of being a teacher was Dan C. Lortie's *Schoolteacher: A Sociological Study* (1975). His 1964 study of the "ethos" of teaching was based on 6,539 surveys of public school teachers in Dade County and 94 interviews with public school teachers in Five Towns, five school districts in the Boston metropolitan area. Twenty years later, we sought a basis for comparison by surveying 2,718 and interviewing 73 teachers in the Dade County Public Schools. In the NIE study, we replicated many of Lortie's survey and interview questions to permit direct comparisons over time. We also developed new questions to probe teacher perceptions of contemporary educational issues and school reform efforts. The timing of the study caught detailed reactions to Florida's comprehensive educational reform program, one that had started earlier but was characteristic of the first wave of reforms triggered by *A Nation At Risk* and other reports on the deficiencies of American education. Our Methodological Appendix contains the details of the setting, sample, survey, and interview questions, and the methods of data analysis, as well as discussions of generalizability, limitations, and other technical matters.

The NIE project generated a varied and voluminous data base that could be analyzed along different substantive dimensions and from multiple philosophical, methodological, and academic orientations. Over several years, different individuals and combinations of the four-member research team wrote numerous articles, chapters, and conference papers that reflected their special interests and research methods. Some of these are cited extensively in this work. Two of the four researchers, Marilyn M. Cohn and Robert B. Kottkamp, have developed this book over the last several years. Although we have profited greatly from earlier years of discussion and collaboration with our co-researchers, Eugene F. Provenzo, Jr., and Gary N. McCloskey, and have been influenced by their thinking and writing, this work represents our own particular approach to the data. It presents a unified argument not found in earlier writings, one that reflects a synthesis of methods, professional backgrounds, and personal experiences that are uniquely ours.

## *Our Perspective and Purpose*

We are former classroom teachers who now work at universities where we are engaged in preparation programs for teachers and administrators, and in research and writing on educational issues. We are deeply concerned with the problems of American education, the general direction of school reform, and the lack of understanding of the challenges and constraints that contemporary teachers confront. With this book, we hope to contribute both to the scholarly literature on teaching and teachers and to the fields of educational policy and classroom practice. While these dual purposes are ambitious and serve to complicate our task, they also provide us with a framework for selecting our focus, targeting what to include and exclude from our vast amount of data, and determining our style of presentation.

Our focus is at the microlevel of the classroom and on the meanings teachers take from their daily work with students, parents, colleagues, and principals in their schools. We seek to determine what they are trying to achieve, the means they use to accomplish their aims, and the rewards they receive when they are successful. We endeavor to learn what supports and what blocks them in their attempts to help students learn. To understand their struggles and successes, we examine forces for stability and change that affect classroom thought and action. Forces for stability lie within the structure of the school and occupation and are deeply socialized into teachers themselves. Forces for change arise from the larger social, cultural, economic, and political spheres in which education is embedded. Teachers experience forces of change most directly from their students and parents and in political distillations of policy and law. These policies and laws result from interaction and conflict among multiple stakeholders with differing perspectives at local, state, and national levels. While we attend to varying perspectives and the changes they create, our interest remains in how teachers perceive and respond to these forces, not the outside views and forces themselves. Within the broader story of change and stability, our attention stays with the perspective of classroom teachers. We describe how their work has become more difficult and less rewarding, so that others might learn from and act upon that knowledge.

Given our aims, we rely heavily on interview data to tell the teacher's story at two levels. At the descriptive level, teachers often speak for themselves. The interview transcriptions are filled with graphic images, emotional reactions, and analytical insights. We use them generously throughout the first two sections of the book. Our goal is to portray vividly the experiences and ideas teachers shared.

Listening to teachers, however, we discover that while they can tell us in exquisite detail what is right and wrong with our schools, they cannot easily tell us how to rethink them. As insiders absorbed in countless all-consuming daily interactions, they are far more adept at describing what succeeds and what fails within the confines of their own classrooms than at designing proposals to alter the entire system. To move toward a more analytical level requires interpretations from those who have experience with the inside realities, but who can also distance themselves from the immediacy of the classroom. In the third section of the book, we take on that interpretive stance. We work toward understanding the implications of what teachers told us to rethink current efforts to reform American education.

Although the key insights come primarily from interviews, the surveys make a significant contribution to our argument. The survey responses, which reflect the perceptions of a much larger sample, are useful in assessing broad trends and evaluating themes that emerged from the smaller interview sample. In presenting our findings, we sometimes start with survey data for a broad overview, and then use the interview data to explain and extend survey responses. Given our dual purposes, in describing and analyzing data from either source we attempt to communicate our findings in language accessible to teachers, administrators, policymakers, and reformers, as well as scholars. Our intent is to present the missing voice of teachers with the clarity necessary for others to recognize the contribution teachers must make toward solving America's educational problems.

## *Organization of the Book*

To tell our story, we have divided this book into three sections. Part I, "Stability and Change over Twenty Years: Purposes, Means, and Rewards of Teaching," examines the general forces for stability and those for change, and their impact on three core components of teaching. Chapter 1 presents an overview of both the societal changes affecting schools and teachers and the continuities in school and occupational structures over two decades. Chapter 2 compares how teachers in 1964 and their counterparts in 1984 expressed their instructional purposes, and the means (knowledge, skills, attitudes, and qualities) required to reach them. Chapter 3 considers how teachers twenty years apart described the rewards they received when their aims were realized. On all three dimensions, teacher voices from both surveys and interviews revealed strong continuity.

In Part II, "The Impact of Change in the Context of Schooling:

The Teacher's Story," the focus is on major changes in today's workplace. Chapter 4 describes changes that teachers perceive in the attitudes and behaviors of both students and their parents, and how these changes have made teaching more difficult and less rewarding. Chapter 5 explores changes that have arisen from public pressure through state-level reforms to hold teachers responsible for students' acquisition of basic skills. We hear how these changes have eroded the professional discretion of teachers as a whole, and then in Chapter 6 we look at some variation in effects related to individual teachers' beliefs and behaviors.

In Part III, "Interpreting and Acting upon the Teacher's Story," we move to an interpretive stance, and consider ways of reframing the problem of educational reform. In Chapter 7, we synthesize what we have learned from the voices of teachers, and conclude that in today's schools, the long-standing tension between learning and control is tipped heavily toward control at the expense of meaningful learning. In Chapter 8, we propose an alternative conception of learning grounded in teachers' views of the instructional process. Chapter 9 identifies three major domains of existing assumptions and the school structures reflecting them, which need to be reconsidered if our educational system is to be significantly improved. Chapter 10 concludes with a proposal for schools as centers of inquiry, where current assumptions can be examined, alternative assumptions and structures developed, and different practices implemented and studied. Our intent is to foster learning environments where teachers and other stakeholders in education can meet the challenge of change by generating new structures and strategies for reaching the students of today and tomorrow.

# Acknowledgments

Our indebtedness is large; we acknowledge it gladly:

To begin with, we are indebted to the citizens of this nation. Their tax dollars made this project possible through funding by the National Institute of Education and Office of Educational Research and Improvement. While our perspective does not represent the position of the United States Department of Education, we hope our efforts through their earlier support will inform policy-making and contribute to the general welfare of this nation, especially of its children.

To "Karen" and the other 72 Dade County teachers who gave irreplaceable time to tell us their stories, and to their 2,718 colleagues and 177 principals who took the time to complete our surveys, we are most deeply appreciative. We hope that their faith in us has been justified and that we have fulfilled our promise by representing them accurately and by making their voices available to a wider audience.

To the Dade County Public Schools, and to the United Teachers of Dade (American Federation of Teachers), especially their leaders, then-Superintendent Leonard Britton and UTD Vice-President Pat Tornillo and their many colleagues, we express our most sincere gratitude. They provided us with access to teachers, helped us to test our research instruments, enabled us to get surveys returned, and offered overall support. Given the nature of our work and its antecedents, it was not possible to keep the site confidential. While it is possible to read certain aspects of our work as critical of these educators, that was not our intention. We found no villains, quite the contrary. We found openness, dedication to finding better ways to educate children amid incredible complexity and constraint, and a willingness to engage in responsible risk-taking demonstrated by the continuing experiments in this district. We only hope the trust in us that led to access to this school district and its personnel has been upheld with integrity.

We owe tremendous debt to Eugene F. Provenzo, Jr., who created the original idea for the NIE project and included us in its development. With him, we constructed the survey and interview forms, collected the data, and wrote many of the earlier articles and papers based on the project. We learned and benefitted much from our years of association. In addition, we owe very special appreciation to Asterie Baker Provenzo. She and Gene allowed their home to become the central processing station for the NIE project and graciously hosted us as live-in guests for too many weeks over several years.

Gary N. McCloskey, O.S.A., initially assisted us by conducting several interviews and later joined the NIE project as a co-researcher. We are thankful for his many contributions, especially for his insights into legislated learning and for helpful feedback on our work.

Dan C. Lortie generously provided us with his 1964 survey data, much encouragement, and critical commentary on earlier analyses. At one point he gave us an entire workday away from interruptions to discuss analytical approaches, false starts and subsequent insights gleaned from his own work, and conceptual frameworks for uniting various types of data. To him we owe our largest conceptual debt, for his *Schoolteacher: A Sociological Study* is the very foundation of our work. Although we wrote a book that differs from his in many ways, he set a scholarly standard toward which we have continually strived.

We extend special thanks to James Steffenson for sponsorship in the early phases of the project, to the Phi Delta Kappa chapters at the University of Miami and at Rutgers University for important small grants, and to Allison Gooding for first-rate work in preparing the computer data and merging data sets. To our many colleagues at Washington, Rutgers, and Hofstra Universities, and to our friends and family outside the world of academe, who provided us with personal encouragement, we are deeply appreciative. Vivian Gellman and Alice Burgess, in particular, selflessly gave their time, assistance, and support, and Murray Bresler consistently lightened the burdens of travel.

For our colleagues, students, and friends who read and responded to earlier drafts, we are extremely thankful. Joyce Bernstein, Michael Lindvall, and Larry Newman gave us helpful feedback. Mary Ellen Finch and Jacqueline Gross provided us with invaluable written critique that deserves special mention. Mary Ellen, who understands teachers better than anyone we know, offered critical validation that we were on target with our description and analysis of teachers' thinking. At the same time, she pointed out weak points of the manuscript and sent us back to the computer to rethink and rewrite final sections. Jackie served us well on three counts. As a teacher in the early stages of her career, she raised provocative questions from the perspective of the beginning teacher. As a former editor, she was an extremely careful and sensitive reader who provided us with both substantive and technical assistance. As a consummate typist, Jackie offered us secretarial help when we needed it most, day or night.

Despite his own time pressures, Louis M. Smith read the manuscript with the insightfulness and thoroughness that are the hallmarks of his scholarship. He raised critical issues, identified inconsistencies, poked holes in our logic, recommended references, provided us with books and papers from his own library, and, most important of all, offered key ideas that found their way into the book. It was, in fact, during one of our many discussions that Lou suggested we have a re-look at Schaefer's *The School as a Center of Inquiry* (1967), which became the core of the final chapter. Although we would still be writing if we had addressed all of his questions, he is singularly responsible for the many sleepless nights and long days we gave to considering his penetrating commentary. For intellectual stimulation and unequalled collegiality past and present, we offer him our deepest gratitude.

With the full support of Bryce B. Hudgins, Chair of the Education Department, the office and administrative staff at Washington University was a mainstay throughout the seemingly never-ending process. Leslie Will, Donna Gardner, Karen Benton, and Cheryl McCrary offered support in countless ways. John Pingree saw us through the maze of incompatible word processing programs, hand-scribbled inserts, faxes, and express mail packages and ultimately typed a technically perfect manuscript.

We received excellent production support from Marilyn Semerad and superb editorial support from Lois Patton and Alan Tom. Alan believed in us deeply and moved things along by encouraging us to "let go of it," while Lois heard us with at least three ears and allowed us to "hang onto it" until we were satisfied. Bravo to an honest, nurturing, unbeatable team!

It may sound like a cliché, but—those who lived it know it is not—our greatest debt goes to our families. We analyzed and wrote though a process of shuffling back and forth between homes in St. Louis and Long Island. Families suffered our physical absence when gone and our physical presence when we were there in body but not in mind. Each of our family members made special contributions, as well. Derek Cohn provided continual encouragement, as well as critical computer assistance and typing support that once went all night. Jeremy Kottkamp gave up his room and bed for many nights without grumbling. Cheryl Cohn and Nathan Kottkamp were our cheerleaders extraordinaire, expressing through a constant stream of cards, calls, and encouraging words a faith in us that we sometimes lost ourselves. In the end, it was our spouses, Jay Cohn and Ginny Kottkamp, who bore the greatest cost of all. They lived through years of missed deadlines, inexplicably strange behavior, homes filled with papers and confusion, and above all being ignored in our preoccupation with analyzing and writing. To them, we say directly and lovingly, "You saw us through to the end. We owe you more than words can say."

ˋ◣　ˋ◣　ˋ◣

Acknowledgment is gratefully extended to the following for permission to reprint their works:

Extracts from Larry Cuban, *How Teachers Taught: Constancy and Change in American CLassrooms, 1890-1980*, copyright © 1984, New York: Longman with permission.

Tables from Robert B. Kottkamp, Eugene F. Provenzo, Jr., and Marilyn M. Cohn, "Stability and Change in a Profession: Two Decades of Teacher Attitudes, 1964-1984," *Phi Delta Kappan, 67*, copyright © 1986, Bloomington, IN: Phi Delta Kappa with permission.

Extract from Sara Lawrence Lightfoot, "Rosemont High School," in Vito Perrone and Associates, *Portraits of High Schools*, copyright © 1985, Princeton, NJ: The Carnegie Foundation for the Advancement of Teaching with permission.

Extracts from Dan C. Lortie, *Schoolteacher: A Sociological Study*, copyright © 1975, Chicago: The University of Chicago Press with permission.

Extract from Linda McNeil, "Contradictions of Control, Part 3: Contradictions of Reform," *Phi Delta Kappan, 69*, copyright © 1988, Bloomington, IN: Phi Delta Kappa with permission.

Extract from Arthur E. Wise, "Two Conflicting Trends in School Reform: Legislated Learning Revisited," *Phi Delta Kappan, 69*, copyright © 1988, Bloomington, IN: Phi Delta Kappa with permission.

Extracts from Seymour B. Sarason, *The Predictable Failure of Educational Reform: Can We Change Course Before It's Too Late?*, copyright © 1990, San Francisco: Jossey-Bass with permission.

Extracts from Lee S. Shulman, "Autonomy and Obligation: The Remote Control of Teaching" in L. S. Shulman and G. Sykes (Eds.), *Handbook of Teaching and Policy*, copyright © 1983, New York: Longman with permission.

# Part I

*Stability and Change Over Twenty Years: Purposes, Means, and Rewards of Teaching*

# Chapter 1

# Stability and Change in Today's Schools: An Overview

---

*Voices from the Classroom: Present and Past*

*October 18, 1984*

*Dear Mom,*

*I can't believe I'm writing you a letter, but don't worry, nothing is seriously wrong. I'm just writing rather than calling because I need to think my way through some pretty heavy career (and life!) decisions. Maybe it's the English teacher in me, but I've always found that writing helps clarify the issues. Since you've always been my best friend and teacher role model, I know you'll listen to my frustrations carefully, ask good questions, and (hopefully) not think of me as a quitter. The last point is really important because I've been feeling very guilty these days. Well, here goes!*

*After nine years in the classroom, I'm actually thinking of quitting. This is even hard for me to say because I have always thought of myself as a teacher. In fact, the matter seemed settled at birth. With you and Uncle Bob being teachers, I always had the sense that everyone just looked through the nursery window and said, "She's a nice girl. She'll make a good teacher."*

*In many ways, the family was right. I am a good
teacher, at least most days. My favorite teachers were
those who took a personal interest in me, and I always
try to do the same with my students. I think it's in my
blood and I really care about the kids, but Mom, it's
also really getting to me. For one thing, I'm never done.
Maybe that's what bothers me most, I'm never finished.
Even last night, I looked at Mark, reading the paper
with his feet up and watching television and I thought
to myself, I'm always in the same position, sitting at the
dining room table with ten thousand papers and books.
It's a good thing he's understanding because I'm not
communicative at night. I would just like, for one
evening, to sit on the couch, watch television, cut
coupons, and not feel guilty. I even feel guilty taking
time to clean my house.*

*The money also bothers me; it just isn't commensu-
rate with the effort I put in. My aspirations were
never to be a millionaire, but this is ridiculous. To add
insult to injury, when Mark and I go to parties, the
response I get from others when they find out what I
do is really depressing. Teaching just isn't respected
anymore. And when I'm working so hard and not
being appreciated, it hurts! I've come home and cried
because I've put so damn much of myself into a lesson
and then one of the kids isn't in a good mood and gets
the class going, and that's it—all that preparation is
down the tubes.*

*I know what you're thinking, Mom. All teachers have
bad days where plans go down the drain; that's part of
teaching. I agree, but kids are not the same as they were
when you taught. I can even see a difference since I
began. I see complete apathy, lack of interest, lack of
motivation! I give an assignment and the next day
maybe five students have done it, always the same five.
The average kid is not like I used to be—loving school
and doing all my homework. In fact, kids who are like
that are laughed at.*

*Getting kids to work is only part of the problem. The
other part is to keep war from breaking out. With the*

*combination of students I have, it's like walking into the United Nations, only no one gets along. To be the only peacemaker among 30 warring nations is no easy task. I actually have fist fights break out among redneck whites who hate blacks, blacks who know the whites hate them, and Mexicans from the migrant camps. Add to the racial and ethnic tensions, the usual adolescent skirmishes within groups, and you have the potentially explosive powderkeg I sit on each day. The first month I don't know if I taught my students anything but to respect the person sitting next to them. So much for the Dade County objectives #1-6 for English Composition! But how can they learn if they're afraid of being ridiculed or attacked?*

*Unfortunately, time devoted to developing tolerance and self-esteem is not understood or valued by my principal. All he cares about is good test scores so he wants every minute spent on drill and practice of basic skills by going page by page through the workbook. He also expects me to write detailed lesson plans, specifying behavioral objectives, procedures, and materials. I wrote them at first, then I rebelled. One reason—and I don't mean to sound arrogant—was that after nine years, I usually know what I am doing without writing everything down. Another was that I didn't want them to see that I wasn't always following the prescribed curriculum. But the greatest frustration was that I never got any feedback. They didn't check for content; they just checked to see if they were done. I'm already drowning in paperwork. I don't need any more secretarial tasks to take my time from the substance of teaching.*

*What I'm agonizing over now is whether to try something else. I have considered both going to law school and becoming an accountant. One of my best friends down here is an accountant and she makes twice what I do and gives, at the most, half the time. But would I really want to work with facts and figures all day? All of this is complicated by my desire to have a baby soon. If I can't take time to clean the house, how will I ever have time to take care of a child properly?*

*Right now, the thought of teaching for the next 20 years
scares me. How did you do it?*

*Love,*

*Karen*

ta ta ta

*October 23, 1984*

*Dear Karen,*

*I was surprised to receive your letter but not shocked to
learn you're considering leaving the classroom. Over
the past few years, particularly since your marriage, I
have sensed a growing dissatisfaction.*

*I don't know how much help I can offer because teaching
in the 60s was clearly different from what you are facing today. It's even hard for me to imagine the students
you describe or the level of prescription you receive on
what to teach and how. I vividly remember my first year
of teaching. Not a single soul came in to observe me, let
alone tell me what to teach. I recall thinking, I could be
teaching the Communist Manifesto and nobody would
know it! My principal didn't judge teachers by students'
test scores. The main criteria for effectiveness were a
quiet classroom and no parental complaints.*

*Still, I can relate to some of what you're saying. I had
students who destroyed lessons, didn't do homework,
and thought Julius Caesar was written in a foreign
language. Believe it or not, most of them saw no point
to learning the distinction between direct objects and
predicate nominatives. I didn't have a lot of record-
keeping, but I did grade 150 essays each week, with no
planning period. Teaching has never been a 9:00 to 5:00
job.*

*So what can I say to my dear daughter whose major
fault may be that she cares too much? I'll just raise a
few questions.*

*First, on the issue of motivation, have you asked students what interests them? I found that you can teach through almost any vehicle, so, if you know what they like, you can probably find materials that will grab them. My most apathetic students got excited about Catcher in the Rye because of the four-letter words. That's not the best rationale for literary selection, but you have to start somewhere.*

*Second, on the matter of misbehavior, can you involve the parents more? When I had problems with discipline, my most potent weapon was threatening to call home. The threat alone was usually enough because when parents found their children were causing trouble, they "grounded" them for the weekend.*

*The money issue has always been frustrating. Will the experiments with merit pay I've been reading about help you gain more recognition and financial reward? I'm biased, but I know you are the kind of teacher who would qualify.*

*Finally, let me talk about staying enthusiastic about teaching over 20 years. I didn't have the career options that you have today; still I would probably make the same choice today. I say this because when I had a good day, which was fairly often, and I could see that the kids really learned something, it was so exhilarating! I knew I was making a difference in the lives of human beings. I don't think I could feel that in an accountant's office. But, times are different, so I can see how you might reach a different conclusion.*

*Now, most importantly, what's this about not having time to take care of my grandchild properly? Just remember, now that I'm retired, I have plenty of time to baby-sit.*

*Love,*

*Mom*

ン ン ン

*October 28, 1984*

*Dear Mom,*

*Your letter gave me just what I needed—encouragement and food for thought. I must admit, though, I started to laugh when I read some of your suggestions. For example, finding relevant novels to read. Read? My students don't know what it's like to pick up a book and read. They just watch television or play video games. The result is they want everything to be immediate and handed to them. One day last week I gave my students an essay to write which started with an open-ended question. You should have heard them! They were upset because they couldn't find the answer in the book. When I told them it wasn't in the book, one of them asked in the most demanding tone, "Well, what are we supposed to do?" I just looked at him and said, "Well, what do you think you're supposed to do?" This kid responded, almost in shock, "You mean we have to think?" Can you believe that? And on the topic of what interests them, nothing—except Michael Jackson, and their friends. In fact, for most of my students, the main attraction of school is that it's a place where they can meet the other kids.*

*But it was your question about the parents that really got to me. The families in our school don't solve problems; they create them. We have mothers who work until they almost drop in the fields; we have mothers who are drug addicts. You can't believe what I have to do to find parents. If I actually do make contact, some say, "Why are you calling me? You should know what to do, you are the teacher!" Some of my colleagues have parents who threaten to sue them.*

*As far as merit pay goes, I hope it goes away—and soon. The competitiveness and hostility that come from one teacher in a building getting merit pay at the expense of someone else can destroy a school. What we need is across-the-board raises, and principals who have the guts to get rid of those who don't deserve to teach.*

*Unfortunately, my principal only thinks about keeping central office happy with higher test scores.*

*Now that I have dismissed all of your suggestions, you're probably wondering what I found helpful. It was what you said about good days. I started thinking about good days I've had. The first thing that came to mind was the mythology unit with my "skills" class. My colleagues in the department couldn't believe I would attempt it. One actually said, "Are you crazy, trying to teach mythology to these kids? They can't even write their own names." Well, they may not be able to write, but they're very imaginative kids, and this unit gave them an outlet for their creativity. They loved learning about the gods and goddesses and what they stood for. At the end, they created their own myths, and some were extraordinary. The best one, written by a black student, was a myth about why black people are black. It was incredible! Some of my students are very artistic, and I displayed their illustrations on the bulletin board. I was so proud of them, and, more importantly, they were proud of themselves. When I showed some of my doubting colleagues what my students had done, they were amazed. But when I offered to work with them in their classrooms to do something similar, I received the cold shoulder. It's really a shame that we all live and work in such separate worlds.*

*Another good day I recalled started as a disaster. Two kids got into a fist fight, with a lot of M-F this and M-F that. As I was trying to break them up, a third student got so incensed at their swearing that he yelled, "You don't talk like that in front of my teacher!" Then he jumped on the pile, so I had three kids rolling around on the floor. Later, when the fight was over, I realized how great it felt to have one of my students trying to protect me.*

*Lately, good days like these seem harder to come by. Still, just thinking about them made me smile. I've been trying to figure out what I could do to make more good days in the classroom. I've also been wondering what a good day is like for an accountant. It's hard to imagine. Maybe if I focus on generating more good days with students, I can, at least, make it through my tenth year. After that, who knows? I love you!*

*Karen*

ả ả ả

## Change and Stability in Teaching over Two Decades

Karen is one of the seventy-three teachers we engaged in lengthy interviews.[1] Her views and experiences are, in a number of important ways, representative of the larger interview sample. Karen also exemplifies much of what our nation desires from its teachers—intelligence, energy, caring, creativity, a sense of mission. Yet she is frustrated and in agony—almost to the point of quitting.

Teaching is in Karen's bones. She literally works day and night to be a good teacher, and she loves what she does. She feels tremendous satisfaction when her efforts result in student learning. But she feels success is increasingly difficult to achieve. Moreover, when she is is successful, it is at great personal cost in terms of time, energy, and emotion.

Karen relates the causes for her frustration to dramatic changes that have occurred since she was a student, since her mother was a teacher, and even since she started her own teaching career. She describes changes in students and parents, changes in the controls exerted upon teachers, and changes in the public's respect for teachers. Her sentiments foreshadow the more general view expressed in varying ways by members of our sample: *teaching today is more difficult and less rewarding than it has been in the past.*

While Karen pinpoints with clarity the changes that have caused her problems, we contend that she fails to recognize another significant but less visible source of her frustration: the forces for stability. She does not appear to see how some of the long-standing school and occupational structures and norms constrain her ability to respond effectively to new situations. For example, while the 1-to-30 teacher-student ratio provokes the complaint that she is the only peacemaker among thirty warring countries, she does not attribute her "order" problems to the large number of students crowded together in a small space. Secondary schools have been organized with this ratio for so long that Karen accepts it as a "given" of school life. Her mother's reference to grading 150 essays suggests her acceptance as well. Karen and her mother are not unusual. For most teachers, structural stability is difficult to see. In fact, some have called the organizational structure of schooling the "world of the more or less invisible" because those who work in schools are so acculturated into the givens that they no longer notice them (Cohn, Kottkamp & Provenzo, 1987; Owens, 1988).

Karen is caught between the challenges of highly visible manifestations of change—different students, parents, and accountability mechanisms—and the nearly invisible constraints of a stable school and occupational structure created for a former time and population. She is expected to confront the realities of moving into the twenty-first century within a school structure designed for the nineteenth century and within an occupational structure that perpetuates a conservative outlook. The pressure to incorporate unsettling changes into existing structures and norms, and the realization that the effort it takes is undervalued has made her consider leaving the only career she ever wanted.

Karen's personal agony introduces the central theme of our work. This book examines how dynamic forces of social change have collided with long-standing forces for stability in the organization of schools and the occupation of teaching and how teachers are absorbing the shocks of this collision. In some instances, teachers have reacted with amazing similarity; in other instances, the impact has been more varied. In most cases, however, the collision of change and stability has not resulted in fiery explosions but in smoldering accommodations. Schools, classrooms, and teachers today look remarkably similar to the way they looked in the past; yet there are fundamental differences that make teaching more difficult and less rewarding than it used to be.

Our vehicle for examining the forces of change and stability is the voices of teachers as they describe their work at two different periods in recent educational history. Our research took as its point of departure Dan C. Lortie's *Schoolteacher: A Sociological Study* (1975). His study of the "ethos" of the occupation—"the pattern of orientations and sentiments which is peculiar to teachers and which distinguishes them from members of other occupations" (p.viii)—grounded in his 1964 data is the baseline for our 1984 study. Using Lortie for historical perspective and context enables us to describe what it is like to teach today as compared to two decades ago, and to analyze how societal changes and school reform efforts of today are inextricably linked to and blocked by structures of the past.

In the sections that follow, we elaborate upon the concepts of change and stability and the ways we will use them as frameworks to hear and interpret the voices of teachers today. Our elaboration includes an overview of some of the dynamic changes that have rocked American society and its schools over the past two decades, as well as some of the structures in school organization and the occupation of teaching that have remained stable for over a century.

## Societal Changes Affecting the Schools

The particular changes that Karen describes in her letters can be closely coupled to major changes in the larger society. Among the social changes that buffeted our nation between 1964 and 1984 were the Civil Rights Movement and Viet Nam War and the responses they inspired; demographic changes within the country, and immigration; opportunities and consciousness-raising brought about by the Women's Movement and the subsequent increase in women working outside the home and in non-traditional occupations; changes in family structure and a rise in the divorce rate; saturation of public consciousness by the media; scientific and technological advances; increasing use of illegal drugs; and shifting values involving sexual behavior and preferences, marriage, and childrearing. Such changes had far-reaching effects on almost every facet of our society, including schools and teachers.

Although most teachers probably have had to contend in one way or another with each of these changes, some of these apparently have had more classroom impact than others. For example, teachers reported that changes in the traditional family structure have had an exceptionally powerful effect on the schools. Between 1965 and 1984 the divorce rate in our country more than doubled, with the numbers increasing from 479,000 to 1,169,000 (U.S. Bureau of Census, 1991, p. 86). From 1970 to 1984, the number of children involved in divorce proceedings in the given year grew from 870,000 to 1,081,000 (p. 88). By 1980, one-fifth (12 million children) of the school population were living in single-parent homes.

Children living in two-parent American families have also experienced significant changes. The increase in working mothers has meant that many children of "intact" families spend less time with parents and have less parental supervision. Duke (1984) argued that living in homes of either divorced parents or two working parents can negatively affect student behavior at school. Students with divorced parents may be less likely to have models of successful resolution of interpersonal difficulties; students of two working parents may exhibit a greater degree of independence but less inclination to conform to school rules, teacher expectations, and close supervision. Karen's frustration with parents who create rather than solve problems refers to some of these problems.

Changes associated with the Women's Movement have had serious implications for education. In addition to the fact that more women work outside the home than in the past, the broadening of work possibilities for women has meant that both potential and practicing teachers have options that garner higher status and higher pay (Carter, 1989; Darling-Hammond, 1984). Karen's consideration of a career in accounting or law in 1984 demonstrates a major shift from 1964, when the majority of college-educated women had only a choice between the "feminized" occupations of nursing and teaching.

Changes related to U.S. immigration and demographics have also dramatically affected schools by creating almost entirely new work contexts. In the 1960s and early 1970s, the student population in schools increased greatly; with the increase in numbers came an increase in the proportion of minority students. Moreover, since the early 1960s, many minority students entering school have not been fluent in English. In addition to language barriers, a host of new challenges have arisen from the dynamic created by a predominantly white, middle-class teaching force facing a growing proportion of minority students, many of whom are of a lower socio-economic background. One such new challenge is that of socializing these students into the school culture while preserving their native culture (Berlak & Berlak, 1981; Duke, 1984). For Karen, the changing school population meant spending weeks of instructional time on getting three different groups, Blacks, "red-neck" whites, and Mexican immigrants to work together within the confines of a single classroom.

While the effects of many cultural changes, such as those in family structure, enter schools directly through the children, others affect schools as policies, laws, or court decisions. In these cases such changes often involve conflicts that are ultimately resolved through the democratic political process at the federal, state, or local level by Congress, state legislatures, school boards, or the courts.

For example, schools and classrooms house a different mix of students since the passage of the federal Civil Rights Act in 1964, which brought about a new, legally backed emphasis on providing equal opportunity to all citizens. In an attempt to achieve equity, many school systems began desegregation programs, which included busing of students and transferring of faculty to obtain more racial balance. Moreover, the Elementary and Secondary Education Act of 1965 led to massive federally initiated and supported programs for disadvantaged youth, including Headstart, bilingual programs, and special education classrooms for students with mental, physical, or behavioral disabilities. The passage of Public Law (PL) 94-142 in 1975 initiated the mainstreaming of most special education students into the regular classroom for at least some part of the school day.

During the late 1960s, as federal programs for disadvantaged youth were being created, the Viet Nam War became another force for change in schools (Tyack, 1990). Student protests on college campuses over the war and over the rigidity of academic requirements, and the writings of "romantic" educators Dennison (1969), Kohl (1967), and Kozol (1967) stimulated efforts to "free the children" and loosen the structure of schooling at every level. "Open" schools and universities, "alternative schools," schools within schools, and "schools without walls" multiplied. The movement toward alternative systems was, however, a short-lived phenomenon, and by the 1970s the country was moving "Back to Basics" and developing accountability measures to "control the children and their teachers" (Wirth, 1983).

The accountability emphasis, which grew out of an interest in maintaining standards along with equity, pressed schools to demonstrate through scores on standardized tests, that all students were acquiring minimum basic skills. These pressures were generated largely through a far-reaching shift in legislative policy-making at the state level and implemented through the central offices of school districts.[2] Although the "reserved powers" clause of the federal Constitution leaves to individual states power over organization and control of public education, the majority of states, until recently, delegated to local school boards most decisions controlling the daily operation of public schools (Tyack, 1990). The degree of autonomy generally accorded to teachers for instructional decision-making, therefore, typically fell within the purview of the local school board. But as Lortie (1969, 1975) pointed out, it was always informally rather than legally grounded, and could be quickly and almost totally withdrawn in times of crisis.

Between 1964 and 1984, states began to reclaim for their central executive and legislative bodies significant portions of the latitude historically delegated to local school boards. Centralization of educational decision-making, which continues today, has come at the expense not only of school boards, but of administrators and teachers who were once in a better position to influence policies that they had to implement (Tyack, 1990; Wise, 1988). With state centralization, important educational decisions have increasingly been rendered by people geographically and experientially removed from specific information about the classrooms and schools they intend to affect (Chubb, 1988).

This increase in state control was coupled with and reinforced by recurrence of an ideology of reform built around the metaphor of the machine for organizations and workers. The ideology has roots in Taylor's "scientific management," an efficiency orientation popular during the period of public school institutionalization in cities (Callahan, 1962). In the late 1960s this ideology resurfaced through evaluation mandates attached to federal legislation for social change. These evaluation procedures were based on Pentagon-inspired input-output systems in relation to cost-benefit analyses (Wirth, 1983).

Wise (1979) demonstrated how this technocratic ideology exerted a powerful influence in the 1970s as it became interwoven with the states' efforts to exercise control over schools in order to get back to basics, create competency-based education, and try to achieve accountability. The technocratic ideology relies on prescribed formal rules and techniques of scientific management to increase efficiency. However, since cause-and-effect relationships between educational input and output are uncertain in some instances and nonexistent in others, such means often fail. These failures have encouraged legislators and bureaucrats to impose "new" and "improved"—but essentially similar—prescriptions, and so the process becomes self-perpetuating (Wirth, 1983; Wise, 1979).

We can see how heavy prescription manifests itself in Karen's classroom as she feels pressured to focus almost exclusively on the acquisition of basic skills through workbook practice so that her students score well on standardized tests. Her complaint about writing long and detailed lesson plans is another example of the more general effort to make teachers more accountable. Moreover, as a nine-year veteran who feels relatively successful in reaching lower-track students, Karen is still expected to produce the same types of plans that novices or failing teachers are required to do.

The immense social change of the last two decades has pushed its way into schools and classrooms with a pervasiveness that most teachers cannot escape. Facing different students who are less willing to accept the traditional curriculum, teachers often find themselves with lessons, activities, and methods that simply don't work any more. At the same time, the different lifestyles of today's parents make them less available or less willing to support teachers. New accountability policies and practices have dramatically altered what teachers are expected to do and how they are expected to do it. Teachers saw these changes; teachers felt these changes; teachers talked about these changes at length in our interviews with them.

## Stability in School and Occupational Structures

While teachers continually emphasized the impact of change on their lives, it soon became apparent that these highly visible changes had to be considered in the context of stability—an almost unshakable and invisible stability of the organizational structures of American schools and of the ethos of the occupation into which they had been socialized. The changes that teachers have experienced in terms of students, parents, and accountability have not been met with corresponding changes in the way schools are organized, teachers teach, or teachers are prepared. To the contrary, the challenges of change have been exacerbated by equally potent forces for stability which significantly constrain teachers' ability to respond.[3]

Teachers, however, did not speak directly or explicitly of problems caused by stability. They did not blame their difficulties on an inflexible school organizational pattern developed over a century ago, on long-standing occupational norms of isolation and privacy, or on unchanging teacher education programs, all of which foster constancy rather than innovation in the classroom. The structure of schools and the norms of the occupation have become so familiar that it is not easy for teachers to recognize how much these shape classroom activities. Still, as teachers talked about problems associated with change, their specific examples often made it clear that their capacity to work successfully with a different student population was hindered or blocked by stable features within the school organization or the "culture of teaching" (Cuban, 1984). We turn now to examine some of the components and forces for stability that interact with change in potent—if less obvious—ways to make teaching more difficult and less rewarding than it has been in the past.

## School Structure as a Force for Stability

The stability of American schools results from their structure, or what Willower (1990, p. 1) called the "organizational characteristics of public schools."[4] Physically, schools are composed of classrooms—small, cellular, isolated structures—containing one teacher and many students engaged in a variety of activities not easily observable by others. Each classroom is the domain of a college-trained, state-certified teacher who has multiple curricular goals to achieve. Student attendance in classrooms is mandatory, which means that teachers often face students who have an agenda that is different from the curricular goals of the teacher, and who, in fact, would rather be elsewhere.

Politically, public schools are officially governed by local boards of education, usually elected and therefore vulnerable to pressures and interventions from various constituencies, including parent organizations and teachers' unions. Because teachers and school administrators report to superintendents who, in turn, report to boards of education, in most cases, the possibilities for change and the probabilities for stability arise from a labyrinth of political maneuvers. While both the representation of various groups on the board and the layers of a bureaucratic organization in a school district tend to be forces for stability, that is not always the case. As Smith, Dwyer, Prunty, and Kleine (1988) pointed out in their in-depth analysis of the Milford School District, events such as the annual school board elections and the hiring and firing of superintendents and principals are forces for change as well as for stability.

Political and physical organizational characteristics affect the attitudes and behaviors of teachers, students, and administrators, and give rise to a shared set of norms and expectations. Two of the strongest teacher norms involve pupil control and teacher autonomy. Pupil control issues arise in large part from the involuntary nature of the student experience and the large number of students crowded into the small space of the classroom. An example of a pupil control norm is "Don't Smile until Christmas," which suggests that teachers have to establish strong behavioral control before they are able to teach (Ryan, 1970). Teacher autonomy arises from the fact that teachers are certified authority figures who have responsibility for their own separate classrooms. Because instruction is always an interactive endeavor and student responses can seldom be fully known when lessons are planned, teachers desire wide-ranging discretionary latitude within the classroom to make on-line decisions (Dreeben, 1973). One result of the autonomy norm is the reluctance of teachers to intervene in or evaluate the activities of their colleagues. Karen's offer to help colleagues develop a mythology unit and their lack of interest in working with her could have a number of meanings, one of which might be their unwillingness to have her involved in their classrooms. It could signal their general discomfort with breaking the norms of well-defined classroom boundaries and teacher privacy and autonomy. Connected to pupil control and teacher autonomy is the matter of time as a highly valued resource. Because of the large numbers of students and activities that teachers have to handle by themselves, they seldom have enough time to accomplish their goals. Karen comments that paperwork expectations reduce her time for the substance of teaching.

Student norms and values are quite different, and often in opposition to those of teachers. Secondary students, for example, tend to develop strong peer groups, many of which center on nonacademic pursuits instead of the academic goals of their teachers. Karen's complaints about students' lack of interest in academics and her view that they see school primarily as a place for being with friends illustrate well the "involuntary client" phenomenon.

School administrators usually take on the role of organizational protectors and conservators (Lortie, 1988). It is their responsibility to be sensitive to various interest groups and to keep the community and their district supervisors reasonably happy with the operations and outcomes of the school. On a daily basis, they are overloaded with multiple responsibilities; thus their day is often fragmented, given to the solution of immediate crises that arise with students, parents, teachers, and the physical plant. Because of work overload, the norm of teacher autonomy, and the absence of agreed-upon criteria for teacher effectiveness, administrators have historically supervised teachers with "a light touch" (Willower, 1990, p. 3). Time constraints plus lack of confidence on the part of high school administrators to judge effective teaching in different subject areas might account for the failure of Karen's administrators to provide useful feedback on her lesson plans. These same factors might also account for the fact that even though she has stopped submitting plans, there appear to be no repercussions. Nonetheless, Karen feels continual pressure from her principal to "cover" district objectives and basic skills for the competency tests. It is highly likely that the pressure levied on Karen and her other colleagues by her principal is, at least in part, related to his need to please the central office administration, the Board of Education, parents, and even the state department of education that monitors and compares districts on the basis of student outcomes.

Despite their complexity, public schools and their organizational arrangements have remained essentially stable because their various interwoven structural elements and the norms they engender are mutually reinforcing. While few individuals in these organizations consciously intend to maintain the organizational status quo—and while the organization *qua* organization certainly can have no "intention" to do so—the various components of the structure and norms work together to create an orderly and consistent environment, one not disposed toward change. Thus, while schools are action-oriented and potentially unpredictable places, many of the commonplace roles, routines, and rules can be understood in terms of the contributions they make to creating controlled and predictable organizations.

To the constituent components of organizational structure, we add one last conception—system. "System" as we use it is a greater abstraction than "organizational structure" and encompasses it. Sarason provided the following definition:

> One can see, touch, and interact with people and things, but not with the abstraction we call a system. System is a concept we create to enable us to indicate that in order to understand a part we have to study it in relation to other parts. It would be more correct to say that when we use the concept *system* it refers to the existence of parts, that those parts stand in diverse relationships to each other, and that between and among those parts are boundaries (another abstraction) of varying strength and permeability. Between system and surround are also boundaries, and trying to change any part of the system requires knowledge and understanding of how parts are interrelated. (1990, p. 15)

The concept of system further illuminates why change is difficult to bring about in an organization. School organization is a system. Every part is connected to every other part in ways that are almost invisible, and it is this set of relationships that give a school its own existence and stability. The connections force us to deal with all of the parts when we desire to change a single part; but, because these connections are almost impossible to see, we generally fail to consider them in reform proposals.

Stinchcomb (1965) argued that organizations continue to reflect the social and historical circumstances of the time in which they became institutionalized long after these circumstances have changed. The organizational characteristics of the current school structure are remarkably similar to those of schools built a hundred years ago. A similar statement can be made for the structure of teaching. We look now more closely at the ethos and stability of the occupation as described by Lortie (1975).

## Occupation Structure as a Force for Stability

In characterizing the ethos of teaching in the United States, Lortie maintained that it emanates from a special pattern of orientations and sentiments that, in turn, "derives both from the structure of the occupation and the meanings teachers attach to their work" (1975, p. viii). Orientations spring from the occupation's external structural aspects, especially those structures that perpetuate the occupation: recruitment, socialization, and the distribution of career rewards. Sentiments include preoccupations (attention given to some aspects of the environment but not others), beliefs (implicit and explicit theories to explain events considered important), and preferences (choices for one way of working rather than another). Sentiments derive from the tasks of the work, are internalized, and are emotion-laden (Lortie, p. 162). Lortie argued that the particular orientations and sentiments in teaching engendered conservatism, individualism, and a focus on the present among teachers.

Lortie (1975) also demonstrated how the current structure of teaching reflects its institutionalized origins in the developing urban schools of the latter half of the nineteenth century. In that era, teaching was low-status work plied mostly by under-educated, single young women who after a few years left the occupation to marry; high turnover of teachers was one result. Further, salaries of teachers were established within the larger societal pecking order of remuneration at a time when women lacked authority and when "women's work" lacked any type of pay equity. Salary levels and social status tend to become relatively fixed in relation to other occupations and their comparative rank is difficult to change.

Today, the occupation of teaching is still "women's work" (the current ratio is two to one) and still offers low pay and low status relative to other occupations that involve similar preparation and responsibilities. Although Karen sounds like a highly dedicated teacher, she still complains that her salary is nowhere commensurate with her workload and that the negative response that she gets socially when she announces she is a teacher is "depressing."

Lortie argued that the stability, or what he called "the tilt toward structural continuity" (1975, p. 21), in teaching stems, in large part, from the ways in which teachers are recruited and socialized into the occupation and rewarded for their efforts. On the issue of recruitment, his study revealed that teachers identify as attractions to teaching the opportunity to (1) work with young people, (2) be of service, (3) stay in school, (4) acquire material benefits (5) have a schedule with time flexibility. He also noted that entry is relatively easy due to highly accessible training, low admission standards, "the wide decision range" (for deciding early or late in life to teach), and a permissive "subjective warrant" (to decide that one is suited for teaching). Moreover, these attractors tend to produce teachers who value the status quo. Those who enter because they like school or the flexible schedule that is conducive to child-care are unlikely to invest time to change the organization. Karen's comments about how she loved school and always did her homework probably reflect a generally positive attitude toward schools as they have been. The problems she confronts are therefore cast in terms of the children who don't fit in, rather than in terms of a school organization that needs restructuring for today's youth. The chances of her becoming a change agent seem unlikely, particularly as she thinks about taking on the added role of motherhood.

In the domain of socialization, Lortie maintained that although prospective teachers are required to have a certain amount of formal preparation, they are not expected to complete a highly demanding program. All teachers must have at least a college degree, and their formal schooling includes both general and special schooling. One unique feature of the general schooling of teachers is that it actually functions in Lortie's terms as an "apprenticeship of observation," in that those who become teachers have, as students, already had at least sixteen continuous years of contact with teachers (1975, p. 61). This apprenticeship encourages the observers to internalize traditional patterns and leads to a widely accepted belief that "we teach as we were taught" (Kennedy, 1991; Porter, 1982). The special schooling, moreover, is relatively short and is "neither intellectually nor organizationally as complex as that found in the established professions" (Lortie, 1975, p. 58). It includes a "mini-apprenticeship" in the form of student teaching, which can be as short as six to eight weeks, and which is highly dependent for its quality on the skill of the supervising classroom teacher. Once hired, a beginning teacher is given the same full load of responsibilities that experienced teachers have and is expected to "learn while doing." The novice typically seeks advice from more experienced colleagues but is disposed to accept or reject suggestions largely on personal grounds. The criteria for acceptance appear to be that they fit one's situation or style and that they "work."

This process of socialization leads, in Lortie's words to an "emergence and reinforcement of idiosyncratic experience and personal synthesis" and to an absence of a "common technical culture" (1975, pp. 79-80). The inability to draw on an accepted body of knowledge in turn affects status and contributes to the individualistic and conservative outlooks of the occupation. Teachers do not feel confident to speak as a group or to respond to the demands of others from an authoritative knowledge base. Further, the overall weakness and brevity of the formal socialization simply cannot counteract the tendencies to absorb and use the ideas and approaches of one's prior personal experience. Thus the occupational structure and its stability link up with the institutional structure and stability as individual teachers selectively and privately continue to employ the models from their past or from their colleagues behind closed classroom doors.

Karen once again illustrates the point. While she doesn't speak about her teacher education in her letters to her mother, she does comment extensively in her interviews on the negative aspects of her preparation for the classroom. One major frustration was the fact that she did not have any extended field experience until she entered student teaching. In her words:

> For three and a half years, I had no idea what it was really like to be a teacher. I "aced" every education course I took, but I didn't know what it was like to be a teacher.

What was even more disturbing was that once she got into her student teaching placement, she had a very unsatisfactory experience with her supervising teacher. Her recollections went this way:

> She was a drill sergeant, and she was very, very structured, very methodical, very sarcastic. . . . She was such a tyrant. . . . The best days that I had were when she left me alone, and I developed a very close relationship with the kids, and she really resented that because they didn't warm up to her because she would not allow them to, and I'm not talking about being buddies, I'm talking about being people. . . . She was very, very sarcastic and very cold to them. . . . I enjoyed the days that I was able to do what I

wanted, and now and then I was allowed to do a project and those types of things.

Karen's experience appears to affirm Lortie's contention that the quality of the apprenticeship is highly dependent on the skill of the supervising teacher. In this case, Karen clashed with her supervising teacher over style and approach, and the result was a competitive situation in which Karen, when she was left alone, seems to have learned primarily "by doing." Moreover, as she indicates in one of her letters, when Karen got into her own classroom, she tended to teach as her favorite teachers taught—by taking a personal interest in each of her students. Thus, as Lortie also pointed out, she consciously and unconsciously was influenced by her "apprenticeship of observation." Her reliance on models of the past also extends to her seeking advice from her mother, who she maintains has always been a strong role model for her. These informal but powerful influences rooted in the past are usually strongly reinforced during student teaching and the first years on the job, as beginners are encouraged to learn from the most experienced teachers in their buildings. Under such circumstances, occupational stability is almost assured.

## *Organizational and Occupational Stability: Relationships and Results*

Although we have discussed stability in the occupation of teaching and school organization separately, their interconnectedness keeps surfacing. Cuban's (1984) analysis of the factors that had maintained a prevailing constancy in the pedagogy of American teachers illuminates the relationships. He concluded that school and classroom structures defined the boundaries within which the ethos or culture of teaching and individual teacher beliefs worked together to develop a "practical pedagogy" for survival. The structural organization of schools has established limits within which teachers must maneuver as they try to teach content, skills, attitudes, and values. The result has been the persistence of teacher-centered approaches that fit reasonably well within the structural limitations. For example, most teachers spend the majority of their time working alone with a group of students in a small space using methods such as lecture, recitation, discussion, demonstration, small group work, and seatwork. At the same time, the structure of the occupation has functioned to attract those who tend to be comfortable with these limitations, rather than those who would seek

129875

to change them. Thus, organizational and occupational structures have mutually reinforced their stability.

From time to time, however, there have been individuals or groups of individuals who have had other visions of how students learn and how schools should be physically arranged. These individuals have managed, for varying periods, to create and sustain alternative structures and pedagogies, particularly at the elementary level. The recurrence of these alternatives within the occupational stability and larger structural stability led Cuban to describe the freedom teachers have in determining their methods as "situationally constrained choice" (1984, p. 249). The narrative we present is basically one of constraints. But in Chapter 6 we look at how the beliefs of individual teachers appear to have altered the more general picture.

## Stability and Change in Today's Schools: Implications for Reform

In the chapters that follow we tell a story of change as it intersects with stability in our public schools. Throughout, we argue that powerful social forces for change have entered American schools and classrooms only to collide with equally strong forces for stability in the structure of schools and the occupation of teaching, and that the classroom teacher has borne the brunt of the impact.

While this story is important on its own terms, the context within which we write adds a critical dimension. Almost daily, we read in the popular press reports of new tests our children have failed, or basic knowledge and skills our children lack—after a decade of intense effort at school reform. Almost as frequently, there are new proposals to improve schools, teachers, and teacher education. The majority of proposals cite the central role of the teacher in improving our educational system, yet they continue to be written primarily by "outside experts" looking inward.

We maintain that if the cycle of failure in our schools and in our attempts to reform schools is to be broken, we must begin with the perceptions, feelings, and viewpoints of the "inside experts," the classroom teachers. It is they who have intimate knowledge of the challenges of change and the constraints of stability. It is they who can tell us about the contradictions and tensions that surface each day in the classroom.

But that is only the starting point. We must also look analytically at the system in which the work of teachers is embedded, with its almost invisible structures and unexamined assumptions. Recognition of the "intractability" of our schools with respect to change is equally critical to breaking the cycle of failure (Sarason, 1990). Our hope is that by listening carefully to teachers and looking closely at the structure and system in which they must work, we may envision a way out of our current educational stagnation. We begin by listening to teachers as they express the purposes they hold and the means they see as necessary to achieve them.

*Chapter 2*

# Teacher Purposes and Means

---

*Interviewer: What do you try most to achieve as a teacher? What are you really trying to do most of all?*

*Karen: I try to turn these kids into people. . . . Kids are selfish and very insensitive and can be very cruel. . . . I try to make them be open-minded and be more toler-ant, and be more flexible and accept change and accept people who are different from themselves . . . also . . . that there is life after high school and . . . that there is a world outside of the small community that they're in.*

ᏋᏋ ᏋᏋ ᏋᏋ

As a teacher, Karen holds ambitious and deeply felt purposes for her students, purposes that are much broader than the prescribed curriculum. She wants to help them succeed as people as well as students. She takes responsibility for their values as individuals and as members of a social group. She tries to influence what they will become after high school. She even seeks to extend their goals and expectations beyond the boundaries of their own community.

At the same time, Karen believes in and works diligently to teach her students the mechanics of grammar, the ability to express themselves in writing, and an understanding and appreciation of Greek myths and William Shakespeare, all of which are part of her district's tenth-grade curriculum. She recognizes that much of their success as persons after high school will hinge on the knowledge, skills, and dispositions they acquire while they are there. Karen is also well aware that many of the students she faces in her skills classes neither want, nor see the future value of, what she is trying to teach them. Therefore, she becomes absorbed in finding approaches to stimulate their interest, connect them to the prescribed curriculum, and lead them beyond it. Part of her approach involves establishing an atmosphere of respect for fellow students as well as the teacher.

Unfortunately, her ideas about purposes and means are often in conflict with those of her principal. The primary goal he holds for low-achieving students is the acquisition of basic skills; his recommended approach is drill and practice in the workbook. Karen claims that neither she nor the students can stand the "tediousness" of "working in a workbook every day," so she tries instead to teach skills in the context of her unit on mythology. Her response to her principal's expectation that she start at page one of the workbook and go to the very end is simply not to turn in her lesson plans.

The fact that Karen and her principal are at odds over purposes and means is neither new nor surprising. The broader purposes and the interpersonal means that teachers formulate grow out of their experiences within classrooms filled with human beings. The narrower goals and technical methods that many principals advocate grow out of pressures for academic outcomes exerted upon them by central office administrators, boards of education, state mandates, and national policy. The agendas and perspectives of the insiders and the outsiders are often quite different.

The conflict is intensified by the fact that in a democracy, there is rarely unanimity within any single external constituency. Historically, particular social forces have led dominant coalitions to press at different times for schools to emphasize academic excellence, vocational competence, preparation for democratic citizenship, scientific accomplishment, social justice and equity, or minimum basic skills. Even more problematic has been the tendency of Americans "to want it all" (Boyer, 1983).

As we write, the debate over purposes and means continues. Today's dominant theme of quality and academic achievement through emphasis on basic skills (Altbach, Kelly & Weis, 1985; Bouton, 1990) is challenged by those who would recommend a focus on a "common core" (Boyer, 1983), those who would favor an emphasis on thinking skills and learning how to learn (Sizer, 1984), those who would stress the acquisition of cultural literacy (Hirsch, 1987), and those who would argue for the importance of developing our "multiple intelligences" (Gardner, 1983; Gardner & Hatch, 1990).

We argue that discussion, debate, and decision-making among outsiders over the ends and means of schooling must seriously take into account the purposes that classroom teachers hold and the methods they believe they must pursue to reach them. As we will show, these goals and means have remained relatively constant over time and stand at the very core of how teachers—past and present—conceptualize their work. If we want to understand contemporary teachers and how they have been affected by change and stability in the workplace, if we want to support teachers in their efforts to help students learn, then we must begin at the beginning—by understanding what they are trying to achieve and how they are trying to achieve it.[1]

## Teacher Purposes: Making the Invisible Visible

As we present teachers' purposes over our twenty-year span, they sound familiar. Teachers then and now hold essentially the same broad aims—to help students grow academically and as whole human beings. Changes are more of degree or emphasis than kind. This continuity, however, can be problematic, for that which is constant is also hard to see. Teachers' goals are, in a sense, so obvious that they have become almost invisible, much like the structures of the workplace and the norms of the occupation. As a result, the full import of what teachers desire to accomplish is frequently disregarded in educational decision-making. Our intention is to bring teacher purposes into close and full view so that we can see with clarity how changes in the workplace have or have not affected their ability to reach them.

In his 1964 study, Lortie (1975) created survey and interview questions that probed for teacher purposes; in 1984, we replicated these questions and developed others. By looking at teacher responses twenty years apart, we can determine how teachers think about their purposes and pinpoint areas of stability and change.

### Teacher Purposes: Survey Analysis

Asking teachers to describe their teaching orientations is one way to determine teachers' purposes. Teachers responded in 1964 and 1984 to a survey question, "If I had to describe my emphasis in teaching I would say . . . ," which posed five gradations of choice between only teaching "subject matter" and only "other things." (See Table 2.1.)

TABLE 2.1

Teaching Orientations of Dade County Teachers, 1964 and 1984

| If I had to describe my emphasis in teaching I would say . . . | 1964 (%) | 1984 (%) |
|---|---|---|
| I'm pretty much the "no-nonsense, get-the-learning-of-the-subject-matter-done" kind of teacher | 5.7 | 15.5 |
| I tend toward the subject matter emphasis, but I think other things are important too. | 73.7 | 67.0 |
| I'm about 50/50 on this. | 17.6 | 16.3 |
| I tend away from emphasis on subject matter, as I consider other things more important. | 2.5 | 1.0 |
| I think that emphasis on subject matter is the mark of a poor teacher. | 0.4 | 0.1 |

*Source:* Kottkamp, Provenzo, & Cohn, 1986b, p. 562, by permission.

There is consistency across time in the teachers' overwhelming selection of the choice that indicates emphasis on subject matter as defined by official curriculum guides, but also acceptance of other goals. But there is also a shift in total responses across time in the direction of the "no-nonsense, get-the-learning-of-the-subject-matter-done" pole of the question. The proportion of "no-nonsense" responses almost tripled over the twenty years, with some erosion from all other choices. The overall pattern reveals an underlying stability in teaching orientation. However, at the same time, it shows that teachers were influenced by the demand for "back to basics" and content orientations that was exerted more forcefully in 1984 than in 1964.

The first survey question does little to elucidate teacher meanings associated with "subject matter" and "other things." Fuller understanding comes from a question that asked teachers to choose, for elementary and secondary students separately, the most important goal from among twelve. (See Table 2.2.)

Several patterns appear in these data. First, within each grade level there is relative stability across the time span. For elementary students the preponderant emphasis is given to two basic skills responses. Secondary level choices are less concentrated. But in both years secondary choices cluster on four student outcomes: using basic skills, desiring to continue learning, weighing evidence to solve problems, and enhancing emotional stability.

The second pattern is an overall movement toward more ele-

TABLE 2.2
Most Important Goals for Elementary and Secondary School Students
Chosen by Dade County Teachers, 1964 and 1984

| Assume that you were in the position of having to decide the single most important thing the school should do for (a) K-6; (b) 7-12. | Most Important Goal for: | | | |
| --- | --- | --- | --- | --- |
| | K-6 Students | | 7-12 Students | |
| | 1964 (%) | 1984 (%) | 1964 (%) | 1984 (%) |
| The basic tools for acquiring and communicating knowledge—the Three Rs | 27.1 | 42.0 | 1.5 | 2.4 |
| Efficient *use* of the Three Rs—the basic tools for acquiring and accumulating knowledge | 44.5 | 35.1 | 14.0 | 24.3 |
| A continuing desire for knowledge, the inquiring mind | 9.3 | 8.5 | 29.5 | 31.0 |
| Ability to live and work with others | 8.8 | 5.4 | 10.4 | 5.8 |
| The habit of weighing facts and imaginatively applying them to the solution of problems | 2.7 | 1.2 | 17.0 | 13.4 |
| A sense of right and wrong—a moral standard of behavior | 2.0 | 4.9 | 3.0 | 5.0 |
| An understanding of the government and a sense of civic responsibility | 0.1 | 0 | 1.4 | 1.2 |
| An emotionally stable person, prepared for life's realities | 4.4 | 2.1 | 16.1 | 10.5 |
| Loyalty to America and the American way of life | 0.6 | 0.2 | 1.8 | 0.8 |
| Information and guidance for a wise occupational choice | 0.3 | 0.1 | 4.8 | 4.6 |
| A well-cared-for, well-developed body | 0 | 0.1 | 0.2 | 0.2 |
| Other | 0 | 0.4 | 0.3 | 0.8 |

*Source:* Kottkamp, Provenzo & Cohn, 1986b, p. 562, by permission.

mental forms of subject matter emphasis. At the elementary level, this is seen in the shift toward more emphasis on acquisition of the "Three Rs" and away from effective use of these skills. At the secondary level this appears as an increase in the focus on use of the basic skills (and consequently a move away from inter- and intrapersonal skills and from creativity in application). These data corroborate the patterns derived from the first question: general stability with some movement toward more elemental forms of subject matter learning. The second question also helps to flesh out the meanings teachers attach to the two categories in the first question. The patterns across both questions suggest important, although certainly not sweeping, effects of pressures toward basic skills and accountability on personal goals of teachers. These patterns might also be read as a slight lowering of expectations for students.

While these findings show teachers moving in the direction of the most powerful external forces and the direction espoused by the school district, they do not tell whether teachers are moving willingly or being pushed. Further insight into the relationship between external and school district attempts to redefine school purposes and teachers' own purposes was gained through new data and reanalysis of the second question. In addition to their personal goal, in 1984 we asked teachers for the single goal most emphasized in their own school. The further analysis (displayed in Table 2.3) compared the individually chosen goal responses with those reported for schools arranged by four grade-level categories. The statistics (in Table 2.3) for each grade level were the perceptions of teachers at that level alone, and only for the top five goals.

These data show that goals emphasized in schools are more focused on acquisition and use of basic skills than teachers desire them to be, and that the discrepancy is considerably greater at the secondary than elementary levels. Further, the top personal choice of both junior and senior high teachers, a continued desire for knowing, received little actual support in the schools. More discrepant yet is the complete lack of emphasis in the secondary schools for developing and weighing facts and applying them to imaginative problem-solving, the goal ranked third highest by teachers at both secondary levels. These data show goals the schools emphasize to be more oriented to basic skills than are those of the teachers who work there. They suggest possible tensions caused by the disjuncture of personal and official goals, especially at the secondary level. Survey data do not allow us to probe this issue, but we return to it later in the examination of interview responses.

## Teacher Purposes: Interview Analysis

Having examined stability and change in teacher purposes through surveys, we plumbed the same issue through interviews. The key questions posed were: "What do you try most to achieve as a teacher? What are you really trying to do most of all?" Lortie had

TABLE 2.3
Dade County Teachers' Identification of Personal Goals for Students
and Goals Emphasized in Their Schools, 1984

| *Assume that you were in the position of having to decide the single most important thing the school should do. Which do you consider . . . most important? Which area is most emphasized in your school?* | | Grade levels | | | | | | |
|---|---|---|---|---|---|---|---|---|
| | | K-3 | | 4-6 | | 7-9 | | 10-12 |
| | | *Most Important Goal* | | | | | | |
| *Teacher/School Emphasis* | T | S | T | S | T | S | T | S |
| *Goal:* | *(%)* | *(%)* | *(%)* | *(%)* | *(%)* | *(%)* | *(%)* | *(%)* |
| The basic tools for acquiring and communicating knowledge—the Three Rs | 43 | 52 | 39 | 47 | 2 | 25 | 4 | 19 |
| Efficient use of the Three Rs—the basic tools for acquiring and accumulating knowledge | 33 | 34 | 39 | 35 | 25 | 39 | 21 | 34 |
| A continuing desire for knowledge, the inquiring mind | 9 | 4 | 8 | 2 | 28 | 6 | 34 | 12 |
| Ability to live and work with others | 7 | 3 | 6 | 4 | 7 | 6 | 5 | 7 |
| The habit of weighing facts and imaginatively applying them to the solution of problems | 1 | 1 | 1 | 1 | 15 | 1 | 17 | 1 |

asked this question of Five Towns teachers twenty years earlier. In analyzing his findings, Lortie found the most frequently expressed response to be "curricular responsibilities" (77%), but noted that teachers also expressed three purposes "beyond the curriculum." He described these as follows: "(1) the moral aspects of teaching, (2) the 'connecting' function of the teacher who instills love of school or a particular subject, and (3) the theme of inclusiveness—of reaching *all* the students in one's charge" (emphasis in original) (1975, p. 111). In our study, we used this question to push teachers to think beyond the countless objectives they formulate for individual lessons and toward their overall priorities. Teacher answers varied substantially, but fell roughly into five categories; each represents an emphasis rather than a completely separate idea.

**Teaching Toward the Prescribed Curriculum.** The first category contained responses focused on course content and the knowledge and skills stipulated, taught, tested, and graded by teachers. Forty percent of respondents made statements under this rubric. This contrasts considerably with the 77 percent, reported by Lortie for this category. The elementary teachers spoke in these terms:

> The basics in academics, to know how to read, to do the basic things in math. (26, F, W, Elem/L, 4th)[2]

≈ ≈ ≈

> I'm trying to bring them up to grade level so that they can pass the tests to get out of the Chapter I class. (14, F, W, Elem/M, 3rd)

Junior high teachers talked this way about curricular purposes:

> Communication of the subject to the students; that they really learned it; not just grades but learning. (53, F, H, Jr/L, Gen. Math)

≈ ≈ ≈

> Make them literate when they leave, that's my overall goal. (59, F, B, Jr/H, Spec. Ed/L.D.)

As might be expected, the largest proportion of subject-matter responses (46%) came from high school teachers. Typical statements were:

> Cover the content. (35, F, W, Sr/H, English/Lang. Arts)

≈ ≈ ≈

> I want them to read efficiently, effectively, communicate like educated people. (30, F, W, Sr/H, Lang. Arts)

That only 40 percent of teachers offered curricular responses is open to multiple interpretations. The most obvious is that curricular goals are taken so much for granted that many teachers failed to mention them. Another interpretation is that the phrasing of the question led respondents to talk about goals beyond the prescribed curriculum. Less obvious is the possibility that the majority of teachers in our sample view the essence of their classroom role as much more than conveying content. In fact, of the teachers who specified curricular aims, only three spoke exclusively of them. Thus, the large picture that emerges is of teachers like Karen, who see their purposes in a broader context than the official curriculum. Whereas Lortie developed three categories "beyond the curriculum," we made sense of our data through four. Similarities and differences among the two sets of categories are explained below.

**Teaching Toward Thinking Skills.** This category, not specifically mentioned by Lortie, is closely connected to curricular aims but extends beyond them. While some teachers regard the explicit teaching of thinking skills as an integral part of their curriculum, interview responses suggested that special efforts are necessary for students to acquire these abilities. It was as if these purposes were part of the ideal academic program, but, at the same time, one step beyond what was, in reality, stressed in the daily course of classroom teaching and learning. Twenty-five percent of the teachers identified this aspect of learning as a priority, nearly 70 percent of whom were in high schools. Their comments revealed two related emphases: logical reasoning and application of subject matter to real-life situations. The following examples capture the substance and flavor of their responses:

To think and not be mesmerized by clichés and statements that are at variance with facts. To think for themselves. (42, M, W, Sr/H, Soc. Stud.)

ια ια ια

To think logically, to say what you mean, answering questions directly. (10, F, W, Sr/M, Eng.)

ια ια ια

To show relevance of subject matter to their daily lives. (47, F, W, Sr/H, Gen. Sci.)

ια ια ια

As a biology teacher . . . if I can somehow affect their future
lives, even if they don't go into medicine or any other bio-
logical field, positively. I'll give you an example. We know
that the cold virus can get into the body primarily through
the nose or eyes. If I can teach them to keep their hands
away from their noses and eyes during flu season, you'll
have a healthy and happy life, and you'll have healthy and
happier children. If you can do something to affect their
future dramatically. (18, M, W, Sr/M, Sci. Bio.)

Both thinking skills and application of subject matter are, of
course, predicated on the acquisition of knowledge. Thinking is
not done in the abstract; one has to acquire and understand information about viruses before applying it. Still, these responses suggest movement beyond the prescribed curriculum. And certainly
these responses go beyond what many teachers perceive to be the
goals emphasized in their schools. (Table 2.3.)

**Teaching for Positive Attitudes Toward Learning.** This third
theme, similar to Lortie's category of "Connecting Children to
School and Learning," was identified as a priority by twenty-four
percent of our teachers:

That they will like school, like themselves. . . . I have seen
over and over again where, as they get this kind of start
and this kind of foundation, they will continue that way. . . .
(61, F, W, Elem/H, Kindergarten)

૱ ૱ ૱

If you instill in them a love of learning, aside from all the
basics . . . they are going to be all right for the rest of their
lives. You know they will go on if they love spending time
in the library. . . . (40, F, W, Elem/M, 3rd)

૱ ૱ ૱

. . . To realize that learning is not just a finite experience,
but it goes on throughout life. (52, M, H, Jr/H, Gen. Math)

According to Lortie (1975), teachers who express serious interest in building positive attitudes toward school, learning, and particular subjects do not believe children are intrinsically motivated

and naturally eager to learn. Instead, they see the teacher as a major stimulus and model for developing and valuing an interest in learning. Among our 1984 interviewees, interest in learning has both present and future dimensions. Thus, while some comments stress the importance of conveying learning as a life-long endeavor, an assumption undergirding others is a strong link between student attitudes or interest and achievement in school. A related assumption is that positive attitudes toward learning must start early; 84 percent of teachers who cited attitudes about learning as a major goal were at the elementary or junior high level.

**Teaching Toward Social and Moral Development.** This category corresponds in some degree to Lortie's "Teacher as Moral Agent." About half of the Five Towns teachers described themselves as striving to achieve moral outcomes. Most of Lortie's examples stressed the teacher's role in developing good citizens who respect one another and contribute positively to society. A considerably smaller proportion, 28 percent of our sample, expressed similar aims:

> I want my students to be better people. . . . Citizenship in social studies covers lots of things. If you hear of somebody being rude to somebody else, you say, look, come on. If we can just love each other, then we'd never have wars. . . . I would like for them to pass tests. I do anything for my students to pass. . . . That's important, but what is really important is getting along with each other. As a social studies person, that's what I like to see, children and teachers getting along. (13, F, W, Jr/L, 6th)

But citizenship goals extend beyond social studies teachers. The following statements by elementary school teachers and a high school English teacher convey the nature and breadth of commitment on the part of some teachers to help young people develop the qualities needed to function in a democratic society:

> I'm trying to cover the content area in my field, and I'm also trying to make better citizens for my community and the United States . . . hopefully inspire students to do the best that they can do in any field, give them self-confidence, teach them respect for themselves and other people because I'm interested in the community in which I live, and it happens to be a very harsh community. I'd like to see it made

better, and these people are our future leaders. (35, F, W, Sr/H, Lang. Arts/Eng.)

❧ ❧ ❧

To treat each other as human beings and to be nice and to care about other people. (48, F, H, Elem/M, 6th)

❧ ❧ ❧

In PE the first thing we try to do is get along, and that is the main thing. Try to get along and try to have respect for others. . . . if you can get along and have respect, and show good sportsmanship, that means a lot. . . . You can't win all the time. If you lose, accept defeat, because that is what life is all about. (11, M, B, Elem/M, Phys. Ed.)

The last two quotations describe citizenship as a goal for the present. This shorter-term emphasis may be related to the organizational characteristics of schools described in Karen's letters and in Chapter 1: crowded places populated by students who do not necessarily wish to be there.

**Teaching Toward Individual Growth and Development.** While some teachers felt strongly committed to helping students develop morally and socially, the largest single group, 57 percent, expressed individual student growth and development as a priority. A number of teachers talked in particular about helping "each child to reach his/her potential":

I have mostly gifted, but I have children that are at the other end of the spectrum. I like to think that by June I have helped each child to reach or realize his potential. . . . just to get as far as he can with the tools he's got. . . . They're all different, . . . and I want to be able to get as much out of them as they are capable of. (11, F, W, Elem/H, Primary)

❧ ❧ ❧

I want my students . . . to succeed. I want them to feel the importance of an education, that they will go out into the world and do the best they can with what they have. And if I can make what they have a little bit better, I can open the door maybe and they can go get it. . . . If they can just make the best person out of themselves that they can. (51, M, W, Sr/L, Lang. Arts/Eng.)

ᴥ ᴥ ᴥ

I have all individual goals, but as a group goal, it is to see some progress in all of them by the end of the year. I have higher goals for the older ones and not as strict goals for the younger ones. (6, F, H, Elem/M, Spec. Ed.)

These teachers appear to assume that in any classroom students come with individual differences and that the teacher's role is to take each of them as individuals just as far as s/he can go.

Self-esteem was a second area of emphasis within the category of individual growth and development. Many teachers who hold self-esteem or self-image as a goal teach younger children or those with special learning problems:

Forgetting academics, the most important thing I do with my kids, whether it be personal or in school, is to make them feel good about themselves. They can leave my class-room and have a decent self-image; then I know I have done my job . . . that's the most important thing for me. (56, F, W, Elem/H, Kindergarten)

ᴥ ᴥ ᴥ

The bottom line, in my field, the most important thing that we can do with these kids, is to make them feel good about themselves. I find that when they come over from the elementary school, they have had sometimes seven years of being told that they couldn't, they can't, they're too dumb, can't learn, you're different, or whatever. Their little egos are so depressed. . . . (07, F, B, Jr/H, Spec. Ed./V.E.)

ᴥ ᴥ ᴥ

You can't accomplish anything if they don't feel good about themselves, or if they don't feel that they can do it. . . . I think you have to deal with the whole student, and you have to work and talk . . . you can't just have such a struc-tured situation that there's no time for personal things. . . .

If a kid has a problem, they can't learn. . . . If you can talk
about things, or if the kid wants to talk about things, it's
appropriate, if it would fit into the group, and if the group
is interested in discussing, then I feel that's as important as
that math objective or the language arts objective for the
day because they have to live in the world. They have to
know these things are out there, and they have to deal with
them. They have to deal with themselves and how they
relate out there.... Content is important too. But I feel that
you have to deal with all these other things. You can't just
deal with content alone. (55, F, W, Sr/L, Spec. Ed./L.D.)

Most surprising were the high school teachers of "regular" students who also claimed to concentrate on self-image:

Art is not just making pretty pictures: It's building self-
esteem in the student, and if a student can express himself
in an individual manner and feel good about it, it helps. . . .
We get students that can only do art, and they're bad in
other subjects. They get recognition from other students.
That's one thing, but if they feel what they put down on
paper is good or expresses themselves and they're pleased
with it, then it reinforces. . . . It's more . . . psychological
than it is visual because there's so much decision-making in
art. What color do I put here? What will I do over there?
There's more decision-making in art in some cases than in
any other subject. (38, F, W, Sr/L, Fine Arts)

A third emphasis within the category of individual growth and
development we labeled the "Pygmalion" strand:

I'm trying to get kids to really make something of themselves, to really be somebody, and not have to depend on
other people. I see so much of that now. It seems like so
many young people are depending on parents, or depending on welfare, or depending on so many other different
things. So I'm trying to get them to be more independent.
(67, F, B, Sr/M, Phys. Ed./Math)

ða  ða  ða

I am very big about keeping a good self-image so you think
well of yourself. I take care of kids who come not dressed

properly and don't look well-groomed. I manage to get them looking like people. (50, F, W, Sr/L, Lang. Arts/Eng.)

Pygmalion comments came mainly from high school teachers who suggested they took enormous responsibility for transforming unsuccessful students into successful people. Karen's statement at the beginning of this chapter falls under this rubric. These comments exhibit interest in bringing about major changes in the lives of the students by molding their attitudes. As one teacher put it:

> You do see a change in attitudes in high school students; there's no question about it. . . . I see a change in attitudes from the beginning to the end of the year. I really see a change in the two weeks that I have been teaching these two groups in summer school. I'm a molder. I get them to do what I want. . . . (50, F, W, Sr/L, English)

Lortie identified an ideal among Five Towns teachers called "Inclusive Teaching: Concern with Universalism," which stresses reaching every student. He found it curious to think of working with *all* students as something "extra." His explanation was that not all teachers did teach inclusively and that, without special effort, some students "fall through the cracks" (1975, p. 115). While the Five Towns teacher's statement, "I'm trying to get every kid to read as well as he can," sounds much like the statement, "I want each child to reach or realize his potential," we sense a subtle but basic difference in emphasis between Lortie's universalism category and our individual growth and development theme. Five Towns teachers appeared to be concerned primarily with equity, but Dade County teachers appeared primarily concerned with diversity. Perhaps the differences in achievement level among Dade County students were serious enough for many teachers to feel a need to individualize efforts and standards. Rather than aiming toward trying to make everyone achieve a single standard, many teachers seemed committed to helping each student maximize his/her unique abilities.

Underlying this effort are several related assumptions. One is that not everyone can achieve the same objective standards set by the district or state. Another is that building the individual's self-esteem and self-worth is a prerequisite to reaching her/his full potential, and is therefore a legitimate purpose for teachers. Still another is that self-esteem and self-worth are linked to the whole child, not just the child as student (Berlak & Berlak, 1981). As one elementary school teacher put it:

I'm teaching children, I'm not teaching reading, writing, math. That's secondary. I really think that if you can't reach them, you can't teach them. (57, F, W, Elem/M, Kindergarten)

## Multiple Purposes of Teachers and Their Meaning

Answers teachers gave to the question of what most of all they are trying to achieve reflect an array of purposes extremely difficult to accomplish and even more difficult to assess. The four purposes beyond the curriculum cannot be accomplished in daily lessons or weekly units; nor can they be evaluated through sporadic or single observations by building level administrators or highly specific behaviorally based assessments such as the Dade County TADS system.[3] They can, in some instances, be assessed over the span of an academic year, if teachers and administrators design alternative evaluation activities. But, given the evaluation measures used in most schools, they are more likely to be seen only years later, if at all. The difficulty in assessing progress toward the achievement of ambitious purposes is one contributor to the "endemic uncertainties" of teaching (Lortie, 1975).

When Lortie asked Five Towns teachers to describe prideful occasions, a delayed gratification theme emerged. Nearly half of the secondary teachers spoke of pride in the educational and vocational success of former students or of pride experienced when students returned to express appreciation for their teaching. We did not ask our sample to describe prideful situations, but their responses to a question on important satisfactions indicated that rewards connected to these larger purposes were often delayed for years. One kindergarten teacher made an important distinction between the daily and the more significant, but necessarily delayed, satisfactions:

About a month ago I had a 22-year-old boy knock on the door. He said, "Miss R?" I said, "Yes." He is now in England, an architect; he's married and has a little girl. I thought, "This is not happening to me. I had you in kindergarten." If you teach high school and a kid comes back and he's married in two or three years, that's expected, but 16 years or 18 years—first year in kindergarten. It's rewarding. . . . be it one year, or ten years down the road. My father kept telling me this. He taught Bob Graham [Governor of Florida] and Bob constantly communicates back and forth with him. That's the reward, it's not on a day-to-day, it's after you completed a year or so. There are daily satisfactions—"She got it!"—that's a reward in itself, but I think it's a little bit down the road that you get your satisfaction. (57, F, W, Elem/M, Kindergarten)

Our data on purposes indicate that the pluralism in personally defined goals found by Lortie (1975) still exists. Attempts to focus and narrow teacher purposes toward basic skills may have had some effect as indicated by the survey responses, but they have neither eliminated broader purposes nor reduced their variety. These findings suggest not only tension between official attempts to move teachers in a direction different from their own personally held purposes, but that teachers may not agree upon common ground if left to themselves.

In sum, we see in survey responses that forces of change from the larger society, focused through state and district mandates for excellence, accountability, and basic skills, have had some impact on teacher goals. We see in interview responses that changes in students themselves may have resulted in greater recognition of their diversity and a shift toward encouraging their individual growth and development. But the interview and survey responses taken together indicate much more stability than change over twenty years. We also see a discrepancy in both survey and interview data between the continuing forces for change, especially official pressures to focus teacher efforts more narrowly on basic skills through accountability, and teachers' broader expression of purposes. This theme reemerges in later chapters.

## *The Means for Accomplishing Purposes: Knowledge, Skills, Attitudes, and Qualities of Good Teachers*

There is perhaps no more controversial issue in education than the specification of the means of reaching goals, especially when the means are supposed to represent the characteristics of good teaching. In casual conversation, students, parents, administrators, teacher educators, and lay people speak freely in intuitive and judgmental terms about teachers they know. When the context is more formal, however, these same people often have difficulty defining "good" and "bad" teaching. Hesitancy increases dramatically when judgments are used to reward or fire individuals.

Nonetheless, we encouraged our interviewees to make explicit their conceptions of the means to successful teaching by asking three different sets of questions:

> What kind of knowledge do you think a teacher must possess—what does s/he have to know to be able to do a good job? What skills must s/he possess—what does s/he have to be able to do—to do a good job? What kind of attitudes must s/he exhibit?

> Please describe one of your own teachers whom you considered outstanding. Are there any teachers with whom you work or have worked that you consider outstanding? Would you describe one for me?

> What are your greatest strengths as a teacher? What are your shortcomings?

These differ not only in the specific content probed but in the method of seeking it: the first and third questions are direct, the second is indirect.[4] We analyzed responses to the three questions through a four-stage process. This began at a concrete, literal level and became more abstract and interpretive with each step.[5] Here we present only the final step in the analysis, a rough quantification of "thought unit" responses about the knowledge, skills, attitudes, and qualities required to be a good teacher.

The concept of teacher "qualities" was not contained in the first set of questions. However, in analyzing the responses we found a number which could not be categorized neatly as knowledge, skill, or attitude.[6] We created the new category, "qualities," to include broad patterns of behavior that arise from personality and are not likely to be easily instilled through typical teacher education programs or staff development approaches. Qualities are simply "of the person."

Statements from the four areas of knowledge, skills, attitudes and qualities were coded into one of five clusters (see Table 2.4). Each cluster referred to a broad dimension of teaching, such as "Pedagogical Processes" or "Interpersonal Interactions."

## Knowledge Good Teachers Possess

Comments on knowledge made up 16 percent of all thought units across the three questions. Of the knowledge statements, the vast majority referred to broad subject matter knowledge, specific

TABLE 2.4
Dade County Teachers' References to Means for
Accomplishing Purposes, 1984

| Dimensions of Teaching | Knowledge (N) | Skills (N) | Attitudes (N) | Qualities (N) | Totals (N) | (%) |
|---|---|---|---|---|---|---|
| Work itself or the job | 0 | 0 | 32 | 34 | 66 | 12 |
| Subject matter | 62 | 0 | 9 | 0 | 71 | 13 |
| Pedagogical processes | 10 | 118 | 4 | 0 | 132 | 25 |
| Interpersonal interactions with students | 6 | 69 | 76 | 67 | 218 | 41 |
| Other* | 9 | 19 | 4 | 12 | 44 | 8 |
| Totals | 87 | 206 | 125 | 113 | 531 | 100 |
| | (16%) | (39%) | (24%) | (21%) | | |

* This cluster was created by collapsing three small, more specific clusters: Reference to Adult Interactions, 0.8%; References to Intellect and Cognition, 2%; and References to Individual Students, 6%. None of the smaller clusters had responses in each means category.

content, a solid foundation in the liberal arts, and such specifics as a good command of standard English. Important but much smaller proportions of comments referred to knowledge of pedagogical processes and interpersonal interactions, such as the psychology of learning, principles of motivation, learning and perception principles, how to relate to students, and how to maintain sensitivity to students.

## Skills Good Teachers Possess

Skills comprised 39 percent of all thought unit responses on teachers' abilities, almost double those on both attitudes and qualities and more than double those on knowledge. Within this category, responses overwhelmingly focused on two clusters, interpersonal interactions (33%) and pedagogical processes (57%). Specific interpersonal skills mentioned included earning respect, empathizing with all people, interacting with and relating to people, building rapport, and getting kids to work cooperatively.

Pedagogical skills included making learning come to life, being dramatic in presentations, stimulating students to the point where they look forward to coming to class, getting students engaged in learning, conveying high expectations, simplifying ideas, constructing logical pathways for learning, communicating in more than one way, developing learning centers, employing a variety of teaching strategies, and organizing and developing structures for learning.[7]

The proportion of skill responses to knowledge responses makes it clear that teachers believe they need to be highly skilled as well as knowledgeable to reach their purposes. The emergent image is one which goes well beyond the subject matter specialist to that of a dynamic conductor who can orchestrate the multiple demands of the job and the needs of diverse learners.

## Attitudes Good Teachers Exhibit

Slightly less than one-quarter of all thought units were coded as relating to attitudes. Most references to attitudes were oriented toward two major dimensions of teaching. One emphasis was related to the job or work of teaching (26%). Examples of these attitudes included wanting to teach and doing it "from the heart," enjoying the work, being dedicated to the job and to children, living up to one's own standards, doing what makes sense in the face of "silly rules," and persisting until students learn. Positive attitudes toward teaching and one's own performance can, in the view of a number of these teachers, significantly contribute to classroom success.

The other major cluster concerned interpersonal interactions with students (61%), which included the tone of relationships, expectations and standards for behavior, and moral and personal development of the students. Viewed broadly, teachers indicated that attitudes toward students were important for effective teaching. In terms of establishing positive interpersonal relationships, they maintained it is necessary to like students, enjoy being with them, care about them, be interested in them, and trust them. In terms of expectations and standards, teachers must believe students can learn, expect the best of them, and accept nothing less.

## Qualities Good Teachers Exhibit

Slightly less than one quarter of the total thought units were coded as qualities. The proportion indicates a solid basis for having created this data-grounded category. Over half of these responses were associated with the interpersonal interaction dimension. Examples of qualities included: supportive, helpful, unselfish, giving, stern and strict, firm but loving, tough, generous, fair, flexible, honest, enthusiastic, consistent, warm, sensitive, sincere, and charismatic. The other dimension well represented in this domain concerned work itself and personal characteristics associated with it. Examples included: conscientious, hardworking, going the extra mile, professional and diplomatic, organized, dedicated, and committed. Half of the qualities responses came from questions about former teachers and exemplary peers; they were more frequently given from the viewpoint of the observer or recipient of instruction than from that of the teacher as actor.

## Dimensions of Teaching

Our focus now shifts to the five clusters of dimensions of teaching whose content cuts across the four categories of means for achieving teachers' purposes—knowledge, skills, attitudes, and qualities. (See the percentage distributions for the clusters arrayed down the right margin of Table 2.4.) What stands out is that 41 percent of all thought units concerned interpersonal relationships with students. Subsumed in this cluster are statements about rapport with students, behavioral expectations for them, and classroom management. The next largest cluster, pedagogical processes, contains a quarter of the total responses, including references to learning, motivation, planning and organizing instruction, and teaching strategies. These responses are heavily concentrated in the skills category, unlike interpersonal relationships, which are spread evenly across skills, attitudes, and qualities. Taken together, interpersonal relationships with students and pedagogy make up two-thirds of the total responses.

## What It Takes to Achieve the Purposes of Teaching

Lortie (1975) asked the Five Towns teachers the same questions about their outstanding peers and former teachers but analyzed the responses for "outcomes" and "criteria of respect," rather than knowledge, skills, attitudes, and qualities. Despite the differences between his approach and ours, it is his findings from these questions that serve to unite the two parts of our chapter. In his analysis, he differentiated between "ultimate, instructional results" and "proximate, relational conditions." In his words:

The first, . . . "instructional" outcomes, are the conventional kinds of educational objectives we find in curriculum outlines, educational specifications, and books and articles on teaching goals. The second, however, can more properly be seen as "means" which contribute to such instructional ends; they consist of interpersonal transactions and states which teachers realize with their students. The latter are usually portrayed not as ends in themselves but as conditions for effective teaching; we do not normally think of schools as existing so that students can be disciplined, work hard, or have a warm relationship with a teacher. I will subsequently refer to the second kind of outcomes as "relational." (1975, pp. 117-118)

Using these distinctions, our teachers' responses to the interview question on purposes expressed the "ultimate, instructional results" they hope to achieve within the curriculum and beyond. We found teacher expressions of "proximate, relational conditions" from our analysis of the other three interview questions. Our overall findings reveal that teachers believe the achievement of their instructional purposes is highly dependent on relational conditions that accent the interpersonal skills, attitudes, and qualities necessary for relating to their students as individuals and for managing their students as a group. Teachers cite pedagogical skills only second in frequency as means to achieve their outcomes. What is noticeably absent is heavy stress on the need for more knowledge of content in order to reach instructional outcomes.

In trying to make sense of these findings in relation to what teachers are trying to do "most of all," we come to several conclusions. First, since teachers identified four purposes that go beyond the prescribed curriculum, they do need something other than "more content" to reach these purposes. Teaching students to think and apply content, to develop positive attitudes toward learning, to be good citizens, and to realize their full potential as individuals requires knowledge of subject matter, but also a great deal more. We believe that teachers mention interpersonal and pedagogical processes so frequently because their experience teaches them that they cannot achieve broad instructional outcomes without the ability to establish rapport with individuals, build a positive group climate for learning, and use a variety of teaching methods to motivate and focus students. To move toward their larger purposes, teachers must relate to students affectively as well as cognitively.

Second, even when teachers are concentrating only on the prescribed curriculum, they place a high value on interpersonal and pedagogical abilities. Isolated, crowded classrooms with students taught in large groups have always made interpersonal and pedagogical skills essential. Today, however, these skills appear to be critical. According to contemporary teachers, students are not the homogeneous group of compliant individuals they tended to encounter in the past. Rather, they are a group of individuals with highly diverse ethnic and academic backgrounds. Many do not want to be in school, see no connection between school and the rest of their lives, find concentration on academic tasks difficult, spend outside time working at jobs rather than doing school work, and live in families with considerable stress and discord (Cohn, Kottkamp, McCloskey & Provenzo, 1987). Most of our teachers, therefore, do not worry about having enough knowledge to impart to their students; they worry instead about motivating these students to want to learn and then having the pedagogical and interpersonal skills to keep them engaged with the lessons they plan.

A third conclusion is that our respondents' stress on interpersonal relationships as a means to achieve instructional and broader outcomes should come as no surprise when we recall that the "interpersonal theme" (Lortie, 1975) led the list of reasons why Five Towns teachers and the respondents of the NEA survey (1967) chose teaching as a career. Most teachers chose the occupation because it is "people work" and they like being with children or adolescents. The second-most-cited attraction Lortie described as the "service theme." Teachers see their work as performing a special mission for society, and since that special mission involves service to others, the people-oriented dimension of choice comes through once again. Our teachers and those in other recent studies (Goodlad, 1984; Johnson, 1990) affirm these two themes. Given this historically stable orientation, it makes sense that most teachers recognize they are teaching people, not subjects, and consistently put skills and attitudes required for relating to students at the top of their list of means to achieve their ends.

What should come as a surprise, however, is that most educational reform proposals fail to acknowledge, let alone address, the relationship between interpersonal and pedagogical processes and instructional outcomes. Instead, they consistently focus almost exclusively on academic or cognitive outcomes with little or no attention to the means required to reach those ends, particularly in the changing context of schooling. What teachers know, however, is that without establishing a positive learning climate and finding the pedagogical strategies to interest students in content, the desired academic outcomes will continue to elude them.

## Stability, Change, and Points of Tension

While our historical examination of teacher purposes and means reveals a pattern of continuity, it also identifies changes that deserve consideration. Within the survey data, there was a shift toward greater emphasis on subject matter and acquisition and use of basic skills. Among the interview themes from "beyond the curriculum," there was a shift from universalism toward more of an emphasis on individual development. The changes in emphasis seem to be related to changes in the larger social context of education. Although we cannot claim causality, there does appear to be a relationship between the teachers' more elemental definitions of goals and the accountability and basics movements teachers had experienced in the ten years preceding our study. As part of the accountability thrust, teachers have found their instructional behavior more closely prescribed and monitored through paper tracking and classroom observations. These issues are more fully described in Chapter 5.

The shift from less stress on universalism toward more emphasis on dealing with students as individuals appears to be linked to changes in the student population. At the same time, changes in students have probably reinforced long-standing teacher beliefs in the importance of interpersonal means to achieve instructional outcomes. As Karen's comments suggest, when student diversity increases, so does the teachers' focus on the need for a classroom learning environment that is comfortable for all students. Thus student change may have contributed simultaneously to modification of teacher purposes and to reinforcement of the perceived centrality of interpersonal means. The specifics of changes in students and how teachers have been affected by them are fully explored in Chapter 4.

These changes and continuities reveal several points of tension that contribute to our understanding of why contemporary teachers find teaching more difficult and less rewarding than in the past. One is the fact that schools are pushing teachers toward more elemental basic skills definitions of purpose than they feel is desirable. Another is the contrast between broad teacher purposes, which can only be accomplished and assessed over long periods of time, and the schools' push for narrow, short-term outcomes and evaluations of teacher performance. Yet another is the conflict between teachers' stress on the importance of individual growth and development and the standardized nature of accountability mandates and their evaluation measures. Such tensions are likely to exacerbate rather than quell the sense of uncertainty among teachers whose purposes are not well-synchronized with the means by which they are assessed.

These tensions indicate significant discrepancies between how contemporary teachers think about the aims and means of instruction and how those who would improve schools and the performance of teachers think about them. While teachers today struggle both to teach academic subject matter and to "turn kids into people," educational policy-makers today press them to concentrate almost exclusively on academics (McCloskey, Provenzo, Cohn & Kottkamp, 1987). While teachers search for the interpersonal and pedagogical processes to make academics meaningful to their students, their administrators focus predominantly on the product. While teachers believe that their success in today's classrooms hinges on their ability to develop interpersonal and pedagogical skills, proposals for reforming teacher education concentrate on the acquisition of more liberal arts and subject-matter knowledge (AACTE, 1985; Carnegie, 1986; Holmes Group, 1986). These discrepancies highlight the tension between the teacher or insider's emphasis on the process of teaching and learning and the outsider's stress on the outcomes of instruction.

## Chapter 3

# Rewards in Teaching

---

*Interviewer: What's a good day like for you? What hap-pens?*

*Karen: A good day is when I'm very organized . . . and the lesson plan that I've spent time planning doesn't go up in smoke because one student isn't in the mood to work or this fight breaks out. . . . More often than not I feel like a referee. . . . A good day is when I can actually teach and get my lesson across, have the students respond, and I get a feeling of satisfaction that I have accomplished something other than just "Turn around," "Sit down," "Get back in your seat," "No, you can't go to the bathroom," "Let go of so and so's head." . . . It's a day when I really got through. . . . What also makes me feel good is when a student who wouldn't read out loud suddenly starts volunteering to read . . . even though he is stumbling. . . . At least he's reading. . . . It's when I see kids' progress. . . .*

❧ ❧ ❧

*Interviewer: If you could choose all over again, would you choose to be a teacher?*

*Karen: That's a hard question. . . . I don't know. I'm more practical now than I used to be and I have to live and eat and survive. As far as the money is concerned, no, I wouldn't teach. I wouldn't choose it again. But*

*then again, I thought about this the other day, would I
be happy . . . ? It's a hard question, I don't know. . . . I
don't think I can do this for another twenty years.*

ᏉᏉ ᏉᏉ ᏉᏉ

Karen receives important rewards when she achieves her purposes
with students. Sometimes success comes from lessons with the
entire class and sometimes it comes from the observable progress
of a single student. These rewards, however, are never certain.
Moreover, the rewards that emanate from success with students do
not always compensate for expenditure of effort and the deficiency
in monetary rewards and prestige. As we listen to Karen, we can
hear that she is in conflict over the rewards she desires. On the
one hand, her work brings her deep internal satisfaction; on the
other hand, she feels she has not received her share of the external
rewards that other occupations offer.

In this chapter we examine more closely the overall reward
structure of teaching and the particular types of rewards teachers
seek.[1] We pay special attention to stability and change in teacher
rewards over twenty years. Rewards, like purposes and means, are
at the core of the task of teaching. Understanding what it is that
rewards teachers is critical to understanding our current educational problems and to determining how to improve the performance of teachers. Brief personal accounts taken from our teacher
interviews provide a concrete starting point.[2]

## Personal Experiences with Rewards in Teaching

### Betty

Now in her twelfth year of teaching, Betty substituted until she
found a school she liked. She has taught primary grades in a high
socio-economic status area for ten years. Betty has "known since
[she] was a youngster" she wanted to teach. She is not exactly certain why, but there was never any doubt. She mentioned wanting
to be around children and liking them, especially "their sense of
humor, wit, and total honesty."

Her primary work rewards come from seeing children grow.
She talked of students who come to her in September "as real
babies, sort of hanging on their mommy's apron strings." She is
rewarded from seeing them "become quite independent and able

to function, from their intellectual growth." She feels special satisfaction in taking in children who are nonreaders and moving them to a second-grade level in first grade.

Today she has more doubt about teaching. If she had to do it again, she is not certain she would teach, and she is toying with the idea of going into school administration. Her career has been tremendously satisfying and she likes the schedule, which allows her to pursue other interests, especially late-afternoon tennis. However, before her parents left her an inheritance, her low salary forced her to use the afternoon and evening hours to moonlight in a real estate office. She also taught summer school for financial reasons. Single and now financially secure, Betty remains upset about her salary. It galls her that good friends make much more money doing work that is easier and of less social value.

## Oliver

The Viet Nam War led Oliver to teaching. He had been substituting during his junior year of college to pay expenses. When his draft deferment changed to 1A, teaching became very attractive. He also wanted to stay in Miami, which teaching allowed. Now after years of teaching junior high students, Oliver comments simply, "I have enjoyed it for fifteen years." He also likes the time off and contrasts it to "working in industry where you only have two weeks off." He is not looking for easy work: "I will not teach unless I feel I am effective. I will stop teaching when I realize I'm not effective. I don't want to do something for the sake of making money. I want to be teaching something or I'll do something else."

His rewards come from "seeing the students benefit from what I have to teach them." He gets satisfaction from positive student reactions to his teaching, especially when they "come back and say that [math] is so easy for them now because of what they've had, or that . . . I'm affecting their future."

Oliver is a partner in an international marketing firm run by his father and brother. He has invested savings in the venture, but this is not moonlighting. "I concentrate on teaching; that's the only thing I do."

## Grace

In her ninth year, Grace teaches reading and language arts in a lower-middle-class junior high school. While a high school senior, she chose as an elective working as a teacher aide in an elementary school. Her attraction to teaching was immediate: the "little kids thought you were great," and she realized she could be "an instrument in helping someone else."

Grace responded to a probe about considering other occupations this way: "I enjoy teaching. As a matter of fact, I love teaching, and I feel that there are few teachers like me . . . that really care about what they're doing. There probably are. I just happen to be surrounded by a lot that don't."

After becoming a teacher she gave serious thought to a career as a physician until she realized that her consideration was for the wrong reason—purely occupational prestige. Her interview is replete with mentions of the status accorded teachers. Her parents didn't attend high school. To them teachers were very special and to have a daughter teaching was a high honor. She approached her own teachers with a similar attitude. But that is not what she receives from students or their parents today. And she speaks of that negative "tone in someone's voice" at social affairs when he or she says, "Oh—you're a teacher."

But Grace reflects, "I get a lot of satisfaction." She associates that feeling with having one of her students, whom she "helped push," become student of the year and one of her Chapter I students chosen as most improved. She also recounts being called in by her principal to be told that a parent she did not know had requested Grace for her child next year. This meant that "some child has thought enough about you to tell his parents and that parent has thought enough about you to tell somebody else's parents—and that's a big fulfillment!"

Like Betty and Oliver, Grace also mentioned school vacations and long summers. But she sees these more as attractions to teaching for "the wrong reasons." It bothers her when teachers spend the minimum number of hours in the school, go home with empty briefcases, and treat what she experiences as very important work as "easy money."

Betty, Oliver, and Grace have viewpoints which both overlap and differ on attractions to teaching and rewards available from it. While they are not necessarily representative of all teachers in this study, they provide examples of rewards discussed in the next section.

## Categories of Work Rewards

Lortie's (1975) conception of work rewards provides the theoretical base for our discussion. In his surveys of Dade County teachers in 1964, Lortie asked questions related to three categories of rewards: extrinsic, ancillary, and intrinsic or psychic. We used some of the same survey questions in 1984 in order to have a twenty-year comparison.

## Extrinsic Rewards

Extrinsic rewards constitute the "earnings" attached to an occupational role, and consist of salary, status, and power or influence over others. "These earnings are 'extrinsic' in the sense that they exist independently of the individual who occupies the role; since they are experienced by all incumbents, they have an 'objective' quality" (Lortie, 1975, p. 101). Betty, Oliver, and Grace all speak of salary in negative terms. Betty is deeply agitated by the comparison of her salary with those of friends in other fields. Her salary is not an incentive to keep her in teaching. Oliver and Grace believe those who seek money as their primary reward are not only poor teachers but give all teachers a bad name. Oliver doesn't teach "for the sake of money," and Grace is angered by those who teach for "easy money."

Grace illustrates multiple understandings of status or occupational prestige. Her family taught her a reverence for teachers. Lately she has received a message through her principal that several parents hold her in high regard. But these instances contrast with condescending responses she receives at social gatherings and the lack of respect she experiences from many students and parents. Negative status assessments exerted strong enough pressure for her to think seriously of going into medicine, even while she was thoroughly enjoying teaching.

Grace illustrates Lortie's (1975) argument that individual teachers have little power to influence extrinsic rewards, which are distributed in an undifferentiated manner. Salary differentials are small and based on slowly accumulated longevity and graduate credits. Individual status is based not on performance, but on the prestige of the occupational group. No matter how skillful and dedicated the individual practitioner, when a spate of national reports blamed teachers for a "crisis" in education, Grace found herself treated as a member of a class—public school teachers—not as an individual. At a party she is still, "Oh—a teacher."

Comparing the importance teachers have attached to extrinsic rewards over twenty years, we find "salary" was and is the most important for relatively few. (See Table 3.1.) "Respect from others" and "wielding influence" each received over a third of the responses earlier; both have declined, "respect" more precipitously.

TABLE 3.1
Dade County Teachers' Extrinsic Rewards, 1964 and 1984

| Of these three, from which do you derive the most satisfaction? | 1964 (%) | 1984 (%) |
| --- | --- | --- |
| The salary I earn in my profession | 14.3 | 14.2 |
| The respect I receive from others | 36.6 | 26.3 |
| The opportunity to wield some influence | 36.0 | 31.7 |
| I receive no satisfaction at all from these things | 13.0 | 27.8 |

Source: Kottkamp, Provenzo & Cohn, 1986b, p. 564, by permission.

Only "no satisfaction" showed growth. In a culture that extols extrinsic rewards, more than one-quarter of contemporary teachers find no satisfaction at all from them.

## Ancillary Rewards

"Ancillary rewards are simultaneously objective and subjective; they refer to objective characteristics of the work which may be perceived as rewards by some (e.g., married women[3] might consider the work schedules of teaching to be rewarding, while men might not)" (Lortie, 1975, p. 101). The work schedule, holidays, and summers off, however, are ancillary rewards that also appeal to people without school-age children. Oliver enjoys the schedule, and Betty finds it provides her an opportunity to play tennis. Karen does not derive reward from the time schedule; quite the opposite. Increased paperwork and papers to grade have led her to see the time demands of teaching as incompatible with motherhood. Thus, while time schedule is "objective," each teacher applies a different subjective meaning to it.

Oliver provides two more examples of ancillary rewards. During the Viet Nam War, teaching gave him a draft deferment unavailable in other work. This feature had very high subjective value for him, but no value for the women. The other ancillary reward for Oliver was geographical stability. Other forms of work such as foreign service, which he had considered, entail frequent relocation. Oliver wanted to stay in Miami, so in comparison to some other lines of work teaching had the subjective reward of place stability.

Lortie (1975) indicated that ancillary rewards tend to be stable across time but become "taken for granted." Their major importance arises during the choice among occupations. They are unlikely to inspire greater effort or commitment since they do not expand beyond what is originally received. Thus, draft deferment probably did not induce Oliver to greater work effort beyond that needed to maintain his employment, but it might have helped to prevent him from leaving teaching.

The relative importance of several ancillary rewards changed over time, as indicated in survey responses (see Table 3.2). In 1964 the most frequent response was the perception of "special appro-

TABLE 3.2
Dade County Teachers' Ancillary Rewards, 1964 and 1984

| *Which of the following things do you like best about teaching?* | *1964 (%)* | *1984 (%)* |
| --- | --- | --- |
| The relative security of income and position | 22.6 | 16.1 |
| The schedule (especially summer), which can permit travel, family activities, etc. | 23.2 | 35.4 |
| The opportunity that teaching offers to earn a living without much rivalry and competition with other people | 4.8 | 2.8 |
| The special appropriateness of teaching for people like me | 34.1 | 28.6 |
| None of these afford me satisfaction | 15.3 | 17.1 |

*Source:* Kottkamp, Provenzo & Cohn, 1986b, p. 564, by permission.

priateness" of the occupation, followed by almost identical proportions of responses for time "schedule" and "security." By 1984, time "schedule" had become the most frequent choice. The "no satisfaction" answer had grown slightly by 1984. The decline in security is probably attributable to the experience of reductions in force dating from the mid-1970s, which had no equivalent prior to 1964. Most interesting in these figures is that time away from work ("schedule") and "no satisfaction" are the only ancillary rewards to show increases over time.

## Intrinsic or Psychic Rewards

"Psychic rewards consist entirely of subjective valuations made in the course of work engagement; their subjectivity means that they vary from person to person. But they are also constrained by the nature of the occupation and its tasks . . ." (Lortie, 1975, p. 101).

Betty's most important subjective rewards come from seeing her own imprint on children's growth. Oliver defines primary rewards as "seeing students benefit" from his teaching. Grace also sees her influence on her students' progress as a reward. Karen's intrinsic rewards come on good days like the ones on which a nonreader volunteered to read or her class became engaged in writing myths. But for her, intrinsic rewards come too infrequently, and they are all that continue to hold her in teaching. All four teachers identify work with their students as the primary source of intrinsic rewards. All four are rewarded by the accomplishment of their purposes.

In contrast to the other two kinds of rewards, psychic rewards "fluctuate" (Lortie, 1975). They may go up or down in both the long and short term, and with their fluctuation goes a parallel variation in enjoyment of work. Furthermore, teaching is structured so that, unlike the other two types of rewards, effort applied directly to its major tasks has the potential for increasing personally chosen rewards. Lortie argued that the structure of teaching "favors emphasis on psychic rewards" (p. 103). Similarly, in her interview study of "very good" teachers, Johnson (1990) concluded, "the ultimate reward that teachers seek appears in fact to be quite simple: the opportunity to teach well and to know it matters" (p. 34). Realization of that goal brings a flood of psychic rewards to most teachers.

Unlike teacher choices among extrinsic and ancillary rewards, teacher choices among psychic rewards over two decades show high stability (see Table 3.3). Two of the six psychic rewards account for 94 percent of the choices in both years. Of these, "reaching students and knowing they have learned" is the overwhelming winner. Second place goes to associating with children and developing relationships with them. The vast majority of teachers—like Karen, Betty, Oliver, and Grace—see their primary intrinsic rewards flowing from teaching-learning interactions with students. Thus, the most important subjectively defined rewards are directly aligned with the occupation's central task, successful teaching.

## The Continued Primacy of Psychic Rewards

Dade County teachers also chose one of the three reward groups as most important (see Table 3.4). In 1964, intrinsic rewards were the overwhelming choice, at 76 percent, while extrinsic and ancillary rewards were divided almost equally. In 1984 the basic pattern remained similar, and the rate of choices for extrinsic

TABLE 3.3
Dade County Teachers' Intrinsic Rewards, 1964 and 1984

| Which of the following is the most important source of satisfaction to you? | 1964 (%) | 1984 (%) |
|---|---|---|
| The opportunity teaching gives me to study, read, and plan for classes | 3.4 | 1.9 |
| The chance that teaching offers me to develop mastery of discipline and classroom management | 1.1 | 1.4 |
| The times I know I have "reached" a student or group of students, and they have learned | 86.2 | 86.7 |
| The chance to associate with children or young people and to develop relationships with them | 7.9 | 7.6 |
| The chance that teaching gives me to associate with other teachers and educators | 1.0 | 0.7 |
| I receive no satisfaction from these | 0.3 | 1.6 |

*Source:* Kottkamp, Provenzo & Cohn, 1986b, p. 565, by permission.
*Note:* Percentages do not total 100% due to rounding.

TABLE 3.4
Dade County Teachers' Choices Among Three
Reward Categories, 1964 and 1984

| Of the features grouped below, I think that the following is most important to me: | 1964 (%) | 1984 (%) |
|---|---|---|
| The salary and respect received and the position of influence | 11.9 | 11.3 |
| The opportunities to study, plan, master classroom management, "reach" students, and associate with colleagues and children | 76.3 | 70.2 |
| The economic security, time, freedom from competition, and appropriateness for persons like me | 11.8 | 18.4 |

*Source:* Kottkamp, Provenzo & Cohn, 1986b, p. 565, by permission.

rewards remained almost identical to the earlier year. However, the intrinsic choice dropped to 70 percent and the choice was transferred to ancillary rewards. Thus, comparative data substantiate the primacy of intrinsic rewards for the great majority of teachers. However, the change that did occur was away from rewards that draw potentially higher levels of teacher effort and toward rewards that are givens at the time of employment, rewards which have little power to induce additional effort.[4] Although the change is rather small, it may be suggestive of growing problems.

## Work Rewards: Insights from Teacher Interviews

In our open-ended interviews with teachers we asked them several questions related to their rewards. Their responses validated the patterns of the survey data and explained the essence of psychic rewards and the uncertainty and fragility associated with them.

### Sources of Satisfaction

One question that revealed teacher rewards was the following: "What are the really important satisfactions that you receive from your work?" We analyzed responses by individual thought units. Each thought was identified and coded into categories that emerged from grouping similar responses (see Table 3.5). Some teachers contributed single thought units, while others contributed multiple thoughts. The category pattern is similar to the survey responses.[5]

The largest category, including half of the thought units and

TABLE 3.5
Perceived Sources of Satisfaction Extrapolated from
Dade County Teacher Interviews, 1984

| What are the really important satisfactions you receive from your work? | Percentage of total responses | Percentage of respondents answering |
|---|---|---|
| Perceived contribution to student learning, growth, or development (short-time span) | 50 | 70 |
| Perceiving one's imprint on a student's learning, growth, or development (time frame of more than one year after having the child as a teacher) | 21 | 30 |
| Associating or interacting with children | 14 | 21 |
| Non-student-related | 15 | 24 |

into which 70 percent of the respondents' answers are coded, indicates satisfaction from teacher contribution to student learning, growth, or development over a time frame extending from a single day to the better part of a school year. Response examples include:

Seeing a child achieve. Absolutely thrilled this year—a little girl that came in and couldn't read at all, and in four months I got her through four preprimers and into a primer. The little girl's beginning to feel good about herself. (24, F, W, Elem/L, Primary)

≥▲ ≥▲ ≥▲

I guess the performance. After you've worked you see your students get out there, whether it's a jazz band or symphonic band or a marching band, to do a good job. That's the biggest satisfaction of all. I guess it is an extension of me out there, and that is the biggest reward. If they are out there doing the best job they possibly can. (54, M, B, Sr/L, Music)

≥▲ ≥▲ ≥▲

My students came in at the beginning of the year. They didn't know the difference between 100's and 1000's on the place value chart. We worked on it, we worked and we worked. Finally they understood what it was. I felt something inside of me. I felt really good. (16, F, B, Elem/M, Intermediate)

These responses convey the meaning of the most frequent intrinsic choice on the survey: "The times I know I have 'reached' a student or group of students, and they have learned" (Table 3.3). In the interview responses, the concept, "they have learned," is interpreted broadly to include the full range of teachers' goals as described in Chapter 2 rather than limited to official curricular outcomes.

The second category is similar to the first in terms of the teacher's own imprint on a child's learning, growth, and development broadly conceived. The difference is a time frame of at least one year after having the child as a teacher. Examples include:

Having former students coming back and tell me what

they're doing. Reading about them in the paper. (32, F, W,
Elem/M, 4th)

≈ ≈ ≈

When students who have been my students come to school
to visit me, and they tell me—like yesterday, Kay. She was in
my 7th grade biology class. "Mrs. M, they gave me an
award . . . and I wanted you to know." And they come to
me, and some tell me, "I got a job." Or, "I'm making good
grades." And some win a scholarship, so they come and tell
me, and that makes me feel very good because they have
left the school and there is no reason why they return, but
they come to tell me. They know that is something that I
will be very proud of. (03, F, H, Jr/L, Gen. Sci.)

It is in this longer time frame that teachers may finally realize the
broad, long-range purposes discussed in Chapter 2.

Reaching students and seeing them learn in the short and long
term accounts for 71 percent of the total interview responses. These
results demonstrate that the primary rewards of teaching come
from direct teacher-student interactions leading to student learning.

A third category of interview responses is close to another survey response: "The chance to associate with children or young people and to develop relationships with them" (Table 3.3). These
responses do not claim authorship of learning or changes in students. Just being with children, loving them, seeing them excited
are enough to bring satisfaction. For example:

I love the students and . . . I have a good rapport with them,
and they all respect me and I respect them as individuals. I
treat them like adults and they treat me with the utmost
courtesy and respect. (29, M, B, Sr/M, Soc. Stud.)

≈ ≈ ≈

The kids: At this age level they are very responsive. You
know, they give you a lot back. You get your little notes
that say "I love you." (40, F, W, Elem/H, 2nd).

If we add this category to the short- and long-term contribution to
learning, we see that 85 percent of the responses cite interactions

with their students as the source of the teachers' satisfaction.

Finally, 15 percent of the satisfaction responses did not involve direct interaction with children. The array of non-student-related responses replicates categories of the survey reward questions, and, by its small proportion of responses, solidifies the survey finding that the primary psychic rewards stem directly from student interaction and learning.

## The Good Day

To probe teacher rewards and satisfactions more closely, we asked our interviewees a question that Lortie had posed earlier to Five Towns teachers: "Now and then, teachers have a really good day. Could you tell me what a good day is like for you?"[6] Lortie analyzed his findings in terms of two broad categories, the role of the teacher and the role of the student. Subsumed under each role were actions, attitudes, and feelings. The Dade County teachers' accounts were quite similar to those of Lortie's Five Towns teachers. In fact, Karen's description of a good day that opens this chapter corresponds closely to the accounts of both interview samples. On a good day, Karen is "organized" and ready; "actually teaches" her plans; "gets through" to students; and ends with a "feeling of satisfaction" that she "had accomplished" something. The similarity of her description to that of Lortie's can be seen in this summary statement by Lortie (1975):

> The teacher starts off ready for work, feeling good and having high energy. The day is marked by getting through to students, finishing one's plans, and effective teaching; plans prove viable and one works hard. At the end of the day, the teacher feels worthy. He [or she] has earned his [or her] way. (p. 172)

Lortie's description of the student role also describes our own findings:

> They participate actively, show interest, and give their full attention. They work hard. They behave themselves by conforming to the teacher's rules. They show positive affect by "wanting to learn," "being in a good mood," and "enjoying the classes." (p. 172)

As Karen explained, a good day occurs when she isn't a referee. Her students follow the rules and respond to the lesson.

Finally, our data supported Lortie's three "invariant themes" of the good day, themes of exceeding importance because there are no exceptions. First, all teachers "readily accepted the assumption of variability" (1975, p. 168) from day to day, indicating that the flow of psychic rewards was erratic. Second, all described only the domain of teacher-student interaction. Third, the actors in the descriptions were invariant: "Positive events and outcomes were linked to . . . the teacher and the students. But all other persons, without exception, were connected with undesirable occurrences" (p. 169). Other teacher role partners—parents, principal, colleagues—were viewed as "intruders" disruptive of the flow of a good day, hence destructive to the teacher's receipt of psychic rewards.

## The Bad Day

On good days, subjectively defined rewards flow freely, and as one teacher said, "Sometimes I feel this is the best job in the world, and I wouldn't do anything else" (22, M, H, Sr/M, Phys. Ed.). But on bad days the same teacher said, "Oh God! I wonder if I could find something else."

We analyzed Dade County teachers' responses to the question: "Sometimes teachers have bad days. What happens on a bad day?"[7] Twenty-four percent of the respondents specifically described themselves as bearing personal responsibility for bad days. Most comments indicated being in a poor mood upon arrival, or being excessively tired or feeling ill, and some indicated being unprepared.

A much larger percentage of teachers (69%) described students as key actors in bad days. Student mood and behavior were described as "rotten," "bad," "apathetic," "insulting," "tuned out," "disruptive," "bananas," "noisy," "unmotivated," "high," "stoned," "squirrelly," "twittery," "antsy," and "hyper." Action descriptions included yelling, fighting, mouthing off, stealing, testing authority, and throwing temper tantrums. Milder terms described lack of interest, flexibility, or understanding, and inability to settle down. All in all, these are attitudes and behaviors that ruin a good day. And, as the respondents also made very clear, in many cases it only takes one student to destroy any possibility of receiving a daily dose of psychic rewards and attendant satisfaction.

The last large category associated with "bad days" contained events that interrupted the flow of lessons or the attention of students, including power failures, fire drills, schedule changes, changing weather, football games, and periodic events such as issuing of the school newspaper. Excessive paperwork and generalized "interruptions" were frequently cited.

## Good Days and Bad: The Uncertainties of Interpersonal Relations

Descriptions of "good" and "bad days" reveal the uncertainties of teaching and how they intersect with the potential for earning psychic rewards. Teachers make different attributions of cause for "good" and for "bad days." For "bad days," they typically blame students, their own lack of energy or preparation, or outside events. Teachers, however, make few attributions for "good days," which suggests little sense of control over the conditions and flow of events which lead to the most valued psychic earnings.

An analysis of the student role in "good" and "bad days" revealed that 85 percent of the thought units could be categorized as concerned with "proximate, relational conditions," as opposed to "ultimate, instructional results." Teachers emphasize relational aspects of the student role in a way that parallels their emphasis on interpersonal knowledge, skills, attitudes, and qualities as factors in effective teaching. The accent on the interpersonal methods to instructional ends underscores the human, unpredictable nature of the enterprise. Good days require a delicate interpersonal balance of the teacher and the whole class working together for the teacher to be rewarded more than meagerly. The teacher, a single student, or a single interruption may crack the relational dynamic and begin what one teacher described as the "contagion" that infects the whole of the classroom. Karen's description at the beginning of this chapter vividly captures the uncertainties of teaching and the "fragility" of relational dynamics. "One student" who "isn't in the mood to work" can make her carefully planned lesson "go up in smoke."

## Money: Substance and Symbol

There is great continuity and clarity over the twenty-year period on the issue of rewards. Direct questions on surveys and both direct and indirect questions in interviews illustrate that teachers desire most of all the psychic rewards that come from helping students learn. Unlike many other occupations, in teaching money is not the primary reward teachers seek. It is, nonetheless, very important both substantively and symbolically. Discussion of money and prestige permeated the interviews. Although there were no direct probes about salaries and only two questions about incentive systems, interviewees talked about salary and status across twenty-three different questions. Not only did discussions of money and prestige flow from almost every question, but they took complex, sometimes seemingly contradictory forms. We proceed now to disentangle the various meanings of money and its ally, status.

## *Substance*

Scholars of both motivation (Herzberg, Mausner & Snyderman, 1959) and compliance in organizations (Etzioni, 1964) have argued that money is not a powerful incentive to improve performance in educational organizations. Herzberg and his colleagues developed the two-factor or motivation-hygiene theory in which salary is considered a hygiene. This means that an insufficient amount of salary leads to dissatisfaction, but once dissatisfaction is eliminated by raising the salary to a high enough point, money does not serve as a motivator to perform better. Dissatisfaction from low salary, however, may result in baleful outcomes, such as leaving the occupation altogether.

Salary is a ritual complaint among teachers; however, there is an objective point in that teacher salaries are not at a level that takes away dissatisfaction. After accounting for inflation, salaries fell from the 1970s through the mid-1980s (Plisko, 1984); beginning salaries fell considerably behind other white-collar occupations with similar entry educational requirements (Sykes, 1984); and blue-collar occupations made gains on or surpassed teacher incomes (Ashton & Webb, 1986).

In national surveys of teachers and former teachers, low salaries consistently ranked first as the reason for good teachers leaving. Raising salaries to levels comparable to other white-collar occupations requiring similar education has consistently ranked first among mechanisms for retaining good teachers and attracting bright and committed ones to the occupation. Proportions of teachers answering such questions in these ways usually run above 80 percent and often into the mid-90s (Gallup, 1984; Metropolitan Life, 1985a, 1985b). Through surveys, we asked teachers to rank first, second, and third from among ten categories why they thought their peers were leaving the classroom. Low salary received the highest total percentage, 72 percent, and the largest first-choice percentage, 38 percent. In the interviews, raising salaries across the board was the overwhelming recommendation for providing increased incentives, for attracting bright newcomers, and for keeping good teachers in the classroom.

## Symbol

In a persuasive historical discussion of the social status of teachers, Lortie (1975, pp. 10-13) used the powerful phrase "special but shadowed" to describe the status of the occupation and those who pursue it. The "special" property derives from middle-class work that is "proper and good," socially necessary, "a special mission honored by society," and possessed of moral importance and rectitude. The "shadowed" property flows from its origin one rank below the clergy, and its transition to "women's work" in the nineteenth century. After listening carefully to our teachers, we conclude that in the eyes of the public teaching has become less special and more shadowed than was true when Lortie wrote. The negative responses that Karen and Grace experienced in social situations were shared by many of our interviewees:

Everyone I go out with says, "Why are you teaching? How can you support yourself? What's wrong with you?" That's the attitude. One of them is a lawyer, and he taught for a while. He said, "I loved it. I was really good. [But] you're crazy to stay there." (10, F, W, Sr/H, Soc. Stud.)

꒰ꀠ ꒰ꀠ ꒰ꀠ

Teacher morale is so low right now because the community as a whole I don't think really respects us the way teachers were once respected. We have to be very careful now because everybody has his or her rights and it just seems that we're liable for lawsuits whichever way we turn, and it just doesn't seem to be a very positive attitude in teaching from the community. . . . When I introduce myself to people at places and tell them I'm a teacher, there's always a negative response like: "Oh—what do you want to do that for?" or, "We know you're poor." (35, F, W, Sr/H, Eng.)

꒰ꀠ ꒰ꀠ ꒰ꀠ

I cannot minimize teaching. Other people do this for me. To anybody, you say you're a teacher, they respond: "Oh, do

you really like it?" They minimize it. (49, F, W, Jr/M, Soc.
Stud.)

There are other devastating reports not based specifically on
social situations among adult peers:

You're not treated as a professional person. You're treated
as a servant. (64, F, W, Elem/H, Spec. Ed.)

ᏺ ᏺ ᏺ

We are treated as if we are not professionals. We are treated
like this is a blue-collar job. (71, F, B, Sr/M, Spec. Ed.)

ᏺ ᏺ ᏺ

I heard words, "Fuck off." I had a boy who told me, just
two days ago, "You make me sick!" I told him to move to his
assigned seat. I'm not telling these kids anything that's terrible. (13, F, W, Jr/L, 6th)

Sometimes the denigration even comes from the family:

My brother-in-law calls me up every month or so from California and tells me how much he's making, and he's just
got a high school education. He says, "Why are you settling
for it? You're a sucker! You're not making any money." He's
out there making surf boards and making a bundle. (22,
M, H, Sr/M, Phys. Ed.)

Not all interviewees reported negative views of their social status. However, those just cited would probably agree that the status
of teaching has become more "shadowed." They experience dep-
recation, put-down, and insult. They report being called crazy,
fools, and suckers. They are treated like servants and blue-collar
workers. Children swear at them and threaten to sue them.

As the comments make explicit, status and salary are closely
linked in our culture. Money is substantive, and the amount that
one has affects lifestyle, the college one's child attends, the car
one drives, and the recreation one enjoys. But money is also a
powerful symbol, and that is the link to social status. Without
being asked, 14 percent of our teachers described a causal link

between the salary and status of teachers. Direct salary or status comparisons with other occupations were made by 39 percent. Most were negative, and while many comparisons were to professions like law, medicine, and engineering, some were made to occupations that not long ago would have been considered lower than teaching—clerks, auto body shop owners, firefighters, and ambulance drivers. Furthermore, 15 percent made comparisons within the immediate or extended family. Mothers reported daughters just out of college with higher salaries than theirs after years of teaching. Daughters reported fathers with grade school educations making more than they after years of experience. Teachers reported high-school-educated spouses making more than they were. Mothers talked of sons and daughters who had started teaching but had moved on to other occupations with 20 percent to 50 percent salary increases. These are puzzling and hurtful comparisons.

Troubling status comparisons are not limited to Dade County. A recent national Gallup poll (Elam, 1989) provided a disturbing indicator of the broad-based discrepancy America's teachers perceive between the services they provide society and the respect it accords them through their occupational prestige. When teachers ranked twelve occupations (e.g., teachers, judges, clergy, physicians, local politicians, bankers, funeral directors, and advertising agents) in terms of (1) "their contribution to the general good of society," and (2) "prestige or status," they ranked themselves last in status and first in contribution (p. 792). The pain of under-appreciation and under-reward is deep and broad (p. 785).

Although the money and status nexus is a consuming and disturbing issue when teachers consider how the larger social order values their work, money takes on radically opposite symbolic meaning when status and legitimacy within the occupation are focal. Our interviews revealed consistent descriptions of poor colleagues as teachers who taught "only for the paycheck" (Cohn, McCloskey, Kottkamp & Provenzo, 1988). "Paycheck teachers" were castigated for lack of "dedication," for not working hard for goals described in Chapter 2. These teachers came late, left right at the close of school, and went through the motions with the least possible expenditure of energy. They were not there for students, but "only for the paycheck." The interviews suggested that there were more than a small number of these teachers, and we interviewed teachers who fit this description. The following statement by a highly frustrated teacher who planned to remain in the occupation illustrates the tradeoff:

If I didn't have . . . some of these monetary obligations, . . .
but I want a little house in Tennessee because I bought
some land there. I have a daughter who graduated from
college and she's working now and I'm helping her a little
bit financially. That makes me feel good.—Okay you little
bastards, I'm going to get my money. You want to kick me,
swear at me, I'm still going to have some nice things in life,
money-wise. (13, F, W, Jr/L, 6th)

Teachers desire improved status and monetary reward for all
members of the occupation. At the same time they deprecate "paycheck" colleagues who focus heavily or solely on monetary reward.
What may seem a paradox can be resolved when we see this circumstance as yet another indicator of the primacy of psychic
rewards, which can only be reaped through successfully reaching
students. Paycheck teachers do not receive many intrinsic rewards
and apparently do not have the incentive to work hard at teaching
in order to earn them. They settle for what is left—money, in relatively small amounts. In doing so, they give those outside of teaching yet another reason to attack all teachers. They are a thorn in the
side of "dedicated" teachers, both daily and in the sphere of occupational status.

Clearly teachers want more money and more status for what
they do; yet they are uncomfortable with the notion that they teach
for money. Their sense of mission and dedicated service comes
into conflict with their desire to be well-paid professionals who
are recognized for their important contribution to society. At the
heart of this conflict is the tension between the intrinsic and extrinsic rewards of the occupation. Teachers want more money and status, but those factors, as Herzberg, Mausner, and Snyderman (1959)
pointed out, don't motivate teachers to teach better. One way to see
this tension in action is to examine what happens when policy-
makers try to promote good teaching, an intrinsically driven activity, with the extrinsic reward of merit pay. In a sense, such an
approach asks good teachers to become "paycheck" teachers.

### Merit Pay: A Failed (Again) Reform Attempt

We now examine merit pay, the Florida legislature's attempt to
use the potential of increased extrinsic rewards as incentives for
better teacher performance.[8] Merit pay is but one part of a broad
reform effort described fully in Chapter 5. We present this piece of
the story here because it is the only portion of the reform agenda

which addressed teacher rewards directly. This discussion is a bridge to the direct examination of the impact of social changes on teachers and schools in the next two chapters.

We encountered this reform attempt in a special way. When interviewing began, the Florida Meritorious Teacher Program was being developed. The first half of our interviews were conducted while merit pay was a future condition, the other half after the results of the first year's decisions on merit were known.

Merit pay is a recurring "answer" for improving education, having been tried in both the 1920s and 1950s (Johnson, 1984; Natriello & Cohn, 1984). Perhaps because it is so deeply ingrained in the dominant business ideology of the country, its prior history of failure has not dissuaded contemporary advocates. Merit pay is also an idea with high-level proponents. President Reagan was a strong supporter, and President Bush has advocated applying lessons from business to education by rewarding excellence through merit pay.

In Florida, the strongest proponent of merit pay was the conservative business lobby, the Associated Industries of Florida (AIF), and its president, Jon Shebel, an influential lobbyist. In 1983, when Florida Governor Robert Graham was working hard to raise the salaries of Florida teachers into the top national quartile, the AIF adopted a no-tax-increase position. Graham then had to deal directly with Shebel and the AIF, which was intent on instituting merit pay for teachers (Provenzo, McCloskey, Cohn, Kottkamp & Proller, 1987). Shebel's rationale was:

> Under the [existing] pay system . . . when the raises came through every year, the outstanding teacher got the same percentage as the incompetent teacher. We thought that was wrong. That wasn't the way you pay people in business, and that wasn't the way to motivate people. You motivate teachers by salaries. (Starobin, 1984, p. 12)

From Presidents of the United States to the AIF, advocates of merit pay believe it is an incentive that will induce greater teacher effort and performance. Some also believe that it can serve as an incentive to remain in the occupation longer (Darling-Hammond & Berry, 1988). However, the requirements and process for being judged meritorious, as established by the Florida legislation, were inconsistent with the ideology that merit pay is an incentive. The requirements for merit included: (1) four years of experience, (2) a superior score on a subject area test (or a Master's degree), and

(3) a rating of superior on a performance evaluation assessment. The first two criteria are not incentives to perform; they merely reward past accomplishments. The third is a potential incentive; but, because the observation instrument (the Florida Performance Measurement System) was developed to assess minimal competencies for beginning teachers rather than excellence among veterans (Darling-Hammond & Berry, 1988), there was little incentive value to it. A further problem with the third criterion is that only two observations were made. It is doubtful that the $9.5 million spent in the first year of operation provided incentive to anyone to become a more productive teacher over the long haul, although it may have kept some in the occupation longer. Thus, from its inception, the Florida merit pay reform plan was flawed because of the discrepancy between its ideological assumptions and the means designed to implement it.

## Teacher Perspectives: Before and After

Dade teachers said much about merit pay when interviewed in 1984 prior to its implementation. While many indicated that in the abstract they favored better teachers receiving rewards, they were unanimous in the belief that fairness was impossible (Cohn, Kottkamp, Provenzo & McCloskey, 1989).[9] Underlying this position were several related assumptions. First, consensus does not exist on what constitutes good teaching. Second, even if consensus were reached, teaching cannot be accurately assessed under existing working conditions and technologies. Third, even if accurate assessment instruments existed, the human element, in the person of the evaluator, could not be depended upon to render informed, bias-free judgment.

Beyond the issue of fairness, teachers wondered how merit would affect school life. The most common concern was disruption of the egalitarian norm for working relationships among teachers by the intrusion of competition. Some worried that parents would compound competitiveness by trying to move their children from the classes of nonmeritorious teachers to those of meritorious ones. Others believed competition would reduce incentive, because unsuccessful teachers would become discouraged and lose interest in their work. Finally, some felt that the limited amount of money available in the plan artificially restricted the definition of merit.

We interviewed about half the teachers after merit decisions were made, some the very week results were announced. Three percent of Florida teachers were awarded merit. We interviewed only one teacher, Neal, judged meritorious and granted the $3,000 one-time bonus. His commentary on the meaning of merit is instructive, especially when juxtaposed with the assumptions and expectations of those who advocate this means for motivating teachers.

> This merit teacher plan . . . hardly anybody passed it, and I embarrassingly got 99.99. I feel embarrassed to tell other teachers because. . . . I feel like I'm my own judge now. I used to have to feel that the students or the faculty . . . had to judge me, but now I feel I'm my own judge. . . . Everybody now believes in me so much that only I know when I'm doing a good job.

Our meritorious teacher confided he has become "untouchable" in the eyes of his colleagues.

Moreover, the process of merit pay detracted from his classroom work:

> Everything they've asked us to do this year, the merit teacher [plan], the improvement of different things, has taken so much time and energy away from the classroom and away from teaching that I look at it as strictly a political thing, that the state administration, the department of education strictly has to do things to show the public that teachers are doing more to teach their children . . . all a political P.R. thing. It has taken so much aggravation, so much anxiety, so much effort, and so much push—it has taken it basically from the energy I would put into my classes. (65, M, W, Jr/H, Sci. Bio.)

Had becoming a master teacher actually made him less of one? we asked. "Yes," Neal said, and then asked if the tape recording was private. We offered to stop the tape, but he proceeded:

> The day that the observers were coming, I put on a performance. It was a big spectacle, and I knew what I was doing. I knew I would impress . . . [but] what is that as far as education? Two times in the classroom to observe a teacher who knows you're coming, who can prepare for it, who can do what they want—what is that? I don't think there is any objective way that you could have an observer come in and

really judge a teacher. A teacher's teaching is a long term thing with an average of things, and any one day and any one time, . . . means nothing. . . . I participated, number one, because there was money in it; number two, because I felt my reputation was at stake; number three, I felt that we were doing it strictly as a public relations thing; and number four, I felt the little counties up north were saying, "Hey, we want our teachers to look good against those big counties." If we didn't compete, they would end up with all the money.

So, Neal saw an opportunity to make $3,000 and took it. Nothing in all of this was an incentive for better teaching. They set out a game; he knew the rules and possessed the skills; he won, and walked away cynical about the whole thing. We then asked for a description of the effect of merit pay on his school:

I'd say tremendous demoralization. . . . Many of the finest teachers didn't make it. They knew they did well in the observation from within the school, and that means that there was only one more observation from outside the school. They had to have gotten basically screwed to have done so poorly.

The test they gave . . . I took the biology . . . was way out of context for my area, the level I teach. . . . I have a Master's in biology; I have four years of [medical] research; I teach advanced kids all the time—a lot of that stuff was just beyond what I would know for this level of teaching. I don't think that it reflected what I'm supposed to know for my teaching at all.

Those who argue for merit pay often claim it is opposed primarily by mediocre teachers who stand to lose. Neal, rated an outstanding teacher, considered both the observation and test invalid. The negative evaluation from this very confident teacher puts such arguments in question.

The process did not serve as a performance incentive to Neal at all, and by his account, getting "screwed" did not encourage his colleagues, either. Furthermore, merit pay did not function as an incentive for Neal to remain in teaching. In the interview, he confided that he was already working on developing a business of his own in the evenings and that he might leave education at any time—a surprise, he could guarantee, to all who knew him at work.

Having heard the cynicism of the "winner," we now listen to some "losers." These reactions illustrate additional problems with merit pay, as well as its devastating psychological outcomes:

> I've been observed for the past two years with TADS and I got excellent recommendations from my principal. When you go for this master teacher program, you have two observations. . . . One [observer] is from your home school and one is from a school in the area. I thought the observations went extremely well. I didn't think I could have done any better if I had known what they were looking for. It was one of those good days, everything went off like clockwork.
>
> When I received my scores, I was in the 50th percentile. My principal said to me, "I saw your evaluation before it was sent out and it was absolutely great—what was on your evaluation doesn't jive with your score." God only knows what they are looking for. I understand there was an article in the paper that the teachers of the year in Dade County didn't make it either. They had below 50%. I've been teacher of the year at our school and I'm a good teacher. There must be somebody that's really good, because I think I'm pretty good.
>
> And if somebody is scoring so much higher, then what's the matter with me? How can I improve? And they will not tell you. You will never see your evaluation. . . . It could be a real problem. If I didn't make it, I would want to blame my principal and that can make for hard feelings. I don't know what the answer is, but the whole thing is a mess.
>
> Then there is . . . a test. Now I know I'm not Albert Einstein, but I could not possibly have done as badly on that test. I got my scores back, and I couldn't believe it. There is nobody in our school that made it, and we have some very fine teachers. (11, F, W, Elem/H, Primary)

For this teacher, the observation criteria were simply a mystery. To complicate the matter, she is a "star" in her school, a person whom her principal both praises and relies upon as a leader. The mixed messages were very troubling.

From a high school teacher in a very different area, the story was essentially the same: a lack of congruence between performance and score:

Get rid of merit pay. That's not a motivational factor. If anything it's been a very divisive factor. The fellow I'm teaching with signed up for it. He is a very good teacher. There are times during my planning period when I've just sat in his class and watched him teach because he is that good. It is a pleasure to watch him. He gets across to students that other teachers can't even get to be quiet in class. They work for him. They do a lot of things, yet he was considered a deficient teacher. I thought that was amazing.

Only two teachers I know of on the entire staff of the twenty something that applied for it were actually above their standard. I find that very hard to believe when I take a look at our school. We are an inner city school that has been winning Ford Foundation grants. It is quite obviously not a very valid way of determining whether these people deserve it. (15, M, W, Sr/L, Gen. Sci.)

Such ratings damage both school and personal pride. The psychological games necessary to keep one's self-esteem going after a low score came through in this pained response:

I decided that I would sign up for the master teacher program. I had observations, and I think that I do a good job of teaching. I just found out, though, that I didn't even make in the upper 50th percentile. I was below the 50th percentile, which makes me wonder. This just happened this week. It was a little crushing to find this out. It took me a day to get over that. I said, look, you know what you're doing in the classroom; be happy with yourself. The children are happy that they are with me. I have to know that I am a teacher, I can't depend on anybody to tell me anymore. That is upsetting to me, but I am not complaining about it. It's not worth it. When people say you're doing a good job, and you get this back in the mail, how would you feel? . . . You have to say, don't worry about that part of teaching, do your best. I will do my best and those children are going to get 100% from me, and that's what really counts. (13, F, W, Jr/L, 6th)

For these teachers and others we interviewed, direct experience with individual merit pay in 1985 only confirmed serious concerns anticipated by colleagues interviewed before the program was implemented.

Thus, through both anticipatory speculation and actual experience, teachers told us concretely why they do not want merit pay. Merit programs are unfair because the criteria are not agreed upon and clear, the observations are not frequent enough, and the evaluators are not consistent and objective. Furthermore, merit pay fosters a competitive rather than cooperative school climate. Neither the "winner" nor the "losers" indicated any sense of motivation to perform better. But these reasons really do not reach the underlying assumptions for rejection; they simply give rise to more fundamental questions. Why do teachers believe that their work is so subjective that there cannot be clear criteria? that several visits are not enough to establish whether someone is a good teacher or not? that most evaluators are neither knowledgeable nor honorable enough to give them a fair assessment? Why do they worry about the feelings of others in the building and feel they cannot explain to parents why one teacher is "meritorious" and another isn't? Answers to these questions do not come from responses to the single direct question on merit pay. They come instead from wide-ranging conversations in which teachers talked more generally about how they think about their work, about what excites and what frustrates them.

## Teacher Sentiments and the Assumptions of Merit Pay: A Wide Gulf

As we have seen, major satisfactions in teaching come from successful interactions with students that result in learning. Teachers put much time and energy into developing rapport with and reaching their students. Their greatest reward is seeing children grow, and feeling instrumental in that growth. For most teachers, growth includes moral and social as well as cognitive development. Teachers see themselves as teaching the whole child, not just the child as student. They view their work as more art than science and believe good teachers are special people, "cut from a different cloth." Because of their strong service and mission norms, teachers describe poor or mediocre colleagues as working "only for the paycheck" and outstanding colleagues as "dedicated."

When these sentiments are considered alongside merit pay, we see that discomfort with merit goes far beyond concern for fairness. The gulf between the belief system of teachers and a business-oriented merit pay system is enormous. While teachers view their work as holistic and artistic, merit pay observations focus on molecular and technical behaviors. While teachers know they may not see important student changes for months or perhaps years, merit programs assume valid results can be assessed in several brief observations. While teachers believe their special qualities lie in their capacities to develop rapport, invest personally in their work, and care deeply, merit programs assume the essence of teaching lies in test scores or lesson plans. While teachers define themselves as "people persons" whose major satisfactions come from positive interactions with others, merit programs ask them to compete, become impersonal, and focus only on an objective "product" or "bottom line." While teachers believe those who work "only for a paycheck" discredit the profession, merit programs assume improvement will come through paycheck incentives. It is hard to imagine a greater and more impassable gulf.

Merit pay is a reform aimed at increasing the extrinsic rewards of money and status for teachers. However, imposed from afar by those who hold assumptions in direct conflict with those of teachers, merit pay does not work. In Florida, it was withdrawn in 1986 after only three years (Arthur & Milton, 1991; Darling-Hammond & Berry, 1988). Those who advocated merit pay simply did not understand that it is much more than a motivational tool. Embedded in its incentive and motivational elements are a host of business-like assumptions, which are antithetical to teacher beliefs, daily modes of practice, and professional sentiments. While teachers often do not articulate the underlying conflict of opposing assumptions, they know in a tacit, marrow-bone way that merit pay conflicts with who they are and what they are trying to do. For teachers to accept the concept, processes, and results of merit pay, they must accept a radical redefinition of their purposes, means, and rewards. For business-oriented outside experts who have little awareness of the ethos of teaching, the refusal of most teachers to accept such a redefinition in exchange for the potential of more money and more status is difficult, if not impossible, to grasp.

Teacher responses to the Florida Meritorious Teacher Program illuminate the complexity of their attitudes toward intrinsic and extrinsic rewards and reveal the connections between rewards, purposes, and means. The centrality of psychic rewards cannot be questioned, but the importance of the extrinsic rewards of money and status cannot be minimized. The two different responses of Karen at the opening of this chapter illustrate this duality. Although these pulls are long-standing, we believe that the desire for both psychic and extrinsic rewards takes on new meaning within the contemporary context of teaching. As psychic rewards become more difficult to garner and teachers work increasingly hard to achieve them, their desires for pay and status commensurate with the newly required effort become more intensified. Any rethinking of the reward structure of teaching must be built upon an understanding of these interrelated factors.

## Conclusion

In Chapters 2 and 3 we have told a story of basic stability in teachers' purposes, means, and desired rewards over a twenty-year period. It is, however, a story with signs that foreshadow major collisions of change with that stability. The growing importance teachers attach to the purpose of meeting developmental needs of individuals signals that students have become more diverse in background and ability. Another indicator of change is the strength of teacher sentiment regarding the crucial role that interpersonal means and motivational strategies play in reaching instructional ends. These beliefs suggest that teachers feel an increasing need to build rapport with today's students and to establish connections with their interests in order to encourage learning. Finally, we have seen frustrations linked to decreased status and money and to an attempt to use extrinsic merit pay rewards to motivate teachers toward better performance. Merit pay has further demoralized teachers because it is completely at odds with their beliefs and because it actually drains time, energy, and morale from the pursuit of learning with students. Taken together, these signs indicate that teachers today are increasingly dissatisfied with their daily work and with their occupational rewards.

In the next section, we move from stability with signs of change to the direct realities of change as experienced by teachers. Chapters 4 and 5 describe in great detail teacher perspectives on changes in children and their attitudes toward schoolwork, in the attitudes of parents, and in the teachers' own capacity to exercise professional discretion over the teaching-learning process in their classrooms. Our story not only documents the changes teachers report but also the ways in which these changes intersect and collide with the strength of stability—stability in the occupation, particularly in teacher purposes, means, and rewards, and stability in the school organization. We find that the resistance from this stability in the face of a changing social context exposes teachers to personal shocks, and leaves most of them in a more vulnerable position than they have ever known. While we also present some evidence of mediating forces in the form of individual teacher characteristics in Chapter 6, we demonstrate in Part II that teachers today generally perceive their work to be more difficult and less rewarding than it was twenty years ago.

# Part II

*The Impact of Change in the Context of Schooling: The Teacher's Story*

*Chapter 4*

# Changes in Students and Parents, and the Decline of Psychic Rewards for Teachers

---

*Interviewer: Are you getting less satisfaction from teaching as the years go by?*

*Karen: The kids are changing. . . . People always tend to look back and say, "Well, when I was in school, we would never do this or we would never do that," but I'm not that old. . . . What I'm saying is, you always hear people talking about young people and how awful they are . . . but the truth of the matter is that the kids are not the same as they were. I've been teaching for nine years, and I don't like what I'm seeing.*

ʽ⍺ ʽ⍺ ʽ⍺

Amid a high level of stability in the purposes, means, and rewards that teachers pursue, we have seen evidence of a decline in extrinsic and psychic rewards, and indicators of growing tensions between what contemporary teachers want to accomplish and what schools expect. In this chapter, we concentrate on what teachers perceive to be a major source of the decline in their psychic rewards—changes in students and parents.[1]

A single interview question probed whether students and parents had changed, but the voluminous commentaries on these changes were not confined to that direct question. Rather, teacher sentiments regarding changed attitudes and values of students and parents came in expanded responses to a variety of other questions, none of which were part of Lortie's interview schedule. The opening statement by Karen in response to a question on satisfaction over time is a case in point.

Throughout the chapter, we identify these indirect questions that prompted the most comments on changing students and parents, but we begin with the direct question:

> In what ways, if any, have the values and attitudes of your students and their parents changed? If there have been major changes, how have they affected your approaches to curriculum, instruction, and evaluation of students?

We were startled to find that 90 percent of the interviewees maintained that students and their parents had changed and that the changes were negative, interfering with their ability to achieve curricular and broader purposes.

Although there is a general tendency to recall the past in more glowing terms than it deserves, and although Lortie's sample in 1964 also cited students and parents as sources of discontent (1975, pp. 176-177), both the number and nature of the teacher concerns expressed in 1984 indicate a serious escalation of the problem. The widely shared perception that students and parents had changed was voiced by teachers in elementary and secondary schools and by those who worked in lower- middle- and upper-class communities, although the problem often revealed itself in differing ways, depending on the community context. Moreover, the expressed frustration came from both veteran and beginning teachers. Novices compared the attitudes of students and parents today with those of their own families.

While most teachers saw close connections between changes in students and changes in parents, for purposes of clarity, we focus first on students and then on parents. Next we examine teacher perceptions of increased vulnerability and decreased status and how these factors affect teachers' ability to exert influence over students and parents. We conclude by considering the particular notion of students as incentives and disincentives and the more general link between changes in students and the decline in psychic rewards for teachers.

## Students as Less Motivated and More Difficult to Teach

### The "Motivation Difficulty"

Although secondary school teachers expressed the sentiment more strongly than elementary school teachers, almost every teacher indicated that current students were more difficult to teach than those of the past. Specific student-related frustrations of elementary teachers were often inseparable from complaints about their parents. Still, elementary teachers expressed surprise, and sometimes even shock, at the attitudes and children encountered in the classroom. The following statements capture variations on this theme:

> I had thought that the parents would be more cooperative, that the kids would be more motivated than they are at such a young age—I guess it has to do with the background of the parents, the incentives that the parents give the kids to go to school and want to learn. . . . A lot of the parents don't have education above elementary school, and therefore can't help the kids. That becomes a problem. I guess the kids feel, "Why do it if mom doesn't really push me at home and teachers have no control over me at 3:00?" (14, F, W, Elem/M, 3rd)

ka ka ka

> The children that I see coming now—I just don't remember coming in contact with children who were bruised with cigarette marks, children that come in crying and are from broken homes. If my teacher had to deal with it, I never realized it. . . . I must have been in a very sheltered environment. Now there are just so many things that children are having to deal with, and it's emotionally draining on the teachers. It's not just academics, but to see children who are hungry. A little girl almost faints, and you ask her why. She doesn't want to tell you, and you take her out in the hallway. She hasn't eaten since Friday; and it's Monday. That kind of thing. (09, F, W, Elem/H, Kindergarten)

Others complained that some children have lost respect for teachers as well as interest in school and have resorted, on occasion, to threatening teachers. One elementary school teacher spoke of students threatening to sue her if she touched them; another talked of almost quitting after a small boy yelled, "I'm going to break your ass" (61, F, W, Elem/H, Kindergarten).

At the secondary level, the difficulty revealed itself primarily in terms of students' lack of motivation and interest in academic achievement. Teachers told us that some unmotivated students would do almost nothing and others would do the bare minimum to pass. In either case, the priority for these students appeared to be sports, social life, or a job, as opposed to school work. When they did put forth effort, the motivating factor was grades rather than a desire to learn. The following statements from veterans in different fields and settings convey the general sentiment:

> Children now do the work for grades. They won't work unless they know you are going to check it. The children in the '50s and '60s would work. They didn't worry about your checking their work. They worked just for the sake of learning, so they could understand how to do these problems. The difference now is the ones who come to me don't give a tear about learning how to do the problem, they simply want the grades. . . . I really don't know what it is, but I'll find so many children who will tell me, I just want to make a D. . . . It's hard to believe that children in a high school geometry class will come in with no paper, no pencil, no books. "Where's your book?" "I forgot it." Now how can you justify that . . . remembering to come to class and not thinking about the book? (28, F, B, Sr/M, Math)

                          ià  ià  ià

> When I decided to become a teacher I think the students then wanted to learn more so than now. Now they don't care about learning. I feel like the kids now come to school because they have to. They are under-age and they have to come, most of them. . . . When I first started teaching [19 years ago] all the kids were gung ho; they wanted phys. ed. They enjoyed it, and we had a good time. Then as the years went on, I could see that the kids did not want to dress, they did not want to do anything. They just wanted to come out and sit and talk under a tree. (67, F, B, Sr/M, Phys. Ed./Math)

                          ià  ià  ià

The kids would rather go out and buy a ghetto blaster—they range anywhere from $79 to $200, depending on the size—rather than buy themselves an instrument for the school band. . . . Also they will get on the bus and go to this mall which has a theater in it, but they won't get on the bus and buy the supplies, like maybe a mouthpiece or a reed. They just don't think that way. . . . I think that those who hold teachers responsible for test scores and mediocrity in the schools really need to come in and try teaching themselves. It's very difficult if the kid is not motivated to learn. You can be a motivating teacher, but there are some kids who just want to get by. They don't see the need and value of education." (54, M, B, Sr/L, Fine Arts/Music)

The fact that so many students didn't "see the need and value of education" was shocking to many of the middle-class, achievement-oriented teachers we interviewed. Even more perplexing was that their offers of additional assistance were often rebuffed. One teacher who had always offered special help before and after school, and even on weekends, became increasingly discouraged and frustrated:

I've almost given up. This last nine weeks I've closed my doors in the mornings. If they want to come, they can come after school. And I've closed them in the mornings because I've found that just a few of them take the opportunity, and the ones who really need it don't. . . . I even invited three kids over this weekend. I said, "Come over to the house Saturday, we'll sit at the table and we'll work. Here's my phone number, call me, we'll get together. I'll make it my business to be there. You need the help." I got no phone call, and I stayed home all day. And that behavior is not like it used to be. When my kids needed help, they came. I have never in my 16 years of teaching failed a kid that really worked and learned. I have 23 kids failing this year in Algebra, out of 96. That's terrible. They don't care. They see me in summer school and they still don't care. (01, F, W, Jr/M, Gen. Math.)

Problems with unmotivated students extended to both advanced and special education classrooms as well:

You hear from every teacher day in and day out . . . the students are not motivated . . . they totally could care less

about being here. . . . When I first came in here, students
chewed up the work. I couldn't get it out fast enough. . . .
The level of what I can teach, and how much I can teach,
and where I'm teaching has just continually drifted right on
down . . . it's like every year I end up teaching less and
less . . . less in depth and less difficult exams. . . . This year I
have a sweet bunch of students, but there is not a bright
star. . . . Last year there were two or three. There were kids
last year who could have cared less about being in an
advanced class. . . . The last few years, you hear, "Oh, there's
a final exam today; Oh, I forgot about a final exam." You
never used to hear things like that. (65, M, W, Jr/H, Sci.Bio.)

ᔑᕭ ᔑᕭ ᔑᕭ

I think my satisfaction is going downhill. Each year I get
fewer and fewer motivated students. At the end of this year,
I actually cried because I felt that I was losing the cream of
the crop and realized what I was going to have when I got
back in the fall. I don't seem to have as many kids who are
motivated, who really want to learn, as I had the first year
of my teaching. (59, F, B, Jr/H, Spec. Ed./L.D.)

The last comment underscores not only the general frustration
with students but also its link to decreasing satisfaction with teaching.

A number of teachers reported that unmotivated students continually need to be given a reason for coming to school. These
teachers felt compelled to stress the importance of education
because the schooling process appeared to hold little meaning for
many of their students. One described the situation in these terms:

Teachers meet opposition from the kids themselves. They
[the teachers] walk in feeling, "Here is all the information
that I have got for you. I am going to educate you, make
you a better person and get you a job." The kids listen and
say, "Nah, I don't want to do that. I want to stay home and
watch TV." This kind of attitude brings teachers back to
Earth. With these kinds of kids you have to work a lot
harder. You have to put your nose to the grindstone. You
have to be constantly there, after them, trying to show them
why they have to do it. It's funny, but these kids don't know
why. Why do I have to do anything? They would rather be

out working in the supermarket, stacking boxes and making a couple of bucks to buy themselves a big radio or something. (22, M, H, Sr/M, Phys. Ed./Dr. Ed.)

Other teachers claimed that unmotivated students almost demand to be entertained. Many teachers told us that television has made students "intellectually passive" and "bored with the classroom."

I think that television has had a very detrimental effect on the make-up of the children. Many children will complain that what you are doing is boring. It's not as exciting as what they see on television. Of course, my answer is that there are many boring things that happen in life, and I am not here to entertain you. (23, M, W, Jr/H, Lang. Arts/Eng.)

ₓₐ ₓₐ ₓₐ

I don't like to have to compete with Mr. Wizard and television. Twenty-five years ago I didn't have this feeling because TV hadn't made its impact. . . . Now they expect bombs and explosions. They are not concerned with learning so that they can protect themselves. I am trying to teach them something so they will have an idea of what it means to be cautious. You don't throw a pound of sodium in a pond and say "Hey guys, look at the fireworks!" But this is what they want to see happen. . . . Accidents have occurred in the classroom and these have been the things that have brought the greatest joy to the kids. . . . I don't think they were being malicious, but the fact is that they were delighted to see things go wrong that would erupt in fire. This is what they are looking for. Entertainment no longer comes from a quiet corner for reading with a fire burning. . . . Down here, I think they may know about burning fires, but they don't know about the quiet corner for reading. This has carried through to the classroom. So you have got some of these vibrant teachers who can entertain. I am sorry, my entertainment days are few and far between. (47, F, W, Sr/H, Gen. Sci.)

Finally, we heard about a growing number of students who find ways to avoid school or particular classes altogether. One teacher reported: "The kids have gotten to be such con artists. If they're out of school they can call in and disguise themselves as their parents and call in sick. This can go on for two weeks" (33, F, W, Sr/M, Sci. Bio.). Another teacher at the same school asserted:

> I've never seen so many children trying to beat the system. A number of students will get their names on the absentee list and then they'll cut the classes that they don't particularly like. A good example is fifth-period class which is right after lunch. Maybe they go off of campus for lunch and instead of taking 30 minutes for lunch, they take 45 minutes or an hour. Then they don't bother to go to that class because they've been marked absent in homeroom. I look on the list and see that the student is absent, and so I don't bother sending in a report for that hour. Then I have looked out in the hallway and I have seen them. Then when you ask the students what is going on, they'll tell you, "Well, we were late coming back from lunch." (28, F, B, Sr/M, Math.)

Other teachers complained that even when students were caught and given detentions and suspensions for their avoidance techniques, the practice often continued. Disciplinary actions had little or no effect. As one teacher put it:

> You say, "Look, get to class on time, you have five minutes to get from one door, walk 30 feet and come in the next one." Well, I have kids that will have 30 tardies, and you can give them two hours in detention after school. They don't show, they're still late to class. Give them SCSI [inside suspension], which is getting them out of class to begin with; they are still late to class when they come back. Give them outdoor suspension; they're still late to class. It seems to be increasing; I've never had so many. (73, M, W, Sr/L, Phys. Ed./Health)

## The Source of the "Motivational Difficulty": Societal Changes

Although most teachers found changes in student attitudes difficult to account for with much specificity, many believe the more general changes in society have greatly affected childhood and adolescence. One societal factor mentioned repeatedly was pervasive use of drugs by young people. In particular, there was concern about the shift from marijuana to cocaine. The following comment, by a teacher in a predominantly middle-class high school is representative:

> I think drug use is widespread. Some schools have it worse than others. I think our school is probably average or above average. It's not so much the marijuana anymore, it's the cocaine that is literally tearing these kids up. (33, F, W, Sr/M, Sci. Bio.)

While drug use is more prevalent in high schools, it clearly exists at every level. A kindergarten teacher who has been teaching for five years in the same school she attended as a child was appalled at the dramatic changes in the values of the community and behavior of children. She described children who bring neither manners nor basic hygiene to kindergarten, but who do bring and use marijuana.

Another societal factor, according to teachers, is the materialism of our culture. Many students, who simply cannot afford to buy all that they want, choose to work as much as they can after school, in the evenings, and on the weekends. For most, the job takes precedence over homework or studying for tests. Other students have, in the opinion of teachers, too much money. One teacher put it this way:

> Many of the students I have just don't seem to have the desire to learn. It is really difficult to pin them down and make them understand that this is important.... One thing that I really think is that the kids today have had too much money. For instance, we have 9th-grade kids who drive to school in an automobile everyday. That was unheard-of years ago. (31, M, W, Jr/L, Gen. Sci.)

Some teachers believe that the development of large urban centers has had an effect. One teacher, for example, linked the changing attitude of students to a loss of community in today's society:

> We are living in a world of strangers. When I began teaching 28 years ago in these small rural towns, everyone knew everyone else, and if John did something wrong, the entire community knew about it, so you had the community pressure. You had peer pressure to do the right thing. Today I don't feel that you have peer pressure or community pres-

sure to do the right thing, and I think that many of the students feel that they can remain anonymous. (23, M, W, Jr/H, Lang. Arts/Eng.)

Still others talked of the growing proportion of children from minority groups and poor families facing white, middle-class teachers in schools (Kottkamp, Cohn, McCloskey & Provenzo, 1987). One veteran white teacher, for example, believed that busing for integration has caused additional burdens for students and teachers, which affect motivation and learning:

In the last three or four years, I've experienced an uncomfortableness. . . . The bus scene and the change where it was a forced kind of integration, that's where I see the problem coming from. I see the white kids trying to act Black and the Black kids trying to act white. In the neighborhood I used to teach in, it was a naturally integrated school and all kids were kids. . . . From there I went to a school where it was push and shove, and Black kids came into the schools in a forced situation. I watched and what I saw was that they were being pushed in situations and it wasn't natural, it wasn't effective. So then we see the conflict and the barriers and the whole bit. Educationally the students have gone down. . . . I have seen too many kids pass through the ranks because of this situation. (01, F, W, Jr/M, Gen. Math.)

This teacher maintained that she has held to her standards, but that, unfortunately, has only meant she has a significant number of students who "hate her" and who fail. She expressed deep frustration:

I will not put my standards down; every child will learn. If they do not learn what they are supposed to learn, they will not pass. . . . But it hurts. About 25% of the kids aren't making it and another 25% are getting C's and D's. That's bad, 50%! If I had 1% not doing well, it used to bother me. But one of my friends said, "It's not you. You're doing what works and it does work. What's happening here is the kids aren't taking your facilitation and using it to best advantage. They'd rather go out and play—you are doing the same kinds of things you always did, but the kids aren't the same kinds of kids, so what do you do? You try to adjust. You try to teach more, spoon feed more—but it's not working." It's not working for me.

According to our interview sample, however, the most powerful societal force affecting student motivation might be broadly labeled as the "changing family structure." Many of our data to support this sentiment came from the following question:

> Here is a list of major events and trends of the past two decades. Would you comment on whether or not each has directly influenced your work as a teacher? How?
>
> - Desegregation
> - Unionization
> - Women's movement
> - Mainstreaming
> - Immigration
> - Changes in the economy
> - Viet Nam
> - State & federal mandates
> - Accountability mandates
> - Back to basics movement
> - Technology/media
> - Demographic changes
> - Changing family structure

In response to this list, almost every teacher picked the changing family structure as the trend that had most directly and negatively affected their work. As teachers explained their choice, they talked about changing attitudes among both students and parents, but in the broader context of changes in the traditional family unit. They spoke at length about how divorce and single-parent families, multiple relationships, and two working parents made life more problematic for children. This general sentiment is reflected in the specific experience of a secondary teacher who recently returned to teaching after her own divorce. She spoke first hand about the emotional effect on her daughter:

> When kids are worried about the finances and hostility and feelings, they are not always tuned into school. . . . I've seen it with my daughter. She gained a lot of weight, she doesn't study. She is social. They like to talk. They need to talk. . . . Lack of being with grandparents, the lack of affection, the anger. They're dealing with anger of parents and shuffling back and forth. Absolutely, that affects people. If your family is wrong, you're not going to sit there and dedicate your-

self to education. You can't concentrate. . . . "What's going to happen to me?" Very traumatic. (10, F, W, Sr/M, Eng.)

Some adolescents not only want to talk about their problems with peers, but also with their teachers:

> In many instances, in this day and age, you've got to be the mother, you've got to be a social worker, you've got to be a friend. I have some who come in and sit at the end of the school day who would simply want to talk, not about math, not about any course, they simply want to sit and talk. And they will sit for as long as I'm here. In fact, I will say sometimes, I'm not rushing, but I've got to go. Then, of course, the next day, if they pass by and see me in the room, they'll come in and talk to me again. . . . They simply want someone to listen. . . . You've got to be a psychologist. (28, F, B, Sr/M, Math./Geom.)

At the elementary level, teachers often discussed changing family structure in terms of the working mother. They expressed concerns with the fact that young children may be "dumped" at school at 7:30 a.m. and not picked up until 6:00 p.m. In addition to the long hours, there were concerns about the quality of before- and after-school programs. One kindergarten teacher felt that all her efforts during school on behalf of students' self-esteem were nullified after school.

> The after-school program is housed in the kindergarten. . . . When I am sitting in my office I can hear the whole thing because the supervisors are screaming and yelling. Sometimes the supervisors are university kids who are majoring in education, and it's a way to pick up money from 3:30 on, but their techniques are nil. They scream and yell at these kids, and here you've gone through a whole day of trying to be positive and then somebody yells at them for two and a half hours. (61, F, W, Elem/H, Kindergarten)

Thus, although teachers were frustrated with the fact that students are more difficult to teach, they also recognized that many children were having their own difficulties, particularly due to family circumstances beyond their control. Teachers often expressed great empathy for children who they felt were victims of the changing family structure, but they never absolved parents of their responsibility to support schools and teachers. To the contrary, they maintained that parents—single, poor, working, or otherwise—must play a crucial supporting role in their children's education.

## Parents as Unsupportive

Although there were a few suburban teachers who spoke of highly supportive parents, most of the teachers gave parents a failing grade in support, and blamed parents as a collective for the general decrease in student motivation. While parental support is something almost all teachers wanted more of, it was clear from their statements that their concept of "support" is a complex one, which involves just the right amount and mix of interest and involvement (Lareau, 1986).

### Unsupportive Parents: Too Little Interest and Involvement

The most frequent complaint was over too little interest and involvement: parents who did not look at report cards, who did not attend school meetings or the performances by their children, who did not supervise homework. Many teachers who bemoaned the changing attitudes of parents did so by comparisons with their own parents. Speaking of her own school days, an elementary school teacher recalled:

> Parents were involved. There wasn't a day you didn't turn around that your mother wasn't trying to find out what you were doing. You didn't do anything wrong because if you did, you knew what would happen. (58, F, B, Elem/L, Kindergarten)

Today, however, in the same neighborhood, she described parents who send their children to school without being toilet trained—parents who have many children but who are never at home to supervise or help them with homework, parents who are "on the streets . . . prostitutes, out mixing with other men, partying," parents "who don't care." Her only explanation: "Their values have changed. They just don't care. They don't know what respect, what a role model is."

We heard similar statements of uncaring or uninvolved parents from secondary school teachers in lower-class neighborhoods:

Way back when I thought about becoming a teacher, the parents were more behind the students than they are now. Now parents use the excuse that they don't have time. They're working. Well, my parents worked, too, but they always kept up with us. Now parents don't keep up with their kids. They don't even look at report cards. They don't know what's going on in school with their kids, and I think this is one of the big problems because, if we had the parents behind the students, then I think we could get more done. (67, F, B, Sr/M, Phys. Ed./Math.)

A music teacher voiced frustration with parents who do not appear for performances because they are too busy, but do find time to come to school when they have a complaint:

I had an altercation with a student in the band. The parent of the student had never attended any band parent meetings, and the child always said the parent had to work. But once we had the altercation and I was threatening to throw her off for one football game, all of a sudden the parent shows up and wants to have a conference with me. It's as if the parents won't come to see the child do anything positive. Only when there is something negative, all of a sudden you have the parent visitation. (54, M, B, Sr/L, Fine Arts/Music)

While the familiar stereotype of parents in poor neighborhoods is that they are uninvolved, the corresponding stereotype of parents in affluent neighborhoods is that they are highly involved in the schools. Our data, however, show that teachers working in all types of neighborhoods condemn parents' lack of interest:

You have to get the people more involved in schools. We had parents' night at school. It's embarrassing because nobody comes. We have a pretty good neighborhood out there, a lot of money, upper middle-class, and we cover a pretty good range. . . . And they go through all kinds of methods to bring the parents in. We even try to find the right time when the average parent gets home from work, try to find the right day because you are not going to compete with Monday-night football. It's crazy. Isn't that silly? You figure your kid, your son or your daughter, is more important than listening to Howard Cosell on Monday-night football. But it's true, they just don't come. We don't get the parents out. This year we had maybe 50, if that many, out of 2,800 students. (02, M, H, Sr/H, Phys. Ed.)

On yet another dimension of too little interest and involvement, teachers faulted parental reactions to teacher telephone calls about school problems. Traditionally, a call home has served as an escalated step on the discipline ladder, one that teachers generally could depend upon for home follow-up. Instead, many teachers reported that today they expect to encounter disinterest, resignation, or belligerence. A veteran teacher who has experienced all of these reactions contrasted this behavior with times past:

Years ago, when I first began teaching, if a student did something wrong, if you ever had to contact the parent, the parent would be furious with the student. I would say in 99% of the cases the student would be in trouble at home. In many situations today, I have called parents, and some parents have told me that they're not interested, you handle it any way you can.

You have different reactions from parents today. Many of the parents are completely cooperative and will talk to the students or punish them or have some kind of action in which they will follow through, but you also have other reactions. Sometimes, some of the parents will throw up their hands and say, I don't know what to do with this person. I never heard that 25 years ago. I think the role of the parent has changed, and this has made it a lot different for the teacher or the school who wants to contact the home.

Some parents are belligerent. Immediately, if you talk about their child being in trouble, they want to blame you, and this was unheard of 28 years ago. . . .

So, to summarize, the role of the parent has changed and . . . the reaction that you receive from some of the parents might even shock you. (23, M, W, Jr/H, Lang. Arts/Eng.)

Some of our respondents were indeed shocked by parents, particularly those who were the model rather than the deterrent for inappropriate student behavior:

We had one young lady who refused to wear a bra and did not like to button her shirt. She was very well endowed and didn't understand why the kids called her "jiggles." We got her mother in for a conference because she refused to dress appropriately, and her mother came in with bright blue hair, dressed exactly the same as her daughter and did not think it was inappropriate. (73, M, W, Sr/L,Phys. Ed./Health)

However, the ultimate in the unexpected and the shocking involved a parent who was called by a teacher and told that her son was selling drugs at school. The teacher gave this account of the response:

The parent came in and gave the kid hell because the kid was taking her stash and selling it. That's what the parent cared about. I started laughing; I said I'm going crazy; I had to leave the office because I broke up laughing. But that was the gist of it. I mean she was mad, not that the kid was smoking, had it in school or anything else, but that it was *hers*. (02, M, H, Sr/H, Phys. Ed.)

## Unsupportive Parents: Too Much Interest and Involvement

At the other end of the scale, teachers also labeled parents who exhibited too much interest and involvement in school affairs as "unsupportive." For example, teachers reported that some parents would cover up or make excuses for students, lie for them, or try to get them out of work. Other teachers reported that wealthy parents could exert enormous power with administrators and with the school board. We heard that parents could get grades, classes, programs, and policies changed. One such teacher in response to the question, "Who has the real power in your school?" asked: "Dare I say, the parents?" She explained:

I really feel that they are telling us what to do . . . more and more. And I think that is what is aggravating me more than anything else. . . . If the youngster comes home with a bad paper, it is the teacher's fault. . . . Then there is the matter of the placement of students in classes. I don't think I'm exaggerating that 150 schedules were rearranged, purely because parents wanted it that way. . . . There are students in the honors program, for example, who have no business being there, but mother actually takes the sheet of paper and writes down, I want my daughter to be in the honors program, and that is it. (25, F, W, Sr/L, Lang. Arts/Eng.)

**Vulnerability to Parental Lawsuits.** Today, the power of parents over teachers manifests itself in an entirely new way that has had a profound effect on teacher behavior—the threat of lawsuits. This issue was brought to the forefront primarily by the following interview question:[2]

> Teachers have always been vulnerable to outside attacks, demands, and pressures. What conditions of the 80s, if any, make teachers especially vulnerable? What particular conditions render you powerless to protect yourself?

We were surprised to find that 93 percent of the respondents to this question said they felt more vulnerable than they had in previous times. Moreover, we were shocked to learn that over half of these respondents (51%) felt their increased vulnerability was tied directly to potential personal liability in lawsuits over student rights and welfare. Although generally expressed by all types of teachers in all kinds of settings, there appeared to be variation in the nature of the concern related to grade level. Elementary school teachers, for example, worried about being sued for accidents on field trips, the playground, or in the classroom, as well as for their written evaluations on the cumulative records of students. The following statement reflects some of these concerns:

> I think there is more stress now by virtue of, maybe, malpractice. I don't know if that's the right word. If a kid fell off the monkey bars and broke his arm, the parents would be inclined to sue you now, whereas at one time, they would not. You have to prove that you were there, and you have done everything, and you had instructed how to climb the monkey bars. The respect for a teacher is not what it was. . . . I have to think of protecting myself from a legal standpoint. (61, F, W, Elem/H, Kindergarten)

The majority of elementary school teachers, however, expressed more fear of unfounded accusations of child molestation and abuse. A kindergarten teacher represented the feelings of many colleagues with this comment:

> Parents are very aware of their rights now too. That makes us very vulnerable. We're also vulnerable to what's been happening in Dade County recently with the child abuse. With the kindergarten kids, if they couldn't zipper their

pants, we would help them zipper. We won't do that any more.

If children needed to be reprimanded, we would never hit them before, but we might grab them by their shirts and put them in their seats. Now we won't do that anymore. . . . If a child throws up or has diarrhea I would always clean them up and then call the parents. I won't touch that kid now. The way he is is the way he is, and he's walked down to the clinic, and we call the parents. . . .

It got to the point that we went to the administration because we wanted clarification as to whether we could still nurture, could we still put our arm around the child, could we put a child on our lap if he was crying, if a child falls down and gets a boo-boo, are we allowed to kiss the boo-boo if it's on their elbow? Our principal said yes, that was nurturing, and that was okay, but yet we do it with a little hesitation. All my teammates and myself included were very affectionate in a loving way and never thought about not putting a child on our laps or holding a child, but now we do it with hesitation. (56, F, W, Elem/H, Kindergarten)

At the high school level, as well, concerns with accusations of sexual abuse have become intensified. The following comments by female and male high school teachers capture the general fear:

We are vulnerable with the school student abuse emphasis. It really worries me because I know we have students who are not beyond making up a story just to get even with the teacher. You gave him or her a failing exam or a failing grade or looked at her cross-eyed or whatever the case may be. I'm sure it has happened. And I think it's going to get worse, because students copy. I think they copy all sorts of things, including lunatics. All sorts of things, and this is the year when you accuse people of child abuse or even sexual abuse. I think some of the stories are true. Whenever I've had an intern, one of the first things I tell them is the first thing that I was told. Never be in the classroom alone with a student, male or female. (67, F, B, Sr/M, Phys. Ed./Math.)

ৈ ৈ ৈ

Now this year, men teachers will be hesitant, and I am too, I think about it, if I'm the last one out and there's a girl in the room, I suddenly have a panicky feeling. What if this girl goes, "poof," and says that "He tried to rape me." It can happen with a boy as well. We are very cautious, and I think that it has become second nature now, never to be alone in a room with a child. (51, M, W, Sr/L, Lang. Arts/Eng.)

The fears these teachers expressed were not hypothetical. Within our interview sample of seventy-three teachers, one had been sued by parents, two reported being falsely accused by children, and one experienced, in his view, a near miss. In the latter case, a junior-high teacher felt his 28-year career was on the line when he attempted to break up a fight:

Last year I broke up a fight between two girls, and in the process of breaking up the fight, I was bitten and hit by one of the girls. . . . Well, I filed charges against the girl but . . . in the process of that girl biting me, if I had hit her or pushed her against the wall. . . . Fortunately, I did the right thing, and . . . I grabbed the girl and put my arm around her and held her, and while I was doing that she bit me and hit me. Well, I got her down to the office and fortunately I kept my cool. If I had lost my temper, which I probably had every right to do . . . if I had hit her, my job could have been in jeopardy, and I don't think this is right. Even in protecting yourself, you can get into a great deal of trouble. So I think that this is a way that [the conditions of teaching] have changed. (23, M, W, Jr/H, Lang. Arts/Eng.)

One of the teachers falsely accused of hitting a child described herself as "quaking in my boots" until the girl finally told the truth. While many teachers said they joined the teachers' union expressly for protection in these situations, they also reported that such protection had limitations. The teacher who was sued told this story:

During a wrestling tournament, one of my students was acting up in the stands while another kid was on the mat wrestling. I went up and grabbed him by the back of the neck and I asked him, "What in the hell is the matter with you? You want to act like a fool, then you sit outside." Well, what happened was that the story got to the point that I had slapped him, that was what the kid said and two other kids attested to it that I had slapped him. Two other people attested that I didn't, but that I grabbed him behind the neck. Then it became a racial thing. I went through the whole ball of wax with the lawyers and everybody else, and the lawyer that the union sent me was horrible. I mean, she was to the point of being pitiful. So anyway, they put me on probation for a year and then it was expunged from my record. (02, M, H, Sr/H, Phys. Ed.)

In addition to deep fears associated with threats of lawsuits, teachers reported serious concerns about their ability to establish authority and to create an orderly classroom environment for learning in this litigious context. They maintained that a newly instituted "hands-off" policy made them feel their "hands were tied" when it came to disciplining students. This frustration was expressed by highly experienced, confident veterans as well as extremely nervous beginners. The following comments by teachers with only a few years' experience reveal the vulnerability of the novice:

The discipline, what we call the hands-off policy . . . don't touch them, don't do this, don't do that . . . it's a lot of restriction that is not necessary. . . . How am I going to teach your child if your child is always disruptive in my classroom? I can't put him in the corner because you're going to holler "abusive." . . . You can never tell what [abusive] is. . . . I made a child walk up the stairs five times because he was running up and down the steps. . . . You can never tell so it's just like you have to walk on pins and needles. . . . There have been quite a few problems in Dade County—we've gotten to the point—just to keep hands off, don't bother the kids, don't touch the kids, because every little thing that you do they want to take you to court, they want to sue you. . . . That's why you take the discipline workshop. . . . It's different methods to go about to get that kid in line . . . different things that you can do with that kid without having to physically handle [him]. (14, F, W, Elem/M, 3rd)

ta ta ta

They need to let the teachers have more control. . . . The students know who has control. . . . Some students will actually tell you, "You better not touch me because if you do, I'm going to tell my mother, and she is going to sue you, and you are going to be fired. . . . " There is nothing we can do. It is like our hands are tied. . . . It is like the parents are running the school and not the teachers or the principals. (16, F, B, Elem/M, Intermediate)

Essentially the same sentiment was expressed by a 27-year veteran teacher who exuded competence and feelings of success:

Parents have an attitude against teachers. They tell kids if the teacher touches you, let me know. Teachers should touch, hug kids. . . . Also, teachers should be allowed to discipline kids like second parents, but parents won't allow it. (66, F, W, Elem/H, 4th)

These teachers perceive that their ability to establish an orderly, controlled social environment for achieving academic aims is being seriously undermined by threats from students and parents. Perhaps even more debilitating is the fact that the professional status teachers covet and believe to be central to their self-esteem has been deeply eroded by this abhorrent parental intervention in the instructional process. While teachers generally have had little input into district- and school-level decision-making on matters of curriculum, evaluation, personnel, or school organization, most have typically exercised considerable authority and autonomy within their own classrooms. In particular, teachers have generally felt free to create an interpersonal climate for discipline, control, and learning based on their own style and judgment. Now they increasingly find parents unsupportive of their judgment and taking steps to cross over into what has long been considered the teacher's territory.

## Parents and Teachers: Inherent Tensions

The varying parent behaviors that Dade County teachers labeled as "unsupportive" underscore the complexity of both their concept of support and their relationship with parents. Recognition of this complexity, particularly in terms of the potential for conflict and tension, is certainly not new. Waller (1932) described parents and teachers as "natural enemies" who look at the student quite differently. From the parents' perspective, their child is a special person who needs to be treated individually. From the teachers' perspective, the child is only a member of a group whose individual needs must be subordinated to what is good for the class as a whole. More recently, Lightfoot (1978) similarly argued that the different interests of parents and teachers lead them to different views of what is best for children.

Lortie (1975) also acknowledged this tension and maintained that the conflict between what parents and teachers want is exacerbated for teachers in the sense that students clearly and legitimately "belong" to the parents. Lortie argued that teachers are "doubly dependent" on parents. Because parents have a right to be be involved, teachers are forced to depend on parents to exhibit "voluntary restraint." At the same time, teachers also depend on parents to use their influence to motivate students to behave as teachers want them to in school and to complete their assignments at home. He concluded that teachers desire to be in charge and left alone—unless students are failing to meet the teacher's expectations. It is then and only then that teachers want more parent contact for the purpose of receiving help with student behavior and achievement.

Teachers want to be "gatekeepers," expecting those who are called to respond and those who are not called to keep their distance. Supportive parents are those who show interest in the child's schoolwork and back up what the teacher is trying to accomplish. Although teachers often project an image of wanting to work as partners with parents, Lortie found they do not desire an equal relationship. Instead, he concluded that teachers define the good parent as one who "takes his lead from the teacher—there is no contest for leadership" (1975, p. 191).

Lortie, however, pointed out that teachers do not have the formal status to turn their preferences into policy.

> Upper-middle-class parents can insist on visiting the school without notice and can criticize the teacher to the principal; working-class parents can refuse to honor teachers' requests. Teachers do not possess the status resources to make parents comply or to withstand their attacks; their vulnerability is genuine. (1975, pp. 191-192)

Our data not only support Lortie's findings that teachers generally want more contact with parents of low-achieving students and less with high-achieving students, but also reveal that the desired relationship with each is far more elusive today than in the past. As our respondents told it, there are more students who are less interested in school and less willing to put effort into doing what the teacher wants. Thus, the number of students failing to meet teacher expectations has increased; but the problems of contacting parents and getting them to help have increased even more. In Chapter 1, Karen spoke for the majority of her peers who teach low-achieving students when she exclaimed in her letter:

> The families in our school don't solve problems; they create them! We have mothers who work until they almost drop in the fields; we have mothers who are drug addicts. You can't believe what I have to do to find parents. If I actually do make contact, some say,"Why are you calling me? You should know what to do, you are the teacher!" Some of my colleagues have parents who threaten to sue them.

At the same time, other teachers reminded us that the proportion of educated parents has grown considerably and that many of them feel they have the right to interrupt classroom activities, question teacher decision-making, and even go over the heads of teachers and principals to the district central office or the board of education. The following comment captures the widely held perception of increased aggressiveness and intervention among some parents:

> Parents know right away, "I can go to the district." Years ago, parents were afraid of teachers. . . . We have a P.A. system. . . . they will interrupt me, . . . I am in the middle of a test, "Johnny's mother has a message for him," and the child has to go to the phone to answer the message. . . . this is ridiculous and uncalled for. "Johnny's lunch is here, send him to the office." We have many interruptions during the day when parents can pull a child in and out of a classroom, for whatever reason, and nobody has the right to ask the question. . . . When you do, they go to the district and complain about that. . . . Although our principal . . . is very good about it, still he is put on the carpet. . . . (66, F, W, Elem/H, 4th)

Thus, our findings suggest the long-standing tension between parents and teachers has significantly intensified.

## *Increased Vulnerability and Decreased Status*

Our interview data also dramatically document the degree to which the "status resources" of teachers to gain parent compliance have diminished. The "genuine vulnerability" Lortie found in 1964 has grown immeasurably over the past two decades, and with it has come a decrease in teacher status. The status decline has in turn made teachers even more vulnerable, and so the destructive cycle continues.

While threat of legal action from parents has contributed much to the increased vulnerability, it is clearly not the only factor. Interview data on the vulnerability question revealed other potent sources. For example, 57 percent of the sample maintained that holding teachers accountable for student acquisition of basic skills as demonstrated by test scores made them more vulnerable. As teachers talked about the negative aspects of the accountability movement, they were most critical of being held responsible for student performance when they could not control many of the key variables such as the home lives of students, classroom discipline, allocation of time during the school day, and the content and pedagogy of daily school work. The following expression of frustration is representative:

> Teachers have less control over what they are doing and are held more accountable than ever before. How do you hold a teacher accountable for whether or not a child learns when the child comes to school hungry, when the child comes to school tired, when the child comes to school so disturbed about things that have happened at home that there is no energy left in him? . . . How do you hold a teacher accountable whether or not her entire classroom learns when there is one child who is disrupting the whole classroom to the point that she can't focus on teaching, but is focusing on discipline? Where a child has to be literally threatening the safety of everybody else before something is done about it. They are held accountable for teaching, but yet there are so many other things that don't pertain to the actual teaching process, that take their time and energy that it just seems to be a vicious round robin. (36, F, W, Elem/L, Spec. Ed./L.D.)

While some teachers can apparently ignore the pressure, many others cannot. Teachers reported exhaustion, burnout, paranoia, and even cheating resulting from accountability pressures. Accountability as it evolved in Dade County was so pervasive and central to our story of change and stability in teaching that we devote the entire next chapter to it. Suffice it to say here that large numbers of our sample felt subject to attack from within the school system as a whole for failure to measure up to performance standards, and some felt pressed to respond in unprofessional ways.

Both explicit and implicit references to their principals from 18 percent of the teachers also conveyed a sense of increased vulnerability from accountability pressures. The explicit comments mentioned feeling hassled, humiliated, unsupported, unfairly treated, or placed in an adversarial position. The implicit statements were the refusals by three teachers to answer certain interview questions, particularly those related to principals or dissatisfactions with work. Another teacher asked the interviewer for the tape at the end of the session. The fact that all four of these individuals were Black suggests a heightened vulnerability related to ethnicity, a suggestion supported more generally in our survey data.[3]

In addition, attacks from outside the system were cited by 25 percent of the interviewees as contributing significantly to an increased sense of vulnerability and a decrease in status. Respondents in this category argued there is a growing public perception that teachers are incompetent or lazy based on a combination of media depictions and actions of a few teachers who bring discredit to the entire profession:

> I thought that I was going to get myself a T-shirt when I read an article once. It [was] about teachers being duds, and I was going to wear a T-shirt that said "The Best of the Duds." . . . I find it very disheartening. I think it has produced a certain amount of depression in me over the last several years; I mean real depression. Like . . . am I going to stay in teaching, I don't want to be a teacher, what am I going to be when I grow up? . . . That kind of thing that I've had to work through for my own self and make peace with. I think it's very, very, very difficult. I think it takes a lot . . . to keep your ego intact, especially when you care. (20, F, W, Elem/H, 2nd)

> The media. If one thing happens, it applies to everybody. (58, F, B, Elem/L, Kindergarten)

One respondent who was considering leaving teaching came to understand the low public perception of teachers in a particularly painful way from a private career counselor:

> [We were] told, . . . the first thing you should do is just go
> out and sort of take a little survey, not necessarily to apply
> for any job or to be interviewed, but just to see what's out
> there and what the field is like. . . . I did and . . . the first
> thing they wanted to know . . . naturally . . . where have
> you been? What we were told is don't say that you've been
> teaching because people have a very low respect for teach-
> ers, they just go, "Oh that's all you've been doing," . . . like
> you're not capable of doing anything else. . . . So she said
> just sort of say you're interested and you're looking around.
> (12, F, B, Elem/H, 2nd)

When the predicted scenario was actually realized in one career
interview, and the interviewer asked in a demeaning manner,
"Teaching? Is that what you have been doing?" this teacher was
understandably angered. She defended her profession with vigor
in this way:

> I said . . . do you know how versatile a person has to be . . .
> how well rounded and the wealth of knowledge that one
> has to have . . . especially when you are not in [a] situation
> like high school? . . . You have to have it all, you've got to
> teach it all. . . . You have to be organized. . . . You have to
> plan and you have to budget time. . . . When the person
> said it to me, it offended me . . . "all you've done is teach?"
> And so I really came back at him strong.

Finally, a small percentage thought their low salaries made
them more vulnerable in today's society, but these comments seem
related to the larger issue of public perception. As discussed in
Chapter 3, the implication was that the public respects and accords
higher status and more authority only to those who are highly
paid.

While the various sources of increased vulnerability are
important in their own right, the major point here is that our
interviewees have experienced an enormously heightened sense
of vulnerability, and that the cumulative effect of criticism from
all sectors of society has significantly reduced their status and
capacity to persuade parents as well as students to comply with
their wishes. The vulnerability of contemporary teachers is
more than genuine; it appears to have reached tremendous and
debilitating proportions. The results have been devastating:

decreased status and an increased sense of powerlessness and frustration.

## *Mediocrity in the Schools: Who's to Blame?*

A follow-up question provided more insight into teacher vulnerability today and the prevailing frustration of teachers from being attacked and blamed for failures that should be shared by many:[4]

> Teachers are being blamed today for lower test scores and a general level of "mediocrity" in the schools. How do you feel about these criticisms? Probe: If mediocrity does, in fact, exist, what factors do you think contribute to it? What can be done about it?

Most teachers did not take issue with the indictment of mediocrity, but they did quarrel with being held solely responsible. They saw the problem as a multifaceted one, in which blame is shared by unmotivated students, irresponsible parents, uncommitted teachers, wrong-headed school administrators, local and state policy-makers, and society at large. While they resented bearing the brunt of the blame, 40 percent of the teachers admitted that there were some colleagues who contributed significantly to mediocrity. These are the teachers who peers describe as working "only for a paycheck," teachers we have alluded to in Chapter 3 and who receive fuller treatment in Chapter 6.

Thirty percent of the teachers placed at least part of the blame on the school. They pinpointed such elements as class size, district size, poor administrators, and accountability measures that promoted decision-making far removed from the school site, stifled creativity, promoted minimum rather than high standards, and produced a uniformity that did not fit individuals.

The majority (51%), however, identified once again changes in students, parents, and the home and family as the primary source for mediocrity. The following statements capture the substance and flavor of these counterattacks:

> There are an awful lot of mediocre parents too. I don't think the whole blame falls on the teachers or the schools. I think the mediocrity is due to a bunch of lazy, uncaring parents. (50, F, W, Sr/L, Lang. Arts/Eng.)

&a; &a; &a;

Schools are not mediocre. The home is mediocre. (46, M, B, Elem/M, Phys. Ed.)

ᨠ ᨠ ᨠ

I think it shouldn't just be blamed on teachers, that there are a wide range of variables that contribute to low test scores. . . . First it starts at home. . . . If a parent has taught her kid to behave a certain way in the classroom, then you wouldn't have discipline problems. Also at home, if you emphasize the importance of learning, then you'll know the value of it. . . . You find that most kids don't know the value of education . . . and most teachers—I know that there are some who don't—do everything they can to motivate them, but you can't. (59, F, B, Jr/H. Spec. Ed./L.D.)

ᨠ ᨠ ᨠ

How can you fight against a home where they have one [TV] in every room for each kid to watch the movie they want, and they don't do their homework. (03, F, H, Jr./L, Gen Science)

While the vulnerability question elicited the perceived sources of increased vulnerability and their powerful effects, the mediocrity question enabled teachers to shoot at their own targets for blame. It also revealed the strength and scope of their resentment:

I resent the whole spectrum. I resent the top administration not supporting teachers, being like an adversary. Quite often I feel my union is like administration, and administration is more like a union. That the administration is always trying to beat us down, and it's the union that's trying to say, "Hey wait a minute. Education is important. Education and the teacher mean something." And I quite often feel the administration is just strictly a business. . . . [Administrators downtown] have no comprehension of what the teachers are all about, and I don't think they are supportive, and I really resent some of the things they've done throughout the years. I think the press has been anti-teacher, I think that the public has no concept of what it is like to be in a classroom or what they've asked us to do, what kind of children they're sending to us. I mean they think the education has failed.

I say the parents have failed as far as the children that they are sending to us. Totally. I mean, there's not support at home to turn off the television, no support to make the kids read, to think or whatever. The kids are all passive learners now. Whose fault is that? It's not ours. . . . I resent the students being so inept and so not caring. I resent parents for being so nonsupportive. I resent the whole spectrum. (65, M, W, Jr/H, Sci.Bio.)

## *Changing Student and Parent Attitudes: Reality or Scapegoat?*

At one level, it can be argued that the strong, negative teacher commentary about changing attitudes among students and their parents is little more than "blaming the victim." In response to public criticism of the schools and to statistics showing that achievement of American students is on the decline or is below that of students in other countries, teachers are perhaps saying, "It's not our fault; we simply have less to work with; the job is not possible with these kids." Rosenholtz (1989) in her study of elementary schools in Tennessee found that to keep their self-esteem intact, some teachers who were experiencing failure in certain settings blamed both students and their parents. In discussing the pivotal role of "teacher certainty" or teacher efficacy (Ashton & Webb, 1986) in student achievement, Rosenholtz argued that teachers may attribute to unsupportive parents the source of their own uncertainty. The consequences of such attribution can lead to a downward spiral. As she put it:

And the more teachers complain about uncooperative parents, the more they tend to believe there is little they can do. There is something of a self-fulling prophecy in all of this: Teachers who view parents adversarily often reduce or altogether cease communicating with them, substantially diminishing their opportunities for successful instruction. (1989, pp. 109-110)

While some of our sample responded to the mediocrity question with a defensiveness that tended to scapegoat students and parents, we are convinced that this is not the whole story. Instead, we give considerable credence to the teachers' views, for a number of reasons. First, the perceptions of changing attitudes were voiced by all teachers in our sample, the most enthusiastic, the most disaffected, and all those in between. Although the enthusiastic teachers appeared to have more insight and strategies to deal effectively with the perceived lack of motivation from students and lack of support from parents, they, nonetheless, acknowledged the change and labeled it problematic.

Second, our sample's views on changing attitudes, particularly among parents, are substantiated by other studies (Boyer, 1988; Lareau, 1986). Third, the various factors that teachers cite as giving rise to the changing attitudes are well documented by statistics as well as scholars who focus on societal trends and changes (Boyer, 1988; Cherlin, 1981; Coleman & Hoffer, 1987; Duke, 1984). Moreover, because this teaching force, as in other parts of the country, was older and more experienced in 1984 than the counterpart of 1964 (Kottkamp et al., 1986b; Lareau, 1986), many interviewees were veterans with 15 to 30 or more years in the classroom. Their careers had spanned the period of tremendous change in the school population, whether from abrupt outside forces such as busing or immigration, or from more gradual inside forces such as changing family and community structure or the growing influence of drugs and the media in the society. Such teachers had long-established pedagogical approaches which, in their view, had been successful with a different population. The new population, however, did not respond as positively or as compliantly. Thus, these veterans found themselves working harder, but with less success in the classroom, less cooperation from parents, and less respect from the public. Their present frustration and failure loomed in stark contrast to a vivid recollection of past satisfaction and success. Their complaints reflected their lived reality.

## Students as Incentives and as Disincentives

In the context of our general findings about students and parents, we heard stories from several teachers who recounted changing levels of success and reward associated with changes in their students. For some this phenomenon was related to age- and grade-level changes; for others it was tied to transfer to schools with a different population. For yet others who remained place-bound, the accounts detailed either long-term changes in students' attitudes, values, and motivations, or rapid changes that came with the influx of students from different cultural backgrounds brought there by immigration or desegregation.

Common to these accounts was a sense that the teacher-student mix either "worked," "fit," "clicked," or it didn't. The combination was either congruent or incongruent. In congruent situations, the teacher felt more motivated to teach and more successful; the children learned and rewards flowed back to the teacher. In incongruent situations, the teacher felt frustrated or incapable of teaching, the children did not achieve as expected, and teacher rewards were few or nonexistent. In the latter case, the teacher started thinking about finding options within the school, transferring to another building, or leaving the occupation. In these instances, while the types of rewards teachers desired remained constant, their perception of their ability to achieve them varied in relation to the particular kinds of students they met in the classroom. This finding led us to Mitchell, Ortiz, and Mitchell's (1987) analysis of the differences and interrelationships among the concepts of rewards, incentives, and motivation, concepts often confused in common parlance and even scholarly writing. It also led us to analyze survey data that could speak to the idea of students as incentives and disincentives. While the discussion that follows shifts to a level and type of analysis that differs from the rest of the chapter, our interest remains the same—the relationship between changes in students and their parents and teacher rewards.

## Incentives

In defining incentives, we make use of Mitchell and his colleagues (1987):

> We came to recognize that interpreting incentive systems requires that we grapple with a new perspective on teacher work experiences. To oversimplify, we came to realize that although rewards are "gotten"—and getting them is what is anticipated when a teacher . . . contemplates a task in terms of the rewards to be reaped—incentives moderate behavior in a rather different way. Incentives involve the motivation to "do" something, not just to "get" something for having done it. Thus incentives involve contemplating or imagining the *process* of performing a task, not just anticipating its outcome or consequences. (p. 15)

*Incentive*, Webster's Dictionary tells us, is a transliteration of the old Latin word *incentus*, which means literally "to set the tune." Thus while the term *reward* focuses on the

pleasures or satisfactions gained from an activity or experience, the word *incentive* refers to the fact that contemplating access to those satisfactions leads people to modify
their behavior in order to secure rewards and avoid punishments. In essence, all rewards have both a *reward value*
and an *incentive value*. The reward value refers to the type
and amount of pleasure or satisfaction that is produced.
The incentive value refers to the nature and extent to which
the reward "sets the tune" for one's behavior. Incentives,
therefore, are always contemplated. Other rewards may
come as surprises or happy accidents, but it is only meaningful to speak of incentives when the recipients have contemplated their arrival. (pp. 23-24)

Incentives . . . are destroyed if we cannot concretely
imagine ourselves performing the activities needed for success. . . . [They] involve *imaginatively rehearsing* the performance of a task and finding meaning and pleasure in the
rehearsal as well as in the performance itself. (p. 16) (all
italics in original)

By applying this set of definitions to our stories of increasing or
decreasing rewards related to changes in students, we came to
think of different kinds of students as having potentially different
incentive values for particular teachers. For example, if teachers
were forced to shift from very young to older students (or vice
versa), or from relatively quiet to emotionally draining students, or
from students of their own cultural background to another cultural background, they might find less incentive value in the new
students than in former ones. The teacher might no longer be able
to contemplate the exact processes and to rehearse imaginatively
the exact performance of the tasks necessary to be successful in
teaching these particular students. The students themselves might
provide a weaker "tune setting" or motivation to do some particular things for a teacher who lacks sufficient background, specialized
knowledge, and confidence to imagine what to do. In this case,
such students may actually have disincentive value for that particular teacher.

## Empirical Tests

To test these ideas we used a survey question included in Lortie's 1964 Dade County survey, but not analyzed in his work.[5] This

question asked teachers what kind of students they would choose next year if given a choice. Of the five types identified (see Table 4.1), one category might be identified as "average" students and the other four as having "special needs": the emotionally needy, creative and intellectually demanding, underprivileged, and "slow learners."[6] In addition to repeating the original question on the 1984 survey, we asked Dade County teachers which of the five kinds of students they taught. These are rough categories, and the way the question was posed forced teachers to lump all of their students into a single category. Although a better test of these ideas could be constructed, we decided that comparability in the probe

TABLE 4.1
Dade County Teachers' Preferences for Students, 1964 and 1984,
and Actual Students, 1984

*Preference:* If you could select your students next year, what would be your first choice from among the following alternatives?

*Actual:* Which group best describes your students this year?

|  | Preference 1964 (%) | Preference 1984 (%) | Actual 1984 (%) |
|---|---|---|---|
| Students whose emotional needs are a challenge to the teacher | 6.0 | 3.0 | 16.3 |
| "Nice kids," from average homes, who are respectful and hard-working | 36.2 | 46.6 | 26.1 |
| Creative and intellectually demanding students calling for special effort | 40.0 | 27.9 | 7.8 |
| Underprivileged students from difficult or deprived homes for whom school can be a major opportunity | 12.2 | 13.5 | 23.9 |
| Students of limited ability who need unusual patience and sympathy—sometimes they are called "slow learners" | 5.7 | 9.0 | 26.0 |

*Sources:* Kottkamp, Provenzo & Cohn, 1986b; Kottkamp, 1990c, by permission.

*Note:* Totals do not always equal 100% because of rounding.

over twenty years was important. Even though the tests are crude, we find the results thought-provoking.

Teachers have preferences for different types of students (Table 4.1). These preferences have shifted somewhat from 1964 to 1984. In the earlier year, the most frequently expressed choice, at 40 percent, was intellectually demanding students, while in the later year it was "nice," respectful, and hard-working kids, at 47 percent. The second-place choice in each year was the most frequently expressed choice of the other year. In both years, over three-quarters of teachers chose one or the other of these two categories. (A number of teachers in 1984 underlined the word "respectful" in answering the "nice kids" option.)

The pattern of preference echoes other research findings. Summing up their literature review, Stern and Keislar (1977) noted, "Teachers generally prefer students who are conforming, obedient, compliant, quiet, studious, and passive" (p. 69). From their meta analysis of tracking practices, Gamoran and Berends (1987) concluded that teachers typically have a more positive attitude toward high-track rather than low-track students. Overall, contemporary Dade County teachers prefer students who are not likely to be emotionally or physically draining.

We shift now from preference to the array of students Dade County teachers perceived themselves teaching in 1984. Immediately obvious is the major disjuncture between the preference and actual categories. In fact, two-thirds of the teachers find themselves teaching in the three special needs categories that only a quarter of them prefer. (What the match or mismatch was in 1964 is unknown, because Lortie did not pose the second question.)

To test the hypothesis that preferred students can serve as teacher incentives, we first coded survey respondents as congruent (if their actual and preferred choices matched) or incongruent (if the actual and preferred choices did not match). Then we looked for differences between these sets of teachers on variables such as teacher energy, job satisfaction, and school satisfaction. We found the congruent group had "better" scores.[7] These findings suggest that students as incentives and disincentives deserves further exploration.

Other data suggest that one avenue to pursue is the relationship between teachers' ethnic backgrounds and their preferences in students. Elsewhere (Kottkamp et al., 1987; Kottkamp & Provenzo, 1988) we have explored differential proportions of perceived congruence among teachers of the three dominant ethnic backgrounds found in Dade County: Black, white, and Cuban-born.

Our data showed systematic ethnic differences in student preferences, with Black and white teachers being farthest apart in each category. For example, Black teachers showed a greater preference than whites for teaching emotionally challenging, underprivileged, and "slow" students. Cuban teacher preferences were somewhere in between the other two. In fact, for Black teachers, the second most chosen category was underprivileged students, as opposed to those creative and intellectually demanding preferred by teachers of the other two ethnic groups. Furthermore, Black teachers as a group most desired to teach the kinds of children who actually populate their school system, while the whites showed the largest discrepancy between their actual students and the kinds they desired. However, our data show that even with the pattern just noted, if matches could be made between perceived student categories and teacher preferences, only 55 percent of white, 59 percent of Cuban, and 71 percent of Black teachers could be placed in a congruent situation.

While these findings in and of themselves have important implications for the issue of teacher rewards, they possess even greater significance when related to changes in the teacher and student populations. Demographic figures and forecasts show conclusively that the proportion of teachers with minority backgrounds is falling at the same time that geometrically increasing proportions of students across the country are from ethnic minority backgrounds (Carnegie, 1986). Simultaneously, the proportions of children likely to be perceived as underprivileged, emotionally challenging, or "slow" are increasing, while students in teacher education programs desire to avoid teaching in urban settings where the largest concentrations of these students live (AACTE, 1987). These trends suggest a continuing decline in the incentive value of the students whom many teachers meet daily. In the future, more teachers and students with differing cultural values, norms, and ways of constructing social reality will be brought together in classrooms. Under these conditions, the ability of teachers to find the incentive to teach—to possess enough belief that they can be successful so they rehearse imaginatively their performance of processes and tasks required to reach the students they face—is likely to decline.

## Conclusion

While there is as yet little formal research to document that particular types of students serve as incentives or disincentives for particular types of teachers,[8] this chapter has told a story that generally links perceived changes in the student and parent population to a decline in teachers' psychic rewards. The story starts with the forces for stability and the recognition that teacher satisfaction and reward still depend upon "the times I know I have `reached' a student or group of students and they have learned." It shifts quickly, however, to the forces for change, and the perception that increasing numbers of students are more difficult to reach and less motivated to learn. In concrete and vivid language, we heard teachers maintain that more of their students today are passive learners who desire instant gratification rather than academic preparation for the future. More of their students are driven by drugs, television, and opportunities to make money after school rather than by achieving school success. More students come to school only to be with their friends, and, with a greater mix of different cultures and socio-economic backgrounds, there are more conflicts among students. Of those students who do work in school, more do so only for the grade, and for many only a passing grade at that. When teachers try to help students to do better, they meet, more often than in the past, with disinterest, disrespect, defiance, or disturbing tales of personal and family difficulties.

In search of support, teachers turn to parents, but parents seem more difficult to reach as well—both physically and psychologically. Some parents are impossible to find; others are defensive or belligerent; still others simply throw up their hands and say, "It's your problem. . . . I have given up." Some parents threaten teachers with lawsuits; others go over the heads of teachers and principals to the central office or even the Board of Education. When teachers finally get parents to come to school, they often find parents consumed by their own problems with divorce, single parenting, or two working parents in the family. In some instances, parents are the role models for the inappropriate behaviors and attitudes their children exhibit at school. With these changes in students and parents, it is not surprising that teachers increasingly indicate a preference for "nice kids" from "average homes" who are "respectful and hard-working," and increasingly claim to feel less supported and less respected by parents. Given these changes, it is not hard to understand why teachers find teaching more difficult and less rewarding.

But this is only part of the story. From what teachers have told us, changes in attitudes and behaviors of students and their parents have led both the school and the students to view teachers as surrogate parents and counselors. Parenting and counseling during the school day, however, cut significantly into time available for academics. Moreover, even when teachers don't feel compelled to assume parental roles, they still believe that more than ever they must take time to create interpersonal relationships, work on the self-esteem of individual students, and develop a repertoire of instructional strategies that interest, control, and motivate the entire classroom group. This leads them to formulate purposes that go considerably beyond the prescribed curriculum and to take seriously the distinction between "ultimate, instructional results" and "proximate, relational conditions." It leads them to expend the time and energy necessary to build a positive climate for learning, and to develop the pedagogical strategies required to make the curricular content meaningful to their charges.

Major conflicts and shocks arise, however, when teachers find themselves caught between the strong and pressing demands of accountability from outside the classroom and the equally strong sense of responsibility they personally feel to devote time to purposes beyond the prescribed curriculum and to the development of interpersonal and pedagogical processes. From the teacher's perspective, the pressure to achieve higher test scores all too often ignores the human and individual dimensions, and asks teachers instead to concentrate solely on the cognitive. Karen foreshadowed this conflict in her opening letter when she complained that "time devoted to building tolerance and self-esteem is not understood or valued by my principal." For Karen and the vast majority of our interview sample, building tolerance and self-esteem are not only valuable in and of themselves, but seen as necessary prerequisites for achieving academic outcomes. What happens to teachers when the uniform accountability demands from outside the classroom clash with their professional judgment of what particular students in their classrooms need? The story continues in Chapter 5.

*Chapter 5*

# Competency-Based Education and Accountability: Teacher Responses to Attempts to Change Their Role and Work

*Karen: Every year my amount of paperwork is more and more. . . . I know that my first year teaching I worked like a dog. . . . A lot of time was in preparation and I used to come up with really creative lesson plans. Now that I've been teaching for a while, I don't need to spend as much time in preparation, so it would seem that I would have more time, but I don't. I have less, and everyone I work with complains about the same thing. Every day there's another form. . . . For example, this week progress reports are due; last week there was something about students with excessive tardies. . . . Every week there is something different and I'm spending a lot more time doing paperwork that has nothing to do with teaching. . . . consequently I've cut down on school activities.*

≥ ≥ ≥

Karen's complaint that too much of her time is consumed with paperwork touches only the tip of the iceberg of teacher accountability. Paperwork, as we will see, is a manifestation of a much broader effort to redefine the purposes and means of teaching—

the very nature of the role and the work itself. In this chapter, we examine the effort toward competency-based education and accountability and its effects on teachers as they pursue their long-standing goals and methods in relatively stable school organizations.[1] We find that this attempt at redefinition has produced another wave of shocks—shocks that make teaching more difficult and less rewarding, shocks that lead to increased vulnerability, even dismay and guilt. We begin with an overview of shifts in policy toward public schools, move to teachers' responses to the shifts, and conclude by providing an interpretive frame for understanding changes in teacher sentiments.

## The Historical Context: Social Forces and Policy Shifts Toward Public Schools

The 1950s through the mid-1960s were a period of rapid nationwide school expansion to accommodate the baby boom. School board and administrative attention was generally consumed by the need to provide enough schools and teachers for the burgeoning student population. In Dade County, growth pressures were exacerbated by waves of Cuban immigrants from 1959 to 1976. In addition to growth, the immigrants brought schools the challenges inherent in different language and culture (Provenzo & Provenzo, 1988).

The year of Lortie's survey, 1964, was a period fraught with growth and accommodation of immigrants, but also the calm before the storm of two social movements, Civil Rights and the domestic response to the Viet Nam War. The Great Society legislation arising from the Civil Rights Movement produced the first massive infusion of federal money and attendant regulations into the public schools. The majority of these monies were targeted as equity measures for children of poverty. Federal courts became active in decisions mandating desegregation of specific school systems, an outcome that was stalled by the white power structure in Dade County until the early 1970s. Such changes turned schools into tremendous experiments in social transformation and absorbed much of the energy of local school constituencies.

The Viet Nam War presented a second, concomitant wave of questioning of the existing social order, a questioning that fell with tremendous impact on secondary and post-secondary schools. Pressures for "relevance" were felt in multiple ways: alternative, open, and free schools, expanded numbers of high school courses appealing to the contemporary interests of youth, and an emphasis on "personal transcendence" rather than "social utility" (Sergiovanni, 1980) in the purposes and structuring of schooling. In some extreme cases, a result was deschooling (Illich, 1971). Viet Nam also brought to the forefront issues of free speech and protest, and the rapid growth of drug use among school-aged children. Each of these was disruptive to the existing order of schooling, and in many cases resulted in court decisions that bolstered the individual civil rights of children and prohibited certain traditional means of adult social control in schools. Many of these decisions had the effect of making order and focus on academic learning more difficult to maintain in the crowded social world of the school.

The complex result of the combined forces of the Civil Rights Movement and the Viet Nam War protests was to treat the schools both as a resource for social transformation in the former case and as a means of attempting to preserve a modicum of social order in the latter. In both cases, energy and attention shifted away from traditional concern with academic learning.

Counter-forces soon entered the scene. As SAT scores slid, "excesses" of new freedoms were found to exist. As the economy sank into recession in the mid-1970s, voices of those who wished to use the schools for equity and empowerment were drowned out by a larger and louder group demanding a shift back to a more conservative and elitist agenda of selective mobility embodied in excellence, accountability, back to basics, and competency-based education (Marcoulides & Heck, 1990). These were not new ideas; their roots run back through "scientific management" (Taylor, 1911), and the "cult of efficiency" (Callahan, 1962). But, as noted earlier, in the 1970s they were buttressed with Pentagon-inspired techniques of systems analysis, planning and budgeting, and management-information systems.

Then in the 1980s as the national trade deficit worsened and comparative international test scores showed United States students' lower than those of much of the industrialized world, *A Nation at Risk* (National Commission on Excellence in Education, 1983) trumpeted the failure of our schools and the impending loss of the nation's leading position in international economic competition. Blame was placed on the schools—primarily teachers—for this condition, and the "first-wave" reform movement was off and running at the state level.

A number of states were already moving in the direction of first-wave reform before this highly publicized report galvanized state governments across the country. Florida was in the vanguard of the reform movement, having begun in 1976. The importance of this for our story is that through serendipity we caught the wave of reform in Florida just as it was cresting, a wave which subsequently ran through other states several years later (Cuban, 1988) and produced the predominant policy climate under which most teachers across the nation still work.

## *State-Level First-Wave Reform: The Case of Florida*

Between 1976 and 1984, the Florida Legislature initiated more educational reform than the legislative body of any other state (McCloskey et al., 1987). In fact, by 1984 Florida had enacted laws in sixteen of the twenty categories recorded in *A Nation at Risk.*

The scope and impact of the Florida legislative program were pervasive. In 1976, lawmakers mandated basic skills testing and two years later made a passing score on the high school skills test a criterion for graduation. In 1979 the legislature put through the Florida Primary Education Program, which mandated a comprehensive prescriptive program for primary (K-3) education. By 1980, a statewide assessment program was enacted, which increased student testing. Moving on to encompass the first two years of postsecondary education, the legislature created the College-Level Performance Standards Program, which mandated the College-Level Academic Test as a requirement for upper-division undergraduate study in state-funded colleges. The RAISE bill, enacted in 1983, set curricular and performance standards for high school students. The PRIME bill became law in 1984 to extend the kinds of standards for the primary and high school level to the middle level. Also included in the Florida enactments were performance-based provisions for certification and evaluation of teachers and principals. Finally, while our study was in process, the legislature created the individual-level merit pay mandate (Florida Meritorious Teacher Program) discussed in Chapter 3, and a school-level merit pay mandate (Quality Instruction Incentive Program).

In sum, between 1976 and 1984, the Florida legislature enacted a stream of educational legislation extending from kindergarten through the second year of college. As a whole, this legislative program was an attempt to alter the roles of students, teachers, administrators, and boards of education, and to transform the existing system into a performance-based one in which all four sectors could be held much more tightly accountable. One clear intent of the legislation was to decrease discretion over the ends and means of education at all levels and to centralize decision-making in the state capital. Thus, the role of the teacher was reconceptualized as "one who simply implements policy decided by others" (McCloskey, et al., 1987, p. 21).

In the twenty years between our data points, state government's relationship to local public education changed from acting as a "holding company" that developed broad policies for local implementation under diverse circumstances (Wise, 1988, p. 331) to a centralized decision-making body driving detailed and uniform policies through local school boards and administrations straight into the classrooms. While this process was occurring at the state level, the teaching force in Dade County changed dramatically in terms of attributes teachers perceive as indicating "professionalism." As a group they moved from less than 25 percent to 58 percent with Master's degrees, and their experience base changed from 57 percent with 10 years of teaching or less to 67 percent with 11 years or more (Kottkamp et al., 1986b).

The collision of these two forces, higher formal qualifications and increased experience on the one hand, and greater limitations on their ability to make decisions about their own classrooms and students on the other, led Lortie (1986) to hypothesize, on the basis of our survey data, that decline in teacher satisfaction was attributable, in part, to "structural strain."[2] As he defined it, structural strain is the "increasing tension between qualifications and self-image of teachers in large school districts, their position in the formal system of governance, and their ability to make firm decisions in matters related to their own classrooms and students" (p. 571). Lortie argued that strain was produced by a workplace, especially its decision-making system, that remained the same, while the increased formal preparation and experience of teachers produced their increased expectations for exercising professional discretion.

In the following section, our interview respondents voice their reactions to state and district attempts to reform or redefine the ends and means of teaching. Their collective voices demonstrate that the "strain" was a reality, and that it was far worse than Lortie could imagine from survey data alone.

## Teacher Voices on Accountability

"Accountability," as we use it in this chapter, refers to the combination of state reform mandates covering graduation requirements, curriculum and instruction, teacher evaluation, and district mechanisms in response to the state, including record keeping on students, audits, and test scores. All but two of our interviewees made explicit reference to at least one such mandate or mechanism. The vast majority of comments were negative, although there were positive statements about some aspects of accountability. In response to the interview question: "What are the things you like least about teaching?" 46 percent named paperwork and 22 percent indicated curricular controls and specifications, two direct manifestations of accountability. However, like references to changes in students and parents, and to money and status, talk about accountability spilled over into the entire interview.[3] The effusion of commentary clearly demonstrates the importance of this issue for teachers. The substance of the comments reveals the reasons why this issue has become a key factor in making teaching more difficult and less rewarding over the last two decades.

## Keeping Track of Teachers and Students through Paperwork

Record keeping is a control mechanism commonly used in our culture. One underlying assumption is that record keeping can constrain behavior to limited parameters. Another assumption is that the record is a valid indicator of a completed process or accomplishment. The generic epithet teachers use for this control mechanism is "paperwork." Those with greater analytical bent spoke of paperwork as a means of accountability; those less analytically inclined saw it as a nuisance or worse. In Dade County, as well as in many other school systems, paperwork was a pervasive phenomenon used to keep track of both teachers and students. It provided a base for answering accountability demands from two important constituencies, the state and district administration on the one hand and individual parents on the other.

**Paperwork: Piles, Mounds, and Mountains.** Most teachers go into teaching because they like working with people. One teacher told us she became a teacher years ago to avoid secretarial work. Now, like many of her colleagues, she finds herself spending more and more time functioning as a clerk. Forty-one percent of our teachers indicated a marked growth in paperwork over their careers. All responses were negative; many were visceral:

> It's just the demands, the paperwork, insurmountable piles and piles of paperwork, and all the forms and all the charts, all the schedules you've got to keep. When I first started teaching here 15 years ago . . . you had guidelines and objec-

tives and curriculum to follow. However, so much wasn't mandated to you. You've got to do this, and you've got to have this, and you're accountable to this, and you must do this, and you must have that. . . . You've got to do more, so it's like the pressures of it all, the mounds and mounds of paperwork. Not children's work I'm talking about, but other kinds of forms and charts and things that you have to turn in to the administration. And it's not the administration that's putting it on us. It's coming down through them; it's funnelled down—you must have your teachers do this, and then the administration says teachers must do this and that, and then the state is telling the system what they must do. . . . It gets to be too much. It's like I've had it! I've had enough of it! It's just too much to expect of one person! (12, F, B, Elem/H, 2nd)

ᵗᵃ ᵗᵃ ᵗᵃ

Sometimes you feel like you're teaching paper rather than students here. (04, F, B, Jr/L, Lang. Arts)

ᵗᵃ ᵗᵃ ᵗᵃ

My wife teaches [English]. . . . She spends more time on paperwork than actually what she's supposed to be doing— mountains and mountains of it. (22, M, H, Sr/M, Phys. Ed.)

ᵗᵃ ᵗᵃ ᵗᵃ

One thing that has changed since I came is paperwork. We have to account for so much more than we ever did when I started. That makes it more difficult. I'd rather take that time and use it for teaching than being behind a desk a lot. (06, F, W, Elem/M, Spec. Ed.)

In the last two comments we see not only the growth of paperwork itself, but an indication that it gets in the way of effective teaching, a theme developed later.

**Paperwork: Grade Books and Other "Evidence" Keeping.** "Paperwork" is the generic term of complaint. In some interviews we got beyond the ubiquitous term to specific descriptions of things teachers were required to do on paper. Teachers have traditionally been required to keep record books. But state and district decision-makers gave grade books new meaning by assuming that keeping detailed track of both students and teachers is a means for school improvement. Data put into grade books kept track of three areas: student whereabouts, parental contact, and academic achievement. However, records on students with the specificity required were also records indicating whether teachers had fulfilled all the procedures for which they were accountable. Teachers reacted with amazement and anger to the detailed requirements of this paperwork:

> It's strange. They send us a lot of memos, little notes from downtown. . . . In the plan books this year they wanted us to jot down the conferences we have with parents. This had to be in the plan book. I don't know if you have ever looked at a plan book and seen how small it is. I mean, they wanted us to do this in the plan book. I couldn't believe it! (43, F, B, Elem/M, 4th)

ﻰ ﻰ ﻰ

> We have to have grade books that are arranged just the way they want them. We have to spell out in the grade book what every mark stands for, every plus stands for. Is it green? Is it red? Is it orange? I mean it is getting almost to be a game. I can see where new teachers would become awfully frustrated with the whole thing. (25, F, W, Sr/L, Eng.)

ﻰ ﻰ ﻰ

> It's the grade book for one thing. It's not just grades and attendance anymore. We have to indicate whether the assignment was done inside of class or outside of class. When there is a tardy to class we have to note in a separate part of the grade book that we have talked to the student about it. On the second we have to make a phone call to the parent and so note it. On the third we have to write a referral. Now the referrals are going onto computer forms. It is so complicated; the time has to be military type. Just so complicated: parent contacted yes/no; for this offense yes/no; other offense yes/no; written contact yes/no. It is just a referral. In this grade book you have to have the

dates of the parent contact, the result of the contact, then you have to transfer it to another card. (51, M, W, Sr/L, Eng.)

The information kept in grade books is designed for accountability to the district and state and to parents. It is "evidence" to "protect" teachers and the system. If something is recorded, it is presumed to have happened and in the proper way. But all of this is also altering the teacher role into one of enormous time spent in monitoring and "policing" student attendance and the attainment of learning objectives. This growing process has raised smoldering teacher indignation:

I don't like filing and the admits . . . keeping all the evidence, the paperwork, documentation that I have notified a parent that the kid is failing, that I've called the parent. . . . Another aggravation is that when we go to make a phone call we don't have enough outside lines to call parents so you have to keep dialing and dialing and then you have to write down in the gradebook whether you called them, what you called about. (30, F, W, Sr/H, Eng.)

ə ə ə

Documentation! I have to notify the parents exactly. . . . This, [showing it to the interviewer] is a progress report, and the student has to have this signed. The students carry this home. I had to insist—this is the first time I have ever had to do this—they will lose points from the grade if it wasn't returned signed today. . . . It's my responsibility, . . . if a kid starts to fail, from that point on to notify his parents. I have 170 kids. Parents are never home. Both parents work. When does my responsibility stop? When does my job stop? . . . If the student is cutting class, we are responsible, not the attendance office, because they are already overburdened. Each year more of the paperwork burden and contacting burden is on the teacher. . . . Now they require you to make phone calls home. I made 80 some attempts last year and got through to 30 some parents. If I stayed up all night and stayed home every night and didn't have a personal life or social life of my own—and that's important to me—I may have gotten through to more. (18, M, W, Sr/M, Bio.)

For some teachers the response to evidence-gathering, documentation, and policing has moved beyond smoldering indignation. One analytical high school teacher and department chairperson expressed his cynicism this way:

> According to board policy, if a senior has not received a failure notice, you can't fail him. So what do some teachers do? They make them out by the carload to cover themselves. Isn't that ridiculous?
>
> I think that's a pressure on teachers which causes them to use a lot of time which should be more effectively used in teaching. But if you don't cover yourself by crossing all the "T's" and dotting all the "I's," you will get into trouble. If you don't do a good job teaching, the chances of getting in trouble are infinitesimal, but the chances of getting in trouble if you don't dot an "I" or cross a "T"—they're pretty great! (42, M, W, Sr/H, Soc. Stud.)

This veteran teacher's voice summarizes the feelings of many teachers, namely that though the ostensible purpose of record keeping is accountability for student learning, no such link exists as far as he can see. Rather, paperwork is merely a "game," a requisite means of "covering their behinds." Paperwork was in the end perceived to be a meaningless process of keeping track of teachers. It was meaningless because it had undergone a process of "mystification" in which the symbol became confused with its referent (Allard & Fish, 1990; Burke, 1935). "What is" had become confused with "what's in the records" (Smith, 1974). The purpose of paperwork was inverted. As teachers voiced it, the result was another shock wave, more pressure, and since it took time and energy but produced no visible student learning results, they received less reward.

**Paperwork: Lesson Plans.** As part of the pressure for accountability, lesson plans over time have grown in prescription and specificity, and hence in volume. Planning thus took on a negative association because the new lesson plans required additional paperwork and constituted direct monitoring of teachers. Following are voices of several unhappy teachers, all of them with at least fourteen years of experience:

> I have always had lesson plans. You have to know what you are going to teach. . . . Even after 30 years, I would never go

into a class and just teach off the top of my head. I have to know where I'm going and what I'm doing. But does it have to be spelled out? The student will be able to do Objective Number 10, Objective Number 11, Dade County Objective Number 6? There are some schools that are doing that. (25, F, W, Sr./L, Eng.)

&a &a &a

We have like a Gestapo for [lesson plans.] We do a lot of lesson plans. It's almost like a recipe you find on the back of a Campbell's soup can: the objective, the activity, and the assessment. God forbid we don't have all three of them. . . . They have two little Gestapo agents that come around and sign them. I feel like I'm three years old and I have to be good on the potty or something. (19, F, W, Elem/H, 3rd)

&a &a &a

I was always a very good lesson-plan writer. Lesson plans took me an hour and a half maximum to write. They had the objectives, and they had the activity, and I could under-stand them. Now . . . I have to spend so much time—up to four hours writing lesson plans—that I can't even read when I'm finished because they have to follow these certain guidelines, and I put so much into the plan I have no time to actually sit and plan the lesson. (56, F, W, Elem/H, Kindergarten)

The irony in the last comment is that after completing four hours of "planning," the teacher does not feel she is actually prepared to teach. The "lesson plan," in effect, has little to do with planning a lesson.

Finally, an interview with a very energetic teacher yielded an interesting twist on lesson plans. After indicating that lesson plans, and other forms of record keeping did not bother her, she told the story of receiving an aide in a Chapter I class with 36 children:

On Tuesday I got an aide. . . . Then a couple of days later . . . I got a memo from the department head saying that I had to have lesson plans for my aide. The aide's supposed to help me, not give me more work. So if I have to take another hour to do a lesson plan for another body to be in

there, that's not going to help me at all. . . . I have a hard
time dealing with this paperwork because I have five
classes, and I make five plans because they're all different . . . and now for the hour she's there I have to give her a
special lesson plan! What happened to oral communication?! (21, F, H, Jr/M, 6th)

For this teacher, the potential benefit of an aide to help in an
impossibly large classroom of low-achieving children was nullified by the imposition of a dual lesson-plan requirement.

**Paperwork and Time Control: Beyond "Games" to Harm.** Twenty-
seven percent of the interviewees gave specific descriptions of how
the large amount of paperwork took time away from other more
valuable endeavors, including actual teaching time. In this respect
paperwork was seen as more than meaningless and demeaning—it
proved harmful to students.

There were numerous commentaries describing direct reduction of teaching time due to paperwork. These ranged from calm
statements to outbursts of anger:

The one thing that really bothers a teacher is the amount of
paperwork that you have to do. See, you get so bogged
down in paperwork, you can't really teach, in many
instances. (28, F, B, Sr/M, Math)

ख ख ख

TADS . . . requires so much extra paperwork. You end up
setting it up for the evaluator, not for the children, not for
yourself, not for anything. You have to do all these files . . .
grades . . . records . . . lesson plans like they want you to
do . . . [it] takes so much time out of your day—it would cut
down on my time, what I have to do by 20% to 30%! . . . if I
really did the lesson plans like they're supposed to be done
every day . . . I couldn't do everything that school needs to
be doing. It always drains you. . . . all these things the people above you want you to do are always the type of things
that look good on paper for them to say, "This is what's
going on." But as far as actually contributing in the classroom, it is zero. (65, M, W, Jr/H, Science)

ख ख ख

I actually clocked my teaching time for three days, and the most I taught on one of those days was 54 minutes. . . . I was filling out prep forms that were due by a particular date. I was preparing materials for children for remediation from a 3rd-grade assessment test. I was trying to collate materials the children could use and making up stuff for the other kids—I consider that paperwork. . . . Something for Chapter I also had to be written or looked up. This is taking time away from kids! (24, F, W, Elem/L, Primary)

ᘛ ᘛ ᘛ

Where is the balance of time coming from?! How much do you devote— how much are you expected to devote to paper keeping and how much are you devoting to your students? What are you paid to do, keep records or teach?! (47, F, W, Sr/H, Science)

The most poignant story of harm resulting from paperwork was told by a high school special education teacher about a teacher of her own children:

[Paperwork] puts too much pressure on teachers. The business of this in Dade County, the systems thing, where they have all these checklists—in the elementary level you have to check "Johnny can do this. Johnny can do that."—the teacher is involved in so much bookkeeping that she can no longer teach. I know for a fact that when I taught for a year at L___ Elementary School there was a teacher who was an excellent teacher. This was before the garbage came in. My husband was involved in a pilot program for this, and he said to me, "This isn't going to work. It isn't going to work because it's too much bookkeeping." . . . That same excellent teacher had my son and my daughter and was a lousy teacher. Now what happened to her? Did she lose what she had? No! She had [to give] so much time to checking all this garbage she didn't have time to teach! (55, F, W, Sr/L, Spec. Ed.)

Lortie argued that teachers divide school time into "potentially productive" and "inert" (1975, pp. 175-176). Potentially productive time is direct engagement in instruction or in closely associated activities, time during which students may be "reached" and psychic rewards earned. Inert time is spent on noninstructional tasks during which learning is unlikely and psychic rewards are unavailable. The examples given above indicate how teachers see paperwork turning time that was once potentially productive into inert time. Not only does this process reduce time for student learning, it reduces teacher rewards as well.

## Curricular and Instructional Control: Altering Purposes and Means

While Dade County teachers universally inveighed against paperwork, it is generally something that can be accomplished by coming earlier, staying later, carrying it home. Paperwork saps energy, makes work less rewarding and appealing, and is a potential cause of burnout, but, for the most part, accommodation can be made.

However, paperwork is only the most visible and pervasive secondary effect on teachers produced by the state's performance-based reform initiatives. At a deeper level, and a more noxious one for many teachers, there are even more potent means that seek to control their goals and behaviors. As stated earlier, 22 percent of our interviewees described some form of curricular control when asked directly what they "liked least" about teaching. However, when the total interviews were considered, 42 percent of our teachers reported that, in comparison to earlier times, their professional discretion was being limited by one accountability mechanism or another. Primary among the means was curricular and instructional control, much of which resulted directly and indirectly from the reforms promulgated by the various organs of state government.

Teachers experienced increased mechanisms of control through heavy emphasis on testing of basic and limited objectives and through the mandating of particular programs, packages, "boxes," and other "teacher-proof" materials. Paperwork may be seen as "unprofessional," demeaning, and hurtful, but curricular and instructional control strikes at the very core of how teachers define their work. It limits personal engagement in developing purpose and exercising discretion based on craft experience and minute-by-minute decision-making in the flow of instruction.

Earlier, we saw that teachers have maintained a fairly stable orientation to their purposes, that these extend beyond the basics of the official curriculum, and that teachers place importance on interpersonal interactions as the means to reaching instructional aims. What we see and hear in this section is teachers responding negatively to the systematic narrowing of purpose and the ignoring or denying of many of the means teachers perceive to be central in their work. These are responses to attempts to control and change the very essence of their role and work. Unlike paperwork, these are issues to which accommodation is highly problematic.

The following categories are our analytical imposition on the commentaries of teachers. They are not exclusive; they overlap considerably. However, the particular language teachers used to describe the broader phenomenon of attempts to control curriculum and teacher autonomy does break down into several variations on the larger theme.

**Tightening Control and Limiting Professional Discretion.** This is a broad theme expressed in various ways by 25 percent of the interviewees. We begin with elementary school teachers. Because they teach the basic skills which are heavily targeted in the state performance-based accountability system, they seem to feel the most overall pressure to control their curricula and teaching. One second-grade teacher made the following response to the question of what she "liked least about teaching":

> Being mandated by the state and the county to teach in a certain way that is certainly not creative and just to have to do a tremendous amount of charting and paperwork which are just for audits, that have nothing to do with real performance of children and teachers. (20, F, W, Elem/H, 2nd)

Although she is talking about paper again, the underlying theme is the attempt to control her in ways she considers not productive of good teaching or student learning.

Two elementary school colleagues from other schools express what they see as misguided attempts to control curriculum and teaching behavior in even more specific ways:

> I believe that we have to have some kind of guidelines, but we have taken the word "guidelines" and made them into specifications. A guideline is one thing, but we don't need: "On Tuesday do this; on Wednesday do this, and Friday don't forget to give a test." And it keeps getting worse and worse. I think that on the first teacher workday last year they handed me about four notebooks of guidelines! (26, F, W, Elem/L, 4th)

⁊ª ⁊ª ⁊ª

> It's more than guidelines. It's almost like this is what you
> are to do. Here's the book. It's your Bible, and this is what
> you are to use. . . . I think that if they're going to give teach-
> ers recipes, then they really don't need teachers. They can
> use a master teacher with an aide and get the same thing
> accomplished. (23, F, W, Elem/L, Primary)

This last statement highlights the meaning of mandates for many
teachers: stripping them of autonomy or discretion, the very
essence of teaching as they construe it. Hence, teachers are reduced
metaphorically to aides, functionaries told exactly what to do.

For some teachers, the reduced discretion and control over
their curriculum was almost impossible to handle:

> It seems that the people who make these boxes up and
> think that this [teacher-proof curriculum] is good for chil-
> dren, they just want control. This is the best setting to con-
> trol people. There's no teacher decision, no academic free-
> dom. There's no creative teaching. They don't encourage
> the children to think critically. . . . The change [her growing
> dissatisfaction] came immediately when I saw those boxes.
> There were boxes and then—it's just like a Chinese puzzle.
> When you finish one box, there's another box inside the
> box, and then the box goes within the box—and there are
> boxes till you die. . . . I'm so inundated with boxes that I
> have—I don't want to come back to school anymore. I'd like
> to get another job. I feel that I'm getting so depressed, emo-
> tionally depressed and very angry, that I don't think I'll be
> able to continue. (19, F, W, Elem/H, 3rd)

The perception of curricular control was not limited to the elementary level, though it was more pervasive there. One junior
high teacher expressed a view quite parallel to the elementary
school responses:

> I was much freer to teach sixteen years ago than I am now
> with this requirement and that requirement and the other
> requirement. Take this test and do this thing. They take
> away 30% of my teaching. (01, F, W, Jr/M, Math)

A senior high teacher with thirty years of experience told us:

> Now we have to write one writing assignment per week
> which most of us give, but now they spelled out what that

writing assignment is supposed to look like. We have to give them at least two homework assignments that must be graded, other assignments that we simply check off, and other things have to be graded. You can't do things that way. I know there are schools that actually say that Monday, Tuesday, and Thursday are English assignments, and Wednesday and Friday are science assignments. I can't teach that way . . . with all the years behind me, I'm sorry. (25, F, W, Sr/L, English)

At this point in her career, she simply rejects this kind of external control.

Finally, we hear the voice of a veteran of 15 years' experience, the only one of our interviewees who won a Master Teacher merit award. He told us:

The intention is to make all teachers good teachers by following certain habits. Have your grade book in a certain way, your attendance in a certain way, your files on kids in a certain way. I don't know . . . to me that's not good teaching. Good teaching is what I do in the classroom at that moment, not all this support stuff, not all this grade book stuff, not all that, that to me is pure crap! (65, M, W, Jr/H, Science)

He strongly resents the attempt to produce better teaching and better learning by controlling teachers through record keeping. This is "crap" to him because it has nothing to do with his ability to make good on-line decisions during the flow of lessons.

Although he refers to paperwork rather than curricular control, another high school teacher sums up what he sees as the wrong-headed attempt to control teachers through accountability in this way:

I think they're trying very hard to make great teachers out of some people who are not great teachers, and I don't think paperwork is the way to do it. (22, M, H, Sr/M, Phys. Ed.)

**Control as "Standardization," "Systematization," "Routinization," and "Uniformity."** A more specific subset of the general issue of curricular and behavioral control of teachers was voiced by 15 percent of the interviewees in basically similar terms. These responses came from teachers at all levels. They said:

We have to comply with every minute memo or request
that comes from downtown, but I think more than that
they're trying to—well, they keep talking about standardizing everything, standardizing. I think they're trying to standardize teachers, at least across each grade level, have every
single classroom teacher do the same thing at the same
time. (72, F, W, Elem/H, Librarian)

*ta ta ta*

Power and authority . . . is being taken away from the
teacher. Now, everything is mandated to you. You have no
freedom to venture out; you want to be creative with the
kids, and you want to do things. You don't want to be so
routinized . . . especially with the little ones, they need [cre-
ativity]. But you're accountable for so much, so many things
and within such a framework, amount of time . . . you just
have to keep going. (12, F, B, Elem/H, 2nd)

*ta ta ta*

I feel much less freedom in the classroom than we had
when I first started teaching. I really don't like the fact that
most teachers have to do the same thing just about every
day. We have a yearly calendar, and within that framework
we have to do planning on the same grade level for all the
teachers. To me that stunts my creativity. (35, F, W, Sr/H,
English)

*ta ta ta*

All the systematizing of objectives to a certain degree puts a
lot of pressure on the teacher and takes away some creativity and fun of teaching. (20, F, W, Elem/H, 2nd)

What is striking in these statements is the juxtaposition of the
structural, machine metaphors (Bolman & Deal, 1984; Morgan,
1986), such as "standardized" and "systematized," with "freedom,"
"creativity," and "fun"—the orientations teachers obviously believe
are necessary in teaching and learning. The former words are
goal-oriented in a mechanical way. In them there is no important
place for interpersonal relationships, serendipity, or joy. From
the teachers' perspective, the thrust of accountability-driven man-

dates is to squeeze the juice, the life, the soul out of teaching—even for the "little ones"—and render it dry, routine, repetitious, and boring. Teachers believe they need discretion, and they believe that classrooms need life, creativity, and fun, for both students and themselves.

Deep, special understanding of the tension between tight structure and freedom can be derived from the commentary of a Black teacher who lived and worked through both the separate and unequal dual system and present integrated educational system in Dade County. The tension he felt in the increasing control of his work triggered personal meanings unavailable to those of us who have not lived through recent history as a minority member:

> It is more structured now. You must be on task. You make up your plans and turn them in, and they don't want you to deviate but to go teach and not deviate from the plans. . . . It is just like everyone is teaching the same thing. I disagree with that. Yes, everyone can teach the same subject matter, but not the same way. I am concerned about that, because I think that if you just make everything standard, sooner or later you are going to have a desire to be free.
>
> I will tell you why. I was in Korea in 1951. I had no qualms about getting in the back of the bus in 1951. In 1951 I got shot twice. . . . Then I had qualms about getting in the back of the bus. I was fighting for the Korean to be free, and he's as dark as I am, almost. And if he can be free, surely to God I can be free. He doesn't even understand freedom. What I'm trying to say—freedom is something that you just have to become a part of, live it, and if you make everything standard and you never deviate from it, you lose sight of freedom. (45, M, B, Jr/L, Soc. Stud.)

Finally, although he did not use the language of "standardization" and "systematization," one junior high teacher discussed what he saw as the effects of these orientations as they were manifested through the teacher-evaluation system put in place locally in response to a Florida state mandate:

> According to the TADS [evaluation] system, once you have planned a lesson you should complete the lesson, where before if I was teaching a lesson and found that it wasn't

working to my anticipation, I might stop the lesson and go on to something else. Now this cannot really be done under the TADS system. . . . The rationale, I guess, is that there is a certain pattern that teachers must follow and this pattern has to be judged by an observer, and if the teacher strays from the pattern, then the teacher has not followed the plan.

Now the people who have set up the structure of the TADS—and I say arbitrarily have set up about 120 different check points [actually 81 behavioral indicators], and I would have to disagree with many of them. I feel that many of them are not valid. I feel if you are in a lesson and it's not working, by all means go on to something else, even though it's not on your lesson plan.

Another point that I disagree with as far as TADS is concerned: sometimes a student will ask an absolutely brilliant question, and that is the time to investigate the answer to it, not at a later time, and if you follow through with what you're doing, then you have lost a golden opportunity. (23, M, W, Jr/H, English)

What the last two voices suggest is that to exercise discretion grounded in deep experience and careful attention to student reactions is to become a deviant in the new world of teaching that has enveloped them since the drive for accountability. What this world seems to demand is a mechanical approach and, in some instances, a mindless orientation.

The particulars in this section give added insight into Lortie's (1986) structural strain hypothesis. Some scholars have argued that teaching has never fully warranted the label "profession" (Hoy & Miskel, 1987), and have described it as an "occupation" (Lortie, 1975), or a "moral craft" (Tom, 1984), or a "semi-profession" (Etzioni, 1969). But teachers desire to think of themselves as professionals. Their rationale for professional status has usually been based on the traditionally high level of authority and autonomy they have exercised in classroom decision-making. The comments on paperwork, but especially on curricular and instructional control, indicate a tremendous diminution in their authority and autonomy. This comes at exactly the time when teachers have gained other accouterments of professional status—increased specialized education and greater experience. Lortie hypothesized that they suffer from structural strain. We suggest that "shock" is closer to their own reality.

## Dysfunctional Results of State Mandates and Accountability Mechanisms

The perceived dysfunctions from much of the state's effort to improve education through mandates and accountability mechanisms are implicit in the voices of teachers. Students of organizational change are well aware that any attempt to alter an existing cultural or organizational system is likely to have unanticipated effects (Merton, 1957). Some unanticipated effects are functional, others dysfunctional. A number of our interviewees agreed with the general concept of accountability and especially lauded the movement to have students thoroughly versed in basic skills and learning processes, but a much larger proportion, 58 percent, reported at least one specific form of dysfunction resulting from mandates and accountability measures. (From this proportion we specifically exclude the overwhelming teacher reaction to mandated merit pay as dysfunctional, even harmful.) In the sections that follow, we discuss several subsets of dysfunctions identified by teachers, all of which seem to lead toward an increase in their personal vulnerability.

**Goal and Means Displacement.** Of those who reported dysfunctional outcomes, 55 percent spoke of goals or means displacement. There were actually six different subsets within this category. By means or goals displacement we mean that an intended outcome was not reached. Instead, something to the contrary occurred, or inappropriate means were substituted for appropriate ones.

The first displacement is the simple crowding out of instruction and other important responsibilities by the plethora of paperwork and accountability requirements. This phenomenon documented earlier in the chapter inadvertently forced teachers to spend time that should have been devoted to instruction on paperwork to monitor instruction instead. In the words of one primary teacher:

> I don't want 3rd grade because of all the testing nonsense. . . . I want to get in and teach kids to read and write and to live with themselves. (24, F, W, Elem/L, Primary)

Another displacement occurs when the symbol or "mystification," not the substance, is pursued:

> Third- and fifth-grade teachers at the elementary school, at the beginning of school, do nothing but get children ready for the minimum assessment. Once minimum assessment

is over, they start getting them ready for the Stanford Achievement Test. Once the SAT is in, the results have come back from the minimum assessment, and they are busy remediating all the children in all the areas they missed . . . they never really get a chance to just relax and teach. (36, F, W, Elem/L, Spec. Ed.)

Yet another displacement occurs when the system is standardized to the point that it puts some students into inappropriate learning situations:

When we went back to basics, a lot of kids improved. But for the brighter kids you don't have to go back to the basics. They already have it. (45, M, B, Jr/L, Soc. Stud.)

Still another displacement occurs when joy, creativity, and high levels of engagement in learning are beaten out of kids and teachers by the methodical nature of mandates:

Accountability mandates I think are important. Some of them are silly, but perhaps there are some teachers who just are not accountable and need to be made so. Of course what happens is it filters down. The principal comes under accountability and the assistant principal's under it, and they put the pressure on the teachers so that instead of uplifting us into accountability, it's a pressure that's pushing you down into accountability. I know I'm feeling the loss of a lot of creativity. Friends, they say, "I can't do it all, and something's got to give," so the plays that the children put on and their learning experiences that we all remembered that were not the realm of the "normal"—they were extraordinary things—fall by the side. And the creativity of teaching, the incentives, the sparks are not promoted because of accountability. . . . Enthusiasm for teaching has really gone down, and new teachers come in and they're very enthusiastic, and within a year they're under the pressure of accountability. Instead of being lifted up by accountability . . . the glass is half empty. (69, F, W, Jr/M, Spec. Ed.)

Teachers themselves may also receive displacement effects. In these examples, good teachers are perceived as being harmed most by accountability mechanisms:

I think the intention of TADS is to weed out the good teachers and leave in the ones that are not so good ... because a good teacher is going to finally say: "I'm tired of this. I'm going to give up. This thing is not valid, and I'm going to get just like the other teachers." Sometimes people have that feeling that they are just going to give up. ... It is causing problems. ... The decent teacher would be better left alone to teach than to be hassled with the TADS evaluation. (71, F, B, Sr/M, Spec. Ed.)

 🙚 🙚 🙚

All this stress on accountability in the classroom ends up burdening conscientious teachers. I don't think it bothers those that need to be shaped up. (30, F, W, Sr/H, English)

The final example is a displacement of means. In Chapter 2 we examined teacher perceptions of the importance of interpersonal means for achieving their purposes, and of the tension that results from mandates that stress the cognitive to the exclusion of the interpersonal. The following account is a graphic illustration of that tension:

Just recently a little girl came up to me whose mother has had a series of lovers. She doesn't have a father that lives at home. She wanted my attention. I knew she deserved it, and I had to say, "I'm sorry, Shantara. I can't talk to you now. I have to do charts and then after that I have to work on clusters. After that I have to do the skill pack." I just felt at a loss and it made me very depressed and angry. (19, F, W, Elem/H, 3rd)

**Increase in the Dropout Rate.** Seventeen percent of those citing dysfunctional results mentioned an increased student dropout rate. Specific references were to raising high school graduation requirements and making them uniform, rather than allowing for differential tracks. Teachers said:

I think that the state is fostering a great deal of the dropout rate. We have kids who do not belong—I mean they are trying to put all kids in one bundle. They don't belong in one bundle. There are kids who need to be put in a vocational-type track. They don't need four years of science; they don't need all this math. . . . They're dropping out because they can't go to the vocational school. (55, F, W, Sr/L, Spec. Ed.)

⁂ ⁂ ⁂

I don't know, more requirements for high school gradua- tion—for some kids, and then other kids—if you have more requirements they'll drop out sooner. (61, F, W, Elem/H, Kindergarten)

This is a case in which attempts to make things "better" might actually make them "worse." In fact, given the way negative attri- butions are made, teachers are likely to receive the blame for an increased dropout rate.

**Confusion Caused by Rapid, Almost Ceaseless Change.** As described earlier, the mandates flowing from the Florida legislature were prolific and almost endless. Every year brought a combina- tion of new bills and alterations of existing ones. Nineteen percent of teachers reporting dysfunctional outcomes mentioned the amount and rapidity of change:

One thing I would recommend is not so many changes . . . all these new ideas and new things and new whatever, and they're here for a couple of years and then they disappear. (65, M, W, Jr/H, Science)

⁂ ⁂ ⁂

The system is really moving too fast. What they want to do they're moving too quickly on . . . increasing the things they're doing to new teachers and the things they want to do to the teachers who are in the profession. Things they want to do to upgrade education in the state are fine, but it's just moving too fast—lots of demands on students, a lot of demands on teachers. (29, M, B, Sr/M, Soc. Stud.)

⁂ ⁂ ⁂

Our school system changes so fast. One year we are doing one thing. Then we don't stay with it long enough to see if it's really going to work. They change over to something else. It's just too much changing, for one thing. The requirements have changed so many times it's just unreal. I don't even know the requirements myself now because they change so much. (67, F, B, Sr/M, Math)

       ია ია ია

You're made to do something for a few years, and then they say, "Well, this program, now we're changing it"—it's political. (20, F, W, Elem/H, 2nd)

Teachers are confused by the rapidity of change itself, and they become disheartened, even cynical, when programs and ideas are changed before they are really given a chance to succeed or fail. It is easy to begin to believe that nothing matters because, whatever the issue of the moment happens to be, it too will disappear. Dysfunction appears again.

**Pressure and Stress.** Thirty-three percent of teachers citing dysfunction indicated that mandates for accountability had raised pressure or stress for themselves or students. As they described them, these were not pressures likely to produce positive outcomes:

I hate the word "accountability." It is a word, really, I hear it and I shake a little bit. . . . We have to know what we are going to do, when we are going to do it, and what hour we are going to do it—and now they have thrown this TADS at us where somebody is going to come into the classroom and tell us what we are doing right and what we are doing wrong. Teachers who have been teaching for 15 to 20 years are trembling, literally trembling that somebody is going to walk in at the wrong moment, at the wrong time. (25, F, W, Sr/L, English)

       ია ია ია

I feel a tremendous amount of pressure to get through with the things that I know that I have to do because of state requirements. (32, F, W, Elem/M, 4th)

       ია ია ია

There're a lot more pressures now than there were then. I think when you are given a booklet of required objectives for your particular grade . . . a student has to meet a certain percentage of those objectives by the end of the year, and you are aimed toward that. I think there's a lot of political garbage, and I think there's a lot of foolish stuff going on that we could well do without, especially at the elementary level. They're putting time limits on little kids. They're making little kids do things in kindergarten that they shouldn't be doing until they're in first or second grade. They're doing themselves harm, really, I think. (55, F, W, Sr/L, Spec. Ed.)

**Subversion of Mandates and Accountability Mechanisms.** The final dysfunction of reform mandates was the spawning of outright subversion among those they were intended to affect. Thirty-three percent of those reporting dysfunction claimed to have taken actions to nullify what they saw as harmful elements impinging upon them:

I feel I'm accountable to me. I am the one that really sees children, and I know what my abilities are, and I feel that I am accountable to me first. . . . I have always been a rebel. So I really haven't changed that much [because of accountability]. I have always done what I thought was right, regardless. I say, "Yes, ma'am" and "No, ma'am," but when nobody is looking, I teach it my way. I try to teach what they're saying, and I try to go around it, but when it comes right down to it, if I don't have the feeling for it, it's very hard for me to teach something I don't believe in. (09, F, W, Elem/H, Kindergarten)

ta ta ta

I lie in my lesson plans. . . . I do it quite a bit. . . . Sometimes I think I know better what the kids should be doing. (40, F, W, Elem/H, 2nd)

ta ta ta

You can't get things done if you follow all the rules. I don't break rules that are detrimental to anybody's health or welfare. But I'm not one for following the rules. (01, F, W, Jr/M, Math)

ta ta ta

Subject-matter-wise, the majority of it is determined down-town by somebody I've never met. They say you can talk about this, but you can't talk about that [in life-management skills]. As far as the classroom, with that kind of thing, I've got all the power. I can deal with it in any manner, within reason, that I so desire. (73, M, W, Sr/L, Phys. Ed.)

These are statements of conscience and defiance. In them teachers are asserting their "professional" orientation, asserting from a base of expertise and experience that guides them in knowing the best interests of their students. The fuller context from which a number of these quotations were taken indicates that what was being lied about or what the teacher decided s/he knew better about included the broader definitions of purpose described in Chapter 2, purposes that were often hampered by literal following of the mandated curriculum. These teachers were assertively subversive when the craft knowledge in their very bones was denied by specifications and rules.[4]

## Political Control and Failure of Decisions from a Distance

Teachers who tended to be analytical, some 32 percent of them, were able to stand back a bit and from a larger perspective explain to us why they thought much of the educational reform through accountability directed from the state level was not achieving its intended outcomes. One strong theme was that the reform they were experiencing was essentially a political maneuver put forth by individuals who had little understanding of education or who did not really care about the actual outcomes of their decisions as long as they garnered votes. Teachers told us the following:

I look at it as a political thing. The state administration and department of education has to do things to show the public that teachers are doing more to teach their children. This is all political. (65, M, W, Jr/H, Science)

ء‌ء ‌ء‌ء ‌ء‌ء

Politicians have used education as one of their tools to get votes. Of course parents want better education . . . for their kids, so every politician thinks that he knows better,

and then they write their laws, the laws that they want.
They want to implement them immediately. When you
talk about research, I think less research is done in education . . . The legislators don't push for research to find
out first if that is the correct movement. They do it
because it sounds good for parents, you know . . . to put
so much money into something you haven't found out
about. It is crazy, but that is the way it goes. (03, F, H,
Jr/L, Science)

A second but closely related subtheme is the failure of all prescriptions for reform created at a "distance" from the classroom.
Distance could mean Washington, Tallahassee, or the downtown
central office in Miami. Once the designers of the mandates, regulations, or curricula could no longer see the impact of their decisions on teachers and children, the amount of distance was incon-
sequential. Some of the voices express a combination of the
political and the distant control themes:

I feel that too many decisions are being made in Tallahassee
by people who don't know the first thing about education,
for instance, this merit pay junk. . . . I just feel like the decisions should be made by someone who has some expertise
in the classroom, and I don't mean . . . experience in the
classroom 20 years ago . . . but someone who has been in
the classroom or is in the classroom now. . . . I really don't
think teachers have that much to say about what goes on.
(08, F, B, Jr/H, Spec. Ed.)

ta ta ta

I think it's really kind of hard for some . . . guy in Washington to tell me in my classroom that I should have this
student performing at this level when I sit there for hours
at a time with that kid and the kid doesn't do it. (37, M, W,
Sr/M, Lang. Arts)

ta ta ta

There's absurdity from central office when they're not
totally in tune with what's going on in the classroom and
about what we're up against. It's absurd to sit behind a
desk and not venture into a class and see the reality of

what's going on. I think people are aware that it's absurd, and they're trying not to be caught in that net. (49, F, W, Jr/M, Soc. Stud.)

≈ ≈ ≈

Why don't they come down and ask a few of us, "what do you think about this?" but they don't. They sit up in Tallahassee, and they say, "okay, we're going to require 24 hours instead of 20 or instead of 18. That's going to raise the standards." They're going to require an extra science class; they're going to make the school day longer; they even want to make the school year longer. That I don't think is the way to upgrade education. (23, M, W, Jr/H, English)

*Vulnerability*

In the eyes of many teachers, the final result of the state's attempt to reform education through a competency-based accountability system was to increase their own personal vulnerability. In Chapter 4 we described the heightened sense of vulnerability teachers perceived from threat of legal liability and other sources. The largest source of increased sense of vulnerability, however, was accountability-driven mandates and mechanisms. Fifty-seven percent of the interviewees described this form of vulnerability.

One assumption behind accountability is that it provides some kind of incentive to improve practice. However, we found nothing encouraging in the ways teachers talked about vulnerability from accountability measures. Instead, their voices indicated a decrease in control over their own destinies and an increase in pressure, stress, and feelings of fear and nervousness.

Every time you pick up the paper and somebody decides that their kid doesn't know how to read it's blamed on the teachers. Not on the parents, not on the school system, but on the teachers. Somebody else will come along and try to pass some kind of legislation and put more pressure on the teachers to become great. And there will be more paperwork. . . . I feel it. There's a lot of pressure. (22, M, H, Sr/M, Phys. Ed.)

≈ ≈ ≈

The way the laws are changing, the accountability makes people nervous, makes you nervous. Having taught elementary . . . I know how to teach reading. I mean from step zero I know what it takes to teach a child to read. I've done it . . . but those same skills are almost impossible to teach the child that's 12 years old. The child that didn't get it back then resents your using a technique that he says he knows. . . . Well, when you get these kids [6th-grade remedial] who know how to read somewhat with holes in their skills . . . it's very, very difficult. And when you're being held accountable for that child— that makes you vulnerable. (21, F, H, Jr/M, 6th)

ea ea ea

[Teachers] have less control over what they are doing, and are held more accountable than ever before. (36, F, W, Elem/L, Spec. Ed.)

ea ea ea

[Vulnerability has] become built into the system now. It's built into the things that come down to you as a teacher in memos and so forth. You've got to protect yourself. . . . By mandating that you have to make certain kinds of records, or keep everything you said to kids in a note file and be responsible that the kid is going to make it. Suppose he doesn't make it. What happens to me? Am I going to get sued? Am I going to get fired? Does my credibility go down the tubes? This is what's happening now. You get fearful of it. You get nervous. (02, M, H, Sr/H, Phys. Ed.)

As these comments indicate, accountability-based vulnerability comes not from a single source. It results from the build-up of successive shock waves assaulting teachers. These waves include changes in student and parent attitudes, assumptions, and behaviors, the increased prescription of purposes of education and means for instruction exercised from afar, the imposition of more paperwork, and the clear message of societal distrust. Teachers feel a heightened vulnerability because while these waves are crashing in upon them, they are at the same time held increasingly responsible for specific outcomes that depend upon all of these elements over which they exercise diminished or no control.

The feelings of vulnerability do not lead to concerted effort to improve practice; they are not carrots. Rather, many teachers experience accountability mechanisms as dysfunctional hammers beating them down even further. As we saw earlier, one means of coping is to subvert. Other outcomes are less personally functional: burnout, nervousness, fear. Teachers feeling these emotions are unlikely to work with more dedication, conviction, engagement, and sense of efficacy. Instead, they are likely to become increasingly cynical, tired, and pawn-like in orientation, to search for meaning and invest energy in other sectors of their lives, to teach in mechanical and defensive ways (McNeil, 1988), and ultimately to drop out, either literally or by remaining within the system as "paycheck" or "make do" teachers (Rosenholtz, 1989).

## Competency-Based Education, Accountability and Teachers: An Interpretation

### Integrating Survey and Interview Findings

The responses of Dade County teachers to new policies and procedures in record keeping, planning, curriculum, instruction, and teacher evaluation give credence to our argument that teaching has become more difficult and less rewarding. The interview accounts also illuminate survey results concerning stability and change over two decades in teacher goals, orientations toward work, students they prefer to teach, and, in addition, the means by which they judge their success.

The press toward accountability for the basics led teachers to narrow their focus and lower their expectations (Table 2.2), and to take an increasingly "no-nonsense" approach (Table 2.1). Since outcome measures increasingly took the form of progress charts, audits, test scores, and observations monitored by external sources, teachers began to rely more on the judgments of others and less on their own self-assessment in evaluating personal effectiveness (Kottkamp et al., 1986b, p. 563).[5] And when the daily curricular diet consisted of drill and practice of discrete skills, especially at the elementary level, teachers found it preferable to have students who were "nice kids," "respectful," and "hard-working," as opposed to students who would question the purpose or value of such a curriculum, or students who would either be bored or have difficulty achieving the mandated results (Table 4.1).

With increased insight into how and why the teacher's role and work has changed since 1964 comes increased understanding of the decline of overall satisfaction (Kottkamp et al., 1986b) and of extrinsic rewards (Table 3.1). It also helps to explain why the psychic rewards have declined and ancillary ones have increased (Table 3.4). Teachers found the increased paperwork used to monitor them and their students, their decreased authority and autonomy in curriculum and instruction, and the evaluation decisions made about them both demeaning and debilitating. They also found the pressure to concentrate on limited cognitive goals to the exclusion of broader intellectual, social, and emotional aims for students (Table 2.3) both frustrating and unfulfilling. Under these circumstances, teaching ultimately became more difficult and less rewarding.

## Understanding Dysfunction in Attempts to Change Teachers

In 1979, Wise explored why educational policies "based on seemingly unassailable common sense" not only failed, but brought "profound, unanticipated, and unexamined" dysfunctional changes to American education (p. ix). Wise's theme was stated in the title of his book, *Legislated Learning: The Bureaucratization of the American Classroom.* A decade later, he reexamined his hypotheses in light of the massive educational reform efforts then underway (Wise, 1988). In that article he drew on a paper from our Dade County study (McCloskey et al., 1987), among other sources, to validate his earlier work.

His primary argument was that while it is possible to advance equal educational opportunity by means of regulation from afar, attempts to improve the quality of education through centralized mandates result in reducing it instead. He argued that most recent attempts to improve educational quality are grounded in rationalistic thinking stemming from the assumptions of bureaucratic and scientific management. Moreover, the assumptions of this rationalistic model of organizations are so integral to American culture that they have become part of the subconsciousness of policy-makers and educators.

Starting with actual policy enactments, Wise extrapolated the following embedded rationalistic assumptions about teaching and learning:

1. The child is pliable, at least within the range of normal aptitude and normal expectations.
2. The teacher is pliable and will modify his or her behavior to

comply with legislation, court orders, regulations, or scientific knowledge about education.

3. A science of education exists which yields treatments that can be applied by teacher to student.
4. If shown the way, people prefer cost-effective behavior over behavior which is not cost-effective. (Wise, 1979, p. 57).

The thrust of Wise's argument (1979, 1988) was to demonstrate how these assumptions, when put into policy mandates, resulted in broad dysfunction. The experiences of Dade County teachers provided specific support for his argument (McCloskey et al., 1987).[6]

Our conclusions in this chapter are similar to those of Wise and McCloskey and his "colleagues." However, we present the data and story differently, more from the logic and perspective of teachers who, with rare exception, do not reach the analytical level of understanding displayed in the scholarly analyses. Our purpose here is not to support Wise but to understand how legislated learning has contributed to making teaching more difficult and less rewarding.

Some of the threads that Wise identified are found in Lortie's (1975) earlier analyses. That teachers lack a common technical culture (a concept similar to Wise's "science of education") is a theme that weaves through Lortie's *Schoolteacher*. Lortie argued that without developing a shared and powerful technical culture, teachers would never attain full professional status. In his view, the lack of a shared and developed technical culture lies at the base of much of the endemic uncertainty[7] teachers confront. However, the ethos of teaching he identified mitigates against teachers' developing a powerful technical culture. He also maintained that the gap between high societal expectations of schools and the limited technical culture possessed by teachers leads to excessive demand that make their work even harder. Cuban (1988) and Sarason (1990) argued that educators themselves contribute to this problem by overzealous claims for outcomes of innovations and reforms. We confirm Lortie's estimate of a low level of shared technical culture among teachers. Throughout the interview responses we found very little analytical discussion to indicate a technical culture approaching anything like that of architecture, engineering, medicine, or law.

The teachers' emphasis on the interpersonal realm may be a factor here. Perhaps one of the reasons teachers universally name student teaching as the most important aspect of professional preparation is that only in the real social system of the classroom can novices grasp the significance of the interpersonal dimension as an ongoing stream which underlies everything that transpires on the cognitive level in the classroom. And while this dimension is critical to classroom success, it receives comparatively little attention from those who seek to create a stronger technical culture. Furthermore, the interpersonal is completely ignored by policy-makers who assume that a science of education already exists and that it is through sloth or other failure that school outcomes do not match societal expectations. Any serious effort to construct a shared technical culture for teaching must include the interpersonal focus as an essential element of the whole.

Wise offered the following description of school policy-making:

> Educational policy makers behave as though they believe that schools operate according to the rationalistic model. That model postulates that schools operate by setting goals, and evaluating the extent to which the goals are attained. The goal-oriented process is assumed to be effectuated through a bureaucratic distribution of formal authority and work responsibility. It is further assumed that the attainment of goals provides sufficient incentives to drive the system. Policies emanating from a belief in this model are designed to improve the operation of the goal-oriented process. Policies which promise to increase productivity and equity are imposed on the existing structure of the school in the anticipation that they will improve education. (1979, p. 78)

Wise's statement accurately describes the assumptions underlying the legislated learning experienced by our teachers. But the policies do not produce their intended outcomes. Rather, they produce excessive paperwork, subversion, guilt, pressure, burn-out, anger, disaffection, vulnerability—all disincentives to teaching well and to continuing to teach at all.

The overall outcome, then, of applying rationalistic policies that assume a science of education (TADS, for example) to circumstances in which the assumptions do not pertain is "hyperrationalization." Hyperrationalization results in "more bureaucratic overlay without attaining the intended policy" (Wise, 1979, p. 47). Teachers get more paperwork, and more outside curricular control; students get more testing; but no improvement occurs. In fact, the opposite happens. In the end, the highly rational and the mystical are closely associated. Earlier we wrote of mystification associated with paperwork and testing, where symbol becomes confused with substance. Hyper- or overrationalization produces mystification.

Even worse than the layers of bureaucratic residue deposited on teachers by hyperrationalization is the self-perpetuating process set in motion by the rationalistic assumptions of legislated learning. Failure of policies is interpreted as resulting from insufficient commitment to implementation rather than the disjuncture between the assumptions of the reform model and the realities of the school. The response from policy-makers is not to find a policy congruent with school realities, but "more of the same," and "come down harder." When policies make teachers so angry, so dysfunctional, so "crazy" that they leave or turn to "making do," this is taken as evidence of their laziness and the need for even more stringent controls. Good teachers are driven out, and the rationale for tighter control over the remaining lower-performers is supported.

As teachers told us, only if control continues to be exercised from afar can the mystification of and support for the rationalistic policy itself be maintained. To see these policies through the eyes of teachers is to question them deeply.

Our conclusions and those of Wise are shared by others. Using a Tennessee survey taken at about the same time as ours, Rosenholtz (1989) concluded: "The expectation that bureaucratic control will quickly lead to the promised land of better teaching and student learning cannot be sustained, even by those who most sincerely believe it" (p. 165). On the basis of Texas and Midwestern samples, McNeil (1988) concluded:

> These top-down reforms not only ignore many of the dynamics that produce low-quality instruction, but they actually reinforce them. By applying across-the-board generic remedies, they are dumbing down the best teaching even as they try to raise the bottom. Disclaimers that these will establish "minimums" have little credibility when the best teachers are the ones who feel most alienated and who are talking of leaving. . . .
>
> Good teaching can't be engineered into existence. But an engineering approach to schooling can crowd out good teaching. Instead of holding up a variety of models for practice and learning from strengths, these reforms continue our historically flawed search for "one best way" to run our

schools. These reforms take a cynical view of teachers' ability to contribute constructively to schooling; they choose to make the content, the assessment of students, and the decisions about pedagogy all teacher-proof, so that a standardized model will become the norm. (p. 485)

Finally, we move back to the systemic issues of change and of stability. The focus in this chapter has been the state's attempt to change and standardize the ends and means of education. In Chapter 1 we argued that the essential structure of the schools as developed in the last half of the nineteenth century remains the context for teachers today. Have the change attempts examined here not affected that stability? Cuban's (1988) discussion of the reform puzzle is helpful at this point. He argued that there are two orders of change. First-order changes solve what engineers call "quality-control problems." They are designed to improve efficiency and effectiveness without changing the structure of the organization, thus, preserving the existing system. Second-order changes "alter the fundamental ways in which organizations are put together." They introduce new goals, structures, roles, and ways of solving persistent problems (p. 342).[8] Florida altered teacher recruitment, salary allocation, curricular content, and teacher evaluation, all of which Cuban defined as first-order changes. Thus, while we have viewed, from the teachers' perspective, traumatic changes that inflicted considerable pain, these were not second-order changes. McNeil (1988), in fact, argued that one reason reforms made matters worse is that they did not address the "underlying structural flaws" in education.

In Part III, we consider at length the issues and possibilities of addressing structural flaws and systemic problems in education, but for now we turn to individual variations in responses by contemporary teachers to the changes they experienced with students, parents, and their own roles and work.

*Chapter 6*

# A Teacher is Not a Teacher is Not a Teacher: Differences in Contemporary Teachers' Beliefs and Behaviors

*Karen: I just said, "Look, we're going to do Julius Cae-
sar whether you like it or not—and you're going to
enjoy it—I'm going to make you enjoy it if it kills me,"
and it nearly did....*

*Interviewer: What makes you so persevering?*

*Karen: I don't know ... I am the way I am, and I am
the way I am in the classroom.... But ... I am getting
tired of teaching.... As the years go by, I find that it's
taking an awful lot out of me.... Last year, there were
days I'd come home where I'd just nothing left to give.
See, I also got married, too, so that was another role. I
got married when I was 31, so I was single for a number of years, and I was only responsible for me.... I
think I'm getting tired of it because I'm just getting
tired.*

ۉ ۉ ۉ

Despite the challenge of students who only come to school to see
their friends, and the frustration of instructional controls exerted
from outside the classroom, Karen's drive to connect her students
to the prescribed curriculum appears to be unwavering. The effort

159

to sustain that drive, however, has left her drained and at times, with "nothing left to give." In the course of our study, we met teachers who were equally driven but still energized; we also met individuals who exhibited no drive and had literally given up. In fact, throughout the interview process, we were struck by the remarkable differences among individual teachers.[1]

For example, on a single day, we interviewed an articulate, abstract thinker with a PhD as well as a narrow, concrete thinker who had difficulty understanding our questions and formulating coherent responses. Another day, we interviewed a teacher who loved his work and felt lucky to be in the occupation and a teacher who hated her work and wished she had never chosen teaching for a career. On yet another day, we interviewed a teacher who was open, energetic, dynamic, and dedicated, and a teacher who was fearful, tired, dull, and working only to pay college tuition bills.

These stark differences in ability, personality, commitment, energy, and work satisfaction seemed to suggest significant, interrelated attributes that could offer key insights into contemporary teachers. While it is important to identify commonalities that bind teachers as an occupational group, it seems equally important to recognize differences that separate them, particularly as we consider reforms aimed at recruitment and retention of successful teachers. In addition, we need to examine how individual variations, as well as broader occupational characteristics, interact with differences in school settings and principals to create particular school cultures and learning environments for both students and teachers.[2]

In this chapter, we depart somewhat from the preceding chapters in order to focus on differences among contemporary teachers rather than on differences between the whole occupational group in two different decades. In particular, we examine differences among the ways our interviewees appeared to cope with the major changes in their students and work. Much of the chapter is focused upon two distinctly different subsets of teachers and the patterns of personal attitudes and behaviors that set them apart from others, but we also raise questions as to how differing school environments might contribute to these patterns. Our intention is to reveal and clarify what we found in the way of variations on the general theme of teacher sentiments expressed in the last two chapters.

## Subgroup Variations: Insights from Self-Reports

While our interviews reveal that teachers as a whole believe teaching today is more difficult and less rewarding than in the past, they also indicate that teachers cope with the frustrations and problems in their work in various ways. For a small set of interviewees, teaching was clearly a painful experience. When asked to describe a good day, one teacher in this category could not recall any. For the vast majority of our sample, however, teaching took on the qualities of a roller coaster ride with its ups and downs, its good and bad days. Most teachers in this category talked of more good days than bad days and said consistently that while teaching had its down sides, it also had many high points. Finally, at the other end of what we might call a "work-orientation continuum," there was a small set of teachers who, despite all of the frustrations experienced and expressed, felt highly positive about teaching and looked forward to going to work every day.

Although we initially attempted to identify a number of subsets all along the continuum, in the end we could only speak with assurance about those at the extreme positions. These individuals distinguished themselves by the beliefs and behaviors they exhibited toward the challenges encountered inside and outside of the classroom. Those with a highly positive approach we have labelled "enthusiastic"; those with a highly negative approach we have labelled "disaffected." However, teachers with either of these labels cannot necessarily be assumed to be successful or unsuccessful practitioners. No classroom observations were conducted and no classroom performance data were collected. Information used to construct the categories came only from their self-reports, and we determined the criteria for grouping. We begin with the positive orientation.

## The Enthusiastic Teachers

### Origin and Criteria for Selection

As indicated above, it was obvious that a small set of teachers in our sample was extraordinarily satisfied, despite numerous work-related problems. In search of patterns that offered insights into the high level of enthusiasm, we developed a list of criteria for membership in the subset. These were teachers who:

1. had taught a minimum of eight years;
2. expressed extreme satisfaction with their career choice;
3. displayed a high degree of enthusiasm for their daily work (almost every day is a "good" one);
4. preferred to stay in the classroom rather than become administrators;

5.  would consider becoming teachers if they could choose their profession again.

One elementary, four junior high/middle, and six senior high school teachers met these criteria. Six were women and five were men. As our enthusiastic teachers talked of overall satisfactions and frustrations, goals and aspirations for students and themselves, their language conveyed a shared way of thinking about challenges and acting to confront them successfully. In some instances, their language reflected the responses of the vast majority of interviewees, but to a heightened degree; in others it seemed to represent a totally different set of beliefs and behaviors in the classroom. We now focus on these patterns of thought and action.

## Shared Attitudes

**Deep Sense of Mission.** As noted earlier, Lortie (1975) found that many teachers were attracted by the occupation's service orientation and perceived themselves as "performing a special mission in our society" (p. 28). The prevailing sentiment of contemporary teachers is similar, but with one major difference. Teachers in our study and others (Gallup, 1978, 1984) believe that public regard for them has diminished dramatically in the last two decades and that, generally speaking, neither parents nor students regard teachers as "special" any more. The status decline has, as we have heard, demoralized a large number of teachers. When asked whether they would again choose teaching, many of our interviewees said they would look for something with higher status and respect. When asked on our survey, "Would you like to have a child of yours take up teaching in the public schools as a career?" 72 percent of Dade County teachers answered "No," a response confirmed elsewhere (Gallup, 1986). What distinguishes the enthusiastic subset from the rest of our sample is that the decline in status neither deterred nor discouraged them. They clearly do not like the loss of prestige, but they believe so strongly in the importance of their work that they remain motivated to carry on their mission with enthusiasm and energy.

Among the enthusiastic teachers are those who personally equate their work with the high-status professions:

> I believe that teaching is a profession . . . comparable to law or medicine. We're dealing with the minds of all these children. We're with them all day in the formative years; what could be more important? I've been very conscious of all the teachers of my own children who are good or bad.

I've seen the effect they have had on their lives each year when they've been in school, whether they've walked away from a class highly motivated, or feel, "I can't wait to get out of the class." (21, F, H, Jr/M, 6th)

In a related vein, some described themselves as important because they prepare people for high-status professions:

All of the professions sort of hang on it [teaching] in a sense. . . . Students get a lousy teacher and ten years from now other professions are indirectly affected. . . . You have to teach the doctors. You have to teach the lawyers. You're teaching the other professionals, so if all the teachers are lousy, I don't think we can expect too much in the other areas. (O4, F, B, Jr/L, Lang. Arts/Eng.)

Others in this subcategory simply talked about being an important influence at different points in their students' lives. These teachers viewed themselves as fulfilling a societal "obligation" or "responsibility."

The age that I teach, eleven-, twelve-, thirteen-year olds, they're just discovering themselves. Many of them are forced to discover through good or bad experiences. . . . It's a special time for them, and you have to be cognizant of the fact that you could be very important in their life. They could either hate you and can't wait for sixteen to come . . . or you can be a motivating factor. . . . I know why I want to be a teacher. I know why, and even if I get frustrated when they don't bring their homework or when I call a home and the parents are nasty 'cause they really could care less about their own child, there still have to be people like me. There have to be people that are willing to make that phone call even if you're going to be mistreated or write that note even if you never hear back from those parents. It's my obligation; I feel it is a responsibility. (21, F, H, Jr/M, 6th)

The sense of importance these teachers feel about their work is so strong that they refuse to accept the inferior status often ascribed to teachers:

It's the prestige that I put on myself. I put great emphasis on my status, and I don't let anyone tell me I'm "just a teacher." I don't let people get away with that. I don't let people say, "Oh, you teach, how do you stand to do that?" "Oh, you're a plumber, how can you stand that?" Then they get the idea. I feel that I'm a professional; I'm a college graduate. . . . I'm a very important person to these kids. I'm a very important person in the community. That's a big deal right there. . . . I'm not working for myself. I'm not going to a job, picking up a paycheck when it's over. . . . Somebody who works in a bank, fine if they enjoy it, it's fine for them: It's not good enough for me. I have to be a little bit more involved with the community. (18, M, W, Sr/M, Sci. Bio.)

**Young People: They Give the Mission its Meaning.** Lortie (1975) noted:

One of the most obvious characteristics of teaching is that it calls for protracted contact with young people. To cite this as an attraction almost seems tautological, but this is not so when we compare teaching with other kinds of work; very few occupations involve such steady interaction with the young. (p. 27)

In Lortie's interview sample, and in ours, the opportunity to work with children or people generally led the list of attractions to teaching.

For the enthusiastic subset, however, this interpersonal theme was expressed more often, broadly, and emphatically than in our sample as a whole. Enthusiastic teachers could be described as "child-centered," as opposed to "subject-matter-centered." Although they believe strongly in what they have to offer in their subject fields and spend long hours to make it interesting and clear to their students, their focus is always on the growth and development of the whole child rather than just academic growth. Their students are persons first and students of reading, history, or biology second. Enthusiastic teachers are particularly interested in building students' self-esteem.

An English teacher expressed her goals this way:

I really am interested in teaching them literature and getting them interested in wanting to read. Having . . . a curiosity for the rest of their lives and having the ability to satiate that curiosity, really. I want them to be able to go to a library if they have an interest, know where to find what they're looking for and be able to satisfy that, whatever the need—whether it's research, or whether it's a thought, or an idea. That's really the first uppermost thought in my mind of teaching English.

But I am very big about being a good person. . . . about keeping a good self-image so you think well of yourself. I take care of kids who come not dressed properly and don't look well-groomed. I manage to get them looking like people. (50, F, W, Sr/L, Lang. Arts/Eng.)

In a similar vein, a Social Studies teacher explained:

There's a tremendous amount of self-esteem that has to be developed along with just teaching. This is what I'm constantly working with. I'm working with youngsters that are almost always from divorce situations. They have culture shock.

This one is from Nicaragua, this one is from South America, and they're all of a sudden all put together. You have to build some kind of bridge where we can all work together very successfully. That's why I love world history, because you can pull from each one something, and they have something to contribute. (49, F, W, Jr/M, Soc. Stud.)

Even in a potentially competitive subject such as Physical Education, the enthusiastic teacher works to build everyone's self-esteem:

I believe, and the reason I went into physical education is, that part of being comfortable in learning and achieving things is finding success. In my class every child gets to be a leader and every child is going to find success if I have to cheat for them. That kid that can't walk is going to win, he's going to win one way or another. . . . My satisfaction comes directly from the children. (05, M, W, Elem/H, Phys. Ed.)

The enthusiastic teachers receive tremendous satisfaction from their interpersonal interactions with students, and they appear to respect and value them as persons:

When I took a leave of absence, I really missed it. I realized there was a certain level of student that I really enjoyed teaching and I just flat out missed it. I have a lot of fun teaching. I just enjoy it. . . . I'm there every morning about 45 minutes before school starts and I open my room for a study hall, so I have a lot of students coming in the morning just sitting and studying and asking questions. I tutor. I do it because I like it. . . . I look forward to getting up every day. I enjoy the contact. (15, M, W, Sr/L, Gen. Sci.)

**The Teacher as "Origin" and Motivator of Others.** The enthusiastic teachers hold in common a belief that they can and should control what occurs in their classrooms. This includes taking responsibility for their own actions and those of their students. Compared to the majority of their peers who feel they have lost considerable control over their classrooms, these teachers sound starkly different. They perceive and present themselves as individuals who exert a high degree of influence over their classroom environments. deCharms (1968) described two types of individuals, "origins" and "pawns." "Pawns" see externals—events, situations, people—as controlling their destinies, while "origins" see the locus of causality within themselves. Enthusiastic teachers talk like "origins" who can accomplish the goals they set for themselves and their students. A good day is not dependent on student moods, but upon teacher behavior:

Those considering teaching need to know what it's like. . . . that there are going to be some good and bad days. There are in every profession. Even a housewife can have good and bad days. *You can make your bad days good days.* You're dealing with a spontaneity that's there all the time. It's almost like a volcano. You never know when it's going to erupt, and when it erupts, how high it is going to go and which direction the lava is going to pour. Here you are as this guiding force, and you can create this and you can generate it or you can just let it lie there. (emphasis added) (33, F, W, Sr/M, Sci. Bio.)

ﺩ ﺩ ﺩ

When you're dealing with a hundred and seventy kids, you know, you just can't depend on your good days coming from all those kids, you have to be part of that. *You have to make the day good.* (emphasis added) (21, F, H, Jr/M, 6th)

For the enthusiastic teachers, unmotivated students are not a societal problem; they are a classroom problem to solve. In fact, these teachers take personal responsibility for student motivation. Rather than complain about less motivated students or express a sense of helpless resignation in the face of student apathy, they talk of "turning students around." Their comments consistently have an assertive quality in substance and tone. The message they convey one way or another is, "I am successful because I will it so." One teacher told us:

> You have to stimulate them to the point that they look forward to coming to your class. If they look for ways of getting out of it, then you're not being interesting enough. (33, F, W, Sr/M, Sci. Bio.)

Another teacher saw himself as a "mold breaker."

> I think attitude is more important than knowledge and skill. I think you have to be a *mold breaker* more than an educator. If you can motivate kids to want to do it, they will do it, and I think that's what makes successful teachers and what makes teachers who are not so successful. (emphasis added) (22, M, H, Sr/M, Phys. Ed./Driv. Ed.)

Still another teacher described herself as a molder:

> If they have come in feeling bad about what they have read, I turn them around, and then they feel good about what they have read. . . . You do see a change in attitudes in high school students, there's no question about it. . . . I see a change in attitudes from the beginning to the end of the year—I already see a change in the two weeks that I have been teaching these two groups in summer school. *I'm a molder.* I get them to do what I want. (emphasis added) (50, F, W, Sr/L, Lang. Arts/Eng.)

## Shared Strategies

**Investment of Self: Giving in Order to Get.** Enthusiastic teachers appear to be extraordinarily committed to their work. They come to school early, stay late, take work home, spend their own money on class materials, take a personal interest in individuals, and participate in schoolwide activities. They are willing to do whatever it takes to "turn kids around" and to show them they care:

I'm there at 7:00 in the morning, because I have kids coming in before school to talk, just get my stuff together. I
leave about 5:00 or 5:30. I go back at night for the sports or
meetings, so I have to be totally involved. I've told myself,
"Try to pull out." Just yesterday when I was by the school,
they said, "Do you want to give up volleyball? Are you sure
you want to?" I said, "Look, I don't want to see the sport
go down. If you have somebody good to take it over, I'll let
it go, but I want to know who's going to take it." I don't
just want to give it up to someone as a token. I care too
much about the kids. . . . It's important to be involved in the
school itself, like a club or a sport or an activity where the
kids say, "This person cares about students." They know
who is available and who isn't. (33, F, W, Sr/M, Sci. Bio.)

Motivation for these teachers is intrinsic:

It certainly isn't the money. I think in order to be a teacher
you have to be cut out of a special kind of cloth. You have to
be able to take the work, the hate, the insults, and you have
to be able to take the parent criticism. You have to know
your place. You have to love your work. You have to be
determined that, in spite of all this, you will do a good job
and enjoy it. Because those teachers who don't feel that
way are not really good teachers, and they burn out very
quickly, so they leave for other fields. (25, F, W, Sr/L, Lang.
Arts/Eng.)

The prevailing belief is that you have to give of yourself to get
what you want from your students, and that in the end, you'll
probably get much more than you give:

I realize that, if you just give a little bit of yourself to these
kids, they're going to give a lot more back to you. (21, F, H,
Jr/M, 6th)

ta   ta   ta

It's a two-way thing. You're going to get as much as you put
in. Sometimes you get more back. (33, F, W, Sr/M, Sci. Bio.)

Clearly, enthusiastic teachers thrive on psychic rewards from
reaching students. They recognize that these rewards do not come

automatically. Students also serve as incentives to motivate these teachers to invest heavily their time and energy. The payoff more than justifies the investment.

**Change of Pace: Striking a Balance.** Teachers who invest themselves so heavily day after day run a high risk of burn-out. Similarly, those who teach the same subjects to children of the same age year after year run a high risk of boredom. Enthusiastic teachers consciously work to avoid such effects through change strategies that strike a balance between routine and variety, between work and play.

To stay intellectually stimulated, enthusiastic teachers build variety into their routine in different ways. One teacher achieved variety by teaching different classes:

> It is extremely important for me to teach anatomy because even if I only had one anatomy class a day it would give me a break from the lower-level material, which as a teacher three times a day for fifteen years, you can get pretty stale. No matter how much you embellish it and no matter how much you learn about it, the basics can get pretty stale. Without that switching off, it can get pretty stale. (18, M, W, Sr/M, Sci. Bio.)

Another teacher spoke of changing teaching techniques:

> I never want to get in a rut. I'm always doing different things. Small group activities I've always been afraid of, because it feels like you're losing control when the kids start to talk, and I've always been kind of afraid of them, but the past couple of years I've tried working with them, especially on sensitive issues, and I find that really helps some of the kids. (33, F, W, Sr/M, Sci. Bio.)

Yet another achieved variety by regularly changing the content of lessons:

> Of course, I like to change my lessons. I was just putting a lesson together on the Coliseum in Rome. I bought a book, and just that one particular structure in Rome, there are so many exciting things that I can bring in living in Florida, and how it took sailors the knowledge of sailing skill to build the hull net at the top of the Coliseum. I have pic-

tures, and I'm trying to go into areas in history that can appeal to certain youngsters. I'm always looking for new lessons. I make an interesting window arrangement, Reach Out to the World. I take a map and I make letters out of it. Or I try to collect all kinds of postcards. Can you recognize this type of place? Just lessons before they walk in, that have some kind of visual effect. You have to, otherwise you do the same thing. (49, F, W, Jr/M, Soc. Stud.)

While enthusiastic teachers described deliberate efforts to keep themselves stimulated and energized, they also revealed strategies to prevent overstimulation and eventual burn-out. Those who did not need to work in the summer didn't, and talked of the importance of time away from teaching:

I enjoy the time off. I like the fact that you have an intensity for a period of time and then you have the time that you can relax and rebuild. I could never teach summer school like some of my friends do. I don't think that there is enough time to regroup, because I put so much into it. I play hard and I work hard. (33, F, W, Sr/M, Sci. Bio.)

**Coping with External Pressures: Closing the Classroom Door.** The enthusiastic subset was as vocal about the negative conditions of teaching as the rest of the sample. They had, however, developed successful coping mechanisms. Their basic strategy: "Closing the classroom door." Because their success and satisfaction stem directly from students and their strong sense of mission, they literally and figuratively shut out external influences that might interfere with their primary domain—the classroom.

The following statement captures the essence of the phenomenon as a teacher talks about "building imaginary barriers," rather than "closing the door."

If . . . you are really serious and energetic about your job, then you wake up every morning and say to yourself with a positive attitude: "No matter what bombards me today, it's not going to get to me. I'm not going to fail. I'm going to come through with it." You keep this up as long as you can; you develop. It's when you start thinking all the ill thoughts, "I am going to let this . . . and how dare this person do this to me . . . or this teacher or administrator." You can't. You have to build these imaginary barriers. My job is in the classroom with the children. I have to do the best that I can. I have to help these youngsters. (49, F, W, Jr/M, Soc. Stud.)

This theme is echoed in differing contexts:

If you don't like your first year, it won't get better. It's time to get out. If you do like it, that's half the battle. The worst is paperwork, the principals, the meetings. They aren't important, even your colleagues as far as that goes, are unimportant, 'cause when you close that door it is you and those kids, and if you feel good about being in there, it will come. (21, F, H, Jr/M, 6th)

ૐ ૐ ૐ

I really love what I'm doing. I get a certain sense of power, you know you get behind that lectern and darn it, this is my class and these are my kids, and I see them make progress year after year. . . . There is something about closing the door, these are my kids, that works. (25, F, W, Sr/L, Lang. Arts/Eng.)

These sentiments suggest a disinterest, perhaps an unwillingness to take on some of the broader concerns of "the system" and the profession. Instead of banging down the doors of the principal's office, these teachers close the doors of their classrooms and teach by their own standards. For example, an English teacher working under Title I guidelines that made no sense to her simply ignored them:

State and federal mandates—we have them, but I don't pay much attention to them—I still do what I want to do in English. I do what I feel is necessary to do—they want you to do something, I do it, but I also do what I want to do. (50, F, W, Sr/L, Lang. Arts/Eng.)

This teacher's willingness to take risks to be true to her professional self was typical of the enthusiastic subset. They were confident but not confrontational, risk-takers within their domain, but not active change agents in the school setting. They would avoid making waves as long as their personal classroom situations were under their control. However, when their children were suffering, or they could not do their work effectively, they confronted the appropriate authority. A teacher who conducted classes in the auditorium without complaint was moved to action when he felt his students needed a new text:

> The book that I was teaching out of, for the health class, was a 21-year-old book. . . . I just went ahead and ordered $4,000.00 worth of books, and my principal got really upset. I had to sit him down and make him understand that we're in violation of state law. . . . We were observed by the Southern Accreditation Association this year, and I told him, if they walk into my classroom and take a look at the book I'm using and don't have the books that are state-mandated, we're not going to be accredited, that's first. Second, I'm not going to lie. It's not my place to try to cover up and I'm not going to do it. . . . You have to be real true to your convictions. You can't be pushed around. (18, M, W, Sr/M, Sci. Bio.)

Several enthusiastic teachers found at one point or another in their careers that they were not functioning well at a particular school or grade level. In these instances, they were assertive enough to make the necessary changes. One teacher explained how a transfer can affect satisfaction:

> Last year I had an excellent year. Now, the year before that I had a very down year, but that had nothing to do with the students. I just had to get out of the school that I was in because I had a problem with the administration which was running the school right into the ground. I was powerless to do anything about it, so I left, but I had a very bad year as far as that. As far as the students were concerned, I had a very rewarding year but you don't want to have to keep banging your head with administration. I applied for and got a transfer . . . and I had an excellent year here last year, really a good year. And I mean, at the end of the school I felt great and I was sorry to see the year end. (23, M, W, Jr/H, Lang. Arts/Eng.)

Thus these teachers, who have little inclination to take on the system, will, when their teaching satisfaction or effectiveness is in jeopardy, create a different situation for themselves. If closing the classroom door does not keep out the undesired pressures, they transfer from one school to another.

In sum, enthusiastic teachers have maximized the intrinsic rewards available to teachers in the traditional school structure described by Lortie (1975). For this category, reaching students is a frequent and fulfilling experience, which provides the rewards they desire. They need no external incentives nor accountability system. These individuals continue to work hard at teaching simply because interaction with young people is so pleasurable and the results are so gratifying.

## The Disaffected Teachers

### Criteria for Selection

As we studied the interviews, a small subset at the opposite end of the work-orientation continuum also caught our attention. These teachers were so dissatisfied and overwhelmed by problems that they wanted to leave the profession. In a similar effort to look systematically at this disaffected category, we developed a set of criteria for membership. These were teachers who:

1. expressed extreme dissatisfaction with their career choice;
2. displayed a high degree of frustration with their daily work (many more bad days than good days);
3. would not pick teaching again if they could choose again;
4. wanted to leave the classroom immediately.

Of the eleven who met these criteria, nine were elementary and two were senior high school teachers. All were women. Once we identified this group, we looked for patterns of thought and action; here we found a number of commonalities, but also some differences. We begin with the unifying factors.

### Shared Attitudes

**A Strong Sense of Failure in the Classroom.** The first distinguishing characteristic of the disaffected subcategory is that they experience failure on a regular basis. They reported no success in the classroom, declining success, or less success than they believed they were capable of achieving. Using the "good day" and "bad day" questions, we found these teachers described many more bad than good days. As noted earlier, one disaffected teacher, when asked to describe a "good day," could not think of one. She reported, instead, "a lot of bad days." Another teacher maintained she would have to talk about "an imaginary good day," because she doesn't "have any good days any more." Yet another, when pressed to estimate the number of bad days over a two-week period, responded:

> Oh, boy, not very many [good days in the last two weeks]. I'm going to say . . . seven out of ten were bad—not real pleasant. . . . It's very frustrating. (67, F, B, Sr/M, Math.)

**The Teacher as "Pawn."** Perhaps more significant than a shared sense of failure is the fact that all disaffected teachers saw their failures as caused by external factors they were powerless to control. As emphasized earlier, all teachers in our study experienced many frustrations from the external changes that bombarded them. What separates the disaffected teachers from the rest of the sample, and particularly from the enthusiastic teachers, is their tendency to feel overwhelmed by these frustrations and to believe there is nothing they can do to confront and overcome them.

One disaffected teacher described bad days as those on which the "kids do not respond at all, and *there is nothing you can do*" (emphasis added) and on which students respond in "temper tantrums" and the problem is "getting them quiet." As she and others in this category view it, the responsibility for discipline and control, even in the classroom, rests primarily with the principal:

> It depends on . . . the principal, what she wants. Some principals don't like you to yell. I don't yell at kids too much. . . . I'm getting less satisfaction now because of discipline. Because before when I came, the principal was firm—but now with this lady, they don't learn. When they do go to the office, she isn't firm. . . . The kids can't learn when the classroom isn't quiet or settled—you have to have discipline in order to learn. (58, F, B, Elem/L, Kindergarten)

ta ta ta

> I heard one or another of our administrators say, "We are busy, do not send these children in here." Well, what is a teacher supposed to do with a child who is busy fighting with everybody or yelling or throwing things across the room? The guidance counselor can't be found, and the administrators don't want to be bothered, so you're . . . up a creek without a paddle. (24, F, W, Elem/L, Primary)

For other disaffected teachers, academic achievement is beyond their control. Several teachers placed the blame directly on the children:

> It's a Chapter I class, and that's the next thing to special education, so, I mean, *how much can you do, you know.* (emphasis added) (43, F, B, Elem/M, 4th)

ja ja ja

> I gave a test and I think I had about maybe four in each class that passed, and everybody else failed, and I think, now, it's toward the end of the year, and the students are tuning the teachers out . . . they're not listening. (67, F, B, Sr/M, Math.)

For still others, the imposition of curriculum packages made it impossible to treat children as human beings:

> Because I'm so busy with those things—the crates and the cartons and the clusters . . . I'm having a lot of bad days now. . . . I don't even want to go to school any more; I just don't want to go to school. I'm very depressed, and I'm very angry because I feel we are short-changing children— that we can't get close to them as human beings and that we treat them as automatons. (09, F, W, Elem/H, Kinder-garten)

As we listen to these teachers attribute their failures to people or policies, they sound, in one sense, much like the larger sample. However, the key difference between this set of teachers and the majority of teachers we interviewed is that this set felt completely powerless to act. All disaffected teachers appeared to think and behave as "pawns" (deCharms, 1968).

**Teaching as "Mission Impossible."** Because disaffected teachers experienced high failure and blamed it on sources beyond their control, they all concluded that teaching is "mission impossible." The problems that other teachers express have become, for the disaffected teachers, insurmountable obstacles. They believe that their chosen work is not feasible, and that the situation is getting even worse.

When asked to speculate about the direction of teaching over the next five years, disaffected teacher responses included:

Down the Tubes! (20, F, W, Elem/H, 2nd)

ta ta ta

I see a complete collapse of the teaching profession unless something is done about it, and quick. Need a complete renaissance. It's going downhill all the way, and the teachers are absolutely fed up. (19, F, W, Elem/H, 3rd)

ta ta ta

I think eventually they're going to close all the schools. . . . Kids are going to learn in their own homes, those who want to learn. (67, F, B, Sr/M, Math.)

Many disaffected teachers gave these doomsday conclusions; all believed that the only viable survival strategy was to leave the occupation. For some, however, the means of escape were not clear. Thus, within the disaffected set there was a subcategory which had begun an active search to leave the occupation and another that simply felt trapped into staying.

**Leaving Teaching: A Gap Between Desire and Reality.** In response to where they hoped to be in five years, some of the disaffected teachers were definite and hopeful regarding their decisions to leave, but vague as to where they were headed:

I don't want to be in the classroom in the next five years. I am thinking about going into counseling. (58, F, B, Elem/L, Kindergarten)

ta ta ta

I hope to be in another occupation. I hope to be doing something that I will be well paid for, so that I can live without worrying so much about money. (19, F, W, Elem/H, 3rd)

ta ta ta

I'm tired. I'm tired of the kids; I'm ready to get out. But I don't know what else I want to do with myself. . . . I've looked into real estate, but I'm not a high-pressure salesman. . . . I have started [actively looking]. . . . I had talked about going into a cookie business, but I don't think I'll go into that . . . I don't know. (34, F, W, Sr/H, Media Spec.)

What comes through is not only a desire to leave, but also a genuine question as to how to make it happen.

Other disaffected teachers shared the same desire to leave, but had replaced questing with resignation. They planned to be in the classroom for the next five years, not because they wanted to, but because they saw no exit. Their sense of entrapment in the classroom because of age, lack of skills, or financial pressure came through in the following statements:

There was a point . . . before my children started college that I used to say I was working because I enjoyed it. Right now, I'm not—I'm working to pay tuition. At the time I worked and enjoyed it, I could have never thought of wanting to retire and to quit, but I tell you now I do, now I do. (36, F, W, Elem/L, Spec. Ed./L.D.)

᪐ ᪐ ᪐

I will probably still be at this school, realistically. Sometimes I think that I would like to get out of here, and I would like to get to that school board and be in the higher echelon and make some real changes . . . from the top. I'd almost like to run for school board, but I'm not a speech maker, and too many people hate me. (09, F, W, Elem/H, Primary)

᪐ ᪐ ᪐

No, because of my age. Starting over in something else I think would be so hard, so I think I would stick it out. But if I had to start over again, I would never choose teaching. (67, F, B, Sr/M, Math.)

These teachers appeared bitter about their career choices, and strong emotions spilled out when we asked how they might feel if their own son or daughter became a teacher:

I said to my daughter, "I'll shoot you in the leg." (19, F, W, Elem/H, 3rd)

᪐ ᪐ ᪐

I wouldn't give her [my daughter] one penny for her education, not one penny. (20, F, W, Elem/H, 2nd)

ᘛ ᘛ ᘛ

My one [daughter] of four is going into teaching, and I told her I would not pay for her education if that is what she is going to do. There is no freedom—it leads you nowhere. (36, F, W, Elem/, Spec. Ed./L.D.)

ᘛ ᘛ ᘛ

I'd get down on my knees and beg God that they wouldn't. . . . It is so emotionally draining. (09, F, W, Elem/H, Kindergarten)

## A Split Along Age and Experience Lines

Amid the shared characteristics of the small disaffected set of teachers, one difference was striking. Eight of the eleven were veterans with considerable experience prior to the advent of heavy state accountability mandates. They held vivid recollections of success and a clear vision of effective teaching, which included professional discretion, creativity, and personal interactions with students. Their pain came from changes in the context of teaching that, in their view, destroyed their capacity to be effective enough to garner the psychic rewards they had once known. With no apparent strategies to cope with the changes, they lost the ability to get the rewards necessary to remain energized. They subsequently became disaffected or even distraught. The highly emotional tone of three interviewees suggested serious psychological damage. At the time of the interview, one was on a leave of absence for what appeared to be some type of mental illness.

In great contrast, the other three disaffected teachers were young and inexperienced. Two were in their second year, the other her fourth. Since none had taught prior to the heavy accountability mandates and curricular controls, none had memories of a more rewarding past. They just felt extremely unsuccessful and unrewarded. All three were in highly challenging assignments for any teacher, Chapter I classrooms in schools with relatively low socioeconomic constituencies. All planned to leave teaching.

Their situation is suggestive of Rosenholtz's (1985) analysis of more and of less effective schools. Less effective schools have higher turnover rates, and new teachers in such schools are given the toughest assignments. Their situation is equally suggestive of recent problems in teacher recruitment and teacher education. With increased opportunities for women and minorities in more financially rewarding and higher status professions, new teachers, as a category, have had lower academic qualifications (Darling-Hammond, 1984).

These three teachers struck us as among the least intelligent, articulate, and competent in the interview sample. They had difficulty answering interview questions, and their responses were often short, choppy, and concrete. They appeared unable to grapple with abstractions and with some of the complex issues of teaching. Moreover, all described themselves as having problems with either basic content or basic teaching tasks. One reported using disciplinary and instructional strategies that would be unacceptable in almost any classroom situation and confided that she had been reprimanded for some of these practices. Nonetheless, each had moved through a teacher education program and become certified without possessing basic skills and an understanding of the complexities of the classroom. Each seemed truly surprised and confused as well as dreadfully disillusioned with the challenges of teaching.[3]

The disaffected teachers stood out among the rest of the interviewees because they were so completely negative about their work. All expressed anger, depression, and pain. Their dreams of making a difference in the lives of young people had been destroyed. They talked as if they were at war with the educational establishment, had fought a slew of impossible battles, and had been defeated finally and decisively by forces too numerous and powerful to overcome. They were all anxious to leave the battlefield, but a viable way out was neither clear nor certain for any of them.

## The Enthusiastic and Disaffected Subsets: Dramatic Differences

Variations within the disaffected subset, pale when we contrast the whole disaffected subset with the enthusiastic subset. On key dimensions, the differences are quite dramatic (see Table 6.1). We present the dimensions horizontally as polar opposites to highlight differences between the subsets. However, the vertical dimensions contain highly interrelated factors that produce alternatively positive or negative cycles. For enthusiastic teachers, exactly where

TABLE 6.1
Characteristics of Enthusiastic and Disaffected
Dade County Teachers, 1984

| Dimension | Teachers | |
| | Enthusiastic | Disaffected |
| --- | --- | --- |
| View of Self: | High self-esteem | Low self-esteem |
| Locus of Causality: | Internal, "origin" | External, "pawn" |
| View of Children: | Source of satisfaction | Source of frustration |
| Daily Classroom Life: | Success | Failure |
| Strategies for Accomplishing the Mission and Coping with External Forces: | "Giving in order to get," "striking a balance," "closing the classroom door" | None |
| Time/Energy Commitment: | More and more | Less and less |
| View of Profession: | Special mission | Mission impossible |
| Future Plans/5 Years: | Remain | Stay reluctantly or leave |

the positive cycle begins is difficult to say with certainty. But, at some point, either by faith or experience, these teachers develop a belief in themselves and their ability to make a difference in their students. This leads to a belief in their students and to a confidence and commitment of time and energy to do what it takes to reach unmotivated students, to communicate with uncooperative parents, or even to ignore district guidelines if they are counterproductive to their purposes. Enthusiastic teachers typically find ways to overcome whatever obstacles they encounter. As they experience success and feel rewarded by their effort, they feel better about themselves and their students.

This sense of satisfaction and reward encourages enthusiastic teachers to put forth greater time and effort, and the reward cycle continues. The more they give, the more they get. They are both motivated and rewarded by their students. At the same time, enthusiastic teachers recognize there is a limit to what they can give without burn-out. They consciously build variety and change into daily and yearly work cycles to strike a balance between routine and variety, work and play. This combination of belief in self and others, hard work, tangible success, feelings of reward, and sense of balance produces a positive cycle that leads to overall career satisfaction, a desire to continue to teach well, and the conviction that their work is important and special.

For disaffected teachers, the cycle is almost the opposite. They begin with failure from changes in students and parents, or in the accountability expectations of their district or from personal inadequacies. The failure produces frustration and lower self-esteem. Because they care deeply about succeeding, they continue to try, doing more of the same. What they do, however, fails again, and eventually they become almost immobilized. Then, believing that there is little they can do, they do little. In effect, their students become disincentives. Instead of assuming responsibility for dealing with change by changing themselves, they look to others. They ask students and parents to change, and they ask principals to help and shield. When change and assistance from others is not forthcoming, they become emotionally upset. Some become angry and bitter; others become depressed and disengaged; still others experience burn-out or have mental breakdowns. They declare their work to be impossible, and do even less to confront their problems. The less time and energy they give, the more failure they experience, and the lower their self-esteem becomes.

Without the confidence to ignore or subvert externally imposed impediments, without the energy to commit to doing what is needed, and without the insight to know and the ability to do what it takes, the negative cycle continues until the only viable solution is to quit. Those who feel they can, actively pursue alternatives; those who feel they cannot, quit psychologically. Thus, despite some commonly held teacher sentiments, our sample also reveals sharply different ways of thinking and acting in relation to the challenges that teachers face today. These differences, in turn, have a significant effect on the amount of satisfaction and reward these individuals receive from their work.[4]

## Complexity between the Extremes

Although our discussion of the enthusiastic and disaffected subsets has led to a focus on individual characteristics and extreme differences, there were other variations that seem equally important, although we cannot document them as decisively as we can describe these two subsets at the extremes. We allude to these other types briefly here to call attention to their existence, but, as we do so, we also recognize the need for more exploration on these groups.

## Other Teacher Subsets

In addition to the teachers at each end of the work-orientation continuum, there were gradations in between. For example, some teachers were almost like the enthusiastic ones, but were different on one or two key defining criteria. Karen is a case in point.

**An Almost Enthusiastic Teacher.** Karen views teaching as a special mission, is child-centered, behaves like an "origin," gives more than she gets, and experiences success and psychic rewards. By teaching all day and grading and planning each night, believing in herself and her students, ignoring some of the basic skill workbook practice her principal expects her to do, creating instead more engaging and meaningful activities, and committing enormous energy to the development of interpersonal relations between herself and her students and among her students of different ethnic backgrounds, she reaches some of the most difficult-to-reach students in the district. The problem is that the cost of this personal investment is extremely high.

Karen lacks the emotional balance and physical pacing that enthusiastic teachers exhibit. During the school year, she describes herself as so consumed by teaching that she feels "guilty" taking time to clean her house. She finds it difficult to stop thinking about her students, even when driving a car or taking a shower. Moreover, for financial reasons, she teaches summer school, where she puts forth as much effort as during the regular school year. She has no time for rejuvenation. Thinking of raising a family, she foresees no way to balance teaching with parenting. In addition she is demoralized by a principal who does not give her any positive feedback, and social acquaintances who look down on teaching as an occupation. Her options: to stay and find a livable, workable balance; or to stay and become disengaged, burned out, or disaffected; or to leave teaching.

**The Paycheck Teacher.** As mentioned in our discussion of monetary rewards, many in our sample spoke negatively of other teachers who worked "only for a paycheck." However, none pinned this label on themselves. Twenty percent of our interview sample used this exact phrase or some close synonym, but another 40 percent described the behavior of others without the accompanying phrase or label. For all of these respondents, there seemed to be consensus that these were individuals very close to being disaffected teachers. The following statements capture the overall sentiment:

Very few teachers get involved. Most of the teachers in our school put in their seven hours and twenty minutes, no more, no less. . . . Kids, they've had kids two and three years, and they don't even know what's happened to those kids or what the problems are. And if you don't know your children, the children know that. We have a few teachers that will take the time if the kid is crying and talk to them. Most would send them to the office or get them out of their hair. Now more than ever teachers have to be both parents to children. . . .

It's very, very sad. The teachers, so many of them don't care. They're *there for the paycheck*. And that's sad. We're all there because we need to work, but there are other fields to work in. If you can't have compassion for children, and work with the kids, the whole child, okay, you really don't belong in education. (emphasis added) (01, F, W, Jr/M, Gen Math.)

ᨠ ᨠ ᨠ

In this school so many teachers are *just drawing a paycheck*, whereas at the other school everybody worked because they were all trying to achieve a goal. But here, they come and they *draw a paycheck*, and if the kid doesn't learn, that's tough, that's the kid. I have mine. (emphasis added) (67, F, B, Sr/M, Spec. Ed./L.D.)

ᨠ ᨠ ᨠ

A lot of us are basically structured people, creatures of habit. If they [teachers] had to go on commission, a lot of people would starve . . . because it's structured and because you have a paycheck coming in,[and] you know that it's almost impossible to get rid of you. We have a lot of people losing that interest and that "go get 'em" that they had in the beginning. Not even burn-out—laziness.

That's what we have a lot of now is a lot of dead wood . . . and a lot of laziness in the system, teachers that have 10-12 years. They have too much in not to leave and not enough to retire. They're that middle of the road, they'll hang in there *for the paycheck*, but they'll do the same thing. They have the same lesson plans and the same tests that they gave ten years ago. They don't want the newness; they don't want the challenge. . . .

A drama show was cancelled last year because they didn't have enough chaperons. The kids had been working on it for two months. . . . That to me is sad, for people to sit home and have a few drinks and watch television rather than coming and supporting the kids for a couple of hours. . . . I think that we are cheating our students. Teaching is not just a 7:00 to 2:30 job; it's a longer job than that. (emphasis added) (33, F, W, Sr/M, Sci.Bio.)

From the teachers' perspective, one of the most insulting statements to be made about peers is that they are in the classroom "only for the paycheck." Those who approach teaching primarily as a job with a salary and benefits, such as long vacations, can expect disdain from their colleagues. The chief reason for this is seen directly and indirectly in the quotes above—working "only for a paycheck" means one doesn't care about or work hard for the welfare of students in at least one of three areas of development—academic, emotional, or social. Those who work only for a paycheck shortchange students by refusing to take time to create new lessons and tests, to get to know them personally, and to support extracurricular activities.

In criticizing their "paycheck" peers, we believe teachers are implicitedly addressing what they see as the inherent moral responsibility of teaching (Tom, 1984) and the ethic of caring that Noddings (1984) argues lies at the core of healthy teacher/student relationships. Time and time again, "paycheck" teachers came through as uncaring individuals disinterested in students as persons or unwilling to do what it takes to connect with them. In a sense they have "given up" in the way disaffected teachers have, but seem to have found a way to survive without the emotional devastation that the disaffected teachers display.

These two additional subsets, the "almost enthusiastic" and the "paycheck," suggest that there are probably a number of other variations, all of which add significant complexity to the general response of teachers to the challenges of change.

## A School Is Not a School Is Not a School

Yet another level of complexity is the relationship between the ways particular teachers or subsets respond to the current challenges and the nature of the schools in which they work. Do particular schools foster enthusiasm, disaffection, or gradations of those feelings? Our study does not allow us to answer that question fully, but there are data that are suggestive.[5]

**Elementary Schools as More Restrictive Environments.** Nine of the eleven disaffected teachers were elementary school teachers, while ten of the eleven enthusiastic teachers were secondary school teachers. Beyond these small numbers, the interview data consistently revealed that elementary school teachers experienced more curricular imposition than their secondary school counterparts. These findings obviously are closely connected to state legislation on basic skills acquisition. As mentioned earlier, in 1979 the Florida Primary Education Program mandated a comprehensive prescriptive program for Kindergarten through Grade 3, and promotion to Grade 3 was contingent on the mastery of state-defined competencies. To fulfill its legal obligations, the Dade County school district adopted and administered a prescribed set of programs. Moreover, the mastery provision led the district to require its primary teachers to teach, test, and track almost continuously. This situation gave rise to a paperwork phenomenon known as "charting," something teachers of young children often found absurd and frustrating:

> You have to make a chart for everything that you do . . . you have to make a little chart of what they mastered, what they didn't master; and when you're teaching, you have to shade that back here, shade that. . . . What does that tell me? If I tested them, I know they've not passed it, then why do I have to make all these different charts? . . . Of course when they come out, they want to see charts, so if your charts look good, does that say you're doing a good job of working with the children? No, it doesn't because you know the people are coming. You do the charts. You show it to them. Okay, what does that tell them? Nothing, right? (12, F, B, Elem/H, 2nd)

Since similar performance specifications did not exist for high school students until the 1983 RAISE Bill and for middle school students until the 1984 PRIME program (McCloskey et al., 1987), we suspect that teachers in elementary schools felt the pressures and pain of legislated learning more than their secondary school counterparts. Furthermore, the stories teachers told suggested that the nature of elementary schools makes it more difficult to "close the door," or to find alternative sources for psychic rewards. For example, a number of secondary school teachers reported being highly rewarded from participation in extracurricular activities (Kottkamp, Cohn & Provenzo, 1986). Elementary teachers told no such stories.

**Principals Can Make a Difference.** There is considerable research showing the principal as the central person in setting the working conditions, social system, climate, and culture of a school (Bossert, Dwyer, Rowan & Lee, 1982; Deal & Celotti, 1980; Hoy, Tartar & Kottkamp, 1991; Rosenholtz, 1985, 1989).[6] Many of our respondents had large repertoires of principal stories, graphic depictions that principals differ and can make a substantive difference in the lives of teachers. The following description of a change in principals reveals how quickly and dramatically the atmosphere of the school may be affected:

> [Principals] can cause tension within the structure. We had a principal for the last few years that was absolutely fantastic. . . . She made you feel relaxed; she was supportive; her whole attitude towards children, towards the community of the school, was that of a family; and she carried that all with her. If you had a problem, you could go to her. This [new] administrator, from day one, has set an atmosphere of tension, of anxiety, and it's not just the fact that she's a new principal. This is the atmosphere she has created. (56, F, W, Elem/H, Kindergarten)

Teachers in schools with faculty-principal tension may become highly discouraged, even depressed; they may even begin to question their own abilities and consider leaving the profession:

> I was having so much trouble with this one administrator, and I let it bother me. I usually don't. Then I got to the point where I was worried with what people thought of me, parents and . . . that was controlling a lot of my abilities. For two years things just weren't right. Every day I went to school it was a drag, although the classroom itself wasn't so much a problem, but just the idea of going. The principal was just so negative, and I thought it was just me.
>     Over the years I found out that it wasn't just me that was having the problem. A lot of people were. He is retired now; they kind of eased him out. It was kind of rough, and I was going to get out of it [teaching] at that time. I was seriously thinking of it because it was really driving me up the wall. Then I transferred to Q__ High School, and a lot of the teachers there had been teaching [at the other school], and I got to talk about that situation. (02, M, H, Sr/H, Phys. Ed.)

As demonstrated above, teachers are dependent upon principals for decisions that make the workplace less or more tolerable, and this is especially important when the overall trend is toward work that is more difficult and less rewarding. Teachers particularly rely upon principals to buffer them from parental intrusion, to control troublesome students, to keep colleagues within acceptable bounds, and to maintain a safe and orderly environment. In short, teachers want principals to take care of extra-classroom conditions and intrusions that cause interruptions in their work and reduce their flow of rewards.

From Five Towns teacher interviews, Lortie (1975) depicted the teachers' view of the ideal principal as:

> an approachable principal who eschews rule-making and close supervision and is equitable in his [/her] dealings with faculty members. [S/he] should be knowledgeable and firm with both parents and students. The qualities teachers mention meet their needs for autonomy and support; the principal should moderate his [/her] use of authority over teachers but assert it in relationships with parents, students, and dilatory colleagues. These teachers did not question the rightfulness of the principal's authority, but they seek to appropriate it to their ends. (p. 198)

We found that our teachers shared the same general view of the ideal principal as had Lortie's teachers twenty years earlier (Cohn & Kottkamp, 1991). Many reported having supportive principals who were well organized, defended teachers having problems with parents, provided strong discipline and order, were a positive presence in the schools, and made strong attempts to shield teachers from excessive paperwork and regulation. We also heard of principals far from the ideal. These were individuals who generated pressure, were inconsistent and unsupportive with discipline, played favorites among the faculty, caused friction among teachers, lacked the knowledge and skills to facilitate instruction, and increased the weight of paperwork by insisting on following every small specification to the letter (Cohn, Kottkamp, McCloskey, & Provenzo, 1987). Our interviewees clearly indicated that principals differ and one's principal mattered a good deal.

**Principals as Victims.** While principals were important in shaping less or more supportive work environments, there were limits to what even the most effective ones could do. A number of teach-

ers volunteered perceptions concerning the role of their principals vis-a-vis state reform mandates. Twenty percent reported that
principals and even the superintendent had little control over the
effect of these outside regulations. Teachers spoke of principals
having "their hands tied," just as teachers did, of being the "victims" of paperwork as teachers were, of being under incredible
accountability pressures like teachers, of having no time to do
classroom supervision because of paperwork, and of simply passing along to teachers the paperwork and mandates they all
thought silly and damaging. The following captures the sense of
empathy:

> I've changed my mind and feel differently about my prin-
> cipal, being that I know all the things that she has to do
> and who she really has to answer to, and so forth. Your
> hands are tied all the way down the line. (26, F, W, Elem/M,
> 4th)

To be sure, the principal may, even in these circumstances,
make some difference. But all principals were under pressure to
comply with mandates; those who did not enforce all mandates
vigorously did so under potential pain of being caught in a surprise audit. We did not hear teachers blaming their principals for
state mandates; the more analytical said that they were all being
buffeted by the same state-driven storm. These legislated and district accountability mandates did not seem to increase the personal animosity between teachers and principals, or to heighten
tensions between teachers' autonomy and principals' control per
se. Clearly, there was heightened animosity among teachers
toward legislated learning and accountability and increased tension between their perceived need for autonomy and their lack of
curricular and instructional control. However, our teachers
seemed to separate the messenger from the source of the bad
news. They seemed to recognize the limits of principals' control in
the face of top-down pressures. Principals could make state mandates and district decisions easier to live with, but they could not
make them go away.

## Conclusion

Against a backdrop of profound change in students and their
parents and in the amount of professional discretion teachers can
exercise within their own classrooms, we have heard the voices of

contemporary teachers, and their message has been clear: Teaching is more difficult today and less rewarding than in the past. In this chapter, however, we have described variations in teachers' abilities to cope with changes and constraints they have encountered. The enthusiastic and "almost enthusiastic" teachers, by virtue of their attitudes and skills, appear to experience much success and reward. On the other hand, the "paycheck" and disaffected teachers appear to go basically unrewarded, the disaffected being almost destroyed in the process. The characteristics of individual teachers can make a difference. Similarly, we have suggested that the type of school one teaches in and the kind of principal one has can make teaching easier or harder, more or less rewarding.

Nonetheless, as we weigh the relative strength of individual teacher and principal differences against the weight of the forces for changes that all teachers face as they work within the stable structures of their occupation and school organization, we see little evidence that individuals can do much to alter the overall collision course. Moreover, we conclude that if we continue to believe that the solution to our educational problems lies with individuals rather than the system as a whole, we will never extricate ourselves from our current difficulty.

On the one hand, it is very easy to believe that finding more enthusiastic teachers is the answer to our educational problems. It is a belief that has great appeal because it reassures us that success and satisfaction can prevail even under the more difficult conditions of today. Further, it offers a roadmap for reform. If we know, for example, that "origins," who are child-centered and have a strong sense of mission tend to be more committed to teaching over time, then our task is to find ways to identify and recruit those individuals. Similarly, if we know that individuals who can "close the door," invest themselves heavily in their work, and still achieve a balance between work and play, routine and variety, have a greater tendency to cope successfully with schools, then our task is to help teachers develop these strategies.[7]

On the other hand, the enthusiastic teacher as a model for change raises important questions. First, is it realistic to work toward placing an enthusiastic teacher in every classroom in America? Our answer: "No!" This subset is an unrepresentative minority, and even with increased attention to recruitment and development, there would be insufficient numbers of them to comprise the majority of the teaching force.

Second, would it be desirable to have an enthusiastic teacher in every classroom? Again, our answer: "No!" Because enthusiastic teachers are thoroughly embedded in the existing structure of their profession, work, and school, they flourish under the status quo. "Building imaginary barriers" and "closing the door" constitute an individualistic, isolated perspective at odds with the current interest in school restructuring and teacher empowerment/leadership through collaboration with peers (Carnegie, 1986; Cohn & Finch, 1987; Lieberman, 1986). Enthusiastic teachers, as we define them, do not desire to be school leaders, change agents, or collaborators. They remain in the classroom because they are high-energy, action-oriented individuals who thrive on interactions with young people and on the rewards of reaching students. Their primary purpose is to make a difference in the lives of their students, as opposed to making a difference in the school as an organization or in the structure of their profession. They are individual entrepreneurs of psychic rewards who would be unlikely candidates for building a systematic, practice-grounded, shared knowledge base or technical culture for the profession. In Joyce and Weil's (1972) delineation of differing teacher roles, enthusiastic teachers are clearly "interactive teachers" rather than "institution builders," "innovators," or "scholars."

Strange as it sounds, if we are interested in substantive changes both in schools and the structure of the profession, it might be more instructive to pay attention to the disaffected subcategory and those close to it than to focus on the enthusiastic. Enthusiastic teachers lead us to believe that the current system is fine, and that the problem is with individuals—with teachers. Disaffected teachers are more likely to lead us to see and to reconsider the system that has become so ingrained in our consciousness that we rarely question or confront it.

# Part III

*Interpreting and Acting Upon the Teacher's Story*

*Chapter 7*

# Interpreting the Voices of Teachers: The Underlying Tension Between Learning and Control

This chapter is a turning point in this book, for it neither begins with Karen nor features the voices of her Dade County peers. From this point forward, our voice becomes dominant as we try to interpret what we heard teachers saying and to apply what we learned from them to the complexities of educational reform. In the interpretive process we broaden our viewpoint to include other data sources and scholars as well as our own experiences with and as school practitioners. While our interpretations are based on what we learned from the teachers in our study, we do not presume to speak for them or claim that they would necessarily agree with all of our conclusions.

First we briefly synthesize earlier themes and then consider the issues of stability and change in a reframed light. The reframing leads us to an in-depth focus upon the systemic and layered nature of control in education and the fragility of teacher autonomy. We find an underlying tension between learning and control which has been tipped toward control to a point where learning becomes meaningless for students and teachers alike. Our conclusion is that if we are to confront the collision of stability and change and the tension between learning and control, we must adopt a systemic perspective toward making learning more meaningful for all students.

## *"Natural" Change and "Constructed" Change*

We begin by describing two forms of change. Teachers, in talking about the changes they experienced, did not differentiate types or causal relationships among them. However, as we listened to teachers, it became apparent that they were telling a story in which a "natural" emergent, culturally derived change in the form of different and more challenging students and parents gave rise to a "constructed," deliberately planned change through which external authorities specified how teachers were to handle the problems resulting from natural change (Cohn, 1991).

## Students and Parents: Source of "Natural Change"

Within the classroom, teachers spend the greater part of their time trying to influence students. But students are not raw material to be pressed into shape, although sometimes they are treated as such. Rather, they are intentional beings with personal histories that influence their own decisions to engage in or reject classroom activities. Moreover, teachers and schools are not the main influences on students. Students spend the greater portion of their lives under the influence of "families" of some definition. Families serve as the filter through which the whole array of major social forces of the time are brought to bear upon children. The filtering and reinforcing of social forces vary with ethnic group, socio-economic status, and value orientation of a given family. However, such social forces as television as medium and message, materialism, drug use as a mode of coping with problems, violence as a means of settling disputes, symbols of status, sexism, and racism come to reside within students through the process of acculturation. Thus, when students walk into the classroom, they are the most immediate carriers of the vast forces of social change.

As noted earlier, schools are organized in terms of role definitions for both students and teachers. Students are expected to "behave," and to engage in academic and other tasks; they are expected to comply with teacher direction within certain bounds. This is, of course, an idealized definition. Given their conscript status (Carlson, 1964), it is well understood that actual student behavior varies from the ideal (Cusick, 1973; Henry, 1963; Jackson, 1968). Every teacher knows that such variance exists and most have experienced it. However, our interviewees told us that the discrepancy between the expected role and actual behavior had grown significantly over time. Especially apparent and problematic for teachers were the attitudes that underlie behavior, especially a lack of "motivation" for schoolwork and an increased "passivity." Students were increasingly not "playing by the rules," rules made up before many of the social forces the students carried within them appeared on the scene. Viewed more analytically, what had happened over time was a reduction of the fit between students influenced by changing social forces and the long-standing role expectations that teachers and schools held for them.

Schools and teachers have expectations for parents as well as for their children. Parents are to be supporters of teachers by preparing their children for school, monitoring and helping with their children's school work, and reinforcing the school's role for their children. But teachers claimed parents had also changed. More parents were single or in nontraditional living arrangements. More of them did not speak English. Changes in the economy, along with the Women's Movement, resulted in more women working outside of the home. Because mothers were out of the home more of the time, they spent less time monitoring their children, and some increasingly relied upon television as a "childcare" device. More of their offspring became latch-key children. Some parents felt powerless to handle and discipline their own children, who came under various nonfamily influences. A growing number of students had become parents when they were teens themselves and had either dropped out of school or become alienated from it. Many more suffered emotional stress and exhaustion simply as part of modern life. Drug use and other self-destructive and family-destructive forces affected parents as well as their children. Some were caught up in the drive for materialism and status. Those who were economically successful sometimes manipulated administrators and treated teachers like servants. The growing litigiousness of society led more parents of all socioeconomic levels to threaten suits against teachers. Thus, a combination of powerful social forces generated changes in parents and their relationships with their children and the schools they attended. With time, many parents, too, increasingly developed a poor fit with the school's expectations for them.

Changes in students were the primary vehicle through which teachers felt the collision between stability—in the schools and themselves—and social change. The direct impact of changes brought on by parents was secondary, although parent changes, of course, were socialized into their children as well. Changes rooted in the evolutionary forces of the larger social order, but experienced by teachers primarily through students and parents, we have come to call "natural changes."

## *Legislated Learning as Reform: "Constructed Change"*

If teachers' work was made more difficult and less rewarding by the collision of natural changes in students and parents with the stability of the school organization and the teachers' own orientations, it was made even more so by reforms, "constructed changes" deliberately created in response to the natural changes. In Florida and elsewhere, as officials watched test scores decline, they designed and enacted through legislation a system of competency-based education driven by accountability mechanisms. In developing these means for improving education, state policy-makers drew upon what other states were doing and upon the general public reservoir of what seemed to make sense, hammering out policies through the democratic political process. Although the legislature passed laws aimed at students, school boards, and teacher preparation programs, the brunt of legislation was aimed at "shaping up" classroom teachers.

Policy-makers generally lack a sense of history (Sarason, 1990). As they often see it, there are problems now, and they need to be rectified—now. The historical view, however, puts much frenetic reform activity into perspective. From that orientation, we learn that prior attempts at educational reform have been initiated primarily by forces external to the schools (Coombs, 1987). Major reform efforts have occurred when there is a perception of crisis afoot (Mitchell & Incarnation, 1984; Murphy, 1990), a broad perception such that "concerns about the state of the society or economy spill over into demands that the schools set things straight" (Tyack, 1990, p. 174). Reform of schools has typically been a means to reach some end other than an affirmation of the intrinsic value of learning and education broadly construed (Warren, 1990).[1]

The end that triggered the first-wave reforms in the 1980s was an attempt to regain the preeminence in international economic competition that the United States seemed to be losing. Declining test scores and rising trade deficits seemed highly correlated in the heads of many lay people. In a rationalistic and reified sense, test scores were taken as the measure of U.S. ability to compete economically. Historically, the public schools never had a "golden age" of student outcomes, a time when test scores were high across the board (McNeil, 1986; Powell, Farrar & Cohen, 1985). In fact, prior school achievement results, especially high school outcomes, had been only passable (Powell et al., 1985), and "passable" has always been determined in relationship to societal need. When the economy was of a different order, able to absorb dropouts because of less demand for highly educated workers, the pre-reform school results would have been considered passable—not optimal, but acceptable. However, the economy had surged ahead to a new order requiring a larger proportion of well-educated workers. Such results at this point were no longer acceptable.

The decline in test scores was, among other factors, the result of changes in students combined with a school organization and teaching force that had not adjusted to the changes in fundamental ways. The response from well-intentioned legislators, however, constrained teachers even more. The reforms, as indicated in Chapter 5, were built on the rational-technical assumptions that both students and teachers were pliable and would respond to "reason" (Wise, 1979). The result was a mandated curriculum that pushed many teachers toward fragmented, repetitious, basic skills lessons that had even less motivational value for children than methods they had been using before. It was as if the state of teaching had been turned back to the late nineteenth century when teachers were young, poorly educated, and had a high turnover rate. In these circumstances, superintendents and other officials designed meticulously detailed lessons that teachers were to follow in uniform, predetermined ways (Callahan & Button, 1964). However, the teachers in our study were better educated and had memories of times when they possessed much more discretion in making classroom decisions.

Declining scores triggered reform or "constructed change" of a highly prescriptive sort, the result of which was to make the teaching-learning process more controlled and less meaningful for both students and teachers. What teachers experienced as reform-born "change" was actually a tightening of central elements—especially some of the latent control elements—of stability in school structure. Traditionally employed "low-constraint decisions" (Lortie, 1969), which set general parameters rather than tight specifications, were replaced by high-constraint decisions developed far from the classroom. Traditional "structural looseness" (Bidwell, 1965) or "loose coupling" (Weick, 1976) between the classroom instructional system and the formal bureaucratic control system was tightened up greatly through the reform mandates. As this tightening occurred, the informal basis of teacher autonomy was eroded, and with its erosion the possibility that teachers and schools could respond to student changes creatively and effectively also decreased. Thus, tightening control over instruction only exacerbated the growing lack of fit between students and the school's long-standing expectations for them. "Constructed change" put in

motion a cycle which made teacher reward and student achievement even less likely. This in turn resulted in more calls for tightening the system. "Natural change" and "constructed change" as a
response to it collided in classrooms, and teachers were caught in
the middle.[2]

## The Need to Reframe

On all sides the immediate response to the sense of crisis during this period of reform has been to find villains to blame. While
there have been multiple targets, teachers have been consistently
singled out as the group to reform. Moreover, the way teachers
have been targeted fits into a larger pattern. As a result of general
socialization, most people in our culture seem to hold an implicit
theory of social action that attributes organizational success and
failure to the behavior of individuals. It is a psychological theory
that permeates our thinking about policy and practice at every
level (Bolman & Deal, 1984).

Sarason reported an object lesson. He asked a foundation official who had been pouring a great deal of money into attempting to
improve the New Haven schools what he would do first if he had a
free hand. The official's response: "I would send all of the school
principals to Mexico for a two-year convention." Sarason identified the official's major assumption: "Change the personnel and
improvement will follow!" (1990, p. 14). That is the nub of our
implicit theory, the "Fire 'em" theory. When something is seriously amiss, find, blame, and fire the responsible party or parties.

In Florida, legislators wanted to fire school boards, administrators, and particularly teachers in the sense of taking away their
authority and decision-making. The controls that were exerted on
teachers eliminated much of their professional discretion, if not
their physical person, and the result was a teacher force both
diminished in authority and deskilled in practice. Such is our
widely shared theory of turning failure to success: If things are
wrong—fire 'em, if you can't fire 'em, then at least "fix 'em!"

We are patently *not* saying that individuals have nothing to do
with success and failure. Individuals matter a great deal, as we
illustrated with the variations in teachers in Chapter 6. What we
are saying is that when "fire 'em" becomes "fire 'em all," "send
'em all to Mexico," "control 'em all" through state mandates—when
failure becomes a class action problem—it is time to question our
implicit theory. It is time to turn from a strictly individualist explanation toward an organizational perspective. It is time to reframe

the problem, to view it in different terms (Cuban, 1988; Bolman & Deal, 1991), to make the taken-for-granted more problematic (Sarason, 1971, 1990), and to make the almost invisible world the object of intense scrutiny.

## Reframing: Multiple Perspectives

We begin to reframe by attending to Sarason's (1990) observations. In a passionate and not altogether optimistic personal statement at the end of a distinguished career, he confronted the "predictable failure of educational reform." He faulted reformers, particularly the authors of the spate of first-wave commission reports, for their unwillingness to confront the "intractability" of schools. He described how reformers fail to see their efforts in historical context, a characteristic that results in instituting "new" reforms that are in fact failed old reforms. He described how reformers' attempts fail because they lack sufficient experience with schools to understand what they are really like. They misdefine the problem, seek villains, and in so doing address only parts rather than the whole of the problem.

Sarason suggested we reframe the problem using an old but powerful idea, "system": "At the very least, taking the concept of system seriously is a control against overly simple cause-and-effect explanations and interventions that are based on tunnel vision" (1990, p. 15). The concept of system helps in understanding why change is difficult to bring about in schools. Everything about the school system is connected to every other part in ways that are almost invisible; it is this set of relationships that gives schools their existence and stability. The connections force us to deal with all of the parts when we desire to change one part. But that is precisely what reformers and the rest of us do not usually recognize. We see individual villains, and we often conclude: "Fire 'em! Get some new ones!" (meaning new parts, of course).

Bolman and Deal (1991) would have us consider reframing by looking at the problem from a number of different organizational perspectives—structural, political, symbolic and human resource. In the structural frame we would find no personal villains, only breakdowns in the interconnectedness of parts around central goals. In the political frame we would confront an economic conflict: What are the scarce resources various coalitions are struggling to control? In the symbolic frame we would search for the subjective meaning that people construct from events in order to find villains and assess blame. In the human resource frame we would ask whether the organization is designed with human needs as a major concern. If the answer is no, the organization itself may be a villain.

From Cuban's (1988) perspective, reframing requires a historical perspective. He argued that both practitioners and policy-makers need to look to history to gain an understanding of inherent contradictions and dilemmas embedded in schooling, in what Sarason would call the system.

Our process of reframing to make sense of our teachers' stories utilizes these multiple perspectives. We consider how parts and structures of the existing system were put together in the past, how various dilemmas and contradictions of learning and control were built in, how, as a scarce, publicly owned resource, schools' purposes have been contested by different interests, how we have come to create symbols and invest them with meaning, and how all of these components comprise the institution of schooling.[3]

## Reframing: Learning in the Context of Autonomy and Control

Controls influence, direct, regulate, and restrain. The struggle between control and autonomy generates an embedded tension at the very core of the structure of schools. While control has always been part of schooling (Cuban, 1984; Goodlad, 1984; McNeil, 1986), many of our teachers gave vivid reports of new controls and new pressures to reduce their autonomy, to reduce their use of formal, experience-, and craft-based knowledge in making decisions about students and their learning.

The individual autonomy that teachers desire to exercise inheres in the basic uncertainty central to life in isolated classrooms. The relationship between uncertainty and desire for autonomy has been expressed several different ways. As noted earlier, Dreeben (1973) described it from the standpoint of instruction, which is always an interactive endeavor between teacher and student. Because student responses can never be fully anticipated when lessons are planned, teachers desire wide-ranging discretion to make on-line decisions during instruction. Lortie (1969) maintained that uncertainty arises from the plural nature of educational goals. Teachers must make decisions among goals in the midst of ambiguity. He also argued that much of teacher desire for autonomy is anchored in the dominance of psychic rewards. Students are the primary dispensers of teachers' most important rewards, and teachers desire discretionary latitude to seek and gain these rewards—primarily through seeing their charges learn. For Shulman, autonomy derives from teachers' "multiple competing and conflicting obligations" (1983, p. 497) and the need to make decisions among them. Berlak and Berlak (1981) described multiple dilemmas confronting teachers and argued that these internal conflicting tendencies to act arise from value conflicts within the culture that are socialized into teachers themselves. Many of the dilemmas identified by the Berlaks concern tensions over the locus and extent of control that teachers exercise over students. Thus, the autonomy/control tension is extended into the core of learning in the relationships between teachers and students.

If the desire for autonomy arises because it is a means of dealing with the existing uncertainty, ambiguity, and contradiction found in classrooms, then controls present teachers with preordained resolutions to these kinds of issues, resolutions which discount the details of a given situation. Shulman (1983) noted that highly controlled, highly rational, or tightly structured systems that allow little autonomy may produce individuals who are paralyzed when confronted with uncertainties or contradictions. We argue that when controls on teachers' behaviors become too many and too tight, the teaching-learning process is reduced to a meaningless exchange and becomes a teaching-controlling process.[4]

We turn now to examine the various layers of controls under which teachers work. Some of these layers have a long history and are so much taken for granted that they are almost invisible to teachers; other layers are recent and extremely visible. Each layer puts limits on the decisions teachers can make to adjust to students under increasing conditions of uncertainty, and as the layers accumulate, teachers find their options for creative action diminished. Our broad argument is that the new layers of controls embodied in the constructed change of first-wave reform when added to existing control structures have tipped the balance of autonomy and control too far toward control of both teachers and students. The results have been a teaching-learning process stripped of much of its meaningfulness.

**Control: The Basics.** We begin with the most basic fact of schooling—one teacher and a group of students. With the group comes the need for social control. Control was necessary in the common school with its single classroom, and is dramatically more so in complex "factory model" schools. Crowded classrooms present teachers with behavioral control problems so pressing that until they are solved nothing else can be attempted (Bidwell, 1965; Jackson, 1968; Lortie, 1975; Smith & Geoffrey, 1968; Waller, 1932).[5] We recall Karen devoting the first month of school simply to making peace among the heterogeneous students in her classes. Classroom control is the first skill that a new teacher learns for survival.

Batch processing of students also puts constraints on autonomy and on learning by consuming time for organizing and controlling the work. Goodlad (1984) found that the proportion of classroom time used for instruction ranged between about 73 percent and 76 percent across elementary and secondary schools. Thus, about one quarter of available classroom time is consumed in social, behavioral, and routine organizing functions. Moreover, behavioral control increases with the size and complexity of the school and with the heterogeneity and age of the students.

Thus, behavioral control consumes a very large part of the energies expended in schooling. It is also a phenomenon not well understood or appreciated by outsiders, including policy-makers who design reforms.

> An inestimable gulf lies between teachers and administrators who deal directly with students, and who understand the importance and difficulty of maintaining control, and outsiders who do not deal directly with students and who do not understand the importance and difficulty of the task. (Cusick, 1992, p. 232)

One of the reasons that our teachers put so much emphasis on the interpersonal nature of teaching is precisely that behavioral control is an interpersonal process.

Time control is another basic layer with historically deep effects on both students and teachers. Particularly in secondary schools, time divisions exert tremendous influence on instruction, which is planned for 40 minutes, 47 minutes, 55 minutes—whatever the arbitrary division may be. However, meaningful learning does not necessarily occur in such standardized time spans. Sometimes it takes longer, sometimes less than these standard time divisions. In earlier times, elementary school teachers who had the same children for long periods had autonomy to make decisions on the length of each learning activity within the school day. If more time was spent on one content area one day, other areas could be compensated for on another day. Dade County elementary school teachers, however, reported that with recent reforms they were regulated to the number of minutes per content area daily. Several of them said that they subverted this regulation for the sake of student learning. Addressing individual student needs by pulling them out of regular instruction at the elementary level is another control over time. Yet another view of recent time control comes from the recognition that when Florida encouraged high schools to move from six 60-minute periods to seven 50-minute periods, this actually reduced the total minutes of instructional time per day (Firestone, 1990). Finally, time was also indirectly but significantly controlled by the addition of multiple accountability mechanisms that tracked teacher behaviors. Time spent in these paperwork activities was withdrawn from teachers' time with students, planning, and teaching.

There is another broad but less visible basic layer, custody control, that has been with schools at least from their transformation in the late nineteenth century. The foundational mandate that schools contain and control youth during the normal working hours of the week has deep consequences for teachers, learning, and the organization of schools (Carlson, 1964; Willower, 1977; Willower, Eidell & Hoy, 1973). Compulsory attendance laws formalized the custody-control expectation for schools. The lengthening of the school year, the increasing size of schools, the growing socio-economic, ethnic/cultural, and language heterogeneity of students (McNeil, 1986; Powell et al., 1985), and the rising number of students with disabilities (Dreeben & Barr, 1983) have increased the difficulties of fulfilling the custody-control function. Because the requirement to provide both behavioral and custody control temporally precedes particular learning activities, and because establishing control often focuses on the interpersonal domain, the social learning needed to develop control may preempt academic learning.

Today, the custody-control issue is clearly complicated by the changing student population. Under these circumstances, many teachers tend to define students as the problem. What they have more difficulty seeing is that the stable school structure, along with the need to establish control, inhibits them from adapting their teaching to the specific students, their backgrounds and interests. When teachers define students as problems, especially as control problems, they focus more and more on control. This can become a negative cycle in which greater control focus reduces time for adjusting instruction to particular students' needs, which in turn results in more problems and a perceived need to tighten control even more.

Custody control puts restraints on teachers as well as students.

It is such a taken-for-granted, latent purpose that the work of teachers is simply not assumed to occur unless they are with groups of students. Time for teachers to reflect or to work with colleagues occurs, if at all, during "free periods" or "after school," terms which differentiate these times from legitimate teaching "work." The extent of the embeddedness and interrelatedness of instruction and custody control can be seen in the inability of most schools to structure themselves in other than the Monday through Friday pattern of school days running from 8:30 a.m. to 3:00 p.m. (Sarason, 1971). If, however, we took learning as a purpose of greater priority than custody control, we might structure time in schools much differently.

The custody-control function has, in part, become so interwoven into the fabric of schooling because other institutions and social functions have grown so dependent on it. Keeping youth out of the labor market and providing inexpensive childcare for working parents are but two important functions of schools that are not announced as official goals (Cohn, Kottkamp & Provenzo, 1987). Yet their centrality surfaces every time school officials "call off school" for a day in order for teachers to engage in some activity other than their "regular work."

Custody control as currently exercised so deeply controls teachers and learning that it is time to question this taken-for-granted purpose. Could we imagine stripping the behavioral and custody-control function from the learning function? Could we confront the issue of separating learning from mass childcare and inexpensive "babysitting?" To contemplate the issue is to contemplate massive costs, but perhaps in so doing to recognize the heavy burden for control that education now bears—a burden which, in part, constrains it from producing the kind of graduates the nation is now demanding.[6]

The effects of these three interrelated forms of control on teacher autonomy and instruction, as well as other systemic elements of school structure, were analyzed by Cuban (1984). Driven by the question: "How did teachers teach?", he answered it in a detailed monograph covering the period 1890-1980. In his introduction he cited a powerful image of stability from AFT President, Albert Shanker:

> Ten thousand new teachers each year enter the New York City school system. . . . These new teachers come from all over the country. They represent all religions, races, political persuasions, and educational institutions. But the amaz-

ing thing is that, after three weeks in the classroom you can't tell them from the teachers they replaced. (quoted in Cuban, 1984, p. 1)

Despite some variation, Cuban documented that the strongly predominant behavioral pattern in teaching for over ninety years was "teacher-centered instruction," in which teacher talk exceeded student talk, lessons were taught to the class as a whole, and students sat in rows, facing the blackboard (1984, p. 3). Goodlad (1984) in a study of over one thousand classrooms found essentially the same pattern, which he called "frontal teaching," along with an ambience of "emotional flatness."

Cuban asked why teachers taught as they did. He began with five potential explanations for the behavioral regularities: (1) schooling as social control and sorting; (2) school and classroom structures; (3) the culture of teaching; (4) individual and shared beliefs; and (5) ineffectual implementation of instructional innovations. As noted earlier, his conclusion was "situationally constrained choice" (1984, p. 249):

The school and classroom structures, I believe, established the boundaries within which individual teacher beliefs and an occupational ethos worked their influences in shaping a practical pedagogy. Intertwined as these two influences are, disentangling them and assigning a relative weight to the influence of each I found virtually impossible to do. The constraints, pressures, and channeling that the school and classroom contexts generate is the invisible, encompassing environment that few recognize potentially shapes what teachers do daily in classrooms. How difficult it is to analyze the commonplaces—that which is seen daily and taken for granted as organic, unchanging, brick-hard features of the environment. . . . For public schools, chairs in rows, recitations, whole group instruction, worksheets, and textbook assignments need to be viewed as a series of successful solutions invented by teachers to solve daily problems of managing a score or more of students while they also acquired information and values. Coping with these structures, teachers constructed workable pedagogical solutions that have proved useful in personally maintaining control while carrying out instruction. (1984, p. 250)

It is clear that Cuban assumed behavioral control, custody control, and probably time control in his conception of school and classroom structures. He found teachers who broke the predominant pattern and pursued student-centered instruction, but they were relatively few in number and their alternative instructional modes were anything but contagious. Their "wiggle room" was still contained by the controls already enumerated and by the stability of the organizational structure.[7] Some teachers may have changed their classrooms, but they did not change the whole system. The vast majority of teachers for over ninety years have maintained a solid pattern of stability in instructional methods.

Cuban (1984) also provided a catalogue of instruction-affecting decisions "sealed off" from teachers' own choices for decades: the number and type of students in the class; which students should leave because they are not benefitting from instruction; what extra instruction students receive; the length of the class and the school day; teacher planning time during the day; texts to be used; grades and subjects taught; the format and content of report cards; what standardized tests are given; and the content they teach (1984, p. 252). Restraints on such decisions are definite controls on teacher autonomy and on learning and have helped to channel most instruction toward the teacher-centered mode. These decisions have not been withheld from all teachers, but in general they are constraints or controls around which most teachers have worked out, what in the past were deemed, "successful solutions" to instruction. However, our Dade County data show that teacher-centered instruction is increasingly less "successful" with the recent changes in student population.

**Administrative Emphasis on Behavioral Control.** McNeil (1986) demonstrated how administrative emphasis on controlling student behavior can have unintended negative effects on curriculum, instruction, and learning. In her case studies of four high schools, she described a built-in tension between organizational control and academic instruction in a state having no top-down reform effort and among students more homogeneous than those in our study. While we cannot confirm her findings because we did not observe Dade County classrooms, we speculate that what she described is even more likely to occur with heterogeneous students in a state heavily dominated by top-down reform.

In three of her schools the administrations were distant from instruction and pursued mostly behavioral control of students. The fourth school had an "academic" principal who pervaded the school with concern for learning. Teachers in all schools possessed advanced degrees and were quite knowledgeable. However, in the three schools with administrative focus on control, McNeil saw little evidence of the teachers' solid subject knowledge or interest in content. The teachers dispensed barren, fragmented "school knowledge" separated from their personal knowledge of the subject. "School knowledge" had no meaning for students who experienced disjuncture between what they "learned" in school and the rest of their lives.

The faculty responded to administrative indifference to learning and emphasis on student control by teaching in ways to prevent student discipline problems, which they believed might arise from deep engagement in issues, controversy, and heated discussion. The response was "defensive teaching," which McNeil found to have four elements. "Fragmentation" reduced information to lists and facts having no linkages to anything else and no controversy. "Mystification" indicated the importance of a topic, such as capitalism, but made it unknowable by reducing complexity such that emotional attachment was internalized but students were unable to explain its meaning. "Omission" meant whole historical periods and controversial topics were left out. Finally, teachers' perceptions of lack of student motivation and weak academic abilities led to "defensive simplification." The teacher announced a topic of study, indicated it was complicated, apologized for introducing it, and promised not to demand too much work.[8]

The only value students saw in "school knowledge" was an exchange process in which they traded memorized bits of information for grades and later a diploma. Their response to the boring and defensively taught "school knowledge" was restiveness. Administrators responded to them with yet more emphasis on control, reinforcing the teachers' need for defensive teaching. McNeil expressed the negative cycle this way:

> *When the school's organization becomes centered on managing and controlling, teachers and students take school less seriously.* They fall into a ritual of teaching and learning that tends toward minimal standards and minimum effort. This sets off a vicious cycle. Students disengage from enthusiastic involvement in the learning process, administrators often see the disengagement as a control problem. They then increase their attention to managing students and teachers rather than supporting their instructional purpose. (emphasis in original) (1986, p. xviii)

The important issue for our study is that when students change in fundamental ways and are seen by members of the school's stable organization as potential threats, custody control and behavior management may be heavily emphasized by administrators. In response, teachers actually generate their own increasingly tighter and dysfunctional curricular and instructional controls. McNeil's findings demonstrated how the stability or inflexibility of school structure may contribute to dysfunctional responses to changes in students, responses which only decrease learning and increase control problems.

**Political and Legal Controls.** Public schools are public resources. Their governance is a political process in which various interests compete to influence purposes and activities. At the conclusion of a comprehensive study of innovation in a single school district, Smith and his colleagues (1988) described it as a "political educational entity." Earlier, Smith, Prunty, Dwyer and Kleine (1987) developed a "longitudinal nested systems model." They constructed it primarily to understand change; however, it is useful for analyzing political and legal controls as well. Their model arrays systems nested within each other in a hierarchy of influence: personality, classroom, school, school district, local community, state, national, and international systems. Each system has a political dimension where particular perspectives and beliefs come into conflict and are resolved. These contests and their resolutions exert major or minor influences on school and teachers, often in the form of controls. The nested systems concept is useful because it reminds us that teachers are at the very bottom of many layers, each of which may exert political and other forms of influence on them.

The way democracy resolves conflicts at the school board, state, and national levels potentially controls teachers. Some of the solutions pass through the system quickly, while others leave residues that remain and influence behaviors over long periods. When resolutions come in the form of legislation and court decisions, their controlling effect is increased. Two such political resolutions are racial desegregation, and mainstreaming of the handicapped. In both cases, remedies for individuals were mandated as goals for the public schools. However, there were important unanticipated consequences in both cases, which controlled teachers with the force of law. Dreeben and Barr (1983) argued that in neither case did decision-makers, when coming up with their solutions, understand that the total pattern of school organization influences whether the individual rights of students are actually supported. They concluded that individual students did not receive the direct benefits intended by courts and legislators. What was accomplished was a significant increase in heterogeneity in schools and classrooms, a change which invoked several of the other control means we have described. Our teachers described the effects of both of these policies as putting more controls on them, limiting their autonomy, and making it more difficult to adapt to a wide array of students because some carried specific legal mandates while others did not (McCloskey et al., 1987). The full discussion of the effects of legislated learning in Florida in Chapter 5 is, of course, a major example of controls established through the political process.

Political decisions rendered through legal proceedings contain an additional controlling force. Law brought to bear on education operates from its own rationality, not an educational rationality (Wise, 1979). An aggrieved party brings a claim that educational practice has moved beyond the bounds of law. The court must, within the law's rationality and precedent, find a solution. The focus is narrow: the grievance itself. Courts cannot deal with larger questions, such as the broad effects of a legal decision or set of decisions on learning. We noted, for example, the effects of legal decisions concerning sexual abuse of small children. Among our teachers, these rulings had tremendous and deleterious effects on their relationships with students, especially the very young, and on the effectiveness of instruction. They produced great fear of vulnerability, and severely controlled many traditional modes of interpersonal exchange with children.

**Technical-Rational Assumptions as Controls.** Moving to an even higher level of abstraction and invisibility, we find embedded in schools the same set of technical-rational control assumptions that infuse most organized human endeavor in our culture. Schon (1987) argued that technical rationality grounded in logical positivist epistemology is embedded in the university and so is socialized into all professionals during their preparation. Technical rationality is disposed toward specialization, division of labor, separation of planning and work, distancing of clients from professionals and thought from emotion. It can produce fragmentation, analysis without synthesis, separation without integration. These assumptions and their effects necessitate coordination mechanisms; technical-rational accountability is high among the means in use.

Standard multiple-choice achievement tests are one example.

These are analytical devices based on discrete components of what is presumed together to be a whole, although they do not tap wholeness directly. Widespread acceptance of the use of these types of tests, however, controls availability and use of other forms of assessment grounded in more holistic assumptions and relying upon more holistic means. Subject matter specialization in secondary schools and specialized roles such as guidance counselor and school psychologist are other indications of the pervasive but often unrecognized control over school affairs exerted through technical-rational assumptions.

**Symbolic Controls.** Meyer and Rowan (1977) argued that existing school structure exerts an invisible but powerful control on a symbolic level. They maintained that schools are viewed as legitimate by various stakeholders only when they conform to a culturally held symbolic image, "school." As Meyer and Rowan portrayed the legitimating image, it clearly encompasses custody control and many of the other controls already described. The symbolic strength of this image makes alterations of the basic structure of schooling, including major changes that might be responsive to new and varying kinds of students, very difficult. For example, the symbolic image of school includes age-grading. When schools begin to experiment with putting together multi-age grouping or tearing down walls, they run the risk of losing legitimacy. The power of this symbolic control may also be seen, in part, by the similarity of private to public schools in so many structural respects. Private schools cannot appear to be other than "schools." Even though they have the legal and even financial latitude to be quite different, they are constrained by the societal image of what is legitimate. Symbolic controls, then, place broad limits on what teachers, administrators, and school boards can do to respond to changing students.

**Teacher Unions as Control.** It seems a contradiction to say teacher unions create another layer of teacher and instructional control, but unions limit autonomy for members as well as management. Mitchell and Kerchner (1983) argued that union-structured labor relations produce predictable impacts on teacher work contexts and showed how of four alternative work structures—as labor, craft, profession, or art—unions drive teacher work toward a labor-like condition grounded in technical-rational assumptions. Within these assumptions, tasks become more rationalized, preplanned, routinized, and directed through inspection and monitoring.

One example of this phenomenon is the TADS instrument for

teacher evaluation described earlier. The technical work on this instrument evolved over two years under the oversight of a committee composed of management and union representatives. This assessment tool rationalized the teaching process into 21 key performance indicators and 81 different teaching behaviors; it had the effect of moving toward more textbook and standardized teaching (Peterson & Comeaux, 1990). This was not likely to have been the intention of the committee members but an unintended outcome of an adversarial process in which conflicting concerns for fairness and accountability produced a highly rationalized procedure that further controlled instruction.

While individual school cultures and principals mediate the impact of union contracts, there is also evidence from our data that in some schools teachers were "working to the contract" in terms of hours spent at school and taking work home (Cohn et al., 1988). In such schools, teachers who might not have desired to work to the contract were constrained to do so. Such controls further restricted the ways in which teachers could react to the forces of change carried by their students.

**Curricular and Instructional Control.** Historically, most teachers have experienced curriculum control. Even in situations where districts and states do not mandate particular materials, time pressures and crowded classrooms prevent the majority of teachers from developing their own resources more suited to particular students. All too often teachers use "juiceless," uninteresting commercial materials that result from key states using textbook adoption committees. Critical theorists argue that knowledge control is exerted by hegemonic forces in this process as in others (Apple, 1982, 1986). For example, contributions of women, ethnic minorities, and others are glossed over or omitted. Thus, the process by which curricular materials are generated contributes to cultural reproduction and maintenance of status quo social stratification.

A more instrumental view of learning suggests that many children, especially in places like Miami, find little invitation for intrinsic motivation in materials that build no meaningful bridges to their own experiences. One physical education instructor in a mostly Black and Hispanic high school gave the example of a mandated square dancing unit. Neither he nor his students could find meaning or motivational connection to this anachronism. Once again, changing students clashed with a stable organization—and teachers had to bear the pain of the collision.

With legislated learning in Florida, curriculum control was

pushed until it became control of instruction. Embedded in mandated, teacher-proof "boxes, crates, and cartons" were pedagogical controls. They prescribed a priori instructional methods for standardized teacher and student behaviors. In their interviews, elementary school teachers told of requirements to teach imposed curricula that divided knowledge (in accord with technical-rational assumptions) into bits and arranged them into invariant drill and practice sequences prescribed for a specific number of minutes a day. Mastery on each bit was then tested, and the results charted. Children who did not master skills in the prescribed time were "remediated" with additional worksheets, practice, and tests. High school teachers talked of central-office dictation of content, lesson formats, homework, and test schedules. At both levels, knowledge and skills taught to students were controlled and disseminated by teachers, often in narrow and mechanistic ways without any attempt to connect them to student interests or realities. Not surprisingly, students were unmotivated and disinterested in school work. Not surprisingly, teachers felt frustrated and under-rewarded.

Instruction was also controlled by models of teaching adopted by school districts and monitored through classroom supervision. The TADS evaluation instrument was predicated on a teacher-centered instructional model, in conflict with numerous other models of teaching, such as inquiry, group investigation, and jurisprudential approaches (Joyce & Weil, 1972).

**Control by Testing.** Along with the current climate of dissatisfaction with schools has come a national obsession with raising test scores. The public and many educators look to standardized achievement test scores as the primary indicator of the educational success of students, teachers, districts, states, and even the nation. Almost every attempt at reform in the last decade has been judged a success or failure on the basis of one factor— did the scores go up? We argue that test scores have been subject to mystification, that the assumption that equates scores with achievement and learning is invalid, and that presenting tests as the single arbiter of our educational system is creating yet another negative, "self-sealing" cycle of tightening control that precludes the basic autonomy needed to respond to changing students.

The teachers in our study described how tests took time away from learning, skewed instruction narrowly toward passing them, and even resulted in teachers cheating. Scholars have condemned tests as inaccurate measures of individual and school success

(Wirth, 1983; McNeil, 1986) and have argued that they lead to score inflation through teaching students to pass them while simultaneously lowering actual achievement (Ellwein, Glass & Smith, 1988). Three very recent studies taken together demonstrate how testing is producing a negative cycle of control that deludes all who put trust in them.

First, in an observational study of standardized test effects on instructional practices of Arizona elementary school teachers, Smith (1991) found that making results public initially produced teacher anxiety, shame, loss of esteem, and alienation. In response to these feelings, teachers became determined to do whatever it took to raise scores. One action was to devote throughout the year about one hundred hours previously allocated to instruction to preparing for and giving tests. In addition, they narrowed their content and pedagogical strategies. Faced with a discrepancy between what they taught and what the tests measured, teachers reduced complex content such as math problem-solving to computational skills, and writing and language skills to capitalization and punctuation. Finally, teaching became test-like in approach and teachers became deskilled as "multiple-choice testing [led] to multiple-choice teaching" (Smith, 1991, p. 10). In effect, it was district administrators rather than teachers who actually controlled time, what was taught, and how. Furthermore, the public was completely uninformed about the content and instructional time eliminated in order to produce higher test scores.

Second, in a recent study by Paris, Lawton, Turner, and Roth (1991), students from grades 2 to 11 were questioned on their views about testing. They were asked whether tests motivate them to do better, whether repeated failure affected their perceptions of their abilities, and what strategies they used in test taking. Their responses were surprising. The older they were, the more skeptical the students were about the validity of tests as indicators of their abilities as students and of the effectiveness of teachers. Older students also reported a decreased motivation to perform well on tests and felt they were less prepared to take them. Further, older students reported using more ineffective strategies, such as just filling in choices without reading the questions when tired, or guessing on confusing questions, or even cheating. Finally, low achievers perceived tests as less useful than high achievers and were less motivated to do well on them. Thus, the most vulnerable students who need the most accurate diagnosis for assistance may get lower scores because they lack motivation and testing strategies rather than because they lack ability. Low scores might, in turn, further erode confidence and lead to a self-fulfilling prophesy of lower achievement.

Third, Haladyna, Nolan, and Hass (1991) maintain that a long-standing failure to recognize that test results cannot account for the complexity of achievement and its causes has been exacerbated of late by increasing pressure to produce higher scores. New pressures have led to "test score pollution" (Messick, 1984). Pollution refers to factors that distort test results and mislead those who interpret outcomes. School personnel may pollute scores by the way they prepare students, and by conditions of test administration. Preparation activities can range from "test-wiseness training" to dismissing low-achieving students on test days and practicing verbatim items from tests. While there are disagreements over the ethics of preparation, these scholars make three points not subject to dispute: (1) test pollution practices are widespread, (2) score comparisons are not accurate when some districts have used preparation practices while others have not, and (3) score pollution may raise a student's performance without increasing achievement.

Thus a preoccupation with standardized test results can seriously constrain the curricular and instructional decision-making of teachers and the substantive learning of students. In Florida's "constructed change," the pressures of testing tightened existing controls even more. Moreover, the overemphasis on test scores deflected probing insight into the source of the problem, the collision between stable schools and changing students. It obscured the built-in tension between learning and control by masquerading as the great impetus for learning, when in reality it was the most refined form of control—mystifying and reifying achievement and learning into figures on wall charts. The numbers carried none of the reality of their begetting: hours of teaching for the tests, absence of motivation in those whose learning they purport to measure with validity, and the quite rational pollution that results when the only rule in the game is "Score high!"

## Tightening the Screws

Our purpose thus far has been to illustrate that much of the stability of school organizations comes from the layer upon layer of controls structured into them. In Florida, the existing stability and controls constrained the ability of teachers to respond to the "natural" changes they encountered in their student population. Ironically, the "constructed" changes developed to address the problems associated with the "natural" changes only exacerbated them.

Florida reforms unleashed negative cycles similar to the one described by McNeil (1986). Wise (1979) described the cycle of hyperrationalization, in which an over-rationalized conception of education that did not fit reality—especially student and teacher reality—generated apparent failure, continued accretion of bureaucratic overlay on the schools, and even more tightly legislated controls to "fix" the problem. A corollary of this cycle was the early frustration of the best teachers, whose departure resulted in a less competent total faculty pool, which called forth even more attempts to control the remaining group. A final negative cycle was the narrow emphasis on testing that came with reform. Thus, in unforeseen and unfortunate ways, "constructed" change resulted in additional layers of controls which further strengthened the elements of organizational stability and further weakened the system's ability to respond with alternative approaches to the diversifying student population.

## Learning Reduced to a Meaningless Exchange

When controls become too heavy, especially controls on instruction, the teaching-learning process is reduced to a "teaching-controlling" process that ultimately turns learning into a meaningless exchange. In listening to our interviewees, we heard many instances of meaningless exchanges. However, since we made no direct classroom observations, there were no verbatim transcripts that portray the teaching of our Florida respondents. However, an example of the teaching-controlling process and the meaningless exchange can be found in the transcript of earlier observational research on a Midwestern suburban teacher and her fifth-grade class (Cohn, 1982). The brief excerpt graphically describes the extreme to which teaching may be driven by excessive controls, an extreme which resembles the accounts we heard from many of our interviewees.

Ms. Church's Classroom, 9:15-9:40 a.m., Spelling:

Teacher: Today we are going to review working on dividing words into syllables, I say review because all reading groups have had this.

*Reading from and then following verbatim the directions in the spelling manual, Ms. Church writes on the chalkboard "elections," "welcome," "us," and asks: "How many syllables in each?" Next she writes "fourteen," "be," "perfect," and "enve-lope," and asks: "Where shall we put the dots? . . . A dictionary doesn't put dots between syllables—what does the dictionary do?*

Student: Dashes.

Teacher: No, they leave a space. Every syllable has to have a what sound?

Student: Vowel.

Teacher: Listen to these two words and tell me how they are alike— "sweet" and "sweetly."

Student: Both have "sweet" in it.

Teacher: What do we call that?

Student: The "root."

Teacher: Yes, or "base word." What do we call "-ly?"

Student: "Suffix."

Teacher: Look at these base words. What can we add in each? "Play," "sing," "light," "bright."

*The students correctly add suffixes to the first three, but two make mistakes with the last—"brightless" and "brightful." To each she says simply: "There is no such word." She then makes an assignment in the spelling book, which is practice in syllab-ication and suffixes, goes over the directions and announces: "This is due tomorrow, so you have something to work on dur-ing reading groups." (Cohn, 1982, p. 30)*

This excerpt shows a meaningless presentation of a narrow skill with no effort to connect the knowledge to the students or their writing. No rationale is given for doing the work. Absent is any explanation of the meaning of different suffixes or the useful-ness of syllabication. Content is reduced to fragments with no tran-sitions, as is seen in the shift from syllables to suffixes. Finally, the questions posed seek one-word answers, and incorrect responses receive unexplained correction. In some respects this is the elementary school version of the meaningless "school knowledge" described at the high school level by McNeil (1986).

Ms. Church, a 13-year veteran, was struggling against burn-out. Like teachers in our study, she worked in a school district with many controls: behavioral, time, custody, curricular, political and legal, and symbolic. All of these controls put restraints on her—the ones exerted directly on her but also ironically the controls she exerted on students. Many of these layers of control were probably invisible to her. She had been so thoroughly socialized within the system as a student and teacher that the controls existed within her as well as within the system.

Ms. Church worked in a district similar to the Dade County Public School System, with new pressures to increase student achievement test scores. She returned to school one September to find a "fundamental skills curriculum" mandated by the school board. Their decision had, in turn, been driven by a new state competency test for eighth-grade students. When her students did not improve or exhibit mastery on particular skills, Ms. Church had to "prove" that she had taught those skills and given students ample practice time. Her day-to-day work was increasingly focused on the tested skills and defensive record keeping. She felt extremely vulnerable because her principal began a public posting of test scores of all teachers' classes. She was keenly aware of this new layer of control. Her autonomy was reduced and the tension between learning and control tipped excessively toward control. The teaching-learning process was reduced to exchanges that were meaningless to both her and her students.

Ms. Church's circumstances were compounded by resentments remaining from a recent teachers' strike during which parents circulated a letter declaring that teachers made a reasonable salary for a 7-hour day, 9-month job. This so infuriated her that she began working to the contract, refusing to grade papers at home or to devote evenings or weekends to lesson planning. Her energy went to the teacher association instead. The process was taking a toll; she was burning out. The additional controls had eroded her sources of both intrinsic and extrinsic rewards, and she became, in our terms, a "paycheck" teacher.

In Ms. Church we see a concrete example of a process many of our interviewees described as happening to them or to colleagues. Teachers "taught" by telling or asking factual questions; students "learned" by recording what teachers said or put on an overhead projector, responding to teacher questions with one-word answers, or filling out worksheets; and teachers "assessed" learning through factual tests. Many of our teachers also wistfully recounted "better" days in the past when they had exercised more discretion, felt more creative, and received higher levels of rewards from students.

We may view the negative process Ms. Church was experiencing from a different angle. The school board "taught" her to do her work by mandating the fundamental skills curriculum; she "learned" how to deliver the curriculum and keep additional records; and she was "assessed" by the public posting of her students' test scores. Turning the angle once again, we find that what teachers complain about in students—passivity, disinterest, lack of motivation—also characterizes Ms. Church. Disparate parts of the image converge: Teachers and students alike were fed bits and pieces, "boxes, cartons, and crates" of information.

Much of what our teachers told us can be interpreted by reframing the issue in terms of an inherent organizational tension between learning and control. When control becomes excessive, teacher autonomy is reduced and learning is suppressed for both students and teachers. We do not, however, claim that all teachers react to increased controls in the same way. There was a set of enthusiastic teachers in our sample. Therefore, we do not maintain that most will become disaffected or "paycheck" teachers, although the likelihood seems to increase under the conditions we found. There are probably many teachers like Karen, who continually strive for meaning in their teaching and relations with students, but who are also exhausted by the effort.

Recruiting brighter and more qualified teachers is frequently proposed as a solution to problems of education (Darling-Hammond, 1984). Reformers argue for testing as an entry screen into teaching, along with a more solid liberal arts foundation for future teachers (Carnegie, 1986; Holmes Group, 1986). We too desire greater numbers of bright and liberally educated teachers, but we are troubled by the assumption that more of these teachers alone will solve our problems. To put well-educated teachers, even Phi Beta Kappas and Ph.D.s, into classrooms with the existing controls on time, curriculum, pedagogy, and evaluation is but a somewhat more subtle version of "fire 'em and get some new ones." How, given these controls on time, materials, and methods, can it be assumed that greater teacher knowledge will make a difference in student learning? McNeil's (1986) teachers were, after all, well prepared with content but did not show it in the classroom.

## Conclusion

The core problem with education must be reframed. It is systemic, not individual. The problem arises from the collision of a natural change embodied in students with a tightened and reaffirmed stability embodied in the additional layers of control brought by the constructed change of legislated learning. The stability of the system and its tightening through state action has systematically reduced the possibility of teachers inventing ways to motivate and engage the new kinds of students who meet them daily. We must move beyond blaming individuals and look to changes in the entire system of education, replete with excessive controls on teachers and students.

We are not, however, arguing for abolition of control. Social interaction without control is anarchy. What does concern us is the balance between learning and control. The type, number, and intensity of controls all affect the possibilities for meaningful learning. We believe it is time to raise the tension between control and learning to an explicit level and to consider how we might alter the equation. Unless policies that are aimed at long-distance control of teachers in classrooms are relaxed, there is little likelihood of significant enhancement of learning. Of course, relaxing such controls does not guarantee improvement, but significant change cannot occur without it. In the next three chapters we consider alternatives for enhancing autonomy and learning for both teachers and students.

*Chapter 8*

# Learning as Meaningful Interaction: What is Good for Students is Good for Teachers

In this chapter, we consider how to reconceptualize our educational system to break the cycle of increasing control that reduces the teaching-learning process to a meaningless exchange. Any attempt to alter the existing cycle must confront the basic tensions and complex relationships between external control and teacher autonomy as they function within otherwise stable school and occupational structures. Shulman (1983) put our task into perspective in his portrayal of the differing "fears" and "nightmares" of policy-makers, teachers, and educational scholars over the quality of teaching in our public schools. For policy-makers, the image is of:

> teachers who do not teach, or teach only what they please to those who please them; who prefer the transient kicks of frills and fads to the tougher, less rewarding regimen of achieving tangible results in the basic skills; who close their schoolhouse doors and hide their incompetence behind union-sheltered resistance to accountability and merit increases; whose low expectations for the intellectual prowess of poor children leads them to neglect their pedagogical duties toward the very groups who need instruction most desperately; or whose limited knowledge of the sciences, mathematics, and language arts results in their misteaching the most able. (p. 484)

Not surprisingly, there is a quite different nightmare for teachers who see themselves as:

> a besieged and beleaguered group of dedicated professionals, inadequately appreciated or compensated, attempting to instruct responsibly and flexibly under impossible conditions. They are subject to endless mandates and directives from faceless bureaucrats pursuing patently political agendas. These policies not only dictate frequently absurd practices, they typically conflict with the policies transmitted from other agencies, from the courts, or from other levels of government. Each new policy further erodes the teacher's control over the classroom for which she is responsible: pupils are yanked out of the room willy-nilly for special instruction, disrupting the continuity of their classroom experience while repeatedly upsetting the normal flow of classroom life for everyone else; a larger number of children, or bussed children, or handicapped children, or inexperienced teacher aides must be accommodated in her classroom while she also, by the way, must take on an extra hour per day of reading, a new writing initiative, more rigorous mathematics and science, sex education, bicultural education, and carefully maintain the detailed individual records needed to create the bureaucrat's required audit trail. (p. 485)

Finally, educational scholars envision a totally different nightmare:

> They see both policy-makers and practitioners pursuing their respective chores mindlessly, or at least without the benefit of the carefully collected, sifted, analyzed bodies of knowledge that constitute the stuff of educational scholarship. . . . The scholar's nightmare is of an educational system at all levels uninformed by the wisdom of research, unguided by the lessons of scholarship. Much of this scholarship is directed at understanding not only the enterprises of teaching and of policy per se but also the circumstances arising when these domains of practice collide. (p. 485)

The first two portraits capture well the conflict between outsiders' legitimate interest in control and accountability and the equally legitimate claim for autonomy from classroom teachers. The third portrait expresses our own fear that new reform efforts will continue to ignore the voices of teachers, which report the negative consequences of responding to the challenges of today's students with additional controls. It is this fear that drives the rest of this book. From this point on, we focus on varying ways to penetrate the system of controls that exist within schools and within individuals so that meaningful learning might occur more frequently in today's classrooms.

Our approach begins with the creation of an alternative image of teaching and learning that differs significantly from the current model. This image is grounded in the views expressed by teachers, but it extends beyond the ideas they shared with us. One key assumption that underlies our process of alternative image building is that, for schools to be positive learning environments for students, they must be positive learning environments for teachers as well. Teachers who are not free to construct their own activities, inquire, engage in meaningful learning, take risks, make decisions, and assess their own competence will be unable to create those possibilities for students. Teachers who do not have self-esteem and a sense that they can control their own destinies will find it difficult to foster those beliefs in others. The majority of our interviewees felt neither free nor self-confident.

Sarason expressed the relationship between student and teacher growth this way:

> Whatever factors, variables, and ambiance are conducive for the growth, development, and self-regard of a school's staff are precisely those that are crucial to obtaining the same consequences for students in a classroom. To focus on the latter and ignore the former is an invitation to disillusionment. (1990, p. 152)

Thus, as we explore avenues for making the teaching-learning process in schools a more meaningful and liberating experience, we search for factors that will create a more productive and supportive environment for both teachers and students.

## *Teaching and Learning as Meaningful Interaction: An Alternative Conception*

Although teachers were the source of depressing stories of debilitating controls which too frequently reduced the teaching-learning process to a meaningless exchange, they also offered elements of an alternative approach. The image emerged as they described their goals for students, explained the knowledge, skills, attitudes, and qualities necessary to accomplish these goals, recalled outstanding former teachers and present colleagues, assessed their own instructional strengths and weaknesses, and shared their satisfactions and frustrations. This conception, which emanates from their daily experience with the changing student population, we have labeled "meaningful interaction." Although the basic components of this alternative approach sprang from teachers talking about their own students, we also discuss them as they would apply to teachers themselves. Our purpose is to demonstrate our fundamental premise that what is good for students is good for teachers.

## Meaningful Interaction: Broad Purposes

Our interviewees set the parameters for meaningful interaction broadly. While they recognized responsibility for the prescribed curriculum, an overwhelming majority insisted the teaching-learning process not be so limited. As described in Chapter 2, some argued that the emphasis must be on teaching students to think, and, in particular, to apply curricular content to other situations and to their own lives. Others argued for focusing on developing positive attitudes toward learning. Still others held the social and moral development of their students as a top priority. The majority, however, viewed their role and purpose to be that of fostering individual growth and development. Although different teachers suggested different purposes beyond the prescribed curriculum, 95 percent of them expressed their purposes as being more than teaching academic content. Thus, in one way or another, our interviewees believed that the teaching-learning process could not be reduced only to cognitive outcomes. Teachers were, therefore, understandably frustrated by the narrow cognitive emphasis that dominated direct evaluations of their performance in the TADS and merit pay observations, and indirect evaluations of their performance in the form of student test scores, formal lesson plans, and record keeping. Further, we find it significant that well over half of the interview sample (59%) held as a priority the individual growth and development of students. These teachers maintained the importance of dealing with individual differences in cognitive abilities, self-esteem, and the whole person and, correspondingly, rejected standardized objectives, instruction, timetables, and outcomes for their students.

Taken together, these broad purposes create an alternative image of learning that is more encompassing, more student-centered, and more individualized than the prescribed and uniform basic skills lessons and approaches most teachers felt they were expected to implement. It is an image in which teachers have the discretion to respond to students as people as well as students, and to respect and work toward the development of their individual capacities. Considered as a whole, these purposes also lay the groundwork for a definition of learning as meaningful interaction for both students and teachers.

One way to think of meaningful learning for students is, of course, in terms of the potential meaningfulness of the material and its incorporation into the cognitive structure (Ausubel, 1969). However, we are convinced that to make learning more meaningful for the majority of students in today's classrooms, we must go beyond this. Based upon what teachers told us, we must consider how the material and the cognitive structure are to be connected to the rest of the individual learner's life.

In our conception of meaningful learning, learners are intentional human beings with particular historical, cultural, family, and academic backgrounds that they bring to the classroom. It is essential therefore that the individual learners see some purpose, use, interest, or benefit in the material, and find some opportunity to explore the material actively at their ability levels. Further, our image assumes that learning has social, moral, and personal as well as cognitive dimensions, and it is the interaction of all these dimensions that gives meaning to the instructional encounter. Finally, our model is built on the premise that only in meaningful interactions do students find learning both challenging and satisfying. These dimensions correspond closely to teachers' statements of purpose, and reveal an implicit understanding that meaningful learning, although at its base cognitive, must be much more than that. For students to engage in the learning process, the cognitive must be connected to other dimensions of their lives.

If teacher purposes lay the basis for an alternative conception of student learning, they also have implications for teacher growth and development. If students need to see purpose, interest, or benefit in the material they learn and have opportunities to explore that material, must not teachers have the same needs regarding the material they teach? If students should be recognized as individuals with differing abilities and backgrounds, should not teachers be equally recognized?

Many teachers in our study felt disconnected from the pur-

poses and usefulness of externally selected content that was peda-
gogically designed and sequenced from afar. Some teachers, particularly those with years of experience, also deeply resented the
fact that the specifications and external controls developed to guide
and monitor the work of novices or ineffective teachers were
equally applied to them. They desired individual recognition for
their accomplishments and for the special challenges of their particular classrooms.

In addition, teachers wanted freedom to use their own talents
and creativity rather than a standardized curriculum and time
schedule. Some talked with frustration of having to be on the same
page at the same time as their colleagues and being asked to refrain
from using special materials or activities that were inaccessible to
others. For teachers to feel inspired to make their best contributions to classrooms, their own uniqueness and diversity must be
respected and nurtured.

## Meaningful Interaction:
## Interpersonal and Pedagogical Skills

To accomplish their goals, the majority of teachers stressed the
need for both interpersonal and pedagogical skills. In the interpersonal realm, they spoke of empathizing and building rapport
with students, earning their respect, establishing a system of discipline, and developing a non-threatening classroom environment.
In the pedagogical realm there were three related emphases: setting high expectations, motivating students, and connecting them
to the content. In the area of expectations, teachers stressed the
importance of believing that all students can learn, expecting the
best of everyone, and persisting so that no one was allowed to fail.
In discussing the challenge of motivating the student, teachers
spoke of their making learning come to life, getting students
excited about coming to class, being engaging and dramatic. In
connecting the student to academic content, teachers talked about
their developing active learning experiences, gaining the perspective of the learner, organizing content so its structure was clear
and logical, and knowing how to reach all students through the
use of multiple approaches.

While most teachers felt relatively skilled in the interpersonal
domain, they felt quite deficient in the pedagogical realm, particularly in motivating and connecting learners to the content. Most
also lay the blame primarily on their teacher education. When
asked how universities could prepare preservice teachers better,

our sample recommended more emphasis on pedagogical skills, particularly for generating student motivation, and more time in clinical settings to develop these skills. The priority that teachers gave to these skills reveals that at the core of their "theories-in-use" are the creation of a positive personal climate for teaching and learning and the linkage of the academic curriculum to the interests and lives of their students. The problems and failures cited in creating these links also reveal that this is the most difficult and challenging aspect of their work (Cohn & Kottkamp, 1989).

It is our sense that teachers are in dire need of the same type of nonthreatening work environment that they try to establish for their students. Most felt threatened by almost everyone they encountered in their daily work—students, parents, principals. In situations of merit pay competition or newspaper accounts that focused on the shortcomings of individuals or groups of teachers, they even felt threatened by their peers.

In the pedagogical realm, the importance teachers attach to setting high expectations, motivating students, and connecting them to content is also applicable to their own growth, development, and achievement. The teachers in our study tended to be unmotivated and demoralized by the narrowly focused expectations of superiors. Moreover, they consistently complained about being unconnected to both their subject matter and instructional methods because these were so often prescribed from outside. Rather than being actively involved in the construction of curriculum, they were the dispensers of information selected and arranged by someone else. This detachment from the underlying assumptions about purposes and the choice of materials made learning less meaningful for both teachers and students.

## *Meaningful Interaction: An Attitude of Caring*

One of the most surprising results of our analysis of teachers' perceptions of good teaching and learning was the frequency and intensity of the comments about caring. The word often surfaced in direct responses to the question of what makes a good teacher, but, as we have shown in Chapter 6, it also came through indirectly, but powerfully, as teachers maintained that poor teachers are those who do not care about their students and who therefore work "only for a paycheck." Although no teachers gave specific definitions of "caring," we inferred their meaning by looking at the attitudes they mentioned as central to establishing good interpersonal relationships with students. Teachers talked of liking children and wanting to be with them; of being comfortable and interested in them, getting to know them and their backgrounds, and treating them as individuals; of trusting, listening, recognizing their feelings, and being sensitive toward their perspectives (Cohn & Kottkamp, 1989).

These responses are surprisingly close to some of the meanings that Noddings (1984) attached to her conception of moral education and the ethic of caring. For Noddings, the idea of caring involves a deep, empathic relationship between people, based upon respect, mutuality, receptivity, inclusiveness, and trust. In such relationships, individuals are either the "one-caring" or the "cared-for." In a teaching-learning relationship, the teacher is always the "one-caring" and the students are the "cared-for." Noddings described the one-caring:

> Apprehending the other's reality, feeling what he feels as nearly as possible, is the essential part of caring from the view of the one-caring. For if I take on the other's reality as possibility and begin to feel its reality, I feel, also, that I must act accordingly; that is, I am impelled to act as though in my own behalf, but in behalf of the other. (p. 16)

If the "cared-for" responds ethically in this relationship, he must:

> turn freely toward his own projects, pursue them vigorously, and share his accounts of them spontaneously. (p. 75)

In Noddings' conception of meaningful relationships, teachers must care for their students in the sense that they give themselves fully and freely to their students, come to know them as persons rather than objects or clients, and respect them as equal members of the relationship. When students respond in a caring way, they are intrinsically motivated to pursue learning with seriousness and openness. Teachers seem intuitively to recognize that a caring relationship, as Noddings defined it, is a core element of a meaningful teaching-learning process. Moreover, when teachers talk about caring, they seem to include the moral imperative of Noddings in the sense of recognizing that with the teacher's authority and influence come enormous responsibility (Sirotnik, 1990; Tom, 1984). This may explain why teachers have such disdain for "paycheck" colleagues. They see them as abdicating their moral responsibility to students by no longer engaging in a caring relationship and by doing the minimum for their own selfish (financial) ends.

One theme that underlies much of the dissatisfaction teachers expressed was not being respected, listened to, or trusted—all central components of caring. They believed their feelings and perspectives were often ignored or dismissed, and their work went unnoticed. In Karen's opening letter, she explains why she stopped turning in lesson plans: No one read them. In their relationships with administrators and supervisors, teachers rarely felt cared for. In bureaucracies such as school organizations, the concept of caring is generally nonexistent, but teachers as well as students need a caring environment for their own growth and development.

## *Meaningful Interaction: A Summary of the Model*

If we listen carefully to teachers, we find that most have at least parts of a thoughtful alternative to the meaningless exchange illustrated by Ms. Church. At the center of their meaningful alternative are students—with their capacities, interests, background, perspectives, and personal feelings. Working in a confined area for sustained periods of time with twenty-five to thirty individuals, teachers come to an experience-based understanding that their work is foremost a human endeavor requiring serious attention to student/teacher relationships in a caring, trusting, and accepting environment. Moreover, teachers come to recognize that they are working with whole human beings, not simply their intellects, and that they need to have more than cognitive goals. Teachers appear to have a tacit understanding that the means and ends of instruction are inseparable. In their identification of broad purposes, they are implicitly defining the necessary processes.

For many teachers, ultimate instructional outcomes have to be pursued in a way that shows students how to use what they learn, that develops a desire to learn more, that is collaborative, and that enables each individual to stretch and reach his/her full potential. Some teachers also seem to recognize that if students learn about language by being taught to add suffixes and divide words into syllables divorced from writing and meaning, they may pass the unit test but have neither the ability nor desire to express themselves well. What is worse, students may even grow to hate learning in general and writing in particular. Indirectly, many teachers told us that for the teaching-learning process to be meaningful, students must actively pursue something with a personal connection. Both directly and indirectly, teachers also told us that they themselves needed the same opportunity to become actively engaged in developing a curriculum of interest and value to them, something in which they too could find personal connection.

While teachers could say much about the nature of meaningful learning, there were clearly limits to their knowledge and ability to act on that knowledge in motivating students. A number of teachers, primarily the disaffected ones, told us that meaningful learning had been possible before the students changed and before they lost their curricular and instructional decision-making power. The implication was that meaningfulness depended, in part, on teacher autonomy. However, the "enthusiastic" teachers claimed to have meaningful interactions going on behind closed doors. Without observation, we cannot verify the realities of classroom practice then or now. What we know for certain is that the majority of our interviewees believed it was extremely difficult to make meaningful connections between their students and their curriculum. Furthermore, few outside the enthusiastic group had specific ideas about what they could do to make the students more motivated to learn what they had to teach. They only knew it had to be done. To look more closely at the concept of motivation and relate it to the image of meaningful interaction that we constructed from the views of teachers, we now move to insights from learning theorists who speak to issues of motivation.

## *Intrinsic Motivation: "The Will to Learn"*

Although there is a large literature on motivation (Ames & Ames, 1985; deCharms, 1968; Deci, 1975; Deci & Ryan, 1985; McClelland, Atkinson, Clark & Lowell, 1953), we find more illuminating the work of theorists who consider education and teaching in a broader context. For example, Dewey's (1956) views on the way to make learning interesting and meaningful for students are still worthy of consideration today. In general terms, Dewey argued that education and life must be interconnected; education is part of growth and central to growth is experience; what children are interested in must be a starting point and related to teacher interests; intellectual growth is nurtured in cooperative endeavors; learning comes from doing and acting on the world (Perrone, 1991). Similarly, Bruner's (1963; 1966) recommendations for teaching the structure of a discipline and for providing opportunities for active learning through discovery and problem-solving are at the core of the latest findings in cognitive science (Glaser, 1988; Resnick & Klopfer, 1989). It is, however, Bruner's (1966) analysis of "the will to learn" that we find particularly instructive for the "unmotivated student" of today. As he carefully examined the concept of intrinsic motivation, he illustrated why the current teaching-learning process is often a meaningless exchange and what must happen in classrooms to move toward greater interest and meaning for students and teachers.

For Bruner, intrinsic motivation begins with a curiosity in early childhood that is characterized by a momentary shifting of attention related to change and vividness. The challenge, as children grow, is to encourage them to master their own curiosity in order to sustain it over a longer and more interconnected episodes. The key to sustained curiosity is a problem or uncertainty to be acted upon and a sense of personal ownership or control. Bruner explained:

> Observe a child or group of children building a pile of blocks as high as they can get them. Their attention will be sustained to the flashing point until they reach the climax when the pile comes crashing down. They will return to build still higher. The drama of the task is only its minor virtue. More important is the energizing lure of uncertainty made personal by one's own effort to control it. It is almost the antithesis of the passive attraction of shininess and the vivid. To channel curiosity into more powerful intellectual pursuits requires precisely that there be this transition from the passive, receptive, episodic form of curiosity to the sustained and active form. (1966, pp. 116-117)

Bruner identified "the drive to achieve competence" as another intrinsic motive for learning. Competence is highly related to interest because it is difficult to sustain interest in an activity without the experience of success. As Bruner said, "We get interested in what we get good at" (1966, p. 118). In order to feel a sense of accomplishment, Bruner maintained the task must have a meaningful unity and structure, require more skill than the learner has, but, with effort, still be achievable.

Another intrinsic motive, "identification," refers to the "strong human tendency to model one's 'self' and one's aspirations upon some other person" (1966, p. 122). Bruner argued that teachers are important "competence models," not only for content and skills, but for attitudes toward a subject and toward learning. Desiring to please their competence role models, students also develop an internal sense of whether they are measuring up to the standards of the model, thus becoming less dependent on extrinsic rewards and punishments.

Bruner's final intrinsic motive is "reciprocity," which "involves a deep human need to respond to others and to operate jointly with them toward an objective" (1966, p. 125). Knowledge, he argued, is interdependent, and students are motivated by making their particular contributions to a "community of learners."

Bruner's four components of intrinsic motivation appear to have been derived from watching "motivated" children outside of the formal school system. The problem, as Bruner phrased it, is not in the individual's desire to learn but in the way learning is organized in schools:

> The will to learn is an intrinsic motive, one that finds both its source and reward in its own exercise. The will to learn becomes a "problem" only under specialized circumstances like those of a school, where a curriculum is set, students confined, and a path fixed. The problem exists not so much in learning itself, but in the fact that what the school imposes often fails to enlist the natural energies that sustain spontaneous learning—curiosity, a desire for competence, aspiration to emulate a model, and a deep-sensed commitment to the web of social reciprocity. (1966, p. 127)

Bruner's description of intrinsic motivation and the role of the teacher in providing the environment for it appears to be highly compatible with what many teachers believe the teaching-learning process ought to be. It is, however, at serious odds with much of what happens to students and teachers in the current system. The minimum basic-skills curriculum as teachers described it had little to do with active, student-sustained curiosity, challenging tasks and problems with meaningful unity and structure, aspirational models, and group interdependence. The external controls and prescriptions and the isolated conditions under which teachers were expected to teach discrete skills were equally at odds with Bruner's conception. It is not surprising that both students and teachers found little meaning and motivation in the existing competency-based system.

## Content-in-Context and Developmental Approaches to Learning

Our proposed alternative teaching-learning process is further elaborated by Lieberman and Miller's (1990) concept of "content-in-context" learning, and by Elkind's (1989) developmental orientation to learning. Both described their models in contrast to others. Lieberman and Miller distinguished the content-in-context approach from cultural literacy and core learning approaches. Their process starts with the student, not the content, and the assumption that students bring to school prior knowledge and ongoing experience useful in linking them to the content in personally meaningful ways.

Elkind advocated the developmental approach and contrasted it to the psychometric orientation predominant in most schools. For Elkind, learning is a developmental process, and the task of the schools is to match the curriculum to the existing ability level of the student. Building on the work of Piaget and Inhelder (1969), Elkind argued that learning is a creative and constructivist process that encourages students to interact with content through the manipulation of ideas and materials. Content and skills are integrated and interdependent, and the outcome of learning is individuals who are discoverers, inventors, and critical thinkers.

In contrast, the psychometric approach assumes that the starting point is the curriculum, that the intelligence of students is fixed and measurable, and that students should be matched to each other and to the curriculum. Learning is a series of behaviors acquired through application of general principles such as psychological reinforcement. Skills and content are viewed as independent of each other, and, once learned, skills can be transferred to other disciplines. The aim is to produce individuals with measurable skills, which can be assessed for accountability purposes. It was clearly this orientation that our interviewees found so much in conflict with what they were trying to achieve with their changing student population.

Lieberman and Miller argued that both the developmental approach and content-in-context approach are supported by the latest cognitive research (Devaney & Sykes, 1988; Glaser, 1988; Resnick & Klopfer, 1989) and called for new roles for teachers:

Teaching and learning are interdependent, not separate functions. In this view, teachers are primarily learners. They are problem posers and problem solvers; they are researchers; and they are intellectuals engaged in unraveling the learning process both for themselves and for the young people in their charge. Learning is not consumption; it is knowledge production. Teaching is not performance; it is facilitative leadership. Curriculum is not given; it is constructed empirically, based on the emergent needs and interests of learners. Assessment is not judgment; it documents progress over time. Instruction is not technocratic; it is inventive, craftlike, and above all an imperfect human enterprise. (1990, p. 12)

Much of what Lieberman and Miller found exciting in these new approaches is clearly linked to the complex student-centered, interpersonal, whole-person images portrayed by many teachers. In effect, these approaches, as well as the intrinsic motivation model of Bruner, advise teachers to start with the students' interests and experiences and then provide challenging, relevant, and meaningful tasks to pursue in a sustained and active way. The role of the learner is to discover, construct, and inquire. The role of the teacher is to support, facilitate, and model these processes in a caring and nonthreatening environment where individuals can both work independently and contribute to a larger group learning endeavor. In addition, Lieberman and Miller introduced the notion that teachers are learners enmeshed in figuring out the learning process for themselves and their students. This shift in the definition for the teacher represents an ideal we find extremely important to contemplate but extremely difficult to realize. We address this challenge in more depth in the final chapter.

## *Meaningful Interaction: An Example*

To complete our portrayal of an alternative to the meaningless exchange, we present an observation of a high school English classroom. We suspect that Karen and many of our enthusiastic subcategory developed such meaningful interactions in their classrooms, but since we have no observation data on our sample, we turn to an example from the field notes of Lightfoot's (1985) case study of Rosemont, an eastern urban-suburban high school. The excerpt describes one of the "star" teachers in the school:

In a standard-level American literature class, the students are in the midst of reading and discussing *Death of a Salesman*. The desks and chairs are arranged in a circle and the teacher's style is supportive, thoughtful, and responsive to student needs and direction. Many students in this class have been judged to have learning disabilities, and their behavior shows that they have difficulties in focusing their attention. At the beginning of class, Ms. Dickerson's comments about their written assignments reveal a beautiful balance of empathy and intellectual challenge. She returns their papers and warns, "Now folks, don't panic. Some of you got low grades . . . but consider this a little grade, the equivalent of a quiz. . . . This is like the core of a paper, beginning ideas. . . . If you have a low grade, it is a sign that there has been a misunderstanding." She clarifies the assignment due the next day. "You will need to develop a thesis statement. . . . A thesis statement means it must be a debatable idea or opinion, not a factual statement. . . . Pitfalls for a debatable statement: it can be too huge and expansive [she offers an example]; it can be so obvious that only a ninny would debate it; . . . Virginia Woolf says a writer is one that sticks his neck out . . . a firm stand with some intellectual risk. . . . Then back it up with evidence." The atmosphere is comfortable and unthreatening, even though Dickerson is urging them to be both disciplined and free, careful and courageous in their writing.

When they turn to the discussion of *Death of a Salesman*, many of the students' comments sound confused and inarticulate, but the teacher pushes for clarity. The discussion centers on Willie's decision to commit suicide, and the teacher encourages students to talk to one another rather than direct all their comments to her. To one girl who is having difficulty with the barrage of comments, Dickerson says quietly, "Assert yourself. . . . Get in there. . . . You have something to say." When the conversation becomes scattered and directionless, the teacher breaks in, "We have a whole lot of separate ideas on the floor. Let us take a few minutes of silence to sort these out. . . . If you can't remember anyone's ideas except your own, you haven't been listening. . . . I have heard at least fifteen explanations for Willie's suicide. . . . See if you can reconstruct it." The class grows quiet as students begin to write their ideas down. Dickerson walks around the room, encouraging students who seem stuck or discouraged and restating her question for greater clarity. Then she offers a clue to the whole class: "See if you can remember Cynthia's question. . . . It was a turning point in the discussion. She didn't give an answer, only a question." After several minutes of silent contemplation the teacher says, "Let's combine our reasoning," and students immediately begin to offer reasons for Willie's suicide: "He wanted to quit a world where nothing was going right for him"; "He felt he had failed terribly and was a disgrace to those who loved him"; "He wanted to have people pay homage to him at the funeral"; "He had only half achieved his dream."

The contributions are energetic and fast-paced. When the exchanges become heated and confused, Dickerson intervenes with a tentative and thoughtful voice. "Let me ask you a very hard question. . . . What happens when a dream you've lived by turns out to be a lie? How do you feel about that. . . . Or are you too young?" The responses are charged and unrestrained. One girl speaks with passion: "People shouldn't circle their lives around one idea." Another disagrees: "But it is not just one idea, it is their whole reason for being." A third: "There is always a danger in being too committed, too closed. . . . You should have one or two goals. You should choose. . . . You don't have to die with one ideal." The discussion becomes argumentative but not hostile. The teacher does not direct them toward a tidy conclusion. They are struggling with unanswerable questions, profound dilemmas, and she wants to encourage them in the struggle. She wants them to recognize Willie's pain. Class is over abruptly and there is no closure. (pp. 254-255)

This episode illustrates important components of the Bruner model of intrinsic motivation, the developmental orientation, and the content-in-context approach. When Ms. Dickerson is returning student papers, we see, as Lightfoot describes, "a beautiful balance of empathy and intellectual challenge." Ms. Dickerson acknowledges the complexity of the task and their personal struggle with it, but encourages students to take risks and engage themselves fully in the work. She emphasizes the challenge of the work but also its do-ability, with effort.

When the students discuss *Death of a Salesman*, the approach is directed at both group examination of ideas and individual meaning. Students are asked to talk with one another rather than filter "right answers" through the teacher. The social web and the concept of reciprocity ripples through the interchange. Ms. Dickerson leads when the discussion becomes unfocused, but she doesn't give answers. Instead, she spontaneously comes up with a question and a strategy that enables them to pursue their task and develop some competence in understanding complex issues. Finally, she poses a "hard" question, one which stimulates them to think personally about and respond to a very deep, troubling human dilemma. Students, recognizing the authenticity and meaningfulness of the question, react with unrestrained interest, even passion. Now the students' and the teacher's concerns have become fused with the content. Ms. Dickerson does not try to close with "a tidy conclusion"; rather, she leaves them individually and collaboratively immersed in a struggle for meaning. Our guess is that such guidance makes her a model of competence, a key actor in a dialogue in which students have become personally engaged and intellectually challenged. And all of this has transpired in a climate of openness, spontaneity, respect for one another, and caring.

This excerpt stands in stark contrast to the approach of Ms. Church portrayed in Chapter 7, knowledge control and defensive teaching as discussed by McNeil (1986), and the tight prescriptions and guidelines described by Dade County teachers. It is, instead, close to the intellectually engaged, open-ended inquiry into meaningful topics in a social context led by an aspirational model described by Bruner (1966), Elkind (1989), and Lieberman and Miller (1990). Moreover, it incorporates the different components for good teaching as expressed by our interviewees. Ironically, however, in the context of accountability in Florida, Ms. Church might actually have fared better than Ms. Dickerson on a TADS or merit pay observation. After all, Ms. Dickerson did not (1) have a quiet classroom, (2) write her objectives on the chalkboard, (3) have all the questions she posed written out in her lesson plan, (4) end the lesson with "closure." We suspect that some of the expressed frustration of our interview sample came from the realization that the technical checklist upon which they were evaluated had little to do—and was, in fact, often at cross purposes—with their conception of good teaching.

Lightfoot's description can also be considered on another level. Ms. Dickerson's encouragement of students to engage personally in a safe environment with serious and challenging questions that have no simple answer serves as a model for how teachers need to work with one another. Contemporary teachers in Dade County and elsewhere face the enormously complex task of discovering ways to reach their students and connect them with content, and there are no readily available solutions. They need one or more Ms. Dickersons as administrators to emphasize the challenge but also its do-ability, with effort; to ask hard questions but impose no solutions; to press, but in an atmosphere of openness and respect. Teachers as well as students need a forum for dialogue and learning in a nonthreatening environment.

## Assessment of Learning as Meaningful Interaction

### Assessing Ms. Dickerson

The image we are projecting as an alternative to the narrow basic skills and content-driven curriculum raises the issue of teacher accountability—the bottom line for Florida legislators and district administrators. Simply put: How could Ms. Dickerson assess and communicate to parents the student learning she facilitates in a way that respects what she is trying to achieve? How could a supervisor evaluate Ms. Dickerson's teaching other than by a predetermined checklist of discrete teacher behaviors?

To begin with, the assessment of Ms. Dickerson and her students should be closely tied to her purposes and conception of knowledge. While we have no explicit statement of her goals or epistemology, we infer from her teaching that she believes knowledge is something to act upon, personally relate to, even question, as opposed to a set of truths to be taken as a whole and given back in response to predetermined questions. It is a constructivist and developmentalist view in which ideas are used by all learners in active inquiry. In the "dilemma language" of Berlak and Berlak (1981), her view appears to incorporate "knowledge as process" as well as "knowledge as content;" "knowledge as problematic" as well as "knowledge as given;" and both "personal knowledge" and "public knowledge."

Within this conception, curricular goals would be tied, not to the acquisition of knowledge alone, but to the ability to use knowledge to create personal meaning, develop important intellectual skills with application outside of school, and create an interest in reading as a pleasurable and illuminating activity. Thus, Ms. Dickerson may expect students to identify the theme of *Death of a Salesman*, to analyze the playwright's craft in developing the theme, and to judge the relevance of that theme to their lives in particular and to the human condition more generally.

Given these goals, the all-too-familiar literature test in which students match titles with authors, answer questions about the theme based on what the teacher told them, or remember who said what to whom, and under what circumstances, would be inappropriate. The meaningful interaction that Ms. Dickerson created calls for an alternative assessment that involves purposeful activity or performance by the students. Perhaps students might read another play and then write reviews which discussed both theme and craft for the literary magazine or for fellow students. Students might write a different ending for the play that would still be consistent with the characters and the overall theme. Students might even have the opportunity to select an American play that they believe has a connection to their world and to cast, produce, and direct it for the school or community. Meaningfulness and interest for students tend to be considerably enhanced where there are opportunities to perform for real audiences (Newmann, 1990; Wiggins, 1989; 1990).

In the language of the test maker, the test must have validity. Given Ms. Dickerson's goals and teaching, a valid test would assess the progress of skill development toward critically reading plays and other literature for meaning and connecting that meaning to larger issues. The assessment of student progress in these skill areas would form the basis of communicating with parents.

Supervisors could assess Ms. Dickerson on a variety of skills in this lesson. As defined earlier, the role of the teacher in meaningful interaction is to support, facilitate, and model the processes of student inquiry and to create a caring and nonthreatening environment where individuals can work independently and in groups. Using this role description as a guide, supervisors might not find a better example. Support, caring, and a nonthreatening approach permeate Ms. Dickerson's classroom. Students who received low grades on a writing assignment are told not to panic, but to think of this as a beginning attempt and a misunderstanding rather than as a failure on their part. Her skill as a facilitator is also evident throughout. When the discussion on *Death of a Salesman* is confused, she pushes for clarity; when one girl is having trouble being heard, she encourages her to press forward; when the discussion loses its direction, she intervenes in a way that brings it back into focus. As a model for inquiry, Ms. Dickerson poses questions for textual interpretation and personal reflection, stimulates alternative arguments, and pushes for intellectual risk-taking. As a model for reciprocity, she takes responses offered to her and redirects them to the group; at the end of the lesson, she suggests: "Let's combine our reasoning." Supervisors who understood her conception of knowledge and curricular goals would have little difficulty assessing her performance as stellar. Supervision in this mode, however, requires on-the-spot professional judgment and, thus, is much more sophisticated and demanding than the application of a predetermined check list.

## *The Concepts of Authentic Work, Tasks, and Tests*

This alternative approach to assessment for students and teachers and the conception of knowledge and learning upon which it rests is, in some ways, similar to recent descriptions of "authentic work" (Newmann, 1990; Wirth, 1983) and "authentic tests" (Wiggins, 1989; 1990) built around "essential tasks" (Sizer, 1984). Newmann and Wiggins appear to use the word "authentic" much as we use "meaningful."

Newmann described "authentic work" for students as having the following characteristics: extrinsic rewards, intrinsic interest, a sense of ownership, and connection to the "real world." In terms of the latter, he argued that the authenticity of schoolwork depends largely on students being able to see that it is useful in work settings outside of school. Newmann identified four real-world characteristics that are often missing in school learning: value beyond instruction; clear feedback; collaboration; and flexible use of time. When work is authentic, the curriculum becomes a set of "essential, authentic tasks from which quality products and performances are expected and within which differences of opinion and choice of intellectual direction can exist" (Wiggins, 1990, p. 10). Rather than learning by "covering" certain topics in the academic disciplines, students learn to use the academic disciplines as they engage in issues or projects they find significant and interesting.

For example, students might learn and use the concepts of earth science as part of community service projects; learn the fundamentals of mathematics and measurement by analyzing and comparing the accomplishments of various Olympic winners; develop their research, writing, and verbal presentation skills by producing a video based on study of their community's homeless. The study of literary classics such as *Death of a Salesman* in Ms. Dickerson's classroom also fits within this conception because it is taught in the context of understanding human dilemmas that face us all. Great ideas and great books are not eliminated in this conception; rather, they are taught by an approach that requires students to consider, question, apply, and validate them by personal and group experimentation and inquiry.

This framework for active student learning is clearly embedded in the Deweyan, Brunerian, and Piagetian traditions and in the principle of "learning by doing." It is also the foundation for performance-driven courses for musicians, athletes, artists, lawyers, and engineers. One learns enough to start practicing and then continues to learn in response to performance successes.

The role of assessment in this framework is to measure an individual's progress in the ability to bring together and use knowledge and skill in some performance or product to be judged by high but empirically grounded standards. This means that curriculum and assessment must be developed together around the same authentic, meaningful tasks. It means, as Wiggins (1989) argued, that teachers should actually "teach to the test":

> The catch is to design and then teach to standard setting tests so that practicing for and taking the tests actually enhances rather than impedes education, and so that a criterion-referenced diploma makes externally mandated tests unobtrusive—even unnecessary. If tests determine what teachers actually teach and what students will study for— and they do—then the road to reform is a straight but steep one; test those capacities and habits we think are essential, and test them in context. Make them replicate within reason, the challenges at the heart of each academic discipline. Let them be—authentic. (p. 41)

For public accountability, the assessment challenge in this alternative conception is for students, teachers, schools, and districts to determine the tasks students should be able to perform and the tests that would authentically reveal their development along the way and at graduation. These tests must include clear standards of accomplishment; the students' progress toward meeting those standards would be reported to parents and district officials.[1]

## Assessment as a Stimulus to Motivation and Learning

Although we have discussed alternative approaches to assessment to satisfy the legitimate need for student and teacher accountability, the great strength of these methods is the potential they hold for being both motivational and learning experiences in and of themselves. Producing plays, participating in debates, writing for literary magazines, and creating videos are activities in which learning and evaluation may occur simultaneously and in which students may be motivated to do their best work. If students see the "test" as something worthwhile, their intrinsic drive to deliver a good performance (Bruner, 1966) should come to the fore. The debate, the play, the video, or the book review are then much more than an after-the-fact checkup; they are learning and motivational challenges that matter to students (Wiggins, 1989). In these situations and others, students can set individual mastery goals for themselves as well as goals for group accomplishment. In either case, learning can be viewed as a developmental process, with performances or "tests" as important benchmarks of progress (Paris et al., 1991).

The case for developing a new conception of the teaching-learning process and assessment is strong. Our sample's widely shared view that students today are much less motivated to do schoolwork than in the past is a major reason. The recent research that shows that as students get older, they become increasingly skeptical of the value of standardized tests, feel less motivated to do well on them, and use more inappropriate test-taking strategies (Paris et al., 1991) is another reason. The recognition that teachers' rewards are tied to student interest and success in school is yet another reason. Students today are not unmotivated; just watching them with others in the halls between classes, during recess, on the athletic field or playground is clear evidence of that. Many students today are, however, clearly unmotivated to do the work and take the tests that are currently offered within the classroom, particularly in the isolated and competitive manner in which they are conducted. Similarly, many teachers in today's classroom are clearly unmotivated to work under the current controls and pressures of accountability which have failed to meet the challenges of the new school population.

## *Teachers and the Search for an Alternative Image*

We have spelled out in considerable detail one conception of learning as meaningful interaction, and the kind of assessment that might accompany it. Because the image is almost the opposite of what many of our interviewees described as the reality of their classrooms, we might assume that it represents the solution to the problems teachers face. Both historical insight and awareness of contemporary constraints, however, suggest otherwise. The alternative we have generated to meet the challenges of a changing society at the threshold of the twenty-first century, ironically, resembles the "progressive" model that developed at the turn of the twentieth century. It is a model that has surfaced periodically in American classrooms but never really flourished (Cremin, 1961; Cuban, 1984; Silberman, 1970; Smith & Keith, 1971). Therefore we need to consider, as Cuban (1988) recommended, why the teacher-centered model has predominated, why the student-centered or progressive model has never taken hold, and why, in particular, contemporary teachers might not see our vision as a viable one for today's classrooms.

We start with the recognition that while the alternative image is grounded in individual teacher statements of purposes and means, teachers never directly expressed proposals for change that looked exactly like it. Furthermore, what teachers told us was offered in reaction to what they perceived to be a highly negative situation, and was expressed in a fragmented and indirect way in response to particular questions, as opposed to a coherent proposal for change. We took their pieces, added other pieces, and fashioned a unified alternative. In this case, the whole is clearly more than the sum of its parts.

Second, research (as well as our own experience) has demonstrated that teachers do not have uniform attitudes and beliefs about pedagogy. There are those with more traditional, authoritarian, or teacher-centered beliefs and there are those with more progressive, democratic, or child-centered attitudes (Kerlinger & Pedhazur, 1968; Mitchell et al., 1987). There are also teachers who find these dichotomies to be dilemmas and feel pulled in both directions (Berlak & Berlak, 1981).

Third, while we suspect that a number of interviewees leaned toward a progressive model, we also believe they might also say it is not possible in the existing structure. The fundamental controls of the stable system, with or without the additional legislated layers, serve to constrain both teachers and students from working in more individualized, active, and student-centered ways. As Cuban (1984) argued, teachers have historically relied on a teacher-centered model because it is a practical accommodation to the existing teacher-student ratio and the organizational structure of schools. When he found exceptions to the rule, they tended to be in elementary schools where there was more flexibility in terms of time and the nature of the curriculum and where individual teachers had exceptionally strong beliefs as to the value of a more student-centered approach. Moreover, Cuban pointed out that those teachers who were successfully able to implement and sustain new classroom arrangements and activities in which students took a more active role were those who developed "hybrids of instruction" which combined both teacher- and student-centered approaches that "coped with classroom complexities" (p. 251).

Fourth, for most teachers this model represents a much more difficult approach to do and to do well. If the controls encountered in our Dade County study can be described as external, uniform, formal, and highly specified, the controls as they exist in the alternative model are more internal, individual, ambiguous, and informal. Both teachers and students are active agents whose abilities, goals and interests shape the interaction. With greater freedom and activity come a corresponding lack of guiding frameworks and certainty. With greater student-centeredness comes less teacher control. Our findings suggest the majority of teachers and at least some of their students would feel some discomfort with significant changes in the authority relationships and organizational arrangements in the classroom. As a result of their experience in the workplace and their occupational socialization, teachers have become highly acculturated into the traditional teacher-centered approach as described by Cuban (1984) and Goodlad (1984). As teachers talked with us, we had the feeling that most would, if they could, turn the clock back to the time when students were more compliant and homogeneous and when teachers had more autonomy and less pressure for learning outcomes measured by standardized tests. Never did we get the impression that teachers were looking toward a major restructuring of the overall system or the classroom. Even the enthusiastic teachers who expressed themselves as "origins" with much personal autonomy behind their classroom doors seemed quite willing to take the existing system as given. Our conclusion is therefore that much of the stability and strength of the system comes from the system that is within teachers and in their students as well.

Finally, we believe that the vast majority of teachers would maintain that even if they could positively confront the discomfort that would accompany a major shift from external to internal controls and a shift from teacher- to student-centered pedagogy, they would not have the knowledge or skill to do it. As we have heard, many teachers frankly admitted their lack of understanding or expertise as to how to reach students who spent most of their spare time watching television, playing video games, working, or even getting high on alcohol or drugs; who lived in families with enormous personal problems and financial pressures; who came to school only because they had to or because they wanted to see their friends. Moreover, there was considerable indication that when some teachers tried to engage students in more open-ended and thought-provoking activities, their efforts were often met with strong resistance. Recall Karen's descriptions of students who were outraged when she designed an assignment that required them to "think." Thus, for some teachers, the challenges of today's students would make this "progressive" model even more problematic than it has been in the past.

In the context of these serious reservations, however, we must note that while teachers might quarrel with some or even all of the dimensions of meaningful interaction we have developed, there was, among the majority of our interviewees, virtually no quarrel with the need for change. The belief that the current system was on the wrong track was widespread and deeply felt. The big question was and is: Where should we be going and how might we get there? There were and still are not any easy answers.

On the one hand, our interviewees stated with great certainty that the starting point was a loosening of the controls that had led to demoralized teachers, disinterested students, and learning as a meaningless exchange. At the same time, there was some nagging realization that if suddenly the most onerous controls were lifted, teachers would still face the challenge that initially triggered the controls, a lack of school-defined academic success with a changing population. As we heard in great detail, many contemporary teachers blamed both students and parents for the lack of student motivation, but we also heard some teachers taking responsibility for making content interesting and relevant and many others asking for assistance in this area.

The problem becomes even more complex when we recognize that although teachers will need outside help addressing the challenges, particularly in the form of knowledge of content and pedagogy, they still must be central players in the search for policies, content, and methods that will engage students in academic learning. The experience to date clearly shows that when answers are imposed by outsiders who have little insight into the daily challenges and when teachers are disconnected from curricular and instructional decision-making, the result is failure at all levels. But our experience also suggests the process of involving teachers as central participants in reform will be a long and arduous undertaking. In addition to fighting to be heard among policy-makers, teachers will have to fight the constraints within themselves that inhibit the generation and implementation of alternatives to the status quo. They also have to find the types and degrees of autonomy and control that are optimal for themselves and for their students while still providing the assurances that policy-makers and the general public legitimately expect.

The complexity reaches enormous proportions when we recognize the interrelatedness of the quest. While it cannot be pursued without teachers, it cannot be pursued by teachers alone. The search for meaningful learning in today's classrooms cannot be successful unless there are significant changes within the structure of schools, teacher and administrator preparation, the occupation of teaching, and community and family support.

Thus we conclude that the central question is not whether the particular image of meaningful interaction we have drawn would be endorsed, modified, or even rejected by the members of our interview sample or teachers more generally. Rather, the crucial question is whether some of the majority of teachers who believe our educational system is on the wrong track can be encouraged to engage with their peers and other stakeholders in the search for their own alternative conceptions to the meaningless exchange. Equally important is that teachers and others recognize the search must focus upon the key tensions, dilemmas, and conflicts between autonomy and control in all the nested systems from the national down to the individual level and that multiple resolutions must be conceptualized, implemented, and assessed. Finally, we argue that the process of the search is as significant as the outcome. Harking back to Bruner and to the students in Ms. Dickerson's classroom, we maintain that the teachers' search for greater insight into meaningful learning in contemporary classrooms must be formulated in terms of the problems they face, approached in ways which enable them to take personal control, and pursued in depth with a community of other learners in a caring and risk-free environment. In sum, we repeat that what is good for students is good for teachers, and that teachers must experience positive learning processes and environments first-hand if they are to create them for students in their own classrooms.

*Chapter 9*

# The Challenge of Change: Pausing to Raise Questions

In the concluding two chapters, we consider the challenge of conceptualizing, implementing, and assessing alternative modes of meaningful learning for the American schools of the twenty-first century. The society has changed; the students and their parents have changed; the educational system, schools, and teachers must change as well. But the challenge is one of enormous scope and complexity. We live with a long history of failure in our efforts to change education, with its interlocking, reinforcing, nested systems (Sarason, 1990; Smith et al., 1987; Willower, 1990). Moreover, recent efforts under the imprimatur of national blue ribbon commissions and prestigious foundations and with the force of state legislation have, according to our teachers, only exacerbated problems. Where do we turn now to find more effective new directions to pursue, and what can we do to rekindle the spirit and stamina of discouraged and demoralized teachers to pursue them?

Our proposal is modest and straightforward: (1) Educators, together with other stakeholders, must begin by identifying some of the long-standing but often unrecognized assumptions and structures that have governed our schools and the power relations within them for almost a century; (2) safe and conducive environments for schooling must be created where educators may examine existing assumptions and structures, generate and implement new ways of thinking and working, and study and learn from their efforts to change. This chapter focuses on the first step—the identification and questioning of deeply embedded assumptions and structures.

## Long-standing Assumptions and Structures: Three Domains

If we have learned anything from the voices of teachers, it is that the educational system and the current day-to-day operations of schools and classrooms are no longer positive learning environments for large numbers of students. However, because teachers are part of the system and have the system socialized deeply within them, they cannot necessarily tell us directly or completely which parts of it should be examined, questioned, and changed. Our effort now is turned toward interpreting both what teachers said and what they did not or could not say. Our aim is to delineate those givens of the existing system or of the system of ideas that teachers have internalized, and which need to be reconsidered if learning is to become more meaningful for students and more rewarding for teachers.

Our intention, however, is not to identify a definitive list of assumptions and structures of schooling that need re-examination. Rather we focus on three major domains of assumptions which grow directly out of our study and then consider central structural components related to them. In our discussion we raise issues and delineate tensions that make existing policies, practices, and structures difficult to alter. Our conviction is that the first stage of any change process should involve groups of teachers and other educational stakeholders working together to identify and examine the assumptions and structures within these domains or others that seem most relevant to their specific context.

### Assumptions Related to Expectations of Schools and Teachers

The first domain of assumptions that deserves close scrutiny involves what the public can reasonably expect schools and teachers to accomplish. Sarason (1990) maintained that historically both practitioners and researchers have led the public to unreasonable expectations of schools and teachers. In speaking about practitioners, he argued:

To a significant degree, the major educational problems stem from the fact that educators not only accepted responsibility for schooling, but, more fateful, also adopted a stance that essentially said: We know how to solve and manage the problems of schooling in America. Educators did not say: There is much we do not know, many problems that are intractable to our efforts, and many individuals we are not reaching or helping. Put another way, educators were not calling attention to what was obvious to them in their daily work. (p. 37)

The educational research community has been equally at fault, according to Sarason, by failing to admit that:

The researcher, like the educational practitioner, wrestles with unknowns, trying to do his or her best with extraordinarily complex problems. Like the practitioners, the educational researchers promised the public more than they could deliver, implicitly suggesting a timetable that was wildly unrealistic. Far from seeing his kinship with the practitioner, the educational researcher tended to use the practitioner as a scapegoat. And all the while, both researcher and practitioner knew in their hearts they were seeking their ways through a forest of ignorance that seemed to grow trees faster than they could be cut down. (p. 38)

We strongly agree with Sarason that the public has been led to expect more than is realistic from schools and that there are lessons to be learned in this regard from the field of medicine:

The medical community has made a virtue of its ignorance insofar as its stance with the public is concerned. That community did not say that it would be able to cure cancers next year or twenty years from now. On the contrary, it emphasized the complexity and scope of the problem, the inadequacies of past and present conceptions and practices, the false starts, and disappointments that await it and the public in the future, and the need for patience, forbearance, and the long-term view. In short, scientific medicine said: We will do our best, we will try to learn, but let us not underestimate the obstacles and conundrums we face. (p. 38)

In our view, realistic appraisals of the task of educational reform are critical prerequisites to change. In fact, one of the driving forces behind this book was the commitment and obligation we felt to bring into public discourse the strong obstacles and challenges that

contemporary teachers encounter in the classroom. After listening
to teachers, we are more convinced than ever that this area of expectations and responsibilities is both a serious and internally contradictory one that needs close examination. In the current context, it
is a case of teachers being told simultaneously that they are responsible for student success or failure because they have the knowledge, skill, and authority to make the difference, but, at the same
time, that they must follow the prescriptions of others outside the
classroom because they are basically incapable of making fundamental curricular and instructional decisions. These mixed messages have taken a terrible toll on teachers.

On the one hand, we found that teachers place an enormous
burden on themselves. Most seem to believe that they should be
able to reach successfully the diverse student population they now
find in their classrooms. Their belief appears to come from many
sources: in part, from their deep desire to succeed and their recollections of past success; in part, from underestimating the differences in backgrounds and motives their students now bring to the
classroom; in part, from the expectations parents express (e.g.
"You're the teacher, you should know how to handle my child");
and, in part, from the oversimplified conclusions of researchers
who maintain, for example, that schools and teachers exclusive of
parents can make a difference or that high expectations are the
key to student learning (Edmonds, 1979). In addition, there is a
widespread feeling among teachers that they may be the only
resource left for troubled young people. Many teachers talked of
the parenting and counseling roles they have assumed, as traditional family units and other socializing institutions have deterio-
rated. All of these factors combine to make teachers reluctant to
admit the difficulties of the task or their lack of knowledge of how
to reach the current school population. Instead, teachers take on
the social and personal problems that are largely inseparable from
the problem of achieving academic goals and try to do it all. When
they do not accomplish what those outside the classroom expect
they should, teachers internalize feelings of failure and guilt. Moreover, the attitudes expressed by the public and the media often
work to intensify those feelings.

On the other hand, teachers clearly recognize that, increasingly, they have little control over what they believe to be the key
variables underlying student learning. Many have been given prescribed objectives, curricular packages, and time allotments and
then have been expected to teach engaging lessons and to produce
higher test scores. Many have also found parents unwilling or

unable to support their efforts by serving as role models at home and by establishing a positive environment for homework and a value system that stresses the importance of education. Others have found it difficult to create interpersonal relations in the classroom because of externally determined academic timetables or, in some cases, because of vulnerability to lawsuits from disgruntled students and distrusting parents. Still others have legitimately felt powerless in the face of growing numbers of students who experience some combination of poverty, hunger, violence, divorce, drug and alcohol abuse, teen-age pregnancy, or general alienation from the predominant values of the culture.

All too many of the classroom problems that teachers described to us appeared to be societal problems first and educational problems second, but because teachers encountered them in their classrooms and attempted to address them within the context of the teaching-learning process, they found themselves ultimately held fully responsible for them. In the face of continual blame for what they knew to be a shared responsibility, and continual failure to accomplish what was unfairly expected of them, some teachers in our interviews admitted, with great reluctance, that they did not know how to reach many of their students. Others struck back, with great resentment, at those who wanted them to bear the full burden of responsibility. In many different ways, teachers told us that they could not solve the problems of the whole society in their individual classrooms.

The first domain of assumptions, then, that must be addressed is what teachers can and cannot reasonably be expected to do. The long-standing assumption of teacher knowledge and responsibility, along with its contradictions, should, instead, be turned into a series of questions, such as the following: Should the schools and teachers accept full responsibility for student learning? If not, what level of responsibility should they accept? Who are the other responsible parties, and what do they need to do? Do teachers and schools have the authority and decision-making capacity commensurate with whatever level of responsibility they are expected to accept? How do teachers admit their lack of total knowledge, but still make the case that they are professionals in a better position than outsiders to seek and apply that formal and craft knowledge which does exist? How do educators communicate to the public the complexity of the problems, the dearth of readily available answers or useful models, and the importance of shared responsibility, without appearing to abdicate their legitimate leadership in the educational domain?

Recognition of shared responsibility does not of course absolve educators from working harder to find new and better ways to improve student learning, but it does acknowledge that educational problems arising from larger social forces cannot be successfully confronted as long as they are seen as the sole responsibility of schools and teachers. Again, we find Sarason's (1990) analogy to medicine useful:

> Just as the medical community does not accept responsibility for cancers caused by smoking, pollution, food additives, and scores of other possible carcinogens, the educational community cannot accept responsibility for problems originating in the larger society. Just as the medical community continues to deal clinically as best it can with etiological factors over which it has no control, so must the educational community do its best with problems beyond its control in the sense of prevention. Educators must assume leadership in relation to diverse community groups and institutions, in a way that makes clear that responsibility is shared. . . . For all practical purposes the answer to the question "Who owns the schools?" has been: educators. However understandable that was in terms of seeking professional status and of community compliance, it was a disastrous mistake, confusing leadership with shared responsibility. (p. 39)

Unless shared responsibility is acknowledged and accepted by segments of the larger society, then educational problems associated with drugs, television-watching, violence, family breakup, hunger, and poverty are likely to remain unsolved. As long as serious educational problems remain, educators, particularly teachers, will continue to be blamed. As long as we focus only upon teachers and make them into scapegoats in need of control, we will continue to be blind to the bigger picture of social forces that frame and give shape to the educational puzzle. To break the self-sealing cycle of blaming educators, we must crack apart and examine the strongly held but internally contradictory assumption that the educational community knows how to solve all of the societal problems carried by students and should be held solely responsible for doing so.

## Assumptions About Learning

Another set of issues to be raised and questioned concern our images of learning. While there have long been differing positions on how people learn, retain, and use what they learn (Ausubel, 1967, vs. Bruner, 1966; Gagne, 1968, vs. Piaget, 1964; and Rogers, 1972, vs. Skinner, 1968) the dominant model in schools has been the reception learning model of Ausubel (Hudgins, 1971). In reception learning, the focus is on teacher presentation of content to students and on the outcomes of instruction as measured in terms of what students can recall or explain in verbal recitation (Hoetker & Ahlbrand, 1969) or on written tests. The predominance of this model can be attributed to the fact that it fits well into the generally accepted purpose of schooling as the transmission of knowledge, and its organizational pattern in the factory model.

Furthermore, within this model, learning is generally viewed as the accumulation of separate bodies of knowledge and individual skills which can be "placed in learners' heads through practice and appropriate rewards" (Resnick & Klopfer, 1989, p. 2). Different levels of knowledge and skill complexity are believed to be arranged in hierarchies in which basic activities of learning are separated from thinking and problem-solving. One major assumption is that most or even all students can be expected to master the basics, but that only certain students are capable of the more challenging tasks involving thinking and problem-solving. Another is that learning is an individual activity, and that individuals should compete for grades and class rank. Those who can only do the basics will be aggregated at the bottom, and those who can do the highest levels of thinking will be clustered at the top. In the legislated learning approach experienced by Dade County teachers, these models and assumptions guided classroom instruction, but in a version also characterized by tight external controls. Course or subject content and objectives were often mandated at the district level, and the outcomes of instruction were measured by predetermined standardized tests for each grade level and for high school graduation.

Additional assumptions undergird the tight control by outsiders. One is that by setting standards or minimum acceptable levels for basic skills and information to be acquired, by focusing exclusively on their acquisition through drill and practice, and by close monitoring of progress through testing, it can be assured that all teachers will teach and all students will learn what is expected. This, of course, also assumes that teachers are not subversive and that students are willing to do what schools expect, and will be motivated to achieve either by the desire to perform well and receive good grades or by fear of poor grades and failure to pass. In Chapter 4, however, we heard over and over that students were not motivated by the content taught or by the tests administered.

The long-standing incentives of grades and tests simply did not motivate large numbers of Dade County students. Moreover, in Chapter 5, we learned that the paperwork required to track student outcomes, attendance, and tardiness resulted in less actual time spent on instruction. We also learned that the reduction of teacher input into curricular and instructional decisions resulted in less motivated teachers. The combination proved to be an unanticipated disaster.

While teachers did not have easy remedies, most espoused a conception of learning much broader than the acquisition of the prescribed content, and they emphasized the means or process of learning as opposed to the outcomes. They insisted that pedagogical processes were central, for ways had to be found to connect contemporary students to the curriculum. In effect, teachers had begun to question the assumptions underlying the over-emphasis on content and outcomes. As we argued in Chapter 8, through their statements of purposes and descriptions of means, the teachers offered a starting point for an alternative to the meaningless exchange, which had replaced learning. Moreover, our interview sample believed that there could be no alternative unless teachers had the capacity and right to construct and modify their own lessons and to respond with flexibility to their students as whole persons. To achieve their purposes with students, they insisted upon increased levels of autonomy and responsibility for themselves.

We argue that while teachers appeared to question some of the key assumptions underlying the existing learning model, they ignored others that also need to be questioned. In particular, we believe that while they saw and talked about the need to be actively involved in their own teaching, they did not see or talk much about the need for students to take a more active role in their own learning. As we have heard, teachers spoke frequently and at length about the importance of looking at students as individuals and as whole human beings. But their attention to students as intentional beings with their own backgrounds, abilities, and interests did not necessarily extend to seeing them as active participants in the classroom. Although teacher and student roles in classrooms are inherently different on many dimensions, there are, we believe, strong parallels between what teachers need to be excited about in teaching and what students need to be interested in learning. Just as teachers question their own role as passive implementers and technicians rather than as active creators and decision-makers, they need to question the assumed passive role of the student in the reception model of learning.

The issue of student as passive receiver as opposed to active creator will raise for many the seemingly endless debates on reception learning versus discovery learning, knowledge versus thinking, and content versus process. It is not, however, our desire to reopen those debates nor to argue for discovery, thinking, and process. Our intention instead is to propose, as some of the current cognitive psychologists do, that meaningful learning is the integration of content with active thinking. Resnick and Klopfer put it this way:

> To teach by using concepts generatively is, happily, to teach content and skills of thinking at the same time. This is the real meaning of the Thinking Curriculum, where concepts are continually at work in contexts of reasoning and problem solving. . . . In this vision of the Thinking Curriculum, thinking suffuses the curriculum. It is everywhere. Thinking skills and subject-matter content are joined early in education and pervade instruction. There is no choice to be made between a content emphasis and a thinking-skill emphasis. No depth in either is possible without the other. (1989, p. 6)

It is also our intention to recall and connect what we know about the linkage among motivation, thinking, and problem-solving. Taken together, Dewey (1956), Bruner (1966), Piaget (1964), and current cognitive psychologists (Larkin & Chabay, 1989; Resnick & Klopfer, 1989) strongly suggest that curiosity, challenge, direct and practical experience, ownership, learning communities, and active involvement motivate learners to think and to solve problems. In turn, the challenge and activity involved in thinking and in problem-solving experiences motivate students to learn and apply their knowledge and skills to new situations.

In light of these connections and what appeared to be an almost opposite norm in Dade County classrooms and elsewhere (Cuban, 1984; Goodlad, 1984; Sizer, 1984), we conclude that existing assumptions regarding the roles of teachers and students and the way people learn need to be seriously reconsidered. The excerpts from observations of Ms. Church's and Ms. Dickerson's classrooms may serve as parameters. Most teachers in our study would probably agree that learning in Ms. Church's classroom had been reduced to a meaningless exchange; however, only some of our interviewees might feel comfortable with the discussion in Ms. Dickerson's classroom. The spontaneity and open-endedness of

Ms. Dickerson's approach might be problematic for teachers who desire more advance planning and predictable structure for their lessons.

As we see it, the task of teachers and other stakeholders in the educational community is to develop their own models which feature varying levels of student activity and teacher control based upon their own rationale and comfort level. Such variations, however, should be guided by the following assumptions from motivational theory and cognitive science: Learning is an active developmental process in which new knowledge is constructed by learners; content and thinking skills must be joined together at every level for all learners; the content of learning should include contextualized practice of authentic tasks—as opposed to exercises on discrete skills—and opportunities to watch others do the kind of work expected of them (Resnick & Klopfer, 1989); learning is enhanced in social settings where students interact and engage in cooperative problem-solving (Resnick, 1987); learning must be based on motivation; motivation is linked to student interests or curiosity, challenge, and control (Bruner, 1966; Larkin & Chabay, 1989); and a learner's evolving sense of competence engenders the self-determination, confidence, and desire needed for life-long learning.

These alternative assumptions, however, raise complex questions and dilemmas for teachers. For example: Does one start with a core curriculum for everyone and find ways to connect it with student interests or does one start with student interests and identify appropriate curriculum? Are some subjects more interesting and therefore more intrinsically motivating than others? Does an emphasis on tasks and activities mean more interdisciplinary work, or should subject realms remain separate? Does an emphasis on active construction and thinking mean that knowledge should be treated as "problematic" as opposed to "given" (Berlak & Berlak, 1981)? Are student interests to be considered in individual or group terms? How does one find the extended time it takes to pursue authentic tasks and contextualized practice while still "covering" the content? How does one create authentic tasks and contextualized practice in a classroom setting? If content is to be reduced, on what basis do we select what to keep and what to eliminate? What organizational and pedagogical strategies are necessary for classrooms where students are learning through experience and through group as opposed to individual activities? How should group work, problem-solving tasks, and active learning be evaluated and explained to others?

These are questions with no easy answers. Some ask educators to take value positions; others pose practical issues; still others require new knowledge and skills in the craft of teaching. Most of them suggest the development of new school-wide structures. All of them require time for educators to think, to discuss with others, and to learn new ways of working in classrooms. This leads us to yet another long-standing assumption that needs reconsideration: Schools are places for student learning. We argue that if schools are to be improved as environments for student learning, they will also have to be reconceptualized as places for teacher learning.

Teachers need time and opportunities to unlearn deeply embedded practices from their own schooling experiences as well as from their socialization into the occupation; to identify and question assumptions that have long guided their thinking and behavior but that may be discrepant with what they are trying to accomplish; to formulate, implement, and assess teaching strategies based on new assumptions; and to work individually and collegially on solving some of the challenges that they face in the way of diverse student learners. Porter (1982) maintained that for teaching to be liberating, teachers first need to "liberate the learner" in themselves. But the difficulty and even pain that individuals may have to undergo in the process of identifying and grappling with deeply held assumptions or examining past experiences through new lenses have largely been underestimated or ignored in most reform efforts.

## Assumptions Related to Control

The alternative learning assumptions just described, with their accent on more autonomous decision-making for teachers and a more active role for students, give rise to another domain of assumptions involving the exercise and maintenance of control in schools. As discussed in Chapter 7, control has been pervasive and deeply embedded in school structure. In the past decade, however, as exemplified in Dade County, many school districts have found themselves operating under increased legislated controls as part of a heightened demand for accountability. The operative assumption has been: When results are not as desired, exert more control and permit less flexibility. More specifically, the governing belief has been that the way to keep both teachers and students accountable and under public control is to set uniform standards, policies, and practices, and then hold them responsible for scores on standardized tests.

Because policies based on these assumptions combined with those embedded in the traditional reception model of learning have proven so unsuccessful in Dade County and elsewhere, we have argued for the consideration of different learning assumptions based on the conclusion that students are motivated to learn and do learn more when they have opportunities to influence, construct, and participate in learning experiences. These proposals, however, come into serious conflict with many traditional assumptions about control in schools. Among the most taken for granted are: Bureaucratic organization with its well-defined hierarchy of authority is the most efficient way to run schools; before teachers can teach and students can learn, teachers must establish a firm system of behavior control; teachers must be the major source of knowledge, authority, and order in the classroom; classrooms where students are permitted choice, activity, interaction with peers, and influence are likely to be chaotic and out of control.

In one sense the alternative assumptions about learning are almost completely at odds with deeply ingrained assumptions on school control and governance. In the former, students share some degree of control with the teacher, while in the latter case, students are the objects of teacher control. In another sense, however, the issue is not simply one of students' gaining or teachers' giving up certain kinds of control, but rather one of shifting from external to internal controls. One notion behind the alternative assumptions on learning is that if the learning activity is challenging and meaningful enough to the learner, the learner will be engaged and therefore controlled by the task. External control in the form of teacher rules and sanctions, teacher expertise, and the threat of tests and grades is therefore replaced by internal control in the form of student interest, involvement, and investment in the learning experience itself. Moreover, as students invest more in the learning process, they tend to take more responsibility for it. Thus, external control of students by teachers is also shifted to internal or self-control on the part of the learners.

In our view, there is yet another factor at work under the alternative assumptions of learning that could potentially lead to an ongoing positive cycle of internal controls and intrinsic rewards for both students and teachers. An implicit assumption in bureaucratic organization is the separation of thinking from doing or of planning from work. Someone at the central office or beyond (textbook publisher or state legislator) does the planning and thinking, and the teacher simply executes the plan or follows the prescribed text. Similarly, in the classroom, the teacher plans and organizes the information to be learned, and students respond by listening and following teacher-directed activities. As we envision alternative conceptions of meaningful learning, thinking and doing are interconnected for both teachers and students. Once both are engaged because of greater autonomy and stimulated by more intellectual challenge, both could be more motivated by and more successful in their work. The more successful they all are in the teaching-learning process, the more intrinsically rewarded teachers and students should feel.

More particularly, in the case of students, we have argued earlier that motivation is linked interactively to thinking and challenge. On the one hand, students are motivated to learn by intellectual challenges, but, on the other hand, they must be motivated to use in new situations what they have learned. The joining of thinking and doing for students encourages them to be more motivated to learn, to apply what they learn to new situations, and eventually to develop more positive attitudes toward the learning process itself. Under such circumstances, teachers would find themselves achieving their purposes more often and thereby experiencing more psychic rewards.

Given what we believe to be the potential for more autonomous and intellectually challenged teachers and students as learners in the classroom, we propose a rethinking of the beliefs that more control is better than less in the classroom, that the role of administration is to control the teachers, and that the role of teachers is to control students. Instead, we offer a different set of assumptions regarding control: Teachers are professionals with the power to make significant decisions about the nature of the teaching-learning process in their own classrooms. Students need to exercise some control over their own learning in order to be motivated to invest in the process. Students who are interested in and actively engaged in real tasks become self-controlled and therefore are not discipline problems.

These alternative assumptions about control, like the assumptions about learning, however, raise difficult issues for teachers. For example: What additional knowledge and skill must they have in order to assume greater authority in terms of curricular, instructional, and evaluative decision-making? To what extent and in what areas can or should students exercise choice or control—content, activities, time devoted to different activities, assessment of their own work? What type and degree of control must teachers retain (Berlak & Berlak, 1981)? Can all students be expected to take a more active role in the classroom? How do shifts in control affect roles and power relations in the classroom and in the school? Can the current bureaucratic system accommodate significant shifts in power relations? If not, what changes have to be made? How do we prepare administrators, teachers, students, and parents for such changes?

While there are few obvious answers for these questions, it is clear that the rethinking of assumptions regarding learning and control cannot be a matter for individuals or even groups of individuals. The existing assumptions are inextricably embedded in the structures of the educational system. For teachers and students to operate under different assumptions, some of the long-standing structures must be questioned and changed as well.

## The Structures of Schooling: Questioning the Unquestioned

As noted earlier, the existing organizational framework of schools and the culture of teaching has been highly resistant to the kinds of changes implied in the alternative assumptions we have proposed. Cuban's (1984) analysis suggested that future efforts to shift to more student-centered activities within the existing system are unlikely to succeed, and the firmness of his conviction is revealed by his conclusion, which focused on ways of improving teacher-centered instruction. While his general argument is persuasive, we believe that one of the major problems with past change efforts has been the attempt to fit new approaches within the old system. Our position is that for substantive and widespread change to occur, we must start with a vision of what we want to occur in classrooms and schools and then begin to question which existing structures support or facilitate that image and which must be altered.

Putting aside for the moment the problems associated with developing a shared vision in any single school, let alone a school district, we maintain that the alternative vision must focus on the teaching-learning process and its quality. The majority of recent failed reforms have focused on elements that do not alter the nature of student-teacher interactions during the teaching-learning process. These include proposals for longer school days and school years, better textbooks, tougher graduation requirements, and more testing of students and teachers. In speaking of many of the first-wave reports on improving high schools, Cuban (1984) recognized this point and concluded:

The assumption seems to be that teachers teaching 5 classes a day, and students sitting in those rooms for over 75 percent of the school day are either unchangeable features of the terrain or presumed worthwhile and thereby unsuitable targets for improvement. (p. 261)

In contrast, the alternative images of learning and control that we have projected are based upon assumptions focused directly on what students and teachers do in both elementary and secondary school classrooms. That focus in turn suggests major changes in virtually unquestioned structures and norms: the 1-teacher-to-20 to 30 students ratio in classrooms; the 50-minute period in secondary schools; the fragmented time blocks and pullout programs for remediation, the gifted, music, art, computer, and other special subjects in elementary schools; the division of knowledge and skill by disciplines; the isolation of teachers; the competition among students; the reliance on standardized tests as the dominant and often exclusive indicator of academic success; the faith in the teacher as the sole source of authority and knowledge in the classroom; the practice of increasing controls on students and teachers as a means of achieving higher academic performance; the dependence on outside experts to formulate educational policy; and the design of the school day so that the teacher's time is spent exclusively with students.

For teachers to engage students in the type of meaningful interactions we described in Chapter 8, they need fewer students, much greater flexibility in determining the content and skills to be taught and the time to be devoted to different tasks, more support and assistance from colleagues, more time for planning and reflection, and more latitude to develop authentic projects, foster group work among students, create alternative means of assesssment, and make students active and contributing participants who can be sources of knowledge and who can learn from one another as well as from the teacher. While all of these changes are central to the development of varying conceptions of meaningful learning, we give the highest priority to the reexamination of the authority, autonomy and workday of teachers as linchpins for the others. As a starting point, teachers, as a group, have to possess the authority and autonomy to shape the decisions that affect them, and they need time to determine how to make the process of teaching and learning more meaningful not only in their own classrooms but in their schools as a whole. They need time to plan; time to teach; time to reflect on their teaching; time to consult with others. In sum, teachers as a collective need the opportunity and time to work and grow as professionals.

Although there are clearly individual teachers—perhaps a Ms. Dickerson, perhaps one of our "enthusiastic" teachers—who can, within the existing system, create meaning for their students and rewards for themselves behind the closed classroom door, our study reveals there are far more who cannot. Moreover, our research suggests that among those who have the capacity, there is probably a thin line between those who can prevail and those like Karen who find it very difficult to sustain the effort it takes over time. Moreover, if we focus our change efforts only on the recruitment and retention of individuals like the enthusiastic teachers, we are betting on a strategy built upon teacher isolation rather than collegiality, and subversion rather than improvement of the system. We argue, therefore, that to make meaningful learning a norm rather than an exception in our classrooms and schools, we must question both the assumptions that govern behavior and the longstanding structures that have given rise to those assumptions. We must recognize that the system itself as well as the teachers in it must undergo substantial change, and that such change must be grounded in a more meaningful conception of learning. The concluding chapter pursues this possibility concretely.

*Chapter 10*

# Getting Started Through Inquiry-Oriented Schools

Having argued that both the assumptions and structures of the current educational system must change to make learning more meaningful for the new population, we now face the challenge of getting started. Unfortunately, we have no dramatic and sweeping solutions to recommend, and that gives us pause. However, a recognition of our ignorance about implementation actually provides a point of departure. Because we need to know so much more about how to rethink existing assumptions and structures concerned with teacher responsibility, student learning, and issues of autonomy and control, we argue for an approach that will encourage experimentation at multiple levels. Toward that end, we propose the establishment of special schools that will function as centers of inquiry into the teaching-learning process and the structures that support it in the contemporary context.

Schaefer (1967) a quarter of a century ago coined the term, described the concept, and provided the rationale for the school as a center of inquiry:

> We can no longer afford to conceive of the schools simply as distribution centers for dispensing cultural orientations, information, and knowledge developed by other social units. The complexities of teaching and learning in formal classrooms have become so formidable and the intellectual demands upon the system so enormous that the school must be much more than a place of instruction. It must

also be a center of inquiry—a producer as well as a transmitter of knowledge.

One basic fact is our ignorance of teaching. We simply do not know how to master the abstract knowledge and the analytical skills modern society demands. It seems necessary to transform at least some schools into centers for the production of knowledge about how to carry out the job. (pp. 1-2)

In the years since Schaefer wrote, much has been done to develop a stronger knowledge base about teaching and learning (Resnick & Klopfer, 1989; Reynolds, 1989; Wittrock, 1986), but, at the same time, changes in the society and students have posed many new and more difficult problems for which we desperately need answers.

In addition to its producing more knowledge, Schaefer argued that the school as a center of inquiry could contribute greatly to the "intellectual health" of teachers:

When divorced from appropriate scholarship in substance and in pedagogy, teaching resembles employment as an educational sales clerk. . . . Almost everyone concedes that teaching is or should be an intellectual calling, an occupation emphasizing the transmission of intellectual goods and the use of intelligence in making instructional decisions. But an ever-sharper division of function—between those who contribute to the production of knowledge or to its synthesis for pedagogical purposes and those who routinely distribute it in packaged form in schools—deprives the teacher of his inherent intellectual rights. By concentrating on the distributive function alone, the school effectively imprisons rather than liberates the full power of the teacher's mind. (p. 2)

Given the frustration and demoralization of teachers over the prescription of curricular and instructional programs developed by those external to the classroom, schools that would provide new intellectual challenges for teachers seem more necessary today than ever before.

Finally, Schaefer maintained that in schools organized as centers for inquiry, teachers could serve as role models for students. If one of the major purposes of schooling is to prepare students for life-long learning, then a school characterized by a "pervasive search for meaning and rationality in its work" and by teachers "freed to inquire into the nature of what and how they are teaching" might encourage students to "seek rational purpose in their own studies" (pp. 3-4). We would add a related argument. Schools organized as centers of inquiry could enable teachers to experience growth themselves from the very process that is desirable for their students. Because most teachers have been exposed primarily to the reception learning model in their own schooling, teacher education, and workplace, they often have difficulty envisioning what is involved or possible in an inquiry-oriented approach. Being inquirers themselves in search of important and relevant findings, however, could put them in an excellent position to create comparable situations for students.

Thus, we find Schaefer's conception and rationale of yesteryear amazingly compelling and relevant in the current educational context. In fact, we believe that what may have been an interesting idea two and half decades ago may now be an imperative for the survival of high-quality education in our public schools.

At the same time, we recognize the limitations of this conception for the broader systemic view we have taken. Schaefer's focus is more on pedagogy than on structure, more on classrooms than on systems, more on training teachers to be behavioral scientists than enabling them to be agents of change. Because the transformation of learning into meaningful interaction requires a systemic approach, inquiry must examine not only individual behaviors but also assumptions, structures, and cultures that permit or inhibit behavioral change.

What follows then is our proposal for a contemporary version of Schaefer's school as a center of inquiry. It is a version that focuses on inquiry and activity aimed at changing the system at the school level. However, even as we present this up-dated model, we recognize that it is only a starting point. We are fully aware that the changes we are recommending at the school level must eventually be linked to changes in the broader system. Thus, although we view inquiry into the systems within schools, classrooms, and individuals as a promising beginning, we know that what we learn at these levels must eventually move toward identifying and challenging larger societal assumptions that constrain current and future educational policy and practice.

## *The School as a Center of Inquiry: A Contemporary Version*

Envisioning the school as a center of inquiry, we see a community where teachers can both teach and learn how to create improved learning environments for today's students. The components of such a school might correspond to the components of the inquiry process itself. Thus, inquiry-oriented schools would be places where teachers and other stakeholders might: (1) collaboratively identify problems or questions that are critical for today and tomorrow's concerns, (2) study past efforts of others to solve school problems and bring about structural change, (3) create and study new approaches and structures toward the end of successful reform.

## Problem Identification: "Assumptional Dialogues"

As argued earlier, the first step in the change process is to identify and question long-established assumptions and structures. Inquiry-oriented schools could provide forums for what might be labeled "assumptional dialogues"—opportunities to raise to awareness and examine the largely unrecognized assumptions that currently underlie educational structures and practices and to generate alternatives to them. Such exchanges could in turn identify particular problems to be the foci of inquiry and change efforts.

Assumptional dialogues may come in many forms, all complicated to implement. It is exceedingly difficult to bring to the surface the basic assumptions underlying structures and actions in school settings. Sarason (1990), who has devoted his entire career to practice-informed scholarship on education change, emphasized the importance of making problematic the "behavioral regularities" of schooling, and acknowledged the difficulty in personal terms in the preface of his latest book:

> I wrote to discharge the obligation to myself to state frankly and succinctly conclusions to which I reluctantly have come. If that reluctance, better yet resistance, was strong, it was because I did not want to confront the past inadequacies in my own thinking. No less than most people, I was caught up in a way of thinking about schools that essentially assumed that certain axioms on which reform efforts were based were valid. Once you flush out these axioms you are hoist by your own petard because you now see the educational scene differently, and it makes quite a difference. If it took me years to arrive at this point, I do not expect others to respond enthusiastically.
>
> *The problem is not what to do but how to think* [italics added], how to take seriously the idea that there is a uni-

verse of alternative explanations for past failures of reform. Some wit—I think it was Mencken—said that for any problem there is a simple, direct answer that is wrong. That kind of answer has not been in short supply in the area of educational problems. . . . Problems are constants; answers are provisional. (p. xi)

Nonetheless, there are theories and methods to employ, some directly and others indirectly. We now turn to several possibilities that could be integral elements of the school as a center of inquiry.

**Reflection Seminars: A Direct Approach.** Argyris and Schon (1974, 1978) developed a process of individual and organizational learning generated through awareness of discrepancy between intention and action. If systematically pursued, this process helps educators to identify and question assumptions governing behaviors and structures. Senge (1990) used Fritz's (1989, 1990) "principles of creative tension" to describe Argyris and Schon's learning and growth process through discrepancy analysis. The dimension of intentions, which is the explicit and public statement of individual or organizational philosophy, intent, platform (Kottkamp, 1982, 1990b), or vision (Senge, 1990), Argyris and Schon called "espoused theory." This dimension is not difficult to unearth; it is simply what we say we want to do. The dimension that actually guides individual or organizational action Argyris and Schon called "theory-in-use." It is very difficult to identify theories-in-use because they are deeply embedded in what Polyani (1967) described as "tacit knowledge," by which we know more than we can say. At the core of educators' theories-in-use is a set of assumptions which they cannot easily articulate but which create "the world of the more or less invisible" in schools (Cohn, Kottkamp & Provenzo, 1987).

The problem with theories-in-use is that explicit knowledge of them is virtually inaccessible to the actor, be the actor an individual or organization. It is much easier for an outsider to reach them by carefully observing the actor with full attention applied to extrapolating the assumptions of this dimension. Teachers' being unable to tell us directly how to reform the system is not a "teacher problem." It is, rather, a universal "actor problem." Thus, we may be in a better position to extrapolate the assumptions of the teachers we interviewed than they are, but, in our own work, we also need others to identify unexamined assumptions underlying our own position and conclusions.

Argyris and Schon (1974, 1978) described reflective seminars in which the direct purpose was to uncover and examine assumptions governing behavior. The process works best in groups comprised of members with different roles who are voluntarily committed to the process for the purpose of learning and understanding. Having different role occupants is important, first, because the presence of differing perspectives to reflect on common issues facilitates the work of uncovering and extrapolating one's own assumptions. Second, no single person or even small group of individuals can bring about significant change without the participation of the wide array of stakeholders who ultimately have some say in what happens and what is considered legitimate. Finally, extrapolating assumptions in multi-role groups is a powerful means for developing understanding and appreciation of those in other roles as well as of one's own assumptions. When an individual takes on the task of intense concentration on another, as is required in such extrapolation, the appreciation of the other's position can grow rapidly as the outsider or observer tries to understand the world from the insider's or actor's perspective. With the growth of understanding and appreciation of other roles and perspectives comes the potential for decline of conflict.

The participation in these reflective seminars of individuals who hold differing roles means, of course, that members holding different levels of power are seated around the table. Therefore, processes must be developed to prevent power differentials from being exercised or threatened. Unless all participants feel comfortable enough to speak honestly and openly, there can be no real dialogue. Moreover, without the freedom to participate freely, those with less power may become defensive and eventually disengage from the process (Kottkamp, 1990b). As discussed earlier, some of our most fundamental educational problems stem from existing control and power differentials. Most schools and classrooms today could be characterized, in Freire's (1974) terms, as places which foster "monologues" rather than "dialogues" between administrators and teachers and between teachers and students. If assumptional dialogues are ultimately to produce alterations in the power relations within the educational system, they must begin by functioning as authentic models of the process (Osterman & Kottkamp, 1993).

The centrality of uncovering assumptions lies in two of its functions. The obvious function is that of problem identification. Only by exposing assumptions to the light of analysis can the real issues involved in current practice and reform proposals be acknowledged. This is an important road to the discovery of deeply embedded conflicts such as the one between autonomy and control discussed earlier. Once discrepancies between intention and action are examined, and the underlying assumptions and conflicts are recognized, the participants have reached the stage of problem-finding or problem-setting, a necessary precursor to successful problem-solving.

The other important function of assumption-digging lies in its potential for motivating individuals to act. When the assumptions that lie within the tacit theory-in-use are extrapolated so that they may be compared with what the individual or organization espouses, the incongruence can provide a strong motivational jolt for change. (Argyris & Schon, 1974; Kottkamp, 1990b; Zaltman, Florio & Sikorski, 1977).

One example of this type of assumptional dialogue comes from the current work of colleagues Robert Kottkamp and Janet Miller, who are facilitators for a reflection seminar composed of the superintendent, some central office administrators, and several elementary school principals from a suburban school district. Membership is voluntary, and the broad purpose for meeting is to improve education in the district through stimulating individual and group reflection. The methods used to provoke the uncovering of tacit assumptions include autobiographical writing (Miller, 1990), writing individual educational philosophies or platforms (Kottkamp, 1982, 1990b), and group discussion.

During a meeting in January 1991 a discussion focused on a group of high school students who had visited the Soviet Union and written essays about their experiences. The superintendent asked why the essays seemed hollow, why they were more form than meaning. This triggered a lengthy interchange on the tendency of students to follow form rather than provide substance which led to examination of time control, testing, and the subject-matter focus of high school teachers. Comparisons were made between feeling and meaning in the writing of elementary school students, who were experiencing "writing across the curriculum" and "writing as process," and the less meaningful writing products of the high school students. The session culminated with an intense examination of the metaphor for high school teachers, "dispensers of knowledge." Participants tried to generate a different metaphor that might rechannel teaching at that level. In the course of less than two hours, this group wrestled with a number of the control and testing issues discussed in Chapter 7. It focused participants on what might be done to confront secondary school teaching, which in many respects sounded quite like what McNeil (1986) had reported in her study. Although they did not specifically articulate a preferred approach to learning, the specific depiction of the district's elementary school practices came very close to the image of meaningful interaction we have put forward.

In another session, an elementary principal brought in the problem of insufficient funds in a "materials" account to purchase manipulative materials for the revised math program while, at the same time, there were unexpended monies in the "textbook" account. The eventual resolution was: Define manipulatives as textbooks and purchase them. The group realized that the likely hundred-year-old state category system rested on the unexamined assumption that teaching consisted of a group of students, a teacher, a blackboard, and textbooks. In a related action, the district applied for and received a variance from the state to alter its standard mandated testing of math achievement. The district wished to go further in the direction of a broad problem-solving approach (as opposed to computation) than the state did. This action challenged state assumptions of effective curriculum and testing, and achieved a structural alteration.

Through its probing of issues over a year and a half, this group identified major assumptions lying behind existing structures which cause problems. They are continuing the process of grappling with some of these in an atmosphere of relatively open, unfiltered communication across what would normally be four hierarchical levels of the organization. This experience is changing the structure of communication across the district administrative staff.

In addition, the superintendent is consciously working to change his behavior in decision making. The openness in the reflection group has shown how better decisions can be made when more honest information is available. The superintendent is systematically monitoring his own behavior in decision making situations, deliberately attempting to delay coming to a conclusion while at the same time asking others for more insights and opinions. He is even to the point of saying, "I don't know." more frequently in public. While attempting to change his behavior, he still confronts the expectation of his administrative subordinates that he is the "boss" and knows the answer or, at the very least, is supposed to come up with one. That expectation is grounded in the traditional assumptions of hierarchical and unilateral control with which many of the subordinates have not grappled. In attempting to change his own and his district's decision making process, he has become very aware of unexamined assumptions of power and control underlying his behavior.

Finally, several collaborative school district/university grant proposals are being written to support development of reflection or dialogue groups for teachers. It is hoped that these groups may become vehicles for working on various curricular, instructional, and structural changes that are part of the district's goals, including greater curricular integration and communication across grade levels, and the elimination of "tracking." The administrators also hope to develop some reflection groups with teacher and administrator membership.

**The "Vertical Team": An Indirect Approach.** Marilyn Cohn is a facilitator for a large suburban school district which, for the past four years, has struggled with the processes of decentralization and school improvement (Cohn & Lenz, 1990). The vehicle for this reform effort has been the "Vertical Team," a project developed and sponsored by the Danforth Foundation as part of its School Administrator's Fellowship Program. The district-wide Vertical Team is comprised of key stakeholders in the educational system: a School Board member, the Superintendent, an Assistant Superintendent, the Director of Special Services, the principals of the district's four elementary schools and of the middle and the high school, and one teacher from each of the buildings.

The Vertical Team concept has two major purposes. The first is to develop and model a process in which perspectives held by individuals on different levels of the district hierarchy can be honestly and directly expressed in collegial fashion. The second is to serve as a support and sounding board for the principals on the team whose task it is to develop and implement, with their staffs, improvement plans within their own schools.

Each principal on the Vertical Team has developed a school improvement team comprised of teachers, and, in some cases, parents. On the high school team, students also serve. These teams were created to foster shared decision making at the school level under the leadership of the principals and to shift the role of central office from a source of mandates to a source of assistance.

Monthly, the Vertical Team meets alternatively for a half or whole day to discuss key issues in school improvement. At every session, time is allocated to activities aimed at stripping away titles, roles, and power differentials and encouraging individuals to work collegially in an open and trusting manner. Most of these exercises have involved getting to know each other better on a personal level and have included the sharing of career and family highlights, influential people in one's life, characteristics most admired in colleagues, and famous people team members would like to be for a day. However, the bulk of the agenda is devoted to "school reports" in which principals present what they are trying to accomplish at the school level and ask the Vertical Team for help with the problems they are encountering. Because the Vertical Team members represent various roles, the perspectives and underlying assumptions expressed are usually quite different from each other. Teachers in the group usually help principals understand why some of their actions are not being widely endorsed by teachers in their buildings. Elementary and secondary principals often help each other see problems from other vantage points.

One particular way the Vertical Team offers assistance is through the In-Basket activity developed by the Danforth Program. In this brainstorming process, all members generate possible solutions to problems brought by principals. Often the most creative and viable ideas come from teachers rather than those in positions of greater authority in the school hierarchy, an outcome that has clearly boosted teacher self-esteem and confidence.

As the Vertical Team wrestles with specific problems introduced by principals, larger issues are invariably raised. One February 1990 morning, the first item on the agenda was an In-Basket activity on the "Outdoor Education Counselor Problem." More specifically, the elementary principals wanted the team to grapple with the following question: How can the elementary outdoor education program attract high caliber student counselors from the high school? As one principal explained the problem, the strong leaders from the high school had not been applying because their teachers have told them if they miss a week of school their grades will suffer.

The brainstorming process produced twenty-five possible solutions as well as an emotionally charged discussion. The high school teacher and principal on the team admitted they do not encourage students to apply for counseling positions because they miss too many classes. This position irritated some elementary teachers and principals who believed that strong high school students should have the option to make up the missed work, without penalty, and maintained that a well-rounded education should provide leadership opportunities as well as academics. Because the group members had developed mutual trust, the exchange was direct but not hostile. Different assumptions about the nature of learning and the purposes of secondary education were fully aired, and participants left the meeting with a new understanding of the positions of the others and some possible strategies for addressing the conflict.

More recently, the Vertical Team devoted a full day to discussing a summary report of district scores on international, national, state, and local tests and other achievement information. Before coming to the meeting, principals met with either their school improvement teams or grade level teams to analyze the results and implications for their buildings. The day was spent sharing building level analyses. Members of different schools offered insights and suggestions to others and looked for patterns evident across buildings. At the following half-day meeting, two related In-Basket questions extended the theme of academic achievement and learning in different directions:

1. How can we increase the learning curve of students once the curriculum is in place and textbooks and support materials have been purchased?
2. How can we get students to take more challenging courses and to perform in those classes?

The first question generated over seventy ideas; the second questions yielded more than thirty suggestions. At an upcoming meeting, the Vertical Team will circle back to the testing issue and discuss three articles questioning the validity of standardized testing.

This series of meetings as well as the meeting that addressed the counselor problem reveal that during Vertical Team sessions specific problems move quickly to broader and more complex questions such as what constitutes learning, what is necessary to make learning happen, what standardized tests can tell us about the process and outcomes of learning, and what motivational strategies can stimulate students to set higher standards for themselves? At the heart of each of these questions are tightly held assumptions and existing structures and practices that are being subjected to examination from multiple perspectives.

Thus, although the Vertical Team was not directly constituted as a reflection seminar for assumptional dialogues, it functions indirectly as a means for genuine exchanges among different role players on issues that have systemic implications. In addition, the structure and purpose under which the district Vertical Team and some of the school improvement teams operate have set in motion actual changes in authority, control, and status. On the school level, teachers are actively participating in the setting of goals and the selecting of means to achieve the goals; on the district Vertical Team, teachers, principals, central office administrators, and a board member are openly talking on a first name basis in a setting where principals can feel free to "admit" to problems in front of both their teachers and their "bosses."

**Experiential Learning: A Stimulus for Assumptional Dialogues.** In a participant-observation study of an independent elementary school's attempt to develop and implement a problem-solving curriculum for empowering students, Beyer (1991a) described strategies to help teachers and their principal first think about their own learning. By immersing them in adult problem-solving situations, and then by guiding their reflections, Beyer led the staff both to discover something about their own problem-solving behaviors and to think about what needed to be taken into consideration when planning for students. The sessions following the experiences in which Beyer helped teachers debrief their own learning became, in effect, assumptional dialogues that had implications for the structure of their classrooms and school.

For example, after one problem-solving session, teachers explored how much individualizing is possible for students at different levels of empowerment, how much attention to give students in setting up a problem, and how much structure to provide for the small-group process of solving it (p. 6). In another session devoted to analyzing in small groups their own experiences with collaborative problem-solving, teachers identified issues related to: learning to adjust your own problem-solving style to those of others in the group, establishing a common vision of the problem and of the solution, not allowing an early dominant solution to block other possibilities, supporting risk-taking, and utilizing the different strengths of individual group members. These discussions led Beyer to conclude: "In the midst of solving a problem for which very little direction was given, some important discoveries were made about what these teachers valued for students to experience in a group problem-solving context" (p. 10). Thus, through the experiential process, core assumptions were identified and then analyzed for their implications for changes in the amount of control to be exercised by students and teachers.

Beyer (1991b) also facilitated reflection sessions with groups of principals who participated in a two and a half day Wilderness Experience as part of a Leadership Academy. The experience required risk-taking, group cooperation, and problem-solving, and her role was to help principals connect what they were learning about problem-solving teams in the woods to what might occur with problem-solving teams in schools. For leaders accustomed to exercising considerable power and control in their schools, these experiences and debriefings produced insights into both the struggles and rewards of sharing control with others.

To illustrate the struggle, Beyer quoted Craig, a disgruntled participant:

I've been entirely frustrated this whole weekend. I never know what is going to happen next. I don't have all the information. Everything we do requires getting everyone's opinion. I'm not in control of what I have to do. This would never work in schools. I have to be in control. In my school teachers either get on my wagon or they get left in the dust. (KMB, Principal's Academy notes, 10/19/91, p. 26)

She also documented how different members of the group responded to Craig:

They pointed out the lost potential of teachers who are "left in the dust." They acknowledged the pressures of being forced into taking control when one is in the position of principal. They acknowledged that each of them had been trained to take control. And they reframed the problem I had raised, How do you structure problems in schools to encourage collaborative group problem-solving? (pp. 26-27)

To illustrate the potential rewards of the process, Beyer reported:

Later that evening at an informal campfire, Craig approached me wanting to know . . . how I would work in his school if I were asked to come. . . . The discussion ended with his comment that he would check with his superintendent because, "We've got to get started on something like this." (p. 27)

From this one example, we can observe existing assumptions and practices connected to learning, autonomy, and control becoming problematic at the school level. We think this experiential approach holds promise for helping teachers, administrators, and other stakeholders to confront, examine, and alter some of their long-standing assumptions about the nature of learning and the structures that foster it.

**Assumptional Dialogues: Multiple Possibilities and Common Threads.** We have sketched several approaches to assumptional dialogues we know or have experienced ourselves, although it is we who attach the term "assumptional dialogues" to these activities. In all these instances, the specific concerns or activities, when raised in open and supportive environments and facilitated by sensitive outsiders, moved to broader issues and to the examination of fundamental assumptions and structures regarding teaching, learning, and control. We can imagine many other district-wide or school groups meeting for the purpose of addressing serious problems such as low student performance or teacher morale, for examining and comparing various reform proposals, for trying to develop consensus on their own alternative version of a meaningful teaching-learning and assessment process, or for some combination of all these. We also advocate attempting assumptional dialogues at state and national levels with a wider variety of stakeholders so that they may consider how current unexamined policies constrain meaningful school learning and how new policies might facilitate it.

Whether the dialogues begin with concrete experiences and problems or more abstract visions is probably unimportant. What is important is that they occur, and that the following essential features are present: (1) a forum with individuals who hold varying positions and perspectives; (2) a process that provides the time and climate to establish trust and openness among participants and to foster examination of deeply held assumptions and confrontation between espoused theories and theories-in-use; and (3) an outside facilitator who can sensitively and nonthreateningly help insiders move outside of their individual "boxes" to see a bigger picture and thereby reframe and rethink their problems.[1]

In our view, the questioning of deeply embedded assumptions and long-standing structures among varying stakeholders, particularly in the domains of expectations, learning, and control discussed in the previous chapter, is pivotal to the change process, but rarely a part of it. In the absence of such questioning, well-intentioned reformers often implement programs that appear to be based upon new ways of thinking and acting, but that are actually simply different versions of existing practices. The form changes but the substance remains the same. Further, in many reform efforts, there is a small nucleus of believers and activists who, for their own reasons, are ready to embrace and work under alternative assumptions and a majority who are uncomfortable with or disinterested in doing things differently. Both groups need to participate in assumptional dialogues if they are to understand each other's position on change, as well as to consider the need for and nature of the change itself. Change efforts are often blocked more by a division among educators and other stakeholders over attitudes toward change in general than by specific problems embedded in altering policies and practices.

Two recent studies speak to this issue. Collins & Hanson (1991), in studying the experimental site-based management program in Dade County, found that a feud had developed between two factions, the "activists" and the "provincialists." Activists were enthusiastic about new roles and working arrangements; provincialists were against these innovations and saw the activists as traitors who behaved more like administrators than teachers. Muncey and McQuillan's (1991), study of several schools that belong to the Coalition of Essential Schools (CES) also identified faculty division as a major problem. They consistently found a lack of consensus on the need for changes in structure and teaching practice, even in schools characterized by poor attendance, low scores on standardized tests, and high rates of failure and drop outs. In most schools, they discovered a "vanguard" of faculty who were committed to change; however, instead of serving as role models for others, the "vanguard" was viewed by the noninvolved as receiving preferential treatment. The result was division, which tended to restrict communication and halt the spread of Coalition practices among the faculty.

While time spent in the various forms of dialogue on assumptions is no guarantee of faculty consensus on the complexities of school change, time spent in understanding multiple perspectives and valuing different points of view seems critical to identifying different sets of assumptions that, when tenaciously but unconsciously held, can destroy any substantive change effort. At best, discussions of assumptions hold the potential for rethinking and reframing problems based upon discrepancies between existing pedagogical practices and school structures and espoused purposes. At the very least, they hold the possibility of creating understanding and respect between those who advocate change and those who do not. Without such rethinking or understanding, it is difficult to see genuine possibilities for fundamental and enduring change.

## Literature Review: Lessons from the Past and Present

Most formal inquiry depends upon learning from existing studies before the formulation of new approaches. In schools that function as centers of inquiry, educators and other stakeholders need to spend time looking at past and current efforts to bring about systemic change in schools, particularly those based upon alternative assumptions for learning and assessment as described in Chapter 8. We support Cuban's argument that instead of simply asking how teachers should teach, we need to ask the following types of questions:

What are the goals of proposed changes? What blocks those
goals within and outside of schools? What have previous
efforts achieved? Why did they fail? How do organizational
structures help or hinder these proposed changes? (1988,
p. 344)

This series of questions can lead change agents to discover and
take into consideration the stability of the existing system and the
power of organizational and cultural norms to shape behavior and
ideas.

Typically, researchers know the literature on change better
than teachers and administrators responsible for implementing
it. The findings on the general difficulties and complexities of organizational change (Baldridge & Deal, 1975; Cuban, 1984; Fullan,
1982; Sarason, 1971, 1990) should be available to educators so that
they may realistically appraise the strong forces that work against
such changes. Moreover, specific case studies of failed attempts to
change the traditional roles of teachers and students (Gross, Giacquinta, & Bernstein, 1971; Smith et al., 1987; Smith & Keith, 1971)
should be examined to reduce repetition of failure. Finally, recent
studies of efforts to develop site-based management, teacher
empowerment, and collaborative school change (Cohn & Finch,
1987, 1989; Cohn & Gellman, 1988; Cohn & Lenz, 1990; Collins &
Hansen, 1991; Malen, Ogawa & Kranz, 1990; Muncey & McQuillan, 1991) should be read for insights into attempts at school
improvement in the current social context. These studies can point
to serious barriers to change: lack of time, low faculty morale,
changes in administration (Cohn & Finch, 1989), faculty division,
political naivete, and lack of attention to the ongoing as opposed to
the start-up aspects of change (Muncey & McQuillan, 1991). They
can also identify facilitators of change: strong team leadership,
commitment to process issues, tangible evidence of progress along
the way, and professional treatment of teachers (Cohn & Finch,
1989).

In schools that function as centers of inquiry, there must be
time and opportunity for reading and discussing this literature in
order to encourage informed and realistic expectations based on
lessons from the past. Muncey & McQuillan's (1991) statement captures well our own position:

School reform is going to be extremely difficult to accomplish, it is going to be time- and labor-intensive, and it will
require rethinking and relearning on all parties' parts. To

deny any of this is to believe that there are quick fixes or miracle cures. Our evidence suggests that even where there would seem to be consensus that change is needed and where there are dedicated and well-intended people trying to bring it about, there are issues and problems often unanticipated, that threaten the change process almost from its inception. Structural constraints and power issues are realities in all institutions. Perhaps if others working on creating change in their schools can see themselves or their problems in these observations, they can take heart that they are not alone. Perhaps if others contemplating reform can begin with some awareness of these problems, they might be more prepared to address these concerns if and when they emerge at their schools. (p. 3)

## Developing and Studying New Approaches for Learning: Action Research

After time devoted to examining their assumptions and the available literature on change, we envision teachers in an inquiry-oriented school engaging as members of a collaborative group in the design and implementation of new approaches to learning, including the structural changes necessary to support alternative models. For example, we see experiments that vary the amount of teacher control and student participation, incorporate curricular strands built upon student interests and problem-solving, utilize performance-based assessments, and involve parents and other community members in the teaching-learning process. In some instances, teachers might only modify strategies already in place; in others, they might attempt to create new structures. In either case, the key would be the freedom, opportunity, time, and support from administrators to experiment and to study systematically the results.

Schaefer (1967) maintained that "scholar-teachers" who were properly prepared to study the problems of learning within their own classrooms could make major contributions to the field. In Schaefer's conception, teachers would employ quantitative research methods which would require that they become more "sophisticated in the behavioral sciences" (p. 70). However, as we think of scholar-teachers in contemporary centers of inquiry, we think primarily, although not exclusively, of qualitative methods and of the approach known as "action research" (Stenhouse, 1976; Elliott, 1978, 1988; Somekh, 1989). The following definition illustrates its applicability to classrooms.

> Action research involves the participants in a social situa-
> tion as researchers and co-researchers (in the case of edu-
> cation, the participants are the teachers and the students); it
> involves collaborative inquiry rather than a detached
> observer's stance; it entails careful collection of data which
> directly relates to the professional concerns of the teach-
> ers; it involves the teachers in reflecting on that data and
> planning steps to improve future action; and finally it
> entails putting these actions into practice and beginning
> again on the cycle of data gathering and reflection.
> (Somekh, 1989, p. 8)

Action research is particularly well suited to the dynamic nature of
classrooms. Moreover, it features a type of data collection and documentation that enables teachers to describe the implementation
of different strategies, generate insights, patterns, concepts, and
understandings, and eventually draw some conclusions on making
learning more meaningful for today's students. Finally it is a
methodology that invites teachers to reflect upon their assumptions and practices and to develop alternatives.

Nonetheless, there are also potential problems with this
approach. First, teachers often find it difficult to accept this process
as "real" research. They have become so imbued with and intimi-
dated by the quantitative model pursued by outside "objective"
researchers, who use control and experimental groups and produce statistical findings, that teachers tend to reject at first any
notion of their own subjective perspectives' contributing to a legitimate process of inquiry. Moreover, they don't think of classrooms
as cultures to be studied, and they cannot imagine that others
might be interested in or could learn anything from what happens
there. Finally, they do not conceive of themselves as individuals
with ideas worthy of inquiry, and they don't trust themselves to
know enough to be accurate data collectors.[2]

However, when told that no one is in a better position to assess
or understand their classroom intentions, actions, and students
than they are, teachers begin to nod in agreement. When they find
that they can collect a wide variety of data from observations
recorded in journals, video- and audiotapes, student interviews,
collegial observations, student writing assignments and projects,
test results, attendance records, and parental interviews and ques-
tionnaires, they recognize that they can speak with much more
"scientific" accuracy than they originally imagined. And when they
realize that they can work toward learning something of direct

interest to them, they tend to become highly enthusiastic.

A second limitation is that action research can be an isolated endeavor that is limited in scope and therefore in impact. When conducted as separate studies in traditional settings, action research projects are generally constrained by whatever a single teacher can do within the parameters of his or her classroom. Although individual teachers can clearly learn and grow from research within the confines of their classroom, they cannot alone alter any of the long-standing policies and structures that are major inhibitors of change. Thus, an English teacher who wanted to build a literature curriculum around student interests and study the results might be able to offer some choice within the framework of his existing materials, but he would probably not have the resources nor support for abandoning the district curriculum.

Both the strengths and limitations of the methodology were experienced by Marilyn Cohn, who has worked for the past three years with experienced teachers on action research as part of the St. Louis Teachers' Academy, a leadership group for outstanding teachers (Waskow, 1990). Although teachers worked in different schools and conducted separate studies, the Academy has functioned as a center of inquiry. Collegial endeavors included problem generation as well as practice in descriptive note-taking, interpretation of data, and the critiquing of peers' work in progress. During summer vacation, participants developed final analyses and wrote draft after draft, utilizing facilitator and peer feedback. By September, their action research reports were printed in booklets for dissemination to superintendents, principals and fellow teachers. The discussions that emanated from the sharing of the successes and failures of their studies and the collective sense of satisfaction that came from seeing their joint "publication" have been joyful experiences.

Nonetheless, when teachers conducted their projects in their schools, they were essentially alone and unsupported. Like their counterparts in Dade County, the Academy Fellows have been very concerned with issues of student motivation and learning, and their studies have reflected those concerns but generally within the constraints of the system. Although some studies have involved two or more teachers working on interdisciplinary projects or the development of portfolio or other alternative means of assessment, and others have focused on school-wide structures such as advising systems, most have been focused on altering pedagogy within a single classroom. For example, teachers have studied the process and outcomes of: cooperative learning in a beginning Spanish course; brainstorming and creative problem-solving in secondary art classes; encouraging upper elementary students to become more self-directed learners; varying study strategies for vocabulary building; moving from a chronologically organized, anthology text in American literature to the use of complete novels and full-length plays selected for their relevance to adolescents.

The latter project exemplifies in a number of ways both the limitations and strengths of action research within traditional settings. The author of that study, "Taking Risks," is an English teacher who wanted to find a way to make American Literature more motivating for his students. After years of using a chronological approach with the departmental anthology, he attempted to select full-length novels and plays that might have special appeal to adolescents. The first roadblock he encountered was there were not enough novels in the English department for an entire class. That situation forced him into a cooperative learning strategy with different groups reading different novels, an approach with which he had little experience. The cooperative learning process proved to be somewhat problematic, but the overall results were positive. Thus, the study was ultimately illuminating for a teacher who challenged some of his dearly held practices and personally grew from the experience. As he expressed in his summary statement:

> Primarily this is a picture of a teacher breaking out of a traditional mold and taking the risks to try something completely different. It shows both successes and failure and details the analyses of things which were not successful as well as those which were. (Network for Educational Development, 1990)

That moving out of the text was a risk for this highly competent veteran and that there were not enough materials for him to do it show some of the personal and institutional limitations under which he worked. That he took the risk to break from his "traditional mold" and learned from it, reveals the power of the methodology to help individuals rethink their assumptions about learning. That he was willing to publicly acknowledge his failures as well as his successes shows the confidence that can be gained from the supportive context provided by a strong peer group.

His study as well as the others completed through the Teachers' Academy in relative isolation and under enormous time pressures suggest the potential of this approach under better conditions. While the reports vary in quality, some have, in fact, paved the way for structural changes, most produced changes in teaching methods and insights into student learning, and almost all generated self-reflection, the questioning of deeply held assumptions, and a sense of intellectual accomplishment. In addition, some teachers in the Academy's third year are reading the findings of those in earlier years and building upon their work.

Still, the image we hold goes much farther. We envision schools as communities of scholar-teachers, where everyone, including principals, collaborate on action research projects that have the capacity to change the very structure of schools or significant elements within them. We look toward schools where questions not answers drive the leaders, the teachers, and the students. This does not suggest that everyone has to be or even should be of a single mind as to what constitutes meaningful learning or what kind of action research should be conducted. It does mean, however, that the school, not some outside agency to which individuals belong, is the center of inquiry. It does mean that the research that is conducted is rooted in the assumptional dialogues and the literature on change that has been part of the overall school inquiry process. It also means that groups of individuals within a school who disagree about the amount of control to be given to students or want to try different approaches to assessment might design different studies that would eventually lend credence to or cast doubt on their position. Most importantly, it means that the inside experts rather than outside experts eventually develop the policy and practices of the school.

## Organizing Schools as Centers of Inquiry

What conditions must be present for schools to function as centers of inquiry? Again, we take our lead from Schaefer (1967), since all of our recommendations, except the final one, stem from his original conception.

### Reduced Teaching Loads

The starting point for schools as centers of inquiry is a reduction in teaching load. What teachers need more than anything else is time during the school day and year to read, plan, act, and reflect. Schaefer put it this way:

> If society were to take seriously the job of teaching . . . and, particularly, if teachers were to be encouraged to inquire

into the substance of what they are teaching, or into the
nature of the students with whom they work, or into the
learning process itself, it is apparent that a teaching load of
more than twelve to fifteen hours per week could not be
condoned. . . . No one, not even the most dedicated and
brilliant, can effectively individualize instruction, systematically analyze his own teaching, diagnose learning difficulties, and maintain a vigorous pedagogical and substantive scholarship on a spare-time basis. (p. 61)

In today's teaching context, the diverse population, the
expanded social responsibilities of the schools, and the paperwork
associated with accountability make the teaching load a crushing
one. Moreover, in many schools, as part of a well-intentioned move
toward teacher empowerment, teachers are not only expected to
teach all day but to redesign the workplace after school. As Goodlad
recently so aptly remarked: "We ask teachers to spend forty to sixty
hours a week flying the 727, but, at the same time, we expect them
to invent the 787, especially if we give them a coke at 4 p.m."[3]
Teachers need to participate in the development of new
approaches and structures, but it can only be done properly if they
are provided the time to do so. Dialogues on assumptions, study
toward a better understanding of content, pedagogy, and the process of school reform, and action research projects on innovative
practices must be recognized as central, legitimate, and labor-intensive endeavors requiring reduced classroom responsibilities for
teachers.

## Collegiality as Opposed to Bureaucracy

For inquiry, as we have described it, to flourish in schools,
there must be an end to isolation of teachers from one another
and to hierarchical control. New working arrangements are needed
so that teachers may determine common purposes and work as
colleagues to achieve schoolwide aims. While divergent views and
practices are both inevitable and desirable on any school faculty,
there need to be processes that involve colleagues working toward
a shared conception of meaningful learning and the purposes of
schooling. The challenges of today are too complex and the stakes
too high to be left to individual entrepreneurs and subversives
working behind closed classroom doors. Inquiry must be a collaborative venture with creative individuals working together to generate new assumptions, develop innovative methods based on

those assumptions, and raise broader policy questions for the larger educational system. The road will be long and hard. Finding ways to make schools meaningful learning environments will require the combined talents, wills, and efforts of entire faculties of active professionals.

The image we have drawn of thinking individuals working in concert in turn suggests a fundamental change in the role of school administrators. In schools as centers of inquiry, teachers do not need bosses to tell them what to do; rather, they need facilitators, coordinators of resources, and group process leaders who will support their initiatives.

In replacing old hierarchical relationships and individual isolation with collaborative action, the concept of autonomy will inevitably change. As discussed earlier, teacher autonomy is presently a fragile and individually held form of authority which teachers desire because of their isolation and need to adjust to the ambiguous and unpredictable nature of their work. However, with collaborative work, isolation is reduced and authority can make at least a partial shift toward the group of scholar-teachers. Teachers will increasingly need collective autonomy, a new autonomy based on their new role as collaborative inquirers, as they deviate from the predominant norms, structures, and processes of their work. Thus, while they are opening their classrooms in new ways to each other, they will also likely need to take a collective stand against pressures to push them back into their traditional mold. Collaborative action also offers many new possibilities for intrinsic rewards derived from interaction with colleagues, personal and shared learning from inquiry, and improved student learning.

## School-University Collaboration

Inquiry-oriented schools and scholar-teachers call for strong school-university partnerships built upon shared interests and mutual respect. In the past, the relationship has generally been one of dependence, disjuncture, and denigration. Universities need schools for research sites, student teaching placements, and teachers for enrollment in their programs; teachers and schools need universities for credentials. This recognized interdependence has led schools and universities to work cooperatively in a number of ways, but it has rarely moved them closer together in terms of assumptions, goals, or mutual understanding. In fact, quite the opposite has occurred. Teachers and other school personnel often criticize professors for being too abstract, theoretical, and idealistic, while professors often denigrate school personnel for being overly concrete, practical, and concerned with the immediate at the expense of the long range. Moreover, each blames the other for our educational problems. Teachers maintain that the university failed to prepare them for the school realities they encounter, and professors say that teachers discard the principles they have learned at the university in favor of questionable "practices that work" in the short run.

The relationship should, however, be significantly different with schools as centers of inquiry. With action research as a common bond and with schools reorganized so that teachers have work lives more like those of university professors, greater possibilities for honest communication and genuine collaboration exist. Also, the preparation and continuous nurturing of scholar-teachers will require strong links to university faculty in the disciplines and in education. The development of alternative pedagogical approaches cannot be separated from academic content. Scholar-teachers who seek to create more meaningful learning experiences for students will need a strong command of subject matter, with a firm grasp of the overall structure and key concepts to be taught, as well as a deep grounding in pedagogy. Working closely together, scholar-teachers and professors of education and of the disciplines could determine the fundamental concepts to be taught and how they might be organized in the most meaningful framework for students of different levels and abilities. The task of connecting contemporary students to academic content and skills is clearly one in which both knowledge and pedagogical process are integrated. In similar fashion the new school model will encourage greater collaboration between members of traditionally separate departments of curriculum and instruction and administration within university schools of education. As the interdependent nature of learning and the structure of the school become focal, the need for problem-focused sharing should increase among professors within education. In sum, the same type of collaboration that will be required among school personnel will also be required among university personnel within education and between university arts and sciences and education faculties and school faculties.

The principle of school-university collaboration as opposed to the limited cooperation that currently exists also has far-reaching implications for rethinking teacher education. Traditional role delineations and status distinctions would be blurred, and teacher education would become a shared responsibility of university faculties and the schools. The current emphasis on the design and establishment of Professional Development Schools (Goodlad, 1991; Holmes Group, 1990) represents this approach. In fact, Professional Development Schools could be viewed in some fundamental ways as a revival or at least a variation of Schaefer's original conception, but with a broader community scope and a stronger mission in the field of preservice teacher education.[4]

Moreover, the concepts of scholar-teacher, teachers as collaborative inquirers, action research, and the school as a center of inquiry should have profound effects upon the ways in which educational research has been traditionally conceived, conducted, and taught in many institutions of higher learning. Thus, the rethinking of school systems and the accompanying changes in assumptions, structures, roles, and norms will force the rethinking of the occupation of teaching and of the colleges and universities that prepare teachers for their work. Although this recognition adds yet another layer of complexity to the challenge of change, it may mean that, at last, schools, teachers, and teacher education programs would be working together on the reform of educational policy and practice (Goodlad, 1991).

## A "Safe" Environment

The last condition central to the functioning of schools as centers of inquiry is the creation of an environment where educators are protected from unreasonable time and accountability constraints. Schaefer did not speak to this issue probably because in the late 1960s, pressures to raise scores on standardized tests within particular timelines were virtually nonexistent. Today the picture is quite different. What started as a well-intentioned attempt to encourage and keep track of student achievement has degenerated into a set of vises that constrict the learning of both teachers and students. Schools need the contribution and oversight of parents and community members, as well as state and national officials and accreditation agencies; but schools cannot operate as centers of inquiry if they are saddled with unrealistic expectations and deadlines, "specifications" rather than "guidelines," and predetermined outcomes based on assumptions that have proven to be faulty.

A case in point is President Bush's (1991) *Education 2000: An Education Strategy* and the accompanying Request for Proposals for Designs for a New Generation of American Schools (New American Schools Development Corporation, 1991). In the overview of the report, the strategy for improving America's schools is described as a "bold, complex, and long-range" one which will "spur far-reaching changes in weary practices, outmoded assumptions and long-assumed constraints on education" (p. 5). So far, so good. The plan then proposes a two-track approach to achieve the six national goals developed by the President and the nation's governors. The first track deals with existing schools and the second with a "new generation of American schools" that "break the mold and create their own one-of-a-kind high-performance schools" (p. 19). The key strategy for success in both current and new schools is the establishment of "New World-Class Standards" in the five core subjects, and a means for measuring results. For Track I schools, American Achievement Tests, a voluntary nationwide examination, will be created. It is argued that the results of these tests will matter to students because colleges and employers will be asked to consider them in their selection processes, and presidential citations will be awarded to those who score well. There are also incentives in the form of a Merit Schools Program and "differential pay" for individual teachers whose students score well. Test results will be published in national, state, and local "report cards," and parents can then exercise "choice" by selecting winning and rejecting losing schools.

While the new generation of American schools will have the "flexibility" to pursue the same standards in their own ways, they too will be held accountable for the same ends. According to the Request for Proposals, the new designs must enable students in the proposed schools "to achieve excellent results on these American Achievement Tests or similar measures" (New American Schools Development Corporation, 1991, p. 14). Moreover, the private funding source for these schools has developed a timeline which sets one year for new designs, two years for testing and implementation, and two more years to promote widespread adoption of the designs across the country.

The prescribed core subjects and national standards, the standardized national tests, the merit school and individual "differential pay" incentives, and the highly unrealistic timelines of the President's proposal are exactly the type of constraints from which schools as centers of inquiry must be protected. What we call for, instead, is a climate of trust and a willingness to suspend judgment in the short run, for at least some schools, so that long-run accomplishment might be truly significant. Teachers and administrators who work in such schools must be risk-takers willing to confront deeply embedded assumptions and structures and to try alternative approaches built upon alternative assumptions. Correspondingly, policy-makers and the public at large who are searching for something substantially better than what we have must be risk-takers as well. Inquiry-oriented schools will have no chance to develop new structures or alternative methods of learning and assessment if their hands are tied tightly to the old ones.

## Conclusion

In the context of current educational policy and practice, our renewed call for a contemporary version of schools as centers of inquiry may sound even more idealistic than when Schaefer initially proposed the idea a quarter of a century ago. Given the generally conservative and quantitatively-oriented nature of the times, our alternative conception of meaningful learning may even seem less rigorous and structured than the open education movement of the late 1960s. The present is a difficult period of history in which to advocate less rather than more control of teachers and students and to propose schools which focus on questions rather than answers. Still, there are some promising signs that suggest these may actually be propitious times for such changes in our thinking. For example, the strong interest in the establishment of Professional Development Schools with their emphasis on school-university collaboration and inquiry, the growing strength of the Coalition of Essential Schools with its emphasis on student as worker, teacher as coach (Sizer, 1984), and alternative means of assessment, and the increasing commitment to the "whole language" approach to literacy, with its focus on the interests and abilities students bring to the classroom, are positive indicators that the approaches we advocate can indeed take root and develop in today's climate.

Of all the recommendations we have made, however, we suspect that reducing the teaching load in schools as centers of inquiry will be the most difficult for others to accept, even among those who might find some of our basic ideas attractive. A reduction in teaching load will inevitably incur expenditures of money as well as creative use of existing resources, and we recognize that a proposal with a high price tag is a political disaster. But at the risk of being dismissed as totally unrealistic and impractical, we would go even farther and argue that a reduced teaching load must be the goal for all schools, not just for special schools that are designated as centers of inquiry. In fact, our long-term vision is that eventually all schools will function as centers of inquiry. While many may conceive of them as expensive luxuries, we view inquiry-oriented schools and the broader structural questions they will raise as our best hope for finally turning our entire educational system in a new and positive direction. When all schools become places where inquiry into the assumptions and structures that govern the teaching-learning process can be openly pursued, we will have achieved more than meaningful learning approaches for students of today. We will have succeeded in transforming our nation's long-standing, closed, and stagnant system of education into one that is continually renewed by and responsive to the changing challenges of our larger society.

One way in which we find it helpful to think about their potential is to consider what schools as centers of inquiry might mean to the teachers we encountered in Dade County. In such schools, we ask ourselves: Would the majority of teachers find their work less difficult and more rewarding? Might enthusiastic teachers be willing and able to open their doors? Could disaffected teachers find renewed purpose and be interested in going back to teaching rather than merely keeping school? Would Karen be more inclined to stay in the profession she loves? Obviously we have no answers to these questions, but we would very much like to pursue them. We have no delusions as to the difficulties that lie in the path of such a long-term and costly course; but the possibilities seem well worth the effort. To those who would say our country cannot afford to spend the time and money it will take to turn schools into places where teachers can develop and study new methods and structures to make learning more meaningful for contemporary students, we make one final recommendation: Spend some time in schools, visit and observe in classrooms, talk with students, and most of all, listen to teachers—the missing voice in education.

# Methodological Appendix

## Data Sets and Samples

The data for this study consist of two sets of surveys and interviews, the first collected by Dan C. Lortie in 1964 and the second
collected as part of a National Institute of Education grant (NIE-G-
83-0067) by Eugene F. Provenzo, Jr., Marilyn M. Cohn, and Robert
B. Kottkamp in 1984/85.

### Five Towns Interviews (1964)

Lortie interviewed and tape-recorded 94 of 100 teachers whose
names were randomly sampled from selected schools in five school
districts ("Five Towns") in the Boston Metropolitan Area. He used
an 88-question open-ended interview schedule (Lortie, 1975, pp.
248-256) in probing for the ethos of the occupation. The five districts and the schools within them were chosen to include a variety
of community socio-economic and school grade levels. The Five
Towns interviewees altogether closely resembled a national prob-
ability sample in many respects, but Lortie urged caution in gen-
eralizing from the small sample. He used the interview sample primarily for discovery of broad themes, and he reported only
descriptive statistics on various categories he constructed from
teacher comments. He offered us the typescripts of the Five Towns
interviews, which we declined.

### Dade County Survey (1964)

Lortie constructed and administered a 24-page survey of the
total public school teacher population of Dade County, Florida, a
countywide district encompassing the City of Miami and sur-
rounding areas. Some items were designed to test the generalizability of categories developed from the earlier Five Towns interviews. Questions on work-related attitudes, orientations, and

291

preferences were answered by 6,539 teachers. (See Lortie, 1975, pp. 246-247, 256-259, for more detail.)

Professor Lortie graciously gave us access to the complete 1964 survey data set. His raw survey data served as the base line against which our own survey data could indicate stability or change. His published interview analyses (Lortie, 1969, 1975) were the benchmarks for assessing our interview data for indications of stability and of change.

## Dade County Survey (1984)

We surveyed a 40% sample (N=4,247) of the over eleven thousand Dade County teacher population with a 17-page questionnaire which contained selected questions from Lortie's survey and additional questions developed by the research team or drawn from other studies (Gallup, 1978; Sirotnik, 1979). The 40% sample was stratified by school and randomized within school. A 64% return rate (N=2,718) was achieved after three follow-ups by mail and telephone. Stratification by school was done so that individual responses could be aggregated to the school level. The rule for including a specific school in the aggregated data set was a response by at least 50% of those sampled in that school. Of the 249 schools in the district, 157 were included in the aggregated set. Data on school, staff, and student characteristics and achievement obtained from Dade County School Profiles (Dade County Public Schools, 1985) were also combined with the aggregated teacher data.

## Dade County Interviews (1984/85)

The 38-question open-ended interview schedule drew heavily on Lortie's earlier schedule. At Lortie's suggestion, some of the original questions were deleted, and we condensed several series of questions into single ones. We also developed new questions; one series about the principal was based upon the work of Dwyer, Lee, Barnett, Filby, and Rowan (1985). Other new questions probed teacher perceptions of the effects of major social forces between 1964 and 1984 on their work and orientation toward teaching.

From the 40% survey sample we drew a stratified random interview sample of 100 teachers. Stratification was accomplished by assigning each school to a 3-by-3 matrix consisting of three levels of socio-economic status (based on free lunch counts from school district data) and three grade levels (elementary, junior high, and senior high). We randomly chose 36 schools from the nine cells and then randomly selected teachers within each school. A total of 73 teachers eventually participated in the interviews, which consumed between forty-five minutes and two and a half hours each. Tape-recorded interviews were conducted at schools, homes, and university sites by the NIE principal researchers and by Gary McCloskey. Recordings were transcribed to typescripts, which yielded 1,737 pages of single-spaced teacher commentary. Of the interviewees, 53 were women (73%) and 20 were men (27%). The grade-level figures were 30 elementary (41%), 17 junior high (23%), and 26 senior high schools (35%). The ethnic proportions were 48 white (66%), 15 Black (21%), and 10 Hispanic (14%).

## District and Union Support

Data collection was greatly facilitated by the unqualified support of then-Superintendent of Schools Leonard Britton and his administrative staff, and of Pat Tornillo, Vice-President of United Teachers of Dade County, AFT, and his staff. Leaders of both organizations encouraged teachers to complete the survey forms. In addition, the Dade County Schools provided us with a complete computer tape of the school profiles and the United Teachers of Dade computer specialist developed the stratified random survey sample and created address labels.

## Limitations

Neither our 64% survey return rate nor our 73% interview rate were optimal. The largest disproportion between the survey respondents and the population of Dade County teachers was in ethnicity. Whites were over-represented, while Blacks and Hispanics were under-represented. The percentages of each group in the teacher population and in the survey returns were: Black, 28%/24%; white, 55%/59%; Hispanic, 17%/16%. The interview respondent proportions were even further from the school district population proportions (see previous section). The fact that all four interviewers were white was problematic, and we encourage future researchers to consider the importance of employing as interviewers those who would match the cultural backgrounds of those being interviewed. Two Hispanic interviewees had minimal command of English, and their interviews had limited usefulness. There was also some indication of less openness on the part of some Black interviewees; the proportion of times we were asked to stop the tape for "off-the-record" comments—a request we honored—was higher among this group and seemed concentrated on questions about the school principal. One Black teacher was visibly upset during the interview, and at the end refused to sign the informed consent form. The interviewer handed him the tape, and important data were irretrievably lost. On a different but related dimension, three of the four interviewers were male, while 73% of the interviewees were female. However, Marilyn Cohn completed almost half of the interviews.

There is also the issue that not all interviewees answered all of the questions in the schedule. This occurred for several reasons. In some interview situations, especially those conducted on school sites during the regular school day, there were serious time pressures. In these cases, the interviewer made decisions on which questions to delete based on the flow of the interview and the information uncovered to that point. Under such circumstances, the proportions of responses reported in the text derived from those who answered the particular questions rather than from all 73 teachers. In other instances, interviewees answered several questions on the basis of the probe from only one. Rather than reiterating a question already addressed, the interviewers skipped such questions found later in the schedule. Answers for the various questions then had to be disentangled in the coding and analyses.

Finally, the data for this study were limited to teacher self-perceptions gleaned through survey and interview questions. There were no corroborating observations of classroom or other behavior aside from informal impressions gathered during those interviews conducted within school contexts.

## Generalizability

The issue of generalizability has several components. The first is the return rates noted above. The second and third are location and time. Our data are limited to Dade County, Florida, which we chose because it was the location of Lortie's survey study. It was not the location of his interviews, so we lack comparability in that respect. Lortie (1975) argued that Dade County was a good location for survey work because Miami was an area of immigration from other parts of the country. It has remained so and is now even more culturally diverse as indicated by Table A.1.

The Dade County school system was the fourth largest in the nation at the time the data were collected, and it contained schools which ran the gamut from rural through suburban to inner city. Nevertheless, the experiences reported by teachers in this large

TABLE A.1
Birthplaces of Dade County Teachers, 1964 and 1984

| Birthplace | 1964 (%) | 1984 (%) |
|---|---|---|
| Dade County | 2.5 | 16.9 |
| Florida outside Dade County | 11.1 | 9.8 |
| South (MD, VA, NC, SC, GA, AL, MS, TN, KY) | 21.5 | 3.7 |
| Mid-Atlantic (NY, NJ, DE, PN) | 24.7 | 24.2 |
| New England | 5.2 | 4.1 |
| Mid-West (WS, MI, MN, IL, IN, OH, WV) | 15.2 | 9.4 |
| West of the Mississippi | 6.9 | 4.9 |
| Foreign country (asked in 1964 only) | 2.9 | — |
| Cuba (asked in 1984 only) | — | 13.0 |
| Other foreign country (asked in 1984 only) | — | 4.0 |

and diverse district are probably more representative of teachers working in large metropolitan districts and in states with heavy first-wave reform initiatives than of those in rural or small suburban districts in states without strong reform agendas. We have, however, checked our findings against other studies for which data were collected at about the same time over widely differing geographic regions (Duke, 1984; Freedman, Jackson & Boles, 1983; Gallup, 1984; Goodlad, 1984; Johnson, 1990; McNeil, 1986; Metropolitan Life, 1984, 1985a, 1985b, 1988; Rosenholtz, 1989) and found substantial similarity on most counts.

The final dimension of generalizability is time. The bald question is: Are data collected in 1984/85 "out of date"? This issue, as with Lortie's work, will only be resolved in the longer run. We, however, believe our data are "current" for several reasons. First, because our study occurred in Florida, a precocious state in educational reform, we caught the first wave of reforms that appeared in much of the rest of the country only several years later. Second, while second-wave reforms now receive attention in academic journals, most teachers today still work under state-generated first-wave reform legislation and mandates. A case in point is Dade County itself. There has been broad media coverage of the experiment in school-based management and shared decision-making in 30 schools and more recently of the single school run by an outside for-profit corporation. What goes relatively unrecognized is that, while some pilot schools are indeed under different governance patterns, the majority of teachers and schools in this large district have remained under a governance system not very different from the one in which our data are grounded. Further, a thorough review of school-based management efforts (Malen, Ogawa & Kranz, 1990) as well as recent reports on the Dade County experiment itself (Collins & Hanson, 1991; Morris, 1991) show limited results from this approach to reform.

## Analyses

We analyzed the survey data using standard statistical techniques appropriate for the particular kinds of measures, whether categorical or continuous. Most of the data reported here are comparisons of percentages. Inferential statistics were not generally reported because the N is so large that almost everything comes up statistically significant. We have concentrated on differences large enough to have practical significance beyond the mere statistical condition. Those reported in the book constitute a very small portion of the total statistical analyses run on our data. Although we have not reported all of the additional analyses, they are another part of the context that we have drawn upon in forming our overall argument. Some, but by no means all, of the additional survey analyses were reported in other papers authored by members of the research team.

Analyzing the interview data was more complex and infinitely more time-consuming. One method we used to simplify the process was to produce interview summaries of the 38 questions (and 4 optional questions) based upon broad categories. First, we grouped the questions under the following major headings:

| Topic | Questions |
|---|---|
| Demographics: | 1, 2 |
| Nature and Purpose of the Profession: | 3, 4, 5, 6, 8, 9, 10 13, 14, 15, 16, 30 |
| Rewards, Satisfactions, Dissatisfactions: | 7, 11, 12, 31, 32 |
| Extracurricular Activities: | 18, 19 |
| Collegiality and Authority: | 17, 21, 22, 23, 24, 25, 26 |
| Teaching in the 1980s: | 20, 27, 28, 29, 33, 34 |
| Career Reflections: | 35, 36, 37, 38, (39, 40, 41, 42) |

Next, we developed statements summarizing all responses to each of the questions within the category for each individual. Key quotations or the page numbers for significant ideas or quotations were noted. At the beginning of the summary, we wrote a brief impressionistic statement about the school setting in which the teacher worked from either conducting or reading the interview; at the end, we created a final statement of our overall impressions. As part of the final statement, we ranked teachers on a work-orientation continuum, with 1 being disaffected teachers and 10 being enthusiastic teachers. These summaries were particularly useful for initial identification of themes and for leading us to particular parts of the full interviews. When we needed specifics, we always found ourselves going back to the whole interview.

Using a pattern or theme approach, we either read "across" (i.e., read all responses to a single question in the summaries or full interviews) or read "down" (i.e., each summary or interview was read in its entirety). The strategy of searching across or down was dictated by the particular issue we were seeking to understand. Reading down was more difficult, as Lortie had warned us it would be. However, some issues, such as the discussion of different kinds of teachers in Chapter 6, could only be addressed in this manner, while the purposes and means in Chapter 2 were handled by analyzing across specific questions.

As we analyzed the interview data, wrote, and engaged in wide-ranging conversations, we came to value the certain messiness of these data. In the end, it was often the richness of the less-than-systematic portions of the open-ended responses in which we had followed teacher leads on issues that mattered to them that enabled us to discover major insights. It was often the authenticity of digressions—personal, concrete, and highly affect-laden vignettes—that led us by indirection into the region of teacher assumptions and theories-in-use that they could not state directly. It was when we reached this level that we really began to grasp the interpretive story that we then wove through the book, the story below the surface of direct teacher statements. It was only when we got to this depth that we could be faithful to teacher voices and yet say more than they could directly say themselves. By bringing the teachers' underlying assumptions and tacit knowledge to the surface, we believe that, on some dimensions, we have given voice to the teachers in a way in which they could not represent themselves.

## Interview Questions, Dade County Teachers, 1984

### Origins of the Decision to Become a Teacher

1. How old were you when you decided to become a teacher? What were the major attractions that teaching held for you at the point when you decided to enter the profession?

2. Did you seriously consider other occupations as career possibilities? If so, what and why did they attract you?

### Conception of the Teaching Profession

3. In what way is teaching different from what you expected when you made the decision to go into the field? How is it better or worse than you anticipated?

> Probe: Differences between your pre-teaching expectations and your early teaching experience. Then indicate changes between pre-teaching expectations and realities over course of career.

4. We hear a lot about teacher problems, but there are 2.1 million people working as teachers. What do you think attracts and holds people in public school teaching?

5. To be a good teacher requires both a knowledge base and certain skills and attitudes. What kind of knowledge do you think a teacher must possess—what does he/she have to know to be able to do a good job? What skills must he/she be able to do—to do a good job? What kind of attitudes must he/she exhibit?

### Conception of Self as Teacher

6. Please describe one of your own teachers whom you considered outstanding. Are there any teachers with whom you work or have worked that you consider outstanding? Would you describe one for me?

7. Now and then, teachers have a really good day. Could you tell me what a good day is like for you? What happens? What doesn't happen? Sometimes teachers have bad days. What happens on a bad day? How many bad days do you recall in the last two weeks?

8. What do you try most to achieve as a teacher? What are you really trying to do most of all?

9. How important is it for you to teach your particular grade

level or your particular subject? How painful would it be if you were required to change grade level or subject area?

10. What are the main ways you monitor how well you are teaching? Have your methods of self-assessment changed over time?

Probe: Student focus? Self-focus? Is it difficult to assess your teaching? If so, why is it difficult?

11. For you, what are the really important satisfactions that you receive from your work? Were any of these unexpected? Have the things that bring you satisfaction changed over time.? Has your level of satisfaction changed over time?

12. What are the things that you like least about teaching? the things that bother you most about your work? Have these changed over the course of your career?

13. What are your greatest strengths as a teacher? shortcomings?

14. What experiences have most influenced the way you teach? How have family and personal issues affected you over time?

15. Here are four descriptions of teachers. Which is most like you?

Card No. 1—Teaching Orientations

Teaching is a complex and subtle activity. We acknowledge that much of the complexity and subtlety is not captured in the simplified statements which follow. However, these statements do contain core indicators which differentiate among four general approaches to teaching.

Difficult as it is, please choose the paragraph which best describes your typical orientation to teaching. You may wish to indicate a secondary orientation if you feel that it is difficult to portray your teaching with only one of the descriptions.

Orientation # 1:

My primary goal is the production of high levels of academic achievement. I accomplish this through demanding hard work from students and instilling in them dedication to the learning tasks at hand. I maintain high expectations for the mastery of curriculum content. Learning is a serious, sometimes hard process. In my classroom there is a definite atmosphere of getting down to business and no nonsense.

Orientation #2:

My primary goal is to help students to learn to cope with the demands, both behavioral and curricular, of schooling as preparation for coping with the demands of life after leaving school. I want students to grow as individuals, but they also need to learn to play the game according to the rules so that they are prepared to take their place in the social order after leaving school.

Orientation #3:

My primary goal is to foster intellectual excitement and attainment and to develop a real love of learning among my students. I accomplish this by careful, frequently creative, development of interesting lessons which are appropriate for the students' abilities. I am attentive to student responses to my teaching and often make modifications in my lessons in order to achieve my broad goal. My classroom has a stimulating atmosphere.

Orientation #4:

My primary goal is the total development—intellectual, social, emotional—of each student. I pursue this through a combination of nurturing, pushing and supporting each student in individually appropriate ways. My approach to teaching requires a heavy investment of both personal and emotional energy. Students in my classroom are growing in varied ways because of my attention to their total development.

16. What kind of reputation do you have with your students? How has this reputation changed over the course of your career? Would you like to have a different reputation among students?

17. What kind of reputation do you have with your peers and principal? Has this changed over time?

18. Are you active in professional organizations and other activities associated with teaching? What specifically? Has your involvement in such activities changed over time?

Probe: Include union. Seek rewards received in activities.

19. What are your major interests and activities outside of teaching?

Probe: Second jobs, especially if it seems that more energy goes into the second job than into teaching; competing family issues.

## Working Conditions

20. Have the conditions of work changed over your career as a teacher?

Probe: How have these changes affected your work with students?

21. Whom do you turn to for instructional assistance and inspiration? Who provides you with emotional supports and "strokes?"

22. Who has the real power in your school? Who decides the important issues that affect what you do in the classroom? To whom are you accountable? How has your control over your own teaching changed over the course of your teaching career?

23. If you could imagine the ideal principal, what would you like that person to be like?

Probes: What would he/she do? What difference would that make to your teaching?

24. What about ____ [name of the school's principal] as a principal?

Probe: What do you think ____ tries to accomplish as a principal?

25. We've been talking about different approaches to education, different outcomes that people value for students. What do you think ____ [the principal's] view is about how education should take place?

Probes: What do you think that means?
Does ____ have any long-range goals for the school?
Has ____ had any influence on what you do in the classroom? Can you give me a specific example?

26. How much does ____ [the principal] know about what you are doing in the classroom? How does he/she know?

Probes: Does _____ visit your classroom?
Does _____ talk with you about your teaching?
Do you turn in lesson plans? What happens to them?
How is _____ involved in your professional develop-
ment (including but not limited to staff development)?

27. The principal is often not the only person at a school who acts as an instructional leader. Who else at your school does this? What do they do?

Probes: Is there a certain person or committee that you see about instructional issues (for example, for advice to obtain materials)?

28. In what ways, if any, have the values and attitudes of your students and their parents changed? If there have been major changes, how have they affected your approaches to curriculum, instruction and students?

29. Teachers have always been vulnerable to outside attacks, demands, and pressures. What conditions of the 80s, if any, make teachers especially vulnerable? What particular conditions render you powerless to protect yourself?

30. Teachers are being blamed today for lower test scores and a general level of "mediocrity" in the schools. How do you feel about these criticisms?

Probe: If mediocrity does, in fact, exist, what factors do you think contribute to it? What can be done about it?

31. Teacher education is also under attack today. Critics say that it fails to prepare teachers adequately. Were you prepared adequately? How do you think teachers should be trained at the preservice level? What should inservice training provide for experienced teachers and how should it be provided?

32. There is a lot of talk today about teacher incentives and rewards. If you could restructure an incentive and reward program for teachers, what would it look like? What kinds of incentives and rewards personally motivate you?

33. (If merit pay is discussed in Question No. 32, eliminate Question No. 33). As part of the incentive and rewards discussion, we hear a great deal about merit pay. What does merit pay mean to you, and how do you feel about it? If some form of merit pay were inevitable, how would you like to see it implemented? Do you see

the idea of merit pay as compatible with the fundamental nature of teaching as an occupation or with the sense of "mission" that many teachers have towards their work.

Probes: What could society do that would show a high regard and respect for teachers? Changes required? What could central office personnel and building principals do that would best show their high regard and respect for teachers?

34. Here is a list of major events and trends of the past two decades. Would you comment on whether or not each has directly influenced your work as a teacher? How?

Card No. 2—Major Events Trends (see Chapter 4 for list)

35. There are currently a number of specific proposals being made to improve education. Would you give me your views on the following recommendations?

Card No. 3—Proposals for Reform

Longer school day/year
More homework
More requirements for high school graduation
Core curriculum for everyone (humanities and
    science/math)—fewer electives
Focus on teaching students how to think
Greater emphasis on math/science/technology
Shared decision making between administrators and
    teachers
Increased opportunities to team plan and teach
Lighter loads/smaller classes
More adequate resources—books, equipment, labs, etc.

## Summarizing Questions

36. What have you gained or lost by being a teacher rather than being in some other occupation? If you could do it over again, would you still choose to be a teacher? If not, what other occupation would you choose?

37. Where do you hope to be professionally in 5 years? In 10 years?

38. What do you have to say to young people who are considering going into the teaching profession today? to first year teach-

ers? What suggestions do you have for attracting bright and committed people to teaching?

## Optional Questions

39. How would you respond if your daughter decided to be a teacher? your son?

40. If funding were provided, would you send your children to a public or private school?

41. Are there any comments you would like to make, given the purpose of our study as you understand it?

42. Are there any nagging questions about teaching that you would like to get answers for?

## Survey Questions, Dade County Teachers, 1984

Below are the questions from the 1984 survey to which direct reference is made in the text. (Those taken from Lortie's 1964 survey are marked with an asterisk.)

*1. Taking everything into account, I feel as follows about (a) my particular job and (b) my school as a workplace. (Circle one in each column.)

|  | With My Job | With My School |
|---|---|---|
| Very satisfied | 1 | 1 |
| Satisfied | 2 | 2 |
| More satisfied than not | 3 | 3 |
| Equally satisfied and dissatisfied | 4 | 4 |
| More dissatisfied than satisfied | 5 | 5 |
| Dissatisfied | 6 | 6 |
| Very dissatisfied | 7 | 7 |

2. Public school teachers are leaving the classroom in great numbers. Rank in order (1,2,3) the three main reasons why you think teachers are leaving their jobs? (Rank only three.)

|  | Why Teachers Are Leaving |
|---|---|
| Discipline problems in the schools | ____ |
| Low teacher salaries | ____ |
| Students are unmotivated/uninterested in school | ____ |

*Why Teachers*
*Are Leaving*

Frustration at being unable to achieve one's
  ideals as a teacher                                            ____
Parents don't support teachers                                   ____
A feeling of exhaustion or burn out                              ____
Low standing of teaching as a profession                         ____
Difficulty of advancement                                        ____
Greater job opportunities for women and minorities               ____
Outstanding teacher performance goes unrewarded                  ____


3. Would you like to have a child of yours take up teaching in the public schools as a career?

| | | |
|---|---|---|
| Yes | 1 |
| No | 2 |

*4. Which of the following things do you like best about teaching? (Circle one.)

The relative security of income and position                        1
The time (especially summer) which can permit
  travel, family activities, etc.                                   2
The opportunity it offers to earn a living without
  much rivalry and competition with other people                    3
Its special appropriateness for persons like myself                 4
None of these afford me satisfaction                                5

*5. Teachers can enjoy a variety of things in their work. Which of the following is the *most* important source of satisfaction for you? (Circle one.)

The opportunity teaching gives me to study, read,
  and plan for classes                                              1
The chance it offers to develop mastery of
  discipline and classroom management                               2
The times I know I have "reached" a student or
  group of students and they have learned                           3
The chance to associate with children or young
  people and to develop relationships with them                     4
The chance it gives me to associate with other
  teachers and educators                                            5
I receive no satisfaction from these                                6

*6. Although few would call school teachers a "privileged class," they do earn money, receive a certain level of respect from others, and do wield some influence. Of these three, from which do you receive the *most* satisfaction? (Circle one.)

| | |
|---|---|
| The salary I earn in my profession | 1 |
| The respect I receive from others | 2 |
| The opportunity to wield some influence | 3 |
| I receive no satisfaction at all from these things | 4 |

*7. Of the features grouped below, the following is most important to me: (Circle one.)

| | |
|---|---|
| The salary and respect received and the position of influence | 1 |
| The opportunities to study, plan, master classroom management, "reach" students, and associate with colleagues and children | 2 |
| The economic security, time, freedom from competition, and appropriateness for persons like me | 3 |

*8. Please indicate whether the following statements tend to be true or false of the principal with whom you work: (Circle either true or false for each statement.)

| | True | False |
|---|---|---|
| I can usually count on the principal to support me in my relationship with parents | 1 | 2 |
| I can usually count on my principal to appreciate my best efforts | 1 | 2 |
| My principal provides a sense of direction in the instruction given in the school | 1 | 2 |
| My principal seeks teacher input on decisions directly affecting curriculum or instruction | 1 | 2 |
| You could call my principal an effective administrator | 1 | 2 |
| I can usually count on my principal to provide me with the freedom to do a good job | 1 | 2 |
| The principal usually follows through on discipline problems that I bring to his or her attention | 1 | 2 |

*9. If I had to describe the emphasis in my teaching I would say . . . (Circle one.)

| | |
|---|---|
| I'm pretty much the "no-nonsense, get-the-learning-of-subject-matter-done" kind of teacher | 1 |
| I tend toward the subject matter emphasis, but think other things are important, too | 2 |
| I'm about 50/50 on this | 3 |
| I tend away from emphasis on subject matter, as I consider other things more important | 4 |
| I think that emphasis on subject matter is the mark of a poor teacher | 5 |

*10. If you could select your students next year, what would be your *first choice* among the following alternatives? Then, which group best describes your students this year? (Circle one in each column.)

| | Choice for Next Year | Current Students |
|---|---|---|
| Students whose emotional needs are a challenge to the teacher | 1 | 1 |
| "Nice kids," from average homes, who are respectful and hard-working | 2 | 2 |
| Creative and intellectually demanding students calling for special effort | 3 | 3 |
| Underprivileged students from difficult or deprived homes for whom school can be a major opportunity | 4 | 4 |
| Students of limited ability who need unusual patience and sympathy— sometimes they are called "slow learners" | 5 | 5 |

*11. Assume that you were in the position of having to decide the *single most important thing* that the school should do for: (a) younger students (K-6) and (b) older students (7-12). Which do you consider the single most important task to emphasize at each level? Finally, (c) which area is most emphasized in your school? (Circle only one in each column.)

| | *Most Important for Younger Students | Older Students | Most Emphasized in My School |
|---|---|---|---|
| The basic tools for acquiring and communicating knowledge—the Three Rs | 01 | 01 | 01 |
| Efficient *use* of the Three Rs— the basic tools for acquiring and accumulating knowledge | 02 | 02 | 02 |
| A continuing desire for knowledge—the inquiring mind | 03 | 03 | 03 |
| The ability to live and work with others | 04 | 04 | 04 |
| The habit of weighing facts and imaginatively applying them to the solution of problems | 05 | 05 | 05 |
| A sense of right and wrong—a moral standard of behavior | 06 | 06 | 06 |
| An understanding of government and a sense of civic responsibility | 07 | 07 | 07 |
| An emotionally stable person, prepared for life's realities | 08 | 08 | 08 |
| Loyalty to America and the American way of life | 09 | 09 | 09 |
| Information and guidance for a wise occupational choice | 10 | 10 | 10 |
| A well-cared-for, well-developed body | 11 | 11 | 11 |
| Other | 12 | 12 | 12 |

*12. Which of the following is the good teacher *most likely* to rely on as an indicator of the effectiveness of his or her teaching? (Circle one.)

| | |
|---|---|
| Reactions of other teachers familiar with their work and students | 1 |
| Opinions expressed by students generally | 2 |
| General observations of students in light of the teacher's conceptions of what should be learned | 3 |
| Assessments made by the principal | 4 |
| Assessments made by a "supervisor" or a similar person | 5 |
| Results of objective examinations and various other tests | 6 |
| Reactions of students' parents | 7 |
| Other | 8 |

13. Principals vary in their expectations of teachers. How much *emphasis* does your principal put on the following teacher behaviors?

| | Little ◄——► Much Emphasis Emphasis |
|---|---|
| Maintaining acceptable student behavior | 1 2 3 4 5 6 |
| Bringing the total class up to grade level | 1 2 3 4 5 6 |
| Nurturing the total development of each student | 1 2 3 4 5 6 |
| Holding high expectations for student academic performance | 1 2 3 4 5 6 |
| Helping students to accept the rules of the game | 1 2 3 4 5 6 |
| Meeting the total needs of each student | 1 2 3 4 5 6 |
| Maintaining an organized and disciplined classroom | 1 2 3 4 5 6 |
| Producing high levels of academic achievement | 1 2 3 4 5 6 |
| Providing security and support for student growth | 1 2 3 4 5 6 |
| Getting students to behave well in their role | 1 2 3 4 5 6 |

14. To what degree do you *disagree* or *agree* with the following?

|  | Strongly Disagree ◄──► Strongly Agree |
|---|---|
| Goals and priorities for this school are clear | 1 2 3 4 5 6 |
| I feel energetic about my work | 1 2 3 4 5 6 |
| The principal inspires teachers to work hard | 1 2 3 4 5 6 |
| I feel used up at the end of the work day | 1 2 3 4 5 6 |
| Teachers here trust the principal | 1 2 3 4 5 6 |
| The principal sees to it that teachers perform their tasks well | 1 2 3 4 5 6 |
| I find my job rewarding in other than monetary ways | 1 2 3 4 5 6 |
| I feel emotionally uplifted by my work | 1 2 3 4 5 6 |
| The principal works hard | 1 2 3 4 5 6 |
| I feel burned out from my work | 1 2 3 4 5 6 |

*15. What grade do you teach? (If you teach in more than one, please select the grade range in which you spend most of your teaching time.)

| | |
|---|---|
| Kindergarten, 1st, 2nd, or 3rd | 1 |
| 4th, 5th, or 6th | 2 |
| 7th, 8th, or 9th | 3 |
| 10th, 11th, or 12th | 4 |
| A grade range broader than those above | 5 |

*16. What is your teaching experience? (Circle one in each column.)

| | Years in Dade County Public Schools | Total Years in Teaching |
|---|---|---|
| 1 year or less | 1 | 1 |
| 2 to 5 years | 2 | 2 |
| 6 to 10 years | 3 | 3 |
| 11 to 15 years | 4 | 4 |
| 16 to 20 years | 5 | 5 |
| 21 to 25 years | 6 | 6 |
| 26 years or more | 7 | 7 |

*17. Sex:

|        |   |
|--------|---|
| Male   | 1 |
| Female | 2 |

*18. Are You . . . ?

|                          |   |
|--------------------------|---|
| White Non-Hispanic       | 1 |
| Black Non-Hispanic       | 2 |
| Hispanic                 | 3 |
| Asian American           | 4 |
| Native American (Indian) | 5 |

# Notes

## Chapter 1. Stability and Change in Today's Schools

1. Because Karen seemed, in so many ways, to reflect the most frequently expressed sentiments of the interview sample, we decided to use her thoughts as a unifying thread throughout the book. The content of her introductory "letters" corresponds to what she told us in two extended interviews, but the wording of some of her statements has been altered slightly to fit the letter format. Although she talked at some length during one interview about the fact that her mother was her best friend and role model, her mother's letter is fictional. That response, however, closely captures the experiences of Marilyn Cohn while teaching high school English during 1959-1961. Quotations from Karen also introduce each data chapter in Sections I and II. These sentiments are verbatim statements (except for minor editing) taken directly from the interview transcript.

2. The Reagan administration was responsible for a major shift in federal education policy, from the goal of equity to that of excellence and performance. At the same time, federal policy was focused on devolution of responsibility from federal to state and local educational agencies. (House, 1991)

3. Lewin (1947) analyzed the "equilibrium of change" in terms of driving and restraining forces, and Jenkins (1949) and others applied the idea of "force field analysis" to problems of school and classroom change. In some ways, the forces for change as we discuss them may be thought of as driving forces (factors which are pushing in a particular direction) and the forces of stability as restraining forces (walls and barriers which prevent movement). In other ways, the model seems too narrow and mechanical to capture the social and human dynamics we are describing.

4. In our description of the school as a stable organization, we have drawn heavily on Willower's (1990) succinct and useful account.

## Chapter 2. Teacher Purposes and Means

1. This chapter draws heavily upon Cohn and Kottkamp (1989) and Kottkamp, Provenzo and Cohn (1986b).

2. Each of the quotations from the interviews is identified with a number assigned to each interviewee, a letter for sex (Female, Male), and ethnicity (Black, Hispanic, White), an abbreviation for school grade-level (Elementary, Junior, Senior), and school socio-economic level (Low, Medium, High), and a designation for interviewee's teaching area. The basis for socio-economic designations is located in the Methodological Appendix. Some portions of the quotations may be unclear or grammatically incorrect because they are spontaneous comments rather than edited statements. In the interest of accuracy we presented them as they were transcribed from the tape, but they should not necessarily reflect negatively on the speaker.

3. TADS is the Teacher Assessment and Development System constructed for the Dade County Bureau of Staff Development in 1982, piloted in 1982/83, field-tested in 1983/84 and implemented district-wide in 1984/85. It contains seven categories of teacher performance measured by 21 key performance indicators using 81 specified teacher behaviors. The categories include: preparation and planning; knowledge of subject matter; classroom management; techniques of instruction; teacher-student relationships; assessment techniques; and professional responsibilities. The behavioral observation system is based on technical-rational assumptions about teaching and is used by the principal or designee at every grade level and in every subject area. The instrument is built on criteria from the teaching effectiveness literature. Its focus is on the events of a single lesson. Peterson and Comeaux (1990) found a positive correlation between teachers who gave positive evaluations to TADS and their scores on scales showing their agreement with teacher effectiveness assumptions and with textbook-based teaching. These findings reinforce the technical-rational nature of the instrument.

4. Lortie (1975) discussed differences in questions that result in generalized, ideological responses and those likely to penetrate through ideology to more specific and personal sentiments. He advanced four criteria for assessing questions used to probe teacher sentiments: "(1) indirect versus direct questions; (2) personal versus impersonal referents; (3) concrete versus abstract referents; (4) cathected [high-affect] versus low-affect issues" (p. 110). In each case the first criterion yields a less ideological response. Thus, indirect, personal, concrete, and high-affect questions should produce the most penetrating responses. The first set of questions is direct, personal, abstract, and low-affect. The second set is indirect, personal, concrete, and medium-to-high-affect. The third set is direct, personal, concrete, and high-affect.

5. The first step in analyzing these three questions was to record key phrases from each response to each interview question onto separate pages corresponding to four areas: knowledge, skills, attitudes, and qualities. The second step was grouping similar responses into clusters of similar dimensions of teaching and keeping tallies of the number of responses in each. The third step was to collect the codes from all three questions onto four sheets, one each for knowledge, skills, attitudes, and qualities. The final step was to combine both the four areas of knowledge, skills, attitudes, and qualities and the clusters of dimen-

sions onto a single sheet. In this step the identity of the individual questions disappeared, but the array and density of the dimensions of teaching for each of the four categories were clarified. The results of the final step are detailed in Table 2.4. Full detail on the various levels of analysis may be found in Cohn and Kottkamp (1989).

6. We did not formally define these three concepts for the interviewees but relied upon their own definitions in the context of our first question. In analyzing the responses, we coded cognitions as knowledge; behavioral patterns capable of being learned in some form of systematic training as skills; and emotionally or affectively based beliefs or opinions that indicate tendencies to act as attitudes.

7. The direct skill question elicited responses heavily concerned with pedagogical process and interpersonal relationship skills. The indirect questions concerning exemplary former teachers and peers elicited the lowest number of skills responses, but were coded heavily in subclusters concerning setting expectations for students, and motivating, inspiring, and stimulating them. Responses to the questions of their own strengths and shortcomings showed another pattern. The positive pole of strengths indicated a heavy emphasis on discipline and control, planning and organizing, and interpersonal skills, especially rapport with students. The responses to shortcomings were heavily tilted toward deficiencies in planning and organizing, including completing paperwork.
   What emerged from different skill responses to different questions is important. In the first and third questions, the viewpoint is the actor; in the second, the viewpoint is the recipient of action. When teachers are observers or recipients of instruction, they give much emphasis to skills in setting high expectations and motivating students, and appear to take for granted skills involving planning, interpersonal relationships, discipline, and organization that come to the fore when they are describing themselves as actors. It may be that in teachers' minds the expectational and motivational skills are what differentiate adequate and great performances. It may be that when motivational and expectational skills are powerfully exhibited, they overshadow or reduce the visibility of skills which, although necessary for successful instruction, do not alone lift teaching performance to the highest levels. Whatever the explanation related to different viewpoints encompassed by the questions, the overall picture is that teachers believe it takes much skill in the basic areas of planning, pedagogy, management, and interpersonal relations to achieve their purposes.

## Chapter 3. Rewards in Teaching

1. This chapter draws heavily on Cohn, Kottkamp, Provenzo and McCloskey (1989), Kottkamp, Provenzo and Cohn (1986b), and Provenzo, McCloskey, Cohn, Kottkamp and Proller (1987).

2. Like the letters that begin Chapter 1, these cases were developed from information in Dade County teacher interviews. We condensed responses and made slight alterations, but the essence of their stories has been maintained. The names are pseudonyms.

3. We are sensitive to the dated assumption in this phrase. Lortie has been criticized for such assumptions in reviews of his work.

4. An ANOVA run on a teacher-energy measure across three groups of teachers, those choosing extrinsic, ancillary, and psychic rewards as primary, was significant at $p<.05$. The psychic reward groups had the highest mean energy score. Primary reward choice explained 8% of the variance in teacher energy. This test provides rough support for the claim that psychic rewards are more highly related to teacher effort than other reward types.

5. The first three categories in Table 3.5 are quite parallel to those extrapolated by Plihal (1981) in her interview study of intrinsic rewards of teaching among 30 elementary teachers from the greater Chicago area.

6. This question meets all four criteria Lortie established for getting at the essence of teacher sentiments rather than ideological responses. It is indirect, personal, concrete, and high-affect.

7. Like the counterpart "good day" question, this one is personal, concrete, indirect, and high-affect. It was not asked in the Five Towns interview, but to gain a better overall understanding of rewards, we wanted to hear direct responses as to how teachers construed "bad" or low-reward days.

8. We describe here only the Florida Meritorious Teacher Program merit pay initiative, where competition was among individuals within schools and across the entire state. The predominant merit pay model has been one of individual competition, but in Florida there was, at the same time, the Quality Instruction Incentive Program, a school-level merit pay initiative. In the latter program, competition was among schools within counties. The assumptions underlying the programs were different, and teachers found themselves competing simultaneously against their colleagues on the individual level and with their colleagues against other schools at the school level. Teachers were generally more favorable toward the school-level program, although results were not available during our data collection. Both programs lasted only several years. More detail may be found in Provenzo, McCloskey, Cohn, Kottkamp, and Proller (1987) and Darling-Hammond and Berry (1988).

9. The generally negative attitudes reported here from the interviews were corroborated by survey questions probing attitudes toward merit pay. Further, individual responses were aggregated at the school level. In that analysis it was found that school factors such as perceptions of the principal or student achievement level explained little of the variance in attitudes toward merit pay (Kottkamp, Provenzo & Cohn, 1986a).

## Chapter 4. Changes in Students and Parents

1. This chapter draws heavily on Cohn, Kottkamp, McCloskey and Provenzo (1987).

2. In Lortie's (1975) categories for of interview questions, this one is direct, personal, abstract, and high-affect. Although directness and abstraction can produce ideology, the personal and high-affect dimensions generated emotional and genuine responses, as is evident from teacher quotations that follow.

3. As noted in the Methodological Appendix, we had no Black interviewers in this study. In this case, it may have been the interviewer rather than or as well as the principals that the Black respondents were concerned with when they refused to answer certain questions regarding their dissatisfactions. However, anonymous survey responses, for which the ethnic background of the researchers was less obtrusive, also indicated differences in feelings of vulnerability among the three major ethnic groups on a question concerning behavior beyond the classroom. The survey question was: "Educators sometimes complain they must be careful not to do things, publicly, which they themselves believe are acceptable but others might not." The responses ranged from, "I feel I must be very careful" to "I feel relatively little pressure to be careful." Lortie framed the question, but due to clerical error our statement of it in 1984 contained only four of the original five response categories. This problem renders comparison across the 1964-1984 time frame difficult. However, comparisons within each year show that Black teachers feel they must be more careful than white teachers. The 1984 data show that Hispanic teachers feel they must be more careful than white colleagues but slightly less careful than Black counterparts.

4. This question is direct, concrete, personal, and high-affect.

5. We have analyzed these responses in previous papers (Cohn, 1992; Kottkamp, 1990c; Kottkamp, Cohn, McCloskey & Provenzo, 1987; Kottkamp & Provenzo, 1988).

6. These categories are expressed in outdated terms rather than more contemporary labels like "emotionally disturbed," "gifted," or "learning disabled." Nonetheless, discussion at a professional meeting by teachers who had completed the 1984 survey indicated that they were still useful analytical categories that mirror colloquial categories teachers actually use in thinking about various students. In any case, it was necessary to maintain the original wording for comparability across the surveys of 1964 and 1984.

7. Although the hypothesis was consistently supported with statistical significance generated in T-tests, the proportion of variance accounted for in the analyses was very low, the maximum being 2.5%. Other statistical analyses (chi-squares using other categorical survey questions) did find further evidence of the congruence-incentive hypothesis.

8. Mitchell, Ortiz, and Mitchell's (1987) research is suggestive of the student-as-incentive hypothesis. Cusick's (1981) observations in two high schools yielded a model in which each teacher possessed two "fields." The first was an "interpersonal and egocentric set of forces from which the teacher created his or her approach to teaching and students." The second "was composed of a set of students—real students, past or present, for whom the teacher's particular approach worked" (p. 128).

Cusick then named various categories of students, some quite similar to those in Table 4.1. Teachers in Cusick's study were motivated to develop courses in which they could teach the way and the kinds of students they desired.

# Chapter 5. Competency-Based Education and Accountability

1. This chapter is heavily based on Cohn, Kottkamp, McCloskey, and Provenzo (1987) and McCloskey, Provenzo, Cohn, and Kottkamp (1987, 1991).

2. In making his "structural strain" argument, Lortie had available the first published results of the 20-year comparison of survey data from Dade County. He paid particular attention to data on teachers' experience, formal education, job and school satisfaction, rewards, and sources of help in curriculum and instruction (Kottkamp, Provenzo & Cohn, 1986b).

3. Although other questions elicited accountability responses, the following seven questions were the main sources of comments:

   • What happens on a bad day?
   • What are the things that you like least about teaching?
   • Have the conditions of your work changed over your career as a teacher?
   • Who has the real power in your school? Who decides the important issues that affect what you do in the classroom? To whom are you accountable? How has your control over your own teaching changed over the course of your teaching career?
   • Teachers have always been vulnerable to outside attacks, demands, and pressures. What conditions of the 80s, if any, make teachers especially vulnerable?
   • Teachers are being blamed today for lower test scores and a general level of "mediocrity" in the schools. How do you feel about these criticisms?
   • Here is a list of major events and trends of the past two decades. Would you comment on whether or not each has directly influenced your work as a teacher? (see Chapter 4 for list)

4. Rosenholtz (1989) demonstrated that teachers in schools characterized as having "moving" as opposed to "stuck" faculties (Kanter, 1968) were quick to say that they broke rules when district or state policies contradicted their best professional judgments.

5. For the survey question (not presented in this book) asking teachers what source they thought good teachers relied upon to ascertain the effectiveness of their teaching, there were important shifts in response over the 20 years. In 1964 the modal response, at 59%, was "general observations of students in light of the teacher's conception of what should be learned." By 1984, that response had fallen to 37%. The responses no longer based on self-assessment were distributed across

six different sources of external assessment (other teachers, students, principal, supervisor, exams, parents), each of which showed growth.

6. Wise summarized the significance of the Dade County paper in relation to his argument as follows:

> Gary McCloskey and his colleagues set out to test some of the assumptions that underlie education policies. They found a number of contradictions. They found that teachers questioned scientific management when the solutions it proposed had little correlation with the reality of classrooms. In the face of mandated performance criteria for all students, teachers reported lacking autonomy to deal with variation in student ability and accomplishment. Teachers realized that the demands of increased compliance would never lead to their being recognized as professionals. Teachers also found that the demand that they systematize their work distracted them from the primary tasks of teaching. Moreover, teachers objected to standardized curricula and standardized methods of evaluating teachers and students because they did not match the heterogeneity of classrooms. Teachers believed that efforts to regulate educational quality through the enforcement of uniform standards actually reduced quality by preventing teachers from accommodating differences among students. (Wise, 1988, p. 330)

7. See Schon (1983, 1987) for a different view. He argued that a strong technical or professional culture can never do away with the indeterminacy of problems of practice.

8. Organizational and personal change may be divided into two generic categories: "first-order" and "second-order" (Argyris & Schon, 1974). Cuban (1988) cited Watzlawick, Weakland, and Fisch (1974) as the source for the two-part conception of change. First-order changes have been called "additive reforms." In our terms, educational second-order change entails redesigning teacher education, the basic underlying structure of schooling, and the larger educational system, which we have called "the world of the more or less invisible" (Cohn, Kottkamp & Provenzo, 1987). Plank and Ginsberg (1990) noted that what they termed "structural reform" others have called "system-changing reform" and "institutional reform," as well as "second-order reform."

Argyris and Schon (1974) argued that there is no inherent value hierarchy between the two orders of change in and of themselves, while Cuban (1988) argued that change, whether first- or second-order, is not the same as "progress," a valuation attached by the beholder. Sarason (1990), however, argued strongly that unless they bring second-order changes, contemporary educational reforms are doomed to failure.

# Chapter 6. A Teacher Is Not a Teacher Is Not a Teacher

1. This chapter is heavily based on Cohn, Kottkamp, Provenzo, and McCloskey (1986), and Cohn and Kottkamp (1989).

2. Lortie collected his data in such a way that neither he nor we, in secondary analyses, could construct school-level data sets for school-level analyses of the 1964 data. In contrast, we collected data to perform both individual and school-level analyses. However, we were unable to conduct comparative school-level analyses over the 1964-1984 period.

3. "Disillusioned" was the concept we associated first with the disaffected teachers as a whole. This term is actually more appropriate for the subset of three young teachers. They had illusions about what it meant to be a teacher that were not grounded in reality. Becoming disillusioned or freeing themselves from their illusions was part of their process of becoming disaffected.

4. These findings are somewhat parallel to those of Rosenholtz (1989). In her Tennessee study, Rosenholtz found elementary schools whose faculties bore some resemblance to the teachers in both our enthusiastic and our disaffected subsets. She applied Kanter's (1968) organizational concepts of "stuck" and "moving" to these schools. In "stuck" schools, teachers feel "no sense of progress, growth, or development and so tend to lower their aspirations and appear less motivated to achieve" (p. 149). On the other hand, teachers in "moving" schools reveal a sense of progress and future gain, which encourages them "to look forward, to take risks, and to grow." Rosenholtz's approach assumes that the school unit is the most powerful influence on teachers. By contrast, we assume that both school- and individual-level factors contribute to being stuck or moving, disaffected or enthusiastic. Sederberg and Clark (1990), in a study of "high-vitality" teachers who bear some resemblance to our enthusiastic subset, also suggested such a dual attribution of influence when they asked teachers to discuss what personal factors drive them and what incentives from the school organization encourage them to put forth effort for high performance.

5. We have explored the relationship between systematic variation in school characteristics and the presence of enthusiastic and disaffected teachers (Cohn & Kottkamp, 1991) and we provide a sketch of the results here. Cluster analyses were performed using the school-level data set. Variables included for analysis were: student achievement, teacher engagement, principal engagement, and proportion of students in each ethnic group (Black, white, Hispanic) in a given school in relation to the proportion of that group in the whole district. Each school was categorized in one of the eight clusters. The seventy-three interviews were then coded on a scale of 1 to 10; enthusiastic teachers were scored 1 and disaffected teachers, 10. The coding was based on the attributes of the two polar categories described in this chapter.

The seventy-three interviewees were then allocated to the clusters to which their schools belonged. We compared the teacher-engagement scores taken from the survey responses for each cluster with the average scores of the coded interviewees in that cluster and with their proportion of enthusiastic and disaffected teachers. There was a clear pattern of correspondence between the survey measures and the codings of the interviews. While the numbers of interviewees are too low for any definitive claims, there does seem to be a pattern of school influence on teacher orientation which transcends simple individual variation. We conclude, as have others, that school influence is powerful, but individual variation makes an important difference as well.

6. Robert Kottkamp chaired four dissertations based on the Dade County principal/school level data set. Michael Derczo (1987), Beverly Hetrick (1989), and Martha Pocsi (1987) were integrally involved in constructing and conducting the principal survey. Derczo also co-developed an expectancy motivation measure for principals (Kottkamp & Derczo, 1986). David Church (1990) performed a secondary analysis of the data. Taken together, these dissertations confirmed some general findings in the literature: The principal is influenced by the community context; the principal's personal attributes and leadership orientation have a wide-ranging set of effects on the school, teachers, and students; and the sex of the principal is related to important school variables.

7. There even exist methods designed to identify and develop some of these characteristics. deCharms (1968), for example, has developed measures of "origin" behavior and a training program to increase the "origin" behavior of experienced teachers. Selection Research Incorporated (SRI) has developed interview schedules used as diagnostic tools to identify patterns of belief related to one's capacity for behaviors characterized by "mission," "investment," and "assertiveness" (Golias, 1982). Such measures, however, are only initial forays into the role of teacher attitudes, beliefs, and values.

## Chapter 7. Interpreting the Voices of Teachers

1. Examples of school reforms initiated by concerns external to the schools include the Common School Movement, school reforms of the Progressive Era, desegregation, and curricular reform in response to Sputnik.

2. The first-wave reforms of the 1980s differ from other fairly recent constructed changes and attempts to improve schools in the pervasiveness of their impact on teachers and in the strength of the political coalition supporting them. Various earlier federal educational initiatives, such as the Elementary and Secondary Education Act and the All-Handicapped Children Act (Public Law 94-142) were targeted at specific groups such as children from low-income families or handicapped children and their teachers, and were supported by much more narrowly drawn coalitions. The state-level reforms simply had more penetrating across-the-board effect on teachers than did some of the earlier federal improvement efforts.

3. While we draw upon several sources for reframing, we have by no means exhausted the possibilities. Feminist and critical theory, for example, could also be applied. We might also have taken the perspectives of other role groups such as students, administrators, or parents. However, our story and perspective is that of teachers as a whole.

4. We are aware of the complexity of the autonomy/control issue and are not arguing for complete individual autonomy. Shulman, for example, argued that such freedom to act may be used to advance the interests of the greater society or "merely serve to shield the practitioner's expedient exercise of providing privilege to the powerful" (1983, p. 500).

Such potential conflicts are legion. However, when protection against the potential misuse of autonomy in the form of controls becomes too tight, the controls themselves become dysfunctional in achieving espoused goals; this circumstance was illustrated at length in Chapter 5.

5. It is possible and desirable to provide students with learning activities so motivating and engaging that the behavioral control element is embedded in the learning itself rather than a separate precondition to be established. Chapter 8 addresses issues of motivation and engagement in learning activities.

6. One partial image of how such a stripping away might look comes from extracurricular activities. These often occur under informal conditions with high student motivation and intense engagement, and teachers serving as coaches and mentors. The behavioral and custody-control functions are not absent, but they are relaxed. Learning often takes place even in noisy circumstances. Further, some studies have shown that participation in service-oriented extracurricular activities is actually a more powerful predictor of college completion and other outcomes than grade-point average (Spady, 1971).

7. Cuban (1984) found that the small group of teachers who broke out of the teacher-centered instructional mode were concentrated at the elementary school level. He argued that at this level the external pressures were less and that larger blocks of time were available for teachers to use for different teaching modes. Our data suggest an important change in this historical pattern of greater possibility of deviation from the teacher-centered model at the elementary level. In Florida, the external curricular and time controls came earlier and more forcefully at the elementary level. In Chapter 6, we demonstrated a relationship between the disaffected teacher group and elementary school teaching. We see a major increase in control at the elementary level and a corresponding decline in the ability of teachers to cope with their work.

8. This appears to be a teacher-initiated version of a "treaty," "contract," or "bargain" (Powell, Farrar & Cohen, 1985; Sedlack, Wheeler, Pullin & Cusick, 1986; Smith & Geoffrey, 1968).

## Chapter 8. Learning as Meaningful Interaction

1. As Wiggins (1989) discussed "authentic" assessment, he described performances or products to be designed at the school or district level to fit a locally developed curriculum. We have advocated such an approach as one alternative to the current heavy reliance on standardized tests as measures of academic achievement. Although we have little confidence in state or national tests as a means of assessing the type of meaningful learning we have proposed, it is conceivable that at these broader levels there could be "guidelines" for authentic tasks and outcomes or meaningful standards. Our point is not to take a position on whether assessment should be designed at the local, state, or national level, but to assert the importance of creating a curriculum that both teachers and students see as purposeful and then assessing the learning in ways that fit the purposes.

## Chapter 10. Getting Started Through Inquiry-Oriented Schools

1. For amplification of these issues, see Osterman and Kottkamp (1993), *Reflective Practice for Educators: Improving Schools through Professional Development.*

2. The real difficulty teachers have with accepting the legitimacy of action research as a means to understand and improve their practice is an object lesson in how unrecognized assumptions guide thought and behavior. Teachers and most other individuals are socialized to believe that the dominant research paradigm, positivism, "is research." To take this position does not require any valid understanding of the paradigm. The lay person simply "knows" that research is done by having "scientists," or at least someone from the university, put something under the "microscope" in order to study it, which, of course, involves statistics and other mysteries not available to the common person. Teachers in action research projects must literally confront these assumptions and the way they structure their thinking before they may engage in the work of studying and improving their professional practices.

3. This is a close paraphrase of a statement Goodlad made during a presentation at a conference in St. Louis in 1991.

4. We are well aware that the type of school reform we are proposing cannot occur without corresponding reform in pre-service teacher education. While we have discussed throughout how the current approach to teacher education and occupational socialization fosters stability and constrains change, we have not analyzed the problems of teacher education or made any major proposals for change in this realm. The omission was based on our belief that the subject required an in-depth treatment beyond the scope of this book.

# Bibliography

Allard, J., & Fish, J. (1990). Standardized tests as symbolic improvement: Policymakers' assumptions versus testing-environment realities. *Urban Education, 25*(3), 326-349.

Altbach, P. G., Kelly, G. P., & Weis, L. (1985). *Excellence in education.* Buffalo, NY: Prometheus Books.

American Association of Colleges for Teacher Education (AACTE). (1985). *Educating a profession.* Washington, DC: Author.

American Association of Colleges for Teacher Education (AACTE). (1987). *Teaching teachers: Facts and figures.* Washington, DC: Author.

Ames, C., & Ames, R. E. (Eds.). (1985). *Research on motivation in education (Vol. 2): The classroom milieu.* Orlando, FL: Academic Press.

Apple, M. W. (1982). *Education and power: Reproduction and contradiction in education.* Boston: Routledge & Kegan Paul.

Apple, M. W. (1986). *Teachers and texts: A political economy of class and gender relations in education.* Boston: Routledge & Kegan Paul.

Argyris, C., & Schon, D. A. (1974). *Theory in practice: Increasing professional effectiveness.* San Francisco: Jossey-Bass.

Argyris, C., & Schon, D. A. (1978). *Organizational learning: A theory-in-action perspective.* Reading, MA: Addison-Wesley.

Arthur, G. F. K., & Milton, S. (1991). The Florida Teacher Incentive Program: A policy analysis. *Educational Policy, 5*(3), 266-278.

Ashton, P. T., & Webb, R. B. (1986). *Making a difference: Teachers' sense of efficacy and student achievement.* New York: Longman.

325

Ausubel, D. P. (1969). *Readings in school learning.* New York: Holt, Rinehart & Winston.

Baldridge, V., & Deal, T. (Eds.). (1975). *Managing change in educational organizations: Sociological perspectives, strategies, and case studies.* Berkeley, CA: McCutchan.

Berlak, A., & Berlak, H. (1981). *Dilemmas of schooling.* New York: Methuen.

Beyer, K. (1991a). *Experiential learning and alternative assessment: A focus on problem-solving curriculum.* Unpublished manuscript. Washington University, St. Louis, MO.

Beyer, K. (1991b). *Experiencing change in perspectives of power and power relationships.* Unpublished manuscript. Washington University, St. Louis, MO.

Bidwell, C. E. (1965). The school as a formal organization. In J. G. March (Ed.), *Handbook of organizations* (pp. 972-1020). Chicago: Rand McNally.

Bolman, L. G., & Deal, T. E. (1984). *Modern approaches to understanding and managing organizations.* San Francisco: Jossey-Bass.

Bolman, L. G., & Deal, T. E. (1991). *Reframing organizations: Artistry, choice, and leadership.* San Francisco: Jossey-Bass.

Bossert, S. T., Dwyer, D. C., Rowan, B., & Lee, G. (1982). Effective schools: A qualitative synthesis of constructs. *Educational Administration Quarterly, 18*(3), 12-33.

Bouton, T. A. (1990). *Problem finding: A case study of the origins of reform policy in New York State.* Unpublished doctoral dissertation, Hofstra University.

Boyer, E. L. (1983). *High school: A report on secondary education in America.* New York: Harper and Row.

Boyer, E. L. (1988). *The conditions of teaching: A state-by-state analysis, 1988.* Princeton, NJ: Carnegie Foundation.

Bruner, J. (1963). *The process of education.* New York: Vintage Books.

Bruner, J. (1966). *Toward a theory of instruction.* Cambridge, MA: Harvard University Press.

Burke, K. (1935) *Permanence and change.* Los Altos, CA: Hermes.

Bush, G. (1991). *America 2000: An education strategy.* Washington, DC: U.S. Department of Education.

Callahan, R. E. (1962). *Education and the cult of efficiency.* Chicago: University of Chicago Press.

Callahan, R. E. & Button, H. W. (1964). Historical change in the role of the man in the organization. 1865-1950. In D. E. Griffiths (Ed.), *Behavioral science and educational administration: The 63rd yearbook of the National Society for the Study of Education, Part II* (pp. 73-92). Chicago: National Society for the Study of Education.

Carlson, R. O. (1964). Environmental constraints and organizational consequences: The public school and its clients. In D. E. Griffiths (Ed.), *Behavioral science and educational administration: The 63rd yearbook of the National Society for the Study of Education, Part II* (pp. 262-276). Chicago: National Society for the Study of Education.

Carnegie Forum on Education and the Economy. (1986). *A nation prepared: Teachers for the 21st century.* New York: Author.

Carter, S. B. (1989). Incentives and rewards in teaching. In D. Warren, (Ed.), *American teachers: Histories of a profession at work* (pp. 49-62). New York: Macmillan.

Cherlin, A. J. (1981). *Marriage, divorce, remarriage.* Cambridge, MA: Harvard University Press.

Chubb, J. E. (1988). Why the current wave of school reform will fail. *Public Interest, 90,* 28-29.

Church, D. A. (1990). *The relationship between principals' ambiguity tolerance and measures of school effectiveness.* Unpublished doctoral dissertation, Hofstra University, Hempstead, NY.

Cohn, M. M. (1982). *ThinkAbout: Teacher use and student response in three classrooms: Volume 2, research on the introduction, use, and impact of the ThinkAbout instructional television series.* Bloomington, IN: Agency for Instructional Television.

Cohn, M. M. (1992). How teachers perceive teaching: Change over two decades 1964-1984. In A. Lieberman (Ed.), *The changing context of teaching: The 91st yearbook of the Society for the Study of Education, Part I* (pp. 110-137). Chicago: National Society for the Study of Education.

Cohn, M. M., & Finch, M. E. (1987). *Teacher leadership and collaboration: Key concepts and issues in school change.* Paper presented at the annual meeting of the American Educational Research Association, Washington, DC.

Cohn, M. M., & Finch, M. E. (1989). *The Danforth Improvement of Instruction Project: Case studies of collaborative school-based change.* St. Louis: The Danforth Foundation.

Cohn, M. M., & Gellman. V. (1988). *Increasing teacher leadership and collaboration in schools: Themes from nine case studies.* Paper presented at the annual meeting of the American Educational Research Association, New Orleans.

Cohn, M. M., & Kottkamp, R. B. (1989). *The interrelationship of research, theory, and practice in teaching/teacher education: Insights from interviews with teachers.* Paper presented at the annual meeting of the American Educational Research Association, San Francisco.

Cohn, M. M., & Kottkamp, R. B. (1991). *The challenge of change and the constraint of stability: The teachers' story.* Unpublished manuscript, Washington University, St. Louis.

Cohn, M. M., Kottkamp, R. B., McCloskey, G. N., & Provenzo, E. F., Jr. (1987). *Teachers' perspectives on the problems of their profession: Implications for policymakers and practitioners* (Contract No. ERI-P-86-3090). Washington, DC: U. S. Department of Education, Office of Educational Research and Improvement. (ERIC Document Reproduction Service No. ED 286 828.)

Cohn, M. M., Kottkamp, R. B, & Provenzo, E. F., Jr. (1987). *To be a teacher: Cases, concepts, observation guides.* New York: Random House.

Cohn, M. M., Kottkamp, R. B., Provenzo, E. F., Jr., & McCloskey, G. N. (1986). *Teachers who remain enthusiastic in mid-career: Patterns of thought and action.* Paper presented at the annual meeting of the American Educational Research Association, San Francisco.

Cohn, M. M., Kottkamp, R. B., Provenzo, E. F., Jr., & McCloskey, G. N. (1989). *Merit pay: Why teachers reject a business approach to educational problems.* Unpublished manuscript. Washington University, St. Louis.

Cohn, M. M., & Lenz, O. V. (1990). *A systemic approach to school improvement: An inside/outside look at the vertical team concept as a vehicle for change.* Paper presented at the annual meeting of the American Educational Research Association, Boston.

Cohn, M. M., McCloskey, G. N., Kottkamp, R. B., & Provenzo, E. F., Jr. (1988). *Teachers' perspectives on their interpersonal relationships in school: A focus on peers and principals.* Paper presented at the annual meeting of the American Educational Research Association, New Orleans.

Coleman, J. S., & Hoffer, T. (1987). *Public and private high schools: The impact of communities.* New York: Basic Books.

Collins, R. A., & Hanson, M. K. (1991). *Summative evaluation report: School-based-management/shared-decision-making project, 1987-88 through 1989-90.* Miami: Dade County Public Schools, Office of Educational Accountability.

Coombs, F. S. (1987). *The effects of increased state control on local school district governance.* Paper presented at the annual meeting of the American Educational Research Association, Washington, DC.

Cremin, L. (1961). *The transformation of the school.* New York: Vintage.

Cuban, L. (1984). *How teachers taught: Constancy and change in American classrooms, 1890-1980.* New York: Longman.

Cuban, L. (1988). The fundamental puzzle of school reform. *Phi Delta Kappan, 69*(5), 340-344.

Cuban, L. (1989). The persistence of reform in American schools. In D. Warren (Ed.), *American teachers: Histories of a profession at work* (pp. 370-392). New York: Macmillan.

Cusick, P. A. (1973). *Inside high school.* New York: Hope.

Cusick, P. A. (1981). A study of networks among professional staffs in secondary schools. *Educational Administration Quarterly, 17*(3), 114-138.

Cusick, P. A. (1992). *The educational system.* New York: McGraw-Hill.

Dade County Public Schools. (1985). *District and school profiles, 1984-85.* Miami: Office of Educational Accountability.

Darling-Hammond, L. (1984). *Beyond the commission reports: The coming crisis in teaching* (Report No. R-3177-RC). Santa Monica, CA: Rand.

Darling-Hammond, L., & Berry, B. (1988). *The evolution of teacher policy* (Report No. JRE-01). Santa Monica, CA: Rand.

Deal, T. E., & Celotti, L. (1980). How much influence do (and can) educational administrators have on classrooms? *Phi Delta Kappan, 61*, 471-473.

deCharms, R. (1968). *Personal causation: The internal affective determinants of behavior.* New York: Academic Press.

Deci, E. L. (1975). *Intrinsic motivation.* New York: Plenum.

Deci, E. L., & Ryan, R. M. (1985). *Intrinsic motivation and self determination in human behavior.* New York: Plenum.

Dennison, G. (1969). *The lives of children.* New York: Random House.

Derczo, M. T. (1987). *Effective school leadership: A test of an adapted model from a study of principals and teachers of Dade County, Florida, schools.* Unpublished doctoral dissertation, Rutgers University, New Brunswick, NJ.

Devaney, K., & Sykes, G. (1988). Making the case for professionalism. In A. Lieberman (Ed.), *Building a professional culture in schools* (pp. 3-22). New York: Teachers College Press.

Dewey, J. (1956). *The child and the curriculum.* Chicago: University of Chicago Press.

Dreeben, R. (1973). The school as a workplace. In R. M. W. Travers (Ed.), *Second handbook of research in teaching* (pp. 450-473). Chicago: Rand McNally.

Dreeben, R., & Barr, R. (1983). Educational policy and the working of schools. In L. S. Shulman & G. Sykes (Eds.), *Handbook of teaching and policy* (pp. 81-94). New York: Longman.

Duke, D. L. (1984). *Teaching—the imperiled profession.* Albany: State University of New York Press.

Dwyer, D. C., Lee, G. V., Barnett, B. G., Filby, N. N., & Rowan, B. (1985). *Understanding the principal's contribution to instruction: Seven principals, seven stories: Methodology.* San Francisco: Far West Laboratory.

Edmonds, R. (1979). Some schools work and more can. *Social Policy, 9*(5), 28-33.

Elam, S. M. (1989). The second Gallup Poll of teachers' attitudes toward the public schools. *Phi Delta Kappan, 71*, 785-798.

Elkind, D. (1989). Developmentally appropriate practice: Philosophical and practical applications. *Phi Delta Kappan, 71,* 113-117.

Elliott, H. J. (1978). *What is action research?* Paper presented at CARN (Classroom Action Research Network) Conference, Cambridge, England.

Elliott, H. J. (1988). *Teachers as researchers: Implications for supervision and teacher education.* Paper presented at the annual meeting of the American Educational Research Association, New Orleans.

Ellwein, M. C., Glass, G. V., & Smith, M. L. (1988). Standards of competence: Propositions on the nature of testing reform. *Educational Researcher, 17*(8), 4-9.

Etzioni, A. (1964). *Modern organizations.* Englewood Cliffs, NJ: Prentice-Hall.

Etzioni, A. (Ed.). (1969). *The semi-professions and their organization: Teachers, nurses, social workers.* New York: Free Press.

Firestone, W. A. (1990). Continuity and incrementalism after all: State responses to the excellence movement. In J. Murphy (Ed.), *The educational reform movements of the 1980s: Perspectives and Cases* (pp. 143-166). Berkeley, CA: McCutchan.

Firestone, W. A., & Corbett, H. D. (1988). Planned organizational change. In N. J. Boyan (Ed.), *Handbook of research on educational administration* (pp. 321-340). New York: Longman.

Freedman, S., Jackson, J., & Boles, K. (1983). Teaching: An imperilled "profession." In L. S. Shulman & G. Sykes (Eds.), *Handbook of teaching and policy* (pp. 261-299). New York: Longman.

Freire, P. (1974). *Education for critical consciousness.* New York: Seabury.

Fritz, R. (1989). *The path of least resistance.* New York: Ballantine.

Fritz, R. (1990). *Creating.* New York: Ballantine.

Fullan, M. (1982). *The meaning of educational change.* New York: Teachers College Press.

Gagne, R. (1968). Contributions of learning to child development. *Psychological Review, 75,* 177-191.

Gallup, A. (1984). The Gallup Poll of teachers' attitudes toward the public school. *Phi Delta Kappan, 66,* 97-107.

Gallup, A. (1986). The 18th annual Gallup Poll of the public's attitudes toward the public schools. *Phi Delta Kappan, 68,* 43-59.

Gallup, G. (1978). *A decade of Gallup Polls of attitudes toward education.* Bloomington, IN: Phi Delta Kappa.

Gamoran, A., & Berends, M. (1987). The effects of stratification in secondary schools: Synthesis of survey and ethnographic research. *Review of Educational Research, 57,* 415-435.

Gardner, H. (1983). *Frames of mind.* New York: Basic Books.

Gardner, H., & Hatch, T. (1990). Multiple intelligences go to school: Educational implications of the theory of multiple intelligences. Technical Report No. 4, Center for Technology in Education, New York.

Glaser, R. (1988). Cognitive science in education. In B. Blackwell (Ed.), *Cognitive Science: Education, language, representation, artificial intelligence, neurosciences.* UNESCO.

Golias, Sr. D. (1982). Predicting and developing teacher aptitude in preservice teachers. Report for Selection Research, Inc., Symposium, October 7, 1982.

Goodlad, J. I. (1984). *A place called school: Prospects for the future.* New York: McGraw-Hill.

Goodlad, J. I. (1991). *Teachers for our nation's schools.* San Francisco: Jossey-Bass.

Gross, N., Giacquinta, J. B., & Bernstein, M. (1971). *Implementing organizational innovations.* New York: Basic Books.

Haladyna, T. M., Nolan, S. B., & Hass, N. S. (1991). Raising standardized achievement test scores and the origins of test score pollution. *Educational Researcher, 20*(5), 2-7.

Henry, J. (1963). *Culture against man.* New York: Vintage.

Herzberg, F., Mausner, B., & Snyderman, B. (1959). *The motivation to work.* New York: Wiley.

Hetrick, B. (1989). *Contingencies affecting principals' management behavior and goal setting.* Unpublished doctoral dissertation, Rutgers University, New Brunswick, NJ.

Hirsch, E. D. (1987). *Cultural literacy: What Americans need to know.* Boston: Houghton Mifflin.

Hoetker, J., & Ahlbrand, W. P., Jr. (1969). The persistence of the recitation. *American Educational Research Journal, 6*, 145-167.

Holmes Group. (1986). *Tomorrow's teachers.* East Lansing, MI.

Holmes Group. (1990). *Tomorrow's schools: Principles for the professional development schools.* East Lansing, MI.

House, E. R. (1991). Big policy, little policy. *Educational Researcher, 20*(5), 21-26.

Hoy, W. K., & Miskel, C. G. (1987). *Educational administration: Theory, research, and practice* (3rd ed.). New York: Random House.

Hoy, W. K., Tartar, C. J., & Kottkamp, R. B. (1991). *Open schools/healthy schools: Measuring organizational climate.* Newbury Park, CA: Sage.

Hudgins, B. B. (1971). *The instructional process.* Chicago: Rand McNally.

Illich, I. (1971). *Deschooling society.* New York: Harper & Row.

Jackson, P. (1968). *Life in classrooms.* New York: Holt, Rinehart & Winston.

Jenkins, D. H. (1949). Social engineering in educational change: An outline of method. *Progressive Education, 26* (7), 193-197.

Johnson, S. M. (1984). Merit pay for teachers: A poor prescription for reform. *Harvard Educational Review, 54*, 175-185.

Johnson, S. M. (1990). *Teachers at work: Achieving success in our schools.* New York: Basic Books.

Joyce, B., & Weil, M. (1972). *Perspectives for reform in teacher education.* Englewood Cliffs, NJ: Prentice-Hall.

Kanter, R. M. (1968). Commitment and social organization: A study of commitment mechanisms in utopian communities. *American Sociological Review, 33*, 499-517.

Kennedy, M. M. (1991). *An agenda for research on teacher learning.* East Lansing, MI: National Center for Research on Teacher Learning, Michigan State University.

Kerlinger, F. N., & Pedhazur, E. J. (1968). Educational attitudes and perceptions of desirable traits of teachers. *American Educational Research Journal, 5*, 543-560.

Kohl, H. (1967). *36 children.* New York: New American Library.

Kottkamp, R. B. (1982). The administrative platform in administrative preparation. *Planning and Changing, 13*(2), 82-92.

Kottkamp, R. B. (1984). The principal as cultural leader. *Planning
and Changing, 15*(3), 152-160.

Kottkamp, R. B. (1990a). *The administrative platform as a means of
reflection: A ten-year assessment.* Paper presented at the annual
meeting of the American Educational Research Association,
Boston.

Kottkamp, R. B. (1990b). Means for facilitating reflection. *Education in Urban Society, 22*(2), 182-203.

Kottkamp, R. B. (1990c). Teacher attitudes about work. In P. Reyes
(Ed.). *Teachers and their workplace: Commitment, performance,
and productivity* (pp. 86-114). Newbury Park, CA: Sage.

Kottkamp, R. B., Cohn, M. M., McCloskey, G. N., & Provenzo, E. F.,
Jr. (1987). *Teacher ethnicity: Relationships with teaching rewards
and incentives* (Contract No. ERI-P-86-3091). Washington, DC:
U.S. Department of Education, Office of Educational Research
and Improvement. (ERIC Document Reproduction Service No.
ED 298 078.)

Kottkamp, R. B., Cohn, M. M., & Provenzo, E. F., Jr. (1986). *Shifting
classroom investments among mid-career teachers: Exploratory
cases and evolving questions.* Paper presented at the annual
meeting of the American Educational Research Association,
San Francisco.

Kottkamp, R. B., & Derczo, M. T. (1986). Expectancy motivation
scales for school principals: Development and validity tests.
*Educational and Psychological Measurement, 46*, 425-432.

Kottkamp, R. B., & Provenzo, E. F., Jr. (1988). *Black and white teachers: Patterns of similarity and difference over twenty years.* Paper
presented at the annual meeting of the American Educational
Research Association, New Orleans.

Kottkamp, R. B., Provenzo, E. F., Jr., & Cohn. M. M. (1986a). *Individual and school-level predictors of teacher attitudes toward merit
pay.* Paper presented at the meeting of the Eastern Educational
Research Association, Miami Beach.

Kottkamp, R. B., Provenzo, E. F., Jr., & Cohn. M. M. (1986b). Stability and change in a profession: Two decades of teacher attitudes, 1964-1984. *Phi Delta Kappan, 67*, 559-567.

Kozol, J. (1967). *Death at an early age.* Boston: Houghton Mifflin.

Lareau, A. (1986). *Perspectives on parents: A view from the classroom.* Paper presented at the annual meeting of the American Educational Research Association, San Francisco.

Larkin, J. H., & Chabay, R. W. (1989). Research on teaching scientific thinking: Implications for computer-based instruction. In L. B. Resnick & L. E. Klopfer (Eds.), *Toward the thinking curriculum: Current cognitive research* (pp. 150-172). Alexandria, VA: Association for Supervision and Curriculum Development.

Lewin, K. (1947). Frontiers in group dynamics: Concept, method, and reality in social science: Social equilibria and social change. *Human Relations, 1*(1), 5-41.

Lieberman, A. (Ed.). (1986). *Rethinking school improvement.* New York: Teachers College Press.

Lieberman, A., & Miller, L. (1990). Teacher development in professional practice schools. *Teachers College Record, 92*(1), 105-122.

Lightfoot, S. L. (1978). *Worlds apart: Relations between families and schools.* New York: Basic Books.

Lightfoot, S. L. (1985). Rosemont High School. In V. Perrone (Ed.), *Portraits of high schools* (pp. 195-268). Princeton, NJ: Carnegie Foundation for the Advancement of Teaching.

Lortie, D. C. (1969). The balance of control and autonomy in elementary school teaching. In A. Etzioni (Ed.), *The semi-professions and their organization: Teachers, nurses, social workers* (pp 1-53). New York: Free Press.

Lortie, D. C. (1975). *Schoolteacher: A sociological study.* Chicago: University of Chicago Press.

Lortie, D. C. (1986). Teacher status in Dade County: A case of structural strain? *Phi Delta Kappan, 67,* 568-575.

Lortie, D. C. (1988). Built-in tendencies toward stabilizing the principal's role. *Journal of Research and Development in Education, 22*(1), 80-90.

Malen, B., Ogawa, R. T., & Kranz, J. (1990). What do we know about school-based management? A case study of the literature—A call for research. In W. H. Clune & J. Witte (Eds.), *Choice and control in American education: Vol. II. The practice of choice, decentralization, and school restructuring* (pp. 289-342). London: Falmer Press.

Marcoulides, G. A., & Heck, R. H. (1990). Educational policy issues for the 1990s: Balancing equity and excellence in implementing the reform agenda. *Urban Education, 25*(1), 55-67.

McClelland, D. C., Atkinson, J. K., Clark, R. A., & Lowell, E. L. (1953). *The achievement motive.* New York: Appleton-Century-Crofts.

McCloskey, G. N., Provenzo, E. F., Jr., Cohn, M. M., & Kottkamp, R. B. (1987). *A profession at risk: Legislated learning as a disincentive to teaching* (Contract No. ERI-P-86-3088). Washington, DC: U.S. Department of Education, Office of Educational Research and Improvement. (ERIC Document Reproduction Service No. ED 284 844).

McCloskey, G. N., Provenzo, E. F., Jr., Cohn, M. M., & Kottkamp, R. B. (1991). Disincentives to teaching: Teacher reactions to legislated learning. *Educational Policy, 5*(3), 251-265.

McNeil, L. (1986). *Contradictions of control: School structure and school knowledge.* New York: Routledge & Kegan Paul.

McNeil, L. (1988). Contradictions of control; Part 3. Contradictions of reform. *Phi Delta Kappan, 69*, 478-485.

Merton, R. K. (1957). *Social theory and social structure* (rev. ed.). Glencoe, IL: Free Press.

Messick, S. (1984). The psychology of educational measurement. *Journal of Educational Measurement, 21*, 215-237.

Metropolitan Life Insurance Company. (1984). *The Metropolitan Life survey of the American teacher.* New York: Author.

Metropolitan Life Insurance Company. (1985a). *The Metropolitan Life survey of the American teacher, 1985.* New York: Author.

Metropolitan Life Insurance Company. (1985b). *The Metropolitan Life survey of former teachers in America.* New York: Author.

Metropolitan Life Insurance Company. (1988). *The Metropolitan Life survey of the American teacher, 1988: Strengthening the relationship between teachers and students.* New York: Author.

Meyer, J. W., & Rowan, B. (1977). Institutionalized organizations: Formal structure as myth and ceremony. *American Journal of Sociology, 83*(2), 340-363.

Miller, J. L. (1990). *Creating spaces and finding voices: Teachers collaborating for empowerment.* Albany: State University of New York Press.

Mitchell, D. E., & Incarnation, D. J. (1984). Alternative state policy mechanisms for influencing school performance. *Educational Researcher, 13*(5), 4-11.

Mitchell, D. E., & Kerchner, C. T. (1983). Labor relations and teacher policy. In L. S. Shulman & G. Sykes (Eds.), *Handbook of teaching and policy* (pp. 214-238). New York: Longman.

Mitchell, D. E., Ortiz, F. I., & Mitchell, T. K. (1987). *Work orientation and job performance: The cultural basis of teaching rewards and incentives*. Albany: State University of New York Press.

Morgan, G. (1986). *Images of organization*. Beverly Hills, CA: Sage.

Morris, D. R. (1991). *Initial patterns and subsequent changes in staff characteristics of the SBM pilot 1 schools, relative to those of nonparticipating schools*. Paper presented at the annual meeting of the American Educational Research Association, Chicago.

Muncey, D. E., & McQuillan, P. J. (1991). *Some observations on the possibility of major restructuring in American schools: An ethnographic perspective*. (Working Paper No. 3). Providence, RI: Brown University, School Ethnography Project.

Murphy, J. (1990). The educational reform movement of the 1980s: A comparative analysis. In J. Murphy (Ed.), *The educational reform movements of the 1980s: Perspectives and cases* (pp. 3-55). Berkeley, CA: McCutchan.

National Commission on Excellence in Education. (1983). *A nation at risk: The imperative of educational reform*. Washington, DC: U.S. Government Printing Office.

National Education Association. (1967). *The American public school teacher 1965-66* (Research Rep. No. 1967-R4). Washington, DC: Research Division, Author.

Natriello, G., & Cohn, M. M. (1984). Critical issues in the development of a merit pay system. *Administrator's Notebook, 31*(3), 1-4.

Network for Educational Development. (1990). *Reports on action research*. St. Louis: Author.

New American Schools Development Corporation. (1991). *Designs for a new generation of American schools. A request for proposals*. Arlington, VA: Author.

Newmann, F. M. (1990). Authentic work and student engagement. *National Center on Effective Secondary Schools Newsletter, 5*(3), 2-3.

Noddings, N. (1984). *Caring: A feminine approach to ethics and moral education.* Berkeley and Los Angeles: University of California Press.

Osterman, K. F. (1990). Reflective practice: A new agenda for education. *Education in Urban Society, 22*(2), 133-151.

Osterman, K. F., & Kottkamp, R. B. (1993). *Reflective practice for educators: Improving schools through professional development.* Newbury Park, CA: Corwin Press.

Owens, R. G. (1988). Leadership in educational clans. In L. T. Sheive & M. B. Schoenheit (Eds.), *Leadership: Examining the elusive* (pp. 16-29). Alexandria, VA: Association for Supervision and Curriculum Development.

Paris, S. G., Lawton, T. A., Turner, J. C., & Roth, J. L. (1991). A developmental perspective on standardized achievement testing. *Educational Researcher, 20*(5), 12-20.

Perrone, V. (1991). *A letter to teachers: Reflections on schooling and the art of teaching.* San Francisco: Jossey-Bass.

Peterson, P. L., & Comeaux, M. A. (1990). Evaluating the system: Teachers' perspectives on teacher evaluation. *Educational Evaluation and Policy Analysis, 12*(1), 3-24.

Piaget, J. (1964). Development and learning. *Journal of Research in Science Teaching, 2,* 176-186.

Piaget, J., & Inhelder, B. (1969). *The psychology of the child.* New York: Basic Books.

Plank, D. N., & Ginsberg, R. (1990). Catch the wave: Reform commissions and school reform. In J. Murphy (Ed.), *The educational reform movements of the 1980s: Perspectives and cases* (pp. 121-142). Berkeley, CA: McCutchan.

Plihal, J. (1981). *Intrinsic rewards of teaching.* Paper presented at the annual meeting of the American Educational Research Association, Chicago.

Plisko, V. (1984). *The condition of teaching.* Washington, DC: National Center for Education Statistics.

Pocsi, M. J. (1987). *The effects of elementary school principals' sex, sex-typed personality traits, and classroom experience upon school effectiveness.* Unpublished doctoral dissertation, Rutgers University, New Brunswick, NJ.

Polanyi, M. (1967). *The tacit dimension.* Garden City, NY: Doubleday.

Porter, N. (1982). Liberating teaching. *Women's Studies Quarterly, 10* (4), 19-24.

Powell, A. G., Farrar, E., & Cohen, D. K. (1985). *The shopping mall high school: Winners and losers in the educational marketplace.* Boston: Houghton Mifflin.

Provenzo, E. F., Jr., McCloskey, G. N., Cohn, M. M., Kottkamp, R. B., & Proller, N. (1987). *A comparison of individual and school-level approaches to merit pay: A case study of the Dade County Public Schools.* (Contract No. ERI-P-86-3089). Washington, DC: U.S. Department of Education, Office of Educational Research and Improvement. (ERIC Document Reproduction Service No. ED 292 751.)

Provenzo, E. F., Jr., & Provenzo, A. B. (1988). *The impact of the Cuban immigration on the Dade County Schools: 1959 to 1987.* Paper presented at the annual meeting of the Florida Historical Society.

Resnick, L. B. (1987). *Education and learning to think.* Washington, D.C.: National Academy Press.

Resnick, L. B., & Klopfer, L. E. (1989). Toward the thinking curriculum: An overview. In L. B. Resnick & L. E. Klopfer (Eds.), *Toward the thinking curriculum: Current cognitive research* (pp. 1-18). Alexandria, VA: Association for Supervision and Curriculum Development.

Reynolds, M. C. (Ed.). (1989). *Knowledge base for the beginning teacher.* Oxford: Pergamon Press.

Rogers, C. R. (1972). Learning to be free. In R. Biehler (Ed.), *Psychology applied to teaching: Selected readings.* New York: Houghton Mifflin.

Rosenholtz, S. J. (1985). Effective schools: Interpreting the evidence. *American Journal of Education, 95,* 534-562.

Rosenholtz, S. J. (1989). *Teachers' workplace: The social organization of schools.* New York: Longman.

Ryan, K. (1970). *Don't smile until Christmas.* Chicago: University of Chicago Press.

Sarason, S. B. (1971). *The culture of the school and the problem of change.* Boston: Allyn and Bacon.

Sarason, S. B. (1990). *The predictable failure of educational reform: Can we change course before it's too late?* San Francisco: Jossey-Bass.

Schaefer, R. J. (1967). *The school as a center of inquiry.* New York: Harper & Row.

Schmuck, R. A., & Runkel, P. J. (1972). *Handbook of organizational development in schools.* Palo Alto, CA: Mayfield.

Schon, D. A. (1983). *The reflective practitioner.* New York: Basic Books.

Schon, D. A. (1987). *Educating the reflective practitioner.* San Francisco: Jossey-Bass.

Sederberg, C. H., & Clark, S. M. (1990). Motivation and organizational incentives for high-vitality teachers: A qualitative perspective. *Journal of Research and Development in Education, 24*(1), 6-13.

Sedlak, M. W., Wheeler, C. W., Pullin, D. C., & Cusick, P. A. (1986). *Selling students short: Classroom bargains and academic reform in the American high school.* New York: Teachers College Press.

Senge, P. M. (1990). The leader's new work: Building learning organizations. *Sloan Management Review, 32*(1), 7-23.

Sergiovanni, T. J. (1980). A social humanities view of educational policy and administration. *Educational Administration Quarterly, 16*(1), 1-19.

Shulman, L. S. (1983). Autonomy and obligation: The remote control of teaching. In L. S. Shulman & G. Sykes (Eds.), *Handbook of teaching and policy* (pp. 484-504). New York: Longman.

Silberman, C. E. (1970). *Crisis in the classroom: The remaking of American education.* New York: Random House.

Sirotnik, K. A. (1979). *Development and psychometric analyses of major scales utilized in a study of schooling.* (Technical Report Series No. 4). Los Angeles: University of California Graduate School of Education. (ERIC Document Reproduction Service No. ED 214 874.)

Sirotnik, K. A. (1990). Society, schooling, teaching, and preparing to teach. In J. I. Goodlad, B. Soder, & K. A. Sirotnik (Eds.), *Moral dimensions of teaching*. San Francisco: Jossey-Bass.

Sizer, T. R. (1984). *Horace's Compromise: The dilemma of the American high school*. Boston: Houghton Mifflin.

Skinner, B. F. (1968). *The technology of teaching*. New York: Appleton-Century-Crofts.

Smith, D. E. (1974). The social construction of documentary reality. *Sociological Inquiry, 44*, 257-268.

Smith, L. M., Dwyer, D. C., Prunty, J. J., & Kleine, P. F. (1988). *Innovation and change in schooling: History, politics, and agency*. New York: Falmer Press.

Smith, L. M., & Geoffrey, W. (1968). *Complexities of an urban classroom*. New York: Holt.

Smith, L. M., & Keith, P. (1971). *Anatomy of educational innovation*. New York: Wiley.

Smith, L. M., Prunty, J. J., Dwyer, D. C., & Kleine, P. F. (1987). *The fate of an innovative school: The history and present status of the Kensington School*. New York: Falmer Press.

Smith, M. L. (1991). Put to the test: The effects of external testing on teachers. *Educational Researcher, 20*(5), 8-11.

Somekh, B. (1989). The role of action research in collaborative enquiry and school improvement. In B. Somekh, J. Powney, & C. Burge (Eds.), *Collaborative enquiry and school improvement*. CARN Bulletin 9A. Norwich, England: Classroom Action Research Network, University of East Anglia.

Spady, W. G. (1971). Status, achievement, and motivation in the American high school. *School Review, 79*, 379-403.

Starobin, P. (1984). *Governor Bob Graham and the improvement of Florida's educational system*. (Case Study No. C16-83-574). Cambridge, MA: John F. Kennedy School of Government, Harvard University.

Stenhouse, L. (1976). *An introduction to curriculum research and development*. London: Heinemann.

Stern, C., & Keislar, E. R. (1977). Teacher attitudes and attitude change. *Journal of Research and Development in Education, 10*(2), 63-76.

Stinchcombe, A. L. (1965). Social structure and organizations. In J. G. March (Ed.), *Handbook of organizations* (pp. 142-193). Chicago: Rand McNally.

Sykes, G. (1984). The deal. *Wilson Quarterly, 7*(1), 59-77.

Taylor, F. W. (1911). *The principles of scientific management.* New York: Harper.

Tom, A. R. (1984). *Teaching as a moral craft.* New York: Longman.

Tyack, D. (1990). "Restructuring" in historical perspective: Tinkering toward Utopia. *Teachers College Record, 92*(2), 170-191.

U.S. Bureau of Census. (1991). *Statistical abstract of the United States, 1991* (111th ed.). Washington, D.C.: U.S. Government Printing Office.

Waller, W. (1932). *The sociology of teaching.* New York: Wiley.

Warren, D. (1990). Passage of rites: On the history of educational reform in the United States. In J. Murphy (Ed.), *The educational reform movement of the 1980s: Perspectives and cases* (pp. 57-81), Berkeley, CA: McCutchan.

Waskow, J. (1990). Initiating a teachers' academy. In *Reports in Action Research.* St. Louis, MO: Network for Educational Development.

Watzlawick, P., Weakland, J., & Fisch, R. (1974). *Change: Principles of problem-formation and problem-resolution.* New York: Norton.

Weick, K. E. (1976). Educational organizations as loosely coupled systems. *Administrative Science Quarterly, 21,* 1-19.

Wiggins, G. (1989). Teaching to the (authentic) test. *Educational Leadership, 46*(7), 41-47.

Wiggins, G. (1990). Authentic work: Implications for assessment and school structures. *National Center on Effective Secondary Schools Newsletter, 5*(3), 9-11.

Willower, D. J. (1977). Schools and pupil control. In D. A. Erickson (Ed.), *Educational organization and administration* (pp. 296-310). Berkeley, CA: McCutchan.

Willower, D. J. (1990). *School reform and schools as organizations.* Paper presented at the convention of the University Council for Educational Administration, Pittsburgh.

Willower, D. J., Eidell, T. L., & Hoy, W. K. (1973). *The school and pupil control ideology* (2nd ed.). Penn State Studies No. 24. University Park, PA: Pennsylvania State University.

Wirth, A. G. (1983). *Productive work—in industry and schools: Becoming persons again.* Lanham, MD: University Press of America.

Wise, A. E. (1979). *Legislated learning: The bureaucratization of the American classroom.* Berkeley and Los Angeles: University of California Press.

Wise, A. E. (1988). Two conflicting trends in school reform: Legislated learning revisited. *Phi Delta Kappan, 69,* 328-333.

Wittrock, M. C. (Ed.). (1986). *Handbook of research on teaching.* A Project of the American Educational Research Association. New York: Macmillan.

Zaltman, J., Florio, D., & Sikorski, L. (1977). *Dynamics of educational change.* New York: Free Press.

# Author Index

# Subject Index

349

TEXAS A&M UNIVERSITY, TEXARKANA